Tiger Tales and Ales

A Directory of Leicestershire Brewers 1400 to 1999

by
Mike Brown

A Brewery History Society Publication

INTRODUCTION

IN DEFENCE OF THE COUNTIES

Gourvish and Wilson's phenomenal survey of the brewing industry makes no mention of brewing in Leicestershire and only the occasional reference to Rutland, in terms of Ruddles. And yet, we have Everards, one of the few remaining family-owned breweries, and, remarkably, not only Hoskins in a fine traditional tower brewery, but also a spin-off set up by members of the original family. In addition, there are the growing, both in number and size, micro-breweries, including one which seems to have adopted almost a gypsy like view of location. Other claims to fame include the welcome return of a "brewster" (a female brewer) and the "strongest ale in the world"!

Not only that, but Bass, a national business, first started its concept of pub breweries in bowling alleys in a leisure park to the south of Leicester and we have one of the better brewing Firkins from Allied.

Perhaps the lack of previous references has been caused by the tendency to be over-shadowed by Burton, to such an extent that Everards, like many of the nationals, actually had to go and brew there. This is sad, given that both Leicestershire and Rutland were good malting counties, with water, which at its best, could match that of Burton. Perhaps in these terms, the saddest loss is Ruddle's County which in many ways matched the traditional flavour of Burton IPAs, despite the name being used for a mild before World War Two! You can read this as a failure by both national and international brewers to develop the brand or possibly more simply that once you introduce conical fermenters, no matter who is the owner, the writing may be on the wall.

Historically, Leicestershire had some of the last remaining pubs which brewed for themselves, for example see the entries for the Norths at Loughborough and the Malt Shovel at Barkby. Leicester, like many other Midland towns, had a strong basis of home-brewed pubs until the end of the nineteenth century. However, a particular feature was their support by the local maltsters e.g. Browns, Taylors. George Harrison in particular played an enigmatic role, not only in providing malt for those victuallers still brewing for themselves, but going on to become involved with brewing in the town and at Langham, and providing some of the basis for Leicester Brewing & Malting (LB&M).

Leicester also provides some insights into the balance between competition and collaboration in the brewing industry. For example see the background to RC Allen. How much did the LB&M policy to concentrate on the town trade, leaving Langham to cover the country, represent the previous and continuing influence of the Harrison involvement?

Thankfully, if you are prepared to look around there are still some interesting buildings remarkably intact e.g. All Saints Brewery, LB&M and Sharpes. These are worthy of preservation to mark the involvement of both counties in what is a key industry for understanding the social and economic history of the country.

To give an indication of the importance locally, the following table shows the number of commercial or common brewers operating in Leicestershire:

	Brewery	Maltings
1855	20	83
1864	29	99
1876	38	75
1881	40	60
1895	30	28
1904	32	18
1912	21	10
1922	17	6
1932	11	3
1941	7	2

LIHS Vol 3 1989 pp10-15 extracted from Kelly's directory.

To this must also be added the brewing victuallers producing for a single outlet. The main sources for information are the commercial directory listings, especially those from 1877 onwards, when both common brewers and the brew-pubs can be identified. These were collated by Manfred Friedrich and copies for individual counties are available from the BHS. Where possible Friedrich's original numbering system is indicated, e.g. F62 Anstey.

In most cases locations are identified by the name of the pub and the first clearly identified brewer. Later brewers at the location are included within the entry. The exception is where a family seems to have been associated with the trade at a variety of sites.

The early days of small scale

One of the earliest mentions of brewing in Leicestershire was in 1381, for Roger & Rose Taylour, the latter being a brewster paying a poll tax of 12d at Market Harborough (Davies & Brown p22). The Poll Tax return also recorded a brewer at Hallaton (Millward plate 19).

In terms of what they might have been producing, and how, one needs to bear in mind that it was not until the fifteenth century that there was a transition from medieval ale, which was sweet and fermented for a very short period, to hopped beer, fermented for a week. This was produced by a more industrial process, with a consequent need for capital and technical expertise. However, between the fourteenth and eighteenth centuries, beer was still mainly supplied by publican brewers or victuallers.

For example, Francis' History of Hinckley shows that, according to the Court Roll in 1528, there were seven brewers in the town, all female, and all fined for breaking the ale assize. The principal inn of the town was the Bull's Head, which was run by Richard Hunt, with his wife Elizabeth as the brewer, or to be more precise the brewster.

In 1585 in Leicester, it was said that five full time common brewers dominated the local market. Other early records include a mention in 1663-4 of Edward Read at the Antelope supplying beer to the Town Hall and around 1664-72, Nicholas Smith a brewer in High Cross Street.

One of the earliest records of brewery "marketing" in the actual Borough was in 1690, when Edward Joanes was prosecuted for having kept a common alehouse for some 3 months without a licence. In his statement, he agreed that he had received from John Pratt, the Common Brewer and ale-taster "*20 kilderkins of ale, over and above what he spends and consumes in his own house for his family*". However, he also suggested that Pratt had stated he would not be prosecuted as long as he took ale from him. Clearly brewers were just as aggressive in gaining accounts then as they are today.

In 1628, Charles I issued a Royal Proclamation which was an early attempt to control the industry, in that only brewing would be undertaken by the common brewers. Some have argued this as a possible cause of the Civil War, noting that Cromwell was a brewer and that dissenters and Quakers have traditionally been strong in the industry.

According to Mathias "*brewing victuallers*" produced almost all of the beer which was publicly sold (p213). In contrast, the common brewer could only brew for sale to publicans and customers away from the brewery, except for the one permissible "tap" at the brewery.

The common brewer, especially in London, was associated with the growing sales of Porter. This was due to the need for scale in both brewing and fermentation. Hence, the occasional reference to stocks of such ale in advertisements in the Leicester Journal, not only from London, but later Loughborough. In the case of Loughborough, according to Fletcher's history, in 1650 it was the greatest malting town of the Midlands.

"In some Midland counties there were very few common brewers at all in 1800, household brewing in cottages and brewing victuallers still satisfying local demand in a medieval tradition"
Mathias p241

The majority of houses and farmers would have brewed; however these have only been included where was some evidence of commercial sales e.g. Cropston. For example sale advertisements in 1799 often mentioned brewing utensils:-

- 28th January   Mr Tebbutt's farm at Hinckley included the copper brewing vessels
- 27th May   Swithland Hall sale of brewing utensils
- June   William Sawbridge's estate at Stapleton included brewhouse

In 1886, the licence duty was removed for those households with a rateable value below £8. However, the 1887 Truck Amendment Act stopped estate and private brewers, by making it illegal for employers to pay their workers with beer in kind; hence, the few remaining estate and private breweries disappeared at this time. There was a major decline in the national number of licensed non-duty brewers e.g. farmers and private households:

1881	71,876	
1900	12,734	p26 Monckton

In 1963, the category was abolished, when there were only some 901 left. This had the obvious advantage of promoting the growth of brewing at home from kits.

One of the few remaining examples of this domestic scale of brewing is Avenue House on the corner of Central Avenue and Long Street at Wigston. This was built around 1840 and the outbuildings are thought to include the brewhouse.

Victorian Industrial Production

In the late eighteenth century, some of the background to the common brewers was linked with their role as farmers, who had been brewing to supply the workforce on their estates. They often developed to provide the malt for inns to brew with and capital for their purchase, including brewing utensils from around £25 to £100 depending on size. The major problem was product reliability; hence the importance of the maltster in providing not only the raw material, but also credit facilities. The Harrisons and Taylors played a key role in the survival of small pub breweries in Leicester through to the end of the nineteenth century. This was to lead to a move towards supplying the beer as transport improved, allied with the consistency of large scale brewing. Hence, from 1800, brewers increasingly took out licences to malt as they integrated backwards.

In 1825, a new classification of Retail Brewer was introduced, instead of that of victualler. This was based on a sliding scale which started at not exceeding 20 barrels per annum, but the category did not last long against the competition of the common brewers. Some examples are listed in the Leicester entries.

The 1830 Act retained duty on malt and hops; however, instead of beer duty, brewers paid a small licence duty:-

	£	s
Under 20 barrels pa	10	-
20-50	1	-
50-100	1	10
100-1000	2	-

Then pro rata charges to a maximum of £75. In 1830, the common brewers were thought to have produced around 55% of total output, with the victuallers around 33% and beerhouse keepers some 12.5%, the balance coming from the private and farm brewers (Gourvish & Wilson p67).

Although the Act also made it cheap to open a small beer house and supply oneself, it also enhanced the economies of scale for the larger brewer. At the most, beerhouse brewers only produced a maximum of some 13.4% of beer in 1836. By 1900, the common brewers produced 95% of total output, with the most dramatic changes being in the last two decades of the century, partly linked to the changes in licensing and the growth of the tied trade. For example in 1841, Loughborough had some 17 brewers, but ten years later this had declined to nine. Although this rose again to 16 in 1881, the small local brew-pubs all but disappeared by the turn of the century. This was partly because the brew-pubs' price advantage of around 1d per quart tended to be off-set by their poor extraction rates from the raw materials used. See the entry for Norths of Loughborough, as to why they lasted until the 1970s.

The concentration of production in fewer hands allowed the transfer to a system of duty on beer not malt, rather than the other way round. This made the work of the Customs & Excise easier and was better for controlling the industry, both aspects well-regarded by governments. The change away from the tax on malt also had an impact on the size and scale of maltings. Hence the move towards large malt houses in rural areas near rail access e.g Sleaford and Grantham and the end of brewing in the centres of Leicester and Loughborough. See opening table for evidence of the decline in numbers.

The Product

Where possible, technical terms have been explained in the glossary. However, it may be helpful to explain a little about some of the phrases which often occur in the sale details and relate to the overall scale of the brewery. The term "strike" equated to a bushel of malt, approximately 42lbs. The other term often used for malting was a quarter, which was 8 bushels.

The terms were important to the brewer/ purchaser, since it was generally accepted that a bushel would produce two standard barrels of beer at a gravity of 1055°, or around 5.5% abv (alcohol by volume - the measure of alcoholic strength which is currently used). You may also find the occasional reference to brewers' pounds based on the weight of the raw materials, principally the malt.

This measure worked on the basis that a 36 gallon or standard barrel of water weighs 360 lbs, whereas a similar size of barrel filled with beer would weigh 380 lbs i.e. 20 pounds of material. This would be at a standard gravity of 1055°, nowadays regarded as strong ale rather than average. Hence the brewers, and indeed the excise men, had a reasonable understanding of the relationship between raw materials, brewing process and output in terms of quantity and strength. The brewers who grasped these relationships and other technical developments would clearly be more likely to succeed.

In terms of what they were producing, the eighteenth century sales were mainly of strong and dark vatted old beer and porter, partly resulting from the fact that they were only brewed over the winter months and stored for sale. The only example of the former still available locally would be bottled Strong Suffolk from Greene King at Bury St Edmunds. For example, in 1799 Richard Smith & Sons a wine & spirit merchant at the Hind in Lutterworth was selling porter in 36 gallon barrels for £2 or a dozen bottles for 4s 6d.

Production of London Porter, apart from the obvious economies of scale from dealing with the major urban market, was helped by the nature of the water in the area, which contained relatively high proportion of calcium carbonate and some sodium chloride (p16 Monckton). However, the introduction of isinglass as a finings agent in the mid eighteenth century had set the precedent for the production of the clear pale ales which were to replace the traditional darker beers and lay the foundations for the later growth of Burton.

In terms of raw materials, the 1799 prices in Leicester were Hops £9 per bag and £10 per pocket. Barley was 27s to 31s per quarter and malt 38s to 42s. As ever, producers were looking for ways of reducing their costs. Thus in 1800, G Knowles, a druggist of Coleman Row in Birmingham, was advertising in the Leicester Journal that he was looking to sell hop substitute. Although the county was not a major growing area for hops, there is some evidence of local involvement e.g. Mr King a hop grower at Syston in 1807.

In the August of 1800, the Brewers' Journal was giving a recipe for brewing without malt, using 4lb coarse sugar, 3oz hops, 10 gallons of water, and at one third the price of normal beer.

This period also saw other technical developments which would set the scene for what we take for granted today. For example, on 18th March 1803, L Kirshaw of Manchester was advertising his apparatus for drawing ale and porter. His advertisement in the Journal gave a list of pub owners who were prepared to give references. In Leicestershire the following were listed:-

Mr Bishop	Three Crowns	Leicester
Mr Wolf	White Bear	Leicester
Mrs Spooner	Bulls Head	Leicester
Mr Mansfield	Nags Head	Leicester
Mr Staveley	Bull Inn	Loughborough
Mr Marsh	Denbigh Arms	Lutterworth
Mr Munton	Angel	Market Harborough

In competition, J&R Swinfen were agents for William Dalby's newly invented apparatus for drawing porter, ale, spirits etc. from the cellar to the bar.

In 1803, another advertisement in the Journal was for Brewing with the Thermometer - The Complete Family Brewer price 3s by W Ploughman, brewer at Romsey. He mentions the advantages to be gained by the private brewer in using this new instrument, which he was also selling for 20s.

Other technical developments included a patent in 1864 for dispensing draught beer with a top pressure of CO_2 to maintain it in fresh sparkling condition (p163 Monckton). Such work provided the basis for the chilling and carbonation of bottled beer, rather than allowing it to mature in bottle. Note the investment made by CBB and others as they lost sales and note also the price premium which could be charged for quality bottled products.

However, it was the changes in the style of beer which customers bought which was to have most impact on local brewers. Napoleon's closure of the Baltic ports in 1807 meant that the Burton brewers looked elsewhere for sales. This became allied to the move away from the sweet dark Stout towards Pale Ales from the Burton Union System. Burton in 1830 had some 7 or 8 breweries, with a total output of 50,000 barrels per annum. In 1900, the town's 21 breweries produced some 3.5m barrels roughly 10% of national sales. Proximity to such a brewing centre was to prove crucial for the breweries of Leicestershire and Rutland.

What became known as the Burton Union system for fermentation, relied on lines of wooden casks in which the yeast rose up through piping into troughs. This "cleansed" the product and produced consistent "star bright" pale ales. However, it required a high level of investment, technological expertise and scientific approaches to cleanliness. The Midland Brewery at Loughborough in 1892 had some 72 unions. Marstons at Burton on Trent are the only remaining example of a brewer using such a system.

Monckton points out that the introduction of the saccharometer revealed that curing malt to a darker colour reduced the amount of fermentable sugar available. It also showed that inferior barleys were being used for the coloured malts. Hence in 1812, manufactured coloured compounds from sugar were allowed in the brewing process. Abuses in production led in 1816 to the UK's equivalent of the German Rheinheitsgebot, which specified that only malt, hops and yeast were to be used in brewing. The 1830 legislation put the tax on the raw materials of malt and hops, in order to capture the output of the private brewers. The 1847 Act once again allowed sugar as an ingredient - mainly as a result of political pressure from the owners of plantations in the West Indies.

In 1862, a further act removed the tax on hops. This in turn helped the increase in sales of the bitter hopped pale ales which Burton was producing. Local brewers could either invest in new plant e.g. the Eagle Brewery at Charnwood Street or even consider access to Burton's product such as Everards later purchase of breweries in the town.

In the 1880s, further changes in duty legislation also brought in *"a free mash tun"*, in which brewers were allowed to use any unmalted cereals in the mash, as long as they were not harmful, see the All Saints Brewery purchases around this time.

In 1898, evidence to the Departmental Committee on Beer Materials showed that in the previous ten years, the amount of sugar used in brewing had risen from 10% to 15%. Mr Otto Hehner, public analyst at Nottingham, stated:

> *"The public taste has been created by the brewers and by their chemical advisers, not the public".*

Licensing and the growth of "Tied Trade"

Prior to the eighteenth century, there were three mains types of outlet. The inns provided stabling, accommodation and food and also sold spirits and wine, equivalent to what we would nowadays call a hotel, e.g. the coaching inns of Market Harborough and Loughborough. The tavern was a drinking house, open to a wide variety of customers and selling wine as well as beer. The ale-house, also called tippling houses in earlier years, only supplied ale and beer which they usually brewed on the premises. Not all of the inns and hotels have been included, only those where there is a clear indication of brewing taking place.

Perhaps the earliest trustworthy source for the number of premises is the 1577 Census to raise money for the repairs of Dover Harbour. This revealed a total of 19,579 licences in England and Wales of which locally:-

	Leicestershire	Rutland	
Inns	31	4	
Taverns	2	1	
Alehouses	392	100	p102 Monckton

In the late eighteenth century, the common brewers did not wish to tie up their capital in owning pubs, instead they relied on their traditional links with retailers, particularly those involving credit. However, the decline in sales of porter caused publicans to look to other suppliers. This was particularly important for areas, such as Leicestershire, which were easily supplied by the Burton brewers.

Political involvement in the industry and its outlets was not only at the national level. The Corporation of Leicester is said to have used the grant of licences as a political weapon, strengthened by the freeman monopoly being maintained until 1835 (VCH IV p180).

The 1830 Act allowed the retail (but not production) of beer on payment of £2 annual licence and this is often quoted as leading to a rapid growth in the number of outlets. However, when set against other changes such as the growth in population and the development of urban areas, the growth becomes less dramatic. Consumption per head did rise briefly in the 1830s, but then continued its downward trend to 34.3 gallons per capita per annum in 1900.

One problem with the new beer houses was that the lack of control led to adulteration of the beer e.g. London Porter bought at the brewery averaged 5.25% whilst that bought from pubs averaged only 4.5%. These and other problems instrumental in the passing of the 1860 Food & Drugs Act.

The nineteenth century term public house grew out of these beer houses, primarily built to serve the working class communities of the growing urban areas. The off-sales from the beerhouses were linked to the growth in population. This in turn was linked to the poor quality of the drinking water in many areas.

In evidence to the Royal Commission on Licensing Laws in June 1897, Joseph Barker of 87 Argyle Street, seven years secretary of Leicester & District Off-licence Holders Association, stated that average sales were made up of 2 barrels of 36 gallons per week, which equated to 80 persons per day buying a pint each. Observers saw that over 90% of sales were during meal times and 90% of these were in working class areas.

These sales had their roots in the table beer, which had been defined by Act of Parliament in 1782 (22 Geo 111) as of medium strength for domestic consumption. This was also known as small beer for women and children, and was popular for breakfast. These products, available in small casks, were often major sales for the family brewers mentioned in the text.

However, the 1869 Beer and Wine Act had allowed magistrates to restrict the number of licences in their areas and indeed to reduce them if needed. Hence there was a rush for what became known as "tied trade". This was linked to access to capital through the introduction of limited liability for publicly owned companies.

This change in licensing posed particular problems for the nearby Burton breweries, which had relied on free access. Bass output declined by 100,000 barrels between 1879 and 1885. In 1883, Bass owned only 27 pubs in the UK; in 1888 it went public in order to finance pub purchases, and by 1900 had an estate of 550 pubs. Eadies and Worthington followed their example, but Allsopps believed that the reputation of their own beer meant that they could continue to rely on the free trade. A fall in output of around a third in the late 1880s convinced them otherwise and by 1902 they had rapidly accumulated an estate of 1,200 pubs. Everards which owned only some seven pubs at the start of these changes, although supplying many more, also entered on a major programme of purchases. This may also explain the change in ownership with the introduction of Mr Welldon as a partner, possibly to finance the programme.

In addition, the brewers increasingly purchased run-down pubs for their licences which could be transferred to new premises. In 1891, there 753 licensed houses in the borough of Leicester, a ratio of 1 to 190; new applications were turned down by licensing authorities strengthening the need to capture the outlets.

In Leicestershire, the brewing victualler seems to have had a larger proportion of the trade and lasted longer than in many other counties. Indeed, Pyrah suggests that the majority of Leicester pubs brewed until the end of the nineteenth century (p27).

In 1900, the Brewers' Journal suggested that nationally there were some 120 000 licensed houses, of which the common brewers controlled 90%. However, this was a period in which the number of outlets was to fall dramatically, as can be evidenced by the number of entries for pubs being compensated and closed. Expected 1908 compensation closures were as follows:-

Ashby	14
Leicester	5
Loughborough	1
Lutterworth	3
M Harborough	6

These resulted from the 1904 Act, and there was much fear in the brewing press because of the changes in the proposed 1909 bill e.g. Sunday closing. However, the compensation closures were partly off-set by the growing number of off-licensed premises, which increasingly supplied bottled beer, rather than the traditional jug sales of draught beer.

Part of the pressure for closures came from the Temperance Movement. However, the Brewing Trade Review, fighting back, produced evidence that 422 of 1,133 samples of Temperance beverages, contained from 2% to 12.3% proof spirit, the latter being a dandelion stout!

Twentieth Century and The Tax!

In 1880, the beer duty had been reintroduced, partly because the number of brewers had fallen, making it easier to collect the duty. This was based on the strength of the wort in the vessel before fermentation had started - known as the original gravity (OG), at a rate of 6s 3d per standard barrel of 1057°. This included a 6% waste allowance and was designed to be the equivalent of the malt tax it replaced. Again it tended not to favour the small brewer, since the less efficient might not be able to produce a full barrel from a similar brew and malt.

If in 1899 locals were able to buy beer at 1d per pint, the 1999 equivalent, allowing for inflation, would be 24p compared to an actual average of £1.90 (Office for National Statistics in Daily Telegraph 10th June 1999)!

One might see this in terms of the higher value added of the modern pub, but primarily one must also look at the impact of taxation.

	s	d	
1889 beer duty	6	3	per standard barrel (1055° OG)
1914	23	-	
1918	50	-	
1932	134	-	
1933 changed to bulk barrel up to and including gravity 1027°			
1933	24	-	
1939	48	-	
1947	159	9	
1948	178	10	

One might see some success for the Temperance Movement and the Government, in that rather than outright prohibition one could control through increasing the price and dramatically lowering the strength. Hence, when allowed access to the open market of Europe, the consumer made a mass rush to import either legally or illegally, which was to the detriment of both local producers and retailers.

In 1889, the standard barrel gravity was set at 1055° to help the smaller brewer. This is not much above the strength of Everard's Old Original and Ruddle's County, both of which nowadays are regarded as strong beers. The later decline in beer strength was related to war-time restrictions on raw materials, opening hours and the impact of tax. The decline in average original gravity was:-

1900	1055
1915	1052
1919	1031
1932	1041
1047	1033
1951	1037

The reduction in strength also hastened the switch away from mild and brown beers (the latter being the bottled version) which relied on gaining their taste from their higher gravity towards bitter, which relied more on flavour from hops. The brew-pubs tended to continue to brew their own mild (see Berrington at Loughborough) whilst buying in their pale ales, bitters and stouts. Hence many of the entries, especially for Leicester, show brewing continuing long after the pubs had been purchased by LB&M or the other local concerns.

During World War One, national consumption fell from 35m to 19m barrels pa, and the Depression between the wars created major problems e.g. Everard's sales declined by some 20%. Not surprisingly between the wars the number of common brewers nationally fell from 3,000 to less than 1,000; hence the closures noted in Leicestershire.

There was also a continued growth in the sales of bottled beer (by 1939 30% of total). The importance of bottled trade is often under-estimated e.g. Whitbreads growth from 1870 1,293 barrels bottled to the 1910 figure of 353,936. Their aim was for their product to be available anywhere in the UK at 2/6 per dozen. As late as 1958 70% of the output of Manns, the famous London brewer, was still bottled. The three main sellers were Bass, Guinness and Whitbread. Margins were higher on bottled beer because of consumer demand and there was much investment in plant by the local concerns as they improved their technical expertise in order to capture sales from the big three. The first keg beers were developed elsewhere, but they had an impact on the local breweries as they replaced sales of bottled beer in the pubs.

The World War Two reductions in strength were probably the final nail in the coffin for mild, a product which had become associated with low strength and little flavour. Offilers' directors in 1964 noted the continued fall in sales from 1954, with particular resistance to their mild in Derby and the demand for keg increasing. Initially they considered an agreement with M&B to supply them with beer for 21 years; but they then started looking to be taken-over and the following year Charringtons obliged. The introduction of TV advertising helped strengthen the growth of national markets and national products e.g. the LB&M Eagle brewery becoming supplied from Birmingham or Burton.

There was a also a growing need to invest for lager production e.g. Ruddles. In 1959, lager nationally was some 1% of sales, but by the late 1970s it had grown to around 30% and in 1990 had reached 51%. At first, lager replaced bottled beer and keg, but then it also began to take the share of other draught beers. However, just in case one regards lager drinking as a recent phenomenon, Motts of Leicester were advertising their supplies of German lager ale from Berlin in 1878.

Apart from the further concentration of production in recent years and the impact of the "Beer Orders" in creating the major pub-owning chains, there have also been developments on the taxation front. On 1st June 1993, the UK adopted what is known as factory gate taxation, in line with European practice. Unfortunately we have yet to adopt a sliding scale which would help the new entrants to the industry and indeed the smaller local breweries. In 1974, changes to excise regulations, prior to fermentation, aided the introduction of high gravity brewing, in which one brew could be watered down to produce a variety of products. One spokesman for a national concern accepted that this would lead to further smoothness and blandness. Perhaps an understatement in retrospect and one can only put one's faith in the future of brewing in the hands of the local brewers. Fortunately, both counties have examples which we can drink of and to.

Acknowledgements

To my wife Margaret for her tolerance and to my editor Ken Smith for even greater tolerance.

Those particularly involved in sourcing the material: Richard Bell and Reg Porter for access and guidance to the Allied archives; Andrew Cunningham for access to his collection of memorabilia, many of the illustrations used in the book are his, plus help with the proof reading; Liz Press, Keeper of Documentation at the Bass Museum; Ray Farleigh for tracking the brewers to their pubs; Jack Feast for his wide and deep local knowledge; Eric Folwer for all the help with Marstons; Jim Irving for access to the Smith's papers on Ketton; Ian Peaty for access to his photographic library; David Parry for his assistance with unravelling public house ownership and Tony Diebel for help with the history of Hoskins. The Editor acknowledges the last minute help of Anne Hill, Geoff Birks, Peter Moynihan, Ruth Minett and Michael Jones of the BHS in proof reading the final text. Any typos are now his responsibility. Lastly to the staff of the Leicester Record Office and the numerous local libraries and study sections and the often unknown authors of the many town and village histories.

We are also grateful to Bass and Tom Hoskins plc for their financial support.

REFERENCES

Avis, Anthony:- *The Brewing Industry 1950-1990, 1997*
Barber, Norman:- *A Century of British Brewers, Brewery History Society 1997*
Bateson, M:- *Records of Borough of Leics III - Cambridge 1905 IV p259 Stocks H Cambridge 1923*
Billson, CJ:- *Medieval Leicester - Leicester 1920 p26*
Bone, M:- *Oakham Brewery 1842-1980 - LIHS Bulletin No 6 1983 pp20-28*
Clark, Peter:- *The English Ale House: A Social History 1200-1830 - Longman London 1983*
Davies JC & Brown MC:- *Book of Market Harborough - Barracuda Buckingham 1984 ISBN 0 8602322 62*
Buttery, P & Lount, B:- *Alehouses of Oadby - Oadby Local History Group 1985*
Foss, Peter:- *History of Market Bosworth - Sycamore 1985*
Francis, HJ:- *History of Hinckley - Pickering & Son Hinckley 1928*
Friedrich, Manfred:- *Gazetteer of British Brewers Private publication 1997*
Goodacre, J:- *Lutterworth in C16 and C17 - PhD Thesis Leic Uni 1977 p239*
Goodwin, JM:- *Ketton in Rutland - Spiegl 1993*
Gourvish, TR & Wilson, RG:- *The British Brewing Industry 1830-1980 - Cambridge University Press 1994*
Hunt, P:- *Story of Melton Mowbray - Leicester Libraries*
Jinks, Chris:- *Lost Pubs of Leicester - Leicester Drinker CAMRA Newsletter*
Lee, JM:- *The Rise and Fall of a Market Town - Castle Donington - Leicester Archeological & Historical Society 1956*

Leics Architectural & Archaeological Soc, Vol 1 Part 2 Tradesmens Tokens - Crossley & Clarke Leicester 1863
Mathias, P:- *The Economic Transformation of England - Methuen London 1979*
Millward, Roy:- *History of Leicester & Rutland - Phillimore Oxford 1985*
Mitchell, John W:- *History of Ruddle's Langham Brewery - Rutland Record No 5 1985 pp172-180*
Monckton, HA:- *The Story of the Publican Brewer - Literary Services 1984*
Monckton, HA:- *The Story of British Beer - Literary Services 1981*
Pale Ale and Bitter Beer: Burton Breweries - Staffordshire Libraries
Peaty, IP:- *You Brew Good Ale - Sutton Publishing Stroud 1997*
Pyrah, Chris:- *Inns & Taverns of Leicester - Anderson Publications 1984*
Rae, David:- *Excellence through Independence, The first 150 years of Everard's Brewery. - Taylor Bloxham Leicester 1999*
Rutland LHS:- *Oakham in Rutland - Spiegl Press 1982*
Rutland LHS:- *Villages of Rutland Vol 1 Parts 1 and 2 - Spiegl 1979*
Swift, Eric:- *The Inns of Leicestshire - Leic Research Chamberlain*
The Inns of Leicester during the reign of George III - unpublished MA Leicester University 1976
Tombs, Peter:- *Guide to British Brewers - Sidgwick & Jackson London 1990*
Trayler, AR:- *Life of Gentry from Rutland: Barons, Bankers and Brewers - Spiegl Press 1992*
Victoria County History vol iv

Glossary

Without going too far into technicalities, this glossary covers some of words used in the text in a simplified manner.

Ale - originally used to describe unhopped malt beverage, as distinct from beer, which was brewed from malt with hops as flavouring. Nowadays synonymous with beer and a traditional top-fermented (i.e. the yeast rises to the top during fermentation) product.

Barrel Sizes - Firkin 9 gallons; Barrel 36 gallons; Hogshead 54 gallons.

Beer House - as simple as the term, a house which was licensed to sell only beer. The 1830 Beer House Act made it much simpler and cheaper to set up in business, leading to a rapid expansion, some of which brewed their own beer on a small scale.

Brew House - the actual building, within which would be found the brewing equipment.

Brewery - a term used for both the physical buildings and also the business itself.

Brown Ale - beer brewed from dark malts, bottled and normally of low gravity. The bottled equivalent of mild.

Burton Union System - a particular form of fermentation which originated at Burton on Trent. It involves a series of large connected barrels which circulated the beer during the brewing process.

Burtonised - by adding gypsum to the water (or **liquor**) used to brew, brewers can create a pale ale typical of Burton on Trent.

Cask - general term for all draught beer containers.

Copper - vessel traditionally made of such, nowadays stainless steel, where the "wort" is boiled with hops.

Dray - wagon used to carry casks and bottles from brewery to pub.

Family trade - small or table beer, usually consumed with meals instead of water which was then unsafe. Despite its name and provision for children, the beer was probably as strong as modern day beers.

Fermentation - the process in which yeast converts wort into beer. After brewing, the beer stays in the brewery where the yeast does its work, normally taking from 4 to 8 days.

India Pale Ale (IPA) - first brewed for shipping out to troops in India.

Keg Beer - conditioned at the brewery, chilled, filtered and sealed in containers and served under pressure. Despite the nostalgia for real ale, the evidence is that keg products were welcomed by the majority of drinkers who saw them as providing a consistent taste which did not vary from pub to pub.

Lager - bottom fermented beer initially associated with Europe, which has been available in the county for more than a hundred years. Local brewers attempted to brew top-fermented versions in the 1960s (see Ruddles).

Liquor - the name given to water used in the brewing process.

Long Pull - means of serving additional beer in order to attract custom, particularly prevalent during the "Brewers Wars" at the end of the last century.

Malt Mill - a machine which crushes malt before it is used in brewing.

Malting - the initial stage in the process when the barley is partly germinated and then dried to stop further growth.

Maltster - the individual responsible for malting barley.

Mash Tun - vessel in which the crushed malt and hot water are mixed at precise temperatures to extract malt sugars, which will then be fermented by the yeast.

Mild - previously the main drink of the working male population, usually dark and low in hops. However, do not be misled by present day low gravity versions, since at the turn of the century it would have been 2 or 3 times stronger.

Original Gravity - a measure of the strength of beer used in the UK before European Union. This is now measured as alcohol by volume (ABV). Present day bitter beers are in the region 1036° to 1045° OG compared to some of those mentioned in the text.

Pale Ale - clear, sparkling and well-hopped.

Porter - strong well-hopped dark almost black beer which originated in London. The nearest modern day equivalent is a stout such as Guinness.

Quarter - a measure of the capacity of a brew house, based on the "quarters" of malt which could be brewed.

Stout - dark beer of medium to high gravity, brewed using roasted malt.

Victualler - usually associated with an inn and providing food and possibly accommodation. Only a licensed victualler could serve alcoholic drinks. In the early years, this would probably including brewing beer.

Wort - the unfermented beer at the end of the mashing stage.

Yeast - tiny micro-organism which ferments wort into beer and carbon dioxide.

CONTENTS

ANSTEY	1	KILBY BRIDGE	36
ASHBY de la ZOUCH	4	KNIGHTON	36
BARKBY	6	LANGHAM	36
BARROW upon SOAR	6	LEICESTER	43
BARROWDEN	7	LONG CLAWSON	127
BEEBY	7	LOUGHBOROUGH	127
BELGRAVE	9	LUTTERWORTH	142
BELTON	10	MARKET BOSWORTH	146
BELTON, Rutland	10	MARKET HARBOROUGH	146
BILLESDON	10	MARKFIELD	148
BIRSTALL	10	MELTON MOWBRAY	149
BITTESWELL	10	MOUNT SORREL	155
BLABY	10	NARBOROUGH	156
BOTTESFORD	11	NEWBOLD VERDON	156
BROUGHTON ASTLEY	11	OADBY	156
BURROUGH	11	OAKHAM	157
BURROUGH on the HILL	11	OLD DALBY	161
BURTON OVERY	12	QUORN/QUORNDON	161
CASTLE DONINGTON	12	RATBY	162
CAVENDISH BRIDGE	13	REARSBY	162
COALVILLE	20	ROTHLEY	162
COTESBACH	20	RYHALL	162
COTTESMORE	20	SALTBY	162
CROPSTON	20	SHEPSHED	163
DESFORD	20	SILEBY	163
EARL SHILTON	21	SOMERBY	165
ENDERBY	21	SOUTH LUFFENHAM	166
FLECKNEY	21	STATHERN	166
FOXTON	21	STONEY STANTON	166
FRISBY	21	STRETTON	167
GEESTON	22	SWANNINGTON	167
GILMORTON	22	SYSTON	167
GLENFIELD	22	THURMASTON	169
GREAT DALBY	22	TWYFORD	170
GREAT GLEN	22	ULLESTHORPE	170
HALLATON	22	UPPINGHAM	170
HARBY	22	WALCOTE	171
HATHERN	23	WALTON	171
HILLMORTON	24	WALTHAM on the WOLDS	171
HINCKLEY	24	WHISSENDINE	172
HUMBERSTONE	28	WHITWICK	174
HUNCOTE	28	WIGSTON MAGNA	174
HUSBANDS BOSWORTH	28	WOODVILLE	176
IBSTOCK	28	WORTHINGTON	178
KEGWORTH	28	WYMESWOLD	178
KETTON	31	INDEX	
KIBWORTH BEAUCHAMP	35		

ANSTEY

Burchnall, Samuel.

Burchnall was listed as a brewer and maltster from 1846 to 1855. Prior to this, a Robert Birchnall was an innkeeper living at Anstey in 1826. In 1849, Charles Burchnall was also a brewer and maltster.

Although Samuel was shown only as a farmer in 1870, he was also shown as a brewer 1871-76. However, he reverts to being only a farmer again in 1884, all of which suggests that he may have only been brewing for his own work-force. He is thought to have been related to the family brewing at Broughton Astley (see entry).

Doleman, John, *The Old Brewery.*

The first mention of the Anstey brewery was in 1846. Although Edward Hooke's property included a brewhouse, this was probably for domestic not commercial purposes. In 1867, William Rowbotham was listed as the brewer, maltster and hop merchant, with a depot at 26 Cank Street Leicester, where Joseph H Bailey was the agent. He may have been brewing from around 1862.

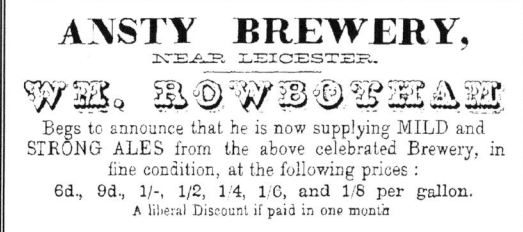

From a commercial directory dated 1867.

His advertising mentioned the Mild and Strong Ales, from the "celebrated" brewery.

The last mention of Rowbotham was in 1871 and in 1875 Doleman was described as a brewer, maltster and hop merchant. The following year the business was called the Old Brewery, which suggests that it had been operating for some time. A Francis Doleman, who had owned property in Anstey from at least 1852, was at the Stamford Arms, Groby 1862-77, where John Doleman lived.

Kelly's directory of 1877 lists Doleman as a large brewer and he was still listed in 1880 (F0062). However, the year after saw William Frederick Coupland & Company at the Old Brewery, but they had left the business by 1884. There is some confusion as to the actual site, but it seems likely that it was then used by Pettifors (see entry). The overlap in the trade directories may be as a result of the information in them often being out-of-date.

The remains of John Doleman's brewery.

Photo: Author

Hughes, Mrs Elizabeth, *Hare & Hounds, 34 Bradgate Road.*

In 1846, George Hughes was the victualler at the Hare and Hounds, but by 1870 Mrs Hughes had become the landlady. Mrs Elizabeth Hughes was then listed as the brewer for the period 1877-1887.

In 1913, it was described as a free house, with Alfred Geary as the licensed victualler, and he seems to have been at the pub from around 1894. The pub features in recent CAMRA Beer Guides.

Pettifor, Daniel, *Steam Brewery, Main Street/Bradgate Road.*

From 1794 to 1815 a Thomas Pettifor was at the Stag & Pheasant, Humberstone Gate in Leicester, from where his son William operated as a carrier, but family links with Anstey have yet to be established. There was also a Mrs Ann Pettifor at the Horse and Trumpet, in nearby Sileby, in 1848. Additionally, around 1864 to 1870, Cooper and Pettifor operated as soda water manufacturers, 19 Charles Street, Leicester. In 1875, Daniel Pettifor was listed as a brewer, baker and grocer, having previously been a baker and beer retailer, but the following year he was only shown as a brewer. Kelly's 1877 directory lists Pettifor as a large brewer, which suggests that he may have taken over the business previously operated by Dolemans.

In 1880, he was described as an ale and porter brewer, although the following year in Wright's directory he was simply listed as a brewer. Three years later he was shown as a brewer and maltster again. In 1891, the business was listed as Daniel Pettifor & Sons (F63). The sons were Daniel junior and George. The family home was at Newtown Linford. Around this time, Pettifor's stout was available from Thomas Fox's ale stores in Church Gate, Leicester. They also had an off-licence at Ratby, which they sold to Leicester Brewing and Malting around this time.

Interestingly, their advertisement in Wright's 1894 Directory states that the brewery was established in 1840. This supports the strong possibility that they were operating on the site previously used by Doleman and the overlap with Coupland may have been caused by the directories being out-of-date.

```
D. PETTIFOR & SONS'
STEAM BREWERY AND MALTINGS,
       1840. ESTABLISHED 1840.
   ANSTEY, NEAR LEICESTER.
   NOTED DOUBLE STOUT AND ALES,
Brewed from Best Malt and Hops, in Casks of 54, 36, 18, 12, 9, and 6 Gallons.
BOTTLED DOUBLE STOUT AND BITTER BEER in Imperial Pints and Half-Pints.
    Branch Establishment at Anstey for the Manufacture of ÆRATED WATERS.
AGENCY AND STORES, HIGH STREET, IBSTOCK.  CIGARS OF THE BEST BRANDS.
    FAMILIES AND THE TRADE SUPPLIED ON THE BEST TERMS.

BRADGATE PARK, THE RUINS, AND "OLD JOHN" HILL.
Pleasure Parties, Artists, Tourists, Cyclists, Schools, and others visiting this Picturesque Scenery, will
find Good Accommodation for Large or Small Parties; also Pleasure Grounds for Games, Cricket, Bowls,
Swings, &c., at the
"BRADGATE" HOTEL & RESTAURANT, NEWTOWN LINFORD.
```
From a commercial directory dated 1894.

```
    D. PETTIFOR'S
ALE & PORTER BREWERY,
        ANSTY,
    NEAR LEICESTER.

FAMILIES AND THE TRADE SUPPLIED.
```
From a commercial directory dated 1880.

The advertisement mentions their Noted Double Stout and Ales. They were also supplying mineral waters and bottled double stout and bitter, in both pint and half pints. The mineral water plant was located at one of the off-licensed premises which was opposite the brewery in the Main Street, and it is possible that this where they had originally started as grocers and brewers. There was also an agency and stores in the High Street at Ibstock.

Their papers show that they were selling their stout at 50/- per barrel to the Bradgate Hotel in Newtown Linford. They were also giving what seems to be the standard 20% on their beers. This was their only leasehold property, with a rent of some £80 pa.

In 1900, as well as beer, Pettifors were producers of stone beer and mineral waters. However, in January 1900, Marston's Directors were looking at the business and they decided to purchase it. The take-over was completed by 26th March, financed by a share issue which took Marstons nominal capital from £208,000 to £325,000. This included the following preference shares:-

George Matts Pettifor	£10,450	1,045 shares
Daniel Pettifor	£10,450	1,045 shares
Rev John Shipley Pettifor, Baston, Lincs	£2,000	200 shares

In 1896, George Matts Pettifor was the licensee of the Melton Hotel in Leicester. Other parties involved were:- Mary Ann Watts Stevenson, wife of William Job Henry Stevenson of King Richard's Road, Leicester - 100 shares. Frances E Nickson wife of James Nickson, Park Hall, Towcester - 100 shares.

In terms of the Pettifor estate, one of the off-licences in Main Street was kept by an Harriet Matts and the Queen's Head Markfield by George Shipley Matts, whilst Henry Shipley ran the off-licence at Station Road, Ratby. These all suggest family links, given the Pettifor first names.

ANSTY, near Leicester.

To BREWERS, BUILDERS, SPECULATORS, and others.

Warner, Sheppard & Wade

HAVE RECEIVED INSTRUCTIONS FROM THE OWNERS,

TO SELL BY AUCTION

At their Mart, Halford Street, Leicester,

On TUESDAY, February 5th, 1901,

At SEVEN o'clock, subject to Conditions of Sale,

IN ONE LOT,

THE

Valuable Freehold Property

COMPRISING

The BREWERY and MALT HOUSES,

for many years in the occupation of Messrs. D. PETTIFOR & SONS, together with the

Dwelling House, Five Cottages and Offices,

AND THE VALUABLE

PLOT of BUILDING LAND adjoining

the whole situate in the main street of Ansty, to which it has a **frontage of 182 feet 6 inches,** the whole site containing an area of

4 ACRES, 2 ROODS, 20 PERCHES,

OR THEREABOUTS.

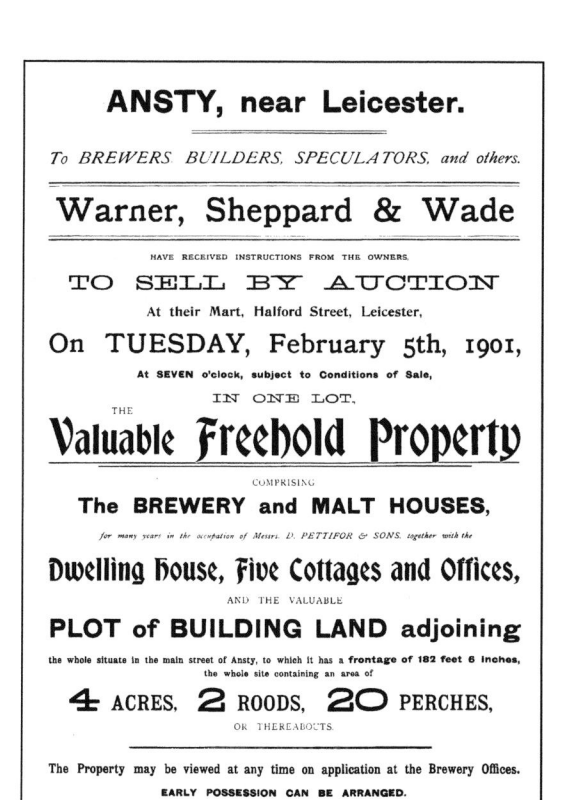

The Property may be viewed at any time on application at the Brewery Offices. **EARLY POSSESSION CAN BE ARRANGED.**

Plans and further particulars may be obtained on application to the AUCTIONEERS, Halford Street, Leicester; or to

Messrs. J. & W. J. DREWRY,

Solicitors, BURTON-ON-TRENT.

PARTICULARS.

The Brewery Premises

Situate at ANSTY, 4½ miles from LEICESTER, for many years in the occupation of Messrs. D. PETTIFOR & SONS,

with extensive Beer Stores, large open Sheds, Store Rooms, Carpenter's Shop, Fermenting Rooms, Engine and Boiler with the Shafting and Gas and Water Pipes throughout the premises, ten ton Weighing Machine, Wine Cellar, Suite of Offices, Garden and Yard with Gateway Entrance.

ALSO

The Three-Storey MALTHOUSE with Kilns,

DWELLING HOUSE in the occupation of Dr. Woolley.

FIVE COTTAGES and

LARGE PLOT OF BUILDING LAND adjoining.

FRONTAGE TO THE MAIN STREET 182 FEET 6 INCHES.

TOTAL AREA:

4 Acres, 2 Roods, 20 Perches,

OR THEREABOUTS.

The Property has a frontage of **37 feet** to the Green, and also to the Hollow Lane **52 feet.**
There is an excellent supply of pure water on the premises.
The Working Plant, comprising the vats, coppers, coolers, refrigerators, hot and cold water tanks, and other fixed or loose plant, can be taken by valuation at the option of the purchaser, or it will be removed or sold by the Vendors.

The Auctioneers beg to call special attention to this Important Property, which is situate in the centre of Ansty, and presents a very favourable opportunity for the erection of Factories, Warehouses, or Cottages, without in any way interfering with the existing premises.

The sale included the brewery, maltings and offices, together with the aerated water factory opposite. The estate, valued at £58,300, included 11 pubs and beerhouses, 10 off-licensed beerhouses and the Working Mens' Club in Anstey. The valuation was originally to be undertaken by Orgill Marks and Lawrence of London, before it was decided a local firm could do it more cheaply; however, the latter's figure of £41,425 seems to have been over-ruled. On the basis of the higher valuation, Marstons were able to raise a £30,000 mortgage with the Law Guarantee & Trust Society. The following values suggest that the business was not very large:-

---

ESTABLISHED 1840.

D. PETTIFOR'S

MALTINGS & STEAM BREWERY,

ANSTY, NEAR LEICESTER.

NOTED DOUBLE STOUT & ALES,

In Casks of 54, 36, 18, 12, and 9 Gallons. Families and the Trade supplied on the best terms.
Double Stout and Bitter Beer in Imperial Pint and Half-Pint Bottles.

ALSO BRANCH ESTABLISHMENT AT ANSTY FOR THE MANUFACTURE OF ÆRATED WATERS.

From a commercial directory dated 1888.

Horses £90   Casks £526   Plant £457

The valuation stated that the properties were generally in a fair state of repair and appeared to be occupied by a very respectable class of tenants. It also said that tenants had reported that they preferred the beer which they were now receiving from Marstons, rather than that which they had previously had from Pettifors. Pettifors had some 5 additional properties, the ownership of which seems to have remained with the family, until they were transferred to Marstons in the 1930s.

On 5th February, 1901, there was a sale by auction in Leicester of the brewery and malt houses, together with a dwelling house, five cottages and the offices. These had been valued previously at £5,100. The sale details state that the brewing plant was also available. The plan shows the site fronting on to Main Street and just down from the Green and Hollow Lane (now Hollow Road). Some of the buildings are now used by Potters Carpets.

However, Pettifors continued to trade until at least 1913 as wine and spirit merchants, bottlers and mineral water manufacturers, presumably as a subsidiary of Marstons. Marstons kept the brewery as a depot on Bradgate Road (Main Street having been renamed), which around 1930 was listed as H Widdowson, Steam Brewery. The depot operated until 1st June 1957, when they sold some of the site, with the remainder being sold in 1969.

> **D. PETTIFOR & SONS'**
> **STEAM BREWERY & MALTINGS,**
> (ESTABLISHED 1840,)
> **ANSTEY, NEAR LEICESTER.**
>
> NOTED DOUBLE STOUT AND ALES, BREWED FROM BEST MALT AND HOPS,
> In Casks of 54, 36, 18, 12, 9, and 6 Gallons.
> **BOTTLED DOUBLE STOUT IN IMPERIAL PINTS AND HALF-PINTS.**
>
> ☛ Branch Establishment at Anstey for the Manufacture of ÆRATED WATERS.
> FAMILIES AND THE TRADE SUPPLIED ON THE BEST TERMS.

From Wright's Directory 1892.

Willett, Mrs Jemima, *Coach & Horses, Market Place.*

In 1846, Richard Arguile was at the pub. Around 1870 to 1875, John Willett was the victualler at the pub, but in 1876 Mrs Jemima Willett was buying her wine and spirits from All Saints Brewery, suggesting that she had taken over from her husband. She was listed from 1877 to 1887 as a brewer. However, she was only shown as a victualler in 1894 and two years later, Thomas Bosworth was running the pub. In 1898, he was shown as paying £80 rent to Pettifors.

In 1900, it was part of the Pettifor's estate bought by Marstons, indeed Daniel Pettifor actually seems to have been living on the premises. With a value of £10,100, twice that of the brewery itself, it was the most expensive piece of property in the take-over. It was fully licensed and had been rebuilt shortly before the acquisition. It was described as doing a considerable and increasing trade, the tenant suggested around £100 per month, and is still trading.

ASHBY-de-la-ZOUCH

Bagnall, Thomas, *King's Head, 52 Market Street.*

In 1848, Mrs Ann Knowles was running the King's Head, whilst Thomas Bagnall seems to have been the owner of the Old George, Market Street and the Shoulder of Mutton, Kilwardby Street. He was also the agent for the Burton Brewery Company. In 1803, John Halford had sold the Old George (rebuilt 1799), when the address was shown as Kilwardby Street.

In 1870, Bagnall was still the agent for the Burton company, that had a maltings on Tamworth Road, but was also a victualler in his own right at the King's Head. The address in 1875 was shown as 52 Market Street.

In 1884, Thomas Bagnall was still shown as the agent for Burton Brewery Company Ltd, but they were also shown as brewers in the Market Place, and two years later he was described as their manager. However, this was probably connected with the maltings which they continued to operate until the mid 1920s. The address of the maltings in 1896 was Packington Road.

There may be a family connection with the Bagnall Brothers Brewery of Little Eaton, who were criticised in 1900 by Offilers for the introduction of ale in one gallon jars, which they were *"hawking around Leicestershire"*. The King's Head was later supplied by Davenports.

Bowmar, Thomas, *Market Street.*

Listed in 1884, this seems to be the only entry for Bowmar, who may have been employed elsewhere. However, a TP Bowmar did operate a beer agency in High Street, Leicester, in 1875, which was continued by the family.

Bradley, Thomas, *Bull's Head, 67 Market Street.*

A very old inn, which originally extended further up the street. Mentioned in W Scott's "Story of Ashby", as where the parliamentarian General Bainbrigg stayed during the siege of the castle in 1646. In 1791, Thomas Brewin was the victualler at the inn.

In 1875, Bradley was at the Navigation (see Swan entry), when Robert Hickinbotham was here, before being listed as a brewer at the Bull's Head in 1877. In 1896, the pub was run by a Thomas Doleman (see Anstey entry), but brewing seems to have stopped earlier.

ASHBY (continued)

It used to have the arms of the Earls of Huntingdon on the front, i.e. the badge of the Hastings family, which was a Bull's Head. It is now the Fayre and Firkin, part of the Allied-Domecq chain, with beers from the Loughborough brewery.

Cooper, George & Field, William, *Acresford Brewery, Donisthorpe.*

In 1848, Oliver Bowley was listed as a maltster and beer retailer at Blackfordby (Acresford), but it is not clear whether this was the forerunner of the Acresford Brewery. There was an entry for an O Bowley as a farmer and miller in 1870 and Friedrich suggests that he may have also involved with brewing. From around 1908 to 1922 a John George Bowley was running the Caves Arms.

Certainly around 1860, a John Harley Berry founded a brewery at Acresford. It is possible that he was related to the Harley family brewing at Loughborough. In 1870, Samuel Cooper was a farmer at Donisthorpe, who by 1876 had taken over the brewery. In 1877, Kelly's directory identified this as a large brewery, but also showed it under Nether Seal. White's directory identified this as the Acresford Brewery at Nether Seal, whilst George's home was in Uttoxeter.

On 15th September 1900, the Acresford Brewery, of George Cooper & William Field & Co (F83), was taken over by Sydney Evershed of Burton and closed in 1902. The purchase included 15 freehold and 4 leasehold licensed properties. G&WF Cooper also had a depot at 352 Fosse Road North, Leicester.

The Coopers became millers, although "Billy" Cooper retired to the Beeches Appleby, where he died around 1902, at what was said to be a fairly advanced age. He was buried at Uttoxeter, his home town. Unfortunately, to get there involved changing trains at Burton and although the mourners were successful, when they arrived at Uttoxeter, they found that no-one had transferred the coffin from one train to the other. Luckily, in those days trains were more frequent and the railway officials were able to put it onto the next service. Whilst waiting, the party adjourned to the nearby hotel for some liquid refreshment. Eventually, the parties were re-united and were able to enjoy the really good lunch which Billy had paid for!

The brewery was near the junction of the A444 and B5002, on the county border (SK299132). The old brewhouse stood in the middle of the yard until recent years, being used as a depot for Staffordshire Farmers Ltd. It has now been demolished and houses built on the site.

Although in 1913 Richard Thomas was listed as a brewer in Moira Road, Donisthorpe, this was probably the same individual shown earlier as Thomas Richardson. Then he had been described as a brewery manager and insurance agent; however, he was also listed as a brewer in 1915. It is also possible that he was employed elsewhere, since the village also housed Richard Douglas Tanner brewer of "Ind Coope".

Farmer, John, *Bowling Green Inn, 22 Brook Street, The Green.*

From around 1800, the Farmer family ran this pub for most of the century. William Farmer was shown at the Bowling Green around 1835 to 1848. By 1870 John was at the pub, where he was listed as the brewer in 1877. It is now supplied by Bass.

Measures, William, *The George, 50 Market Street.*

Pigot's directories of 1835-1855 showed William Measures as a maltster at the pub. In 1835, Thomas Measures was a maltster at Gilmorton. The Measures family ran the George, which stood next to the King's Head, from around 1820 to the 1860s. Around 1870-1875, Arthur Mead was at the pub, but there was no mention of brewing. The building is now an estate agents.

Orgill, John, *The Lamb, 56 Market Street.*

The first Lamb was celebrated for its ale at the end of the eighteenth century, when it was kept by a Mrs Sharpe, who was still there in 1813. In 1835, Ann Matthews was the victualler, and in 1846 to 1848 William Sutton. However, this inn was demolished in 1856 for the new market hall and the name was transferred to what had been the Saracen's Head.

By 1870, John Leedham was at the new Lamb, when Orgill was at the Old George, Market Street (previously run by Thomas Bagnall). In 1848, James Orgill was listed as a beer retailer in Market Street. Around this time, there was also a Francis Orgill, who was a

ASHBY
(continued)

maltster at Loughborough. By 1875, John Orgill was at the Lamb, where he was listed two years later as brewing. He was still the victualler in 1894.

Payne, Peter, *The New Inn, Ashby Woulds.*

The New Inn, perhaps not surprisingly newly built, was for sale by auction on 7th March 1810. Payne was the owner of the pub which, with its convenient brewhouse, was located on the main road. This may be the New Inn, later shown as Peggs Green, Coleorton, which traded until around 1890.

Shaws, *The Queen's Head, 79 Market Place.*

In 1791, Joseph Roe was the victualler at the pub. It was for sale in 1812 by Mr Price (or Rice) who had owned it for some 40 years. He died the following year and the pub was again for sale. This was the great posting house of the town, but in 1822 it was rebuilt by Thomas Shaw and the name was transferred to the Angel. The original site is now a bank.

In 1835, Thomas Shaw was a maltster at the new pub and in 1848 Samuel Shaw was a maltster in Market Street. Samuel Love took over the running of the pub before 1855. In 1870, Love was also a wholesale and retail wine & spirit merchant as well as the Inland Revenue office and agent for Midland Railway.

Sikes, William, *Oddfellows' Arms, 32 Kilwardby Street.*

This pub was initially called the Plumbers/Strugglers. However, in 1870 it was shown as Trinity Street, when run by Sam Jackson. In 1877, Sikes was the brewer, but the pub had closed by 1913. The site is now a garage.

Swan, Isaac, *Navigation Inn, 15 Kilwardby Street.*

In 1801, Henry Farnell was selling the Navigation with its malt office. The pub was named after the proposed canal, which in fact became a railway running at the side of the building. In 1815 to 1835, George Ilsley was running the pub, but with no mention of malting, although a nearby pub was called the Malt Shovel. By 1846, Thomas Cox was the victualler.

In 1870, Thomas Bradley (see entry) was at the Navigation, which in 1875 was shown as 15 High Street and in 1877 Isaac Swan was shown as the brewer. The pub closed, possibly by 1913, and is now the Fallen Knight, a restaurant and hotel.

BARKBY

Carnall, John, *Malt Shovel, 27 Main Street.*

The Malt Shovel was one of the last pubs in the county to brew its own beer. Parts of the building are thought to date back at least 700 years. In 1271, Merton College, Oxford, bought the property from Robert de Percy and the college owned it until 1963, when they sold it to the landlord.

It was kept by William John Charlesworth in 1855, who was shown as an innkeeper, but with no direct reference to brewing. In 1894, John Carnall, the victualler, was shown in capital letters in the directories. In 1904 he was identified as the brewer of the beer retailed.

The pub featured in an article in the Leicester Evening Mail in 1955, which described how Harry Oswin was still undertaking a brew every three weeks. The last brew was in December 1956. The history of the village, published for the 1974 exhibition, described how some of the utensils were still intact, with the masher flails and ladles in the old tap room. However, the 300 gallon copper was being used for flower displays in the foyer of the Dorchester Hotel in London. The pub is now a free house, which features in CAMRA guides.

Berry, Thomas, *Royal Oak.*

In the early 1800s, Berry was leaving the business and selling the pub, with very good malt mill, 40 gallon copper and 7 strike mash tub. There are no signs of a pub of this name, suggesting that it closed or possibly was re-named as what became the Brookside Inn, later supplied from Beeby.

BARROW upon SOAR

Simpson, William, *Bishop Blaize.*

The Bishop was for sale on 3 February 1812, with detached brewhouse, partly newly created, with nearby malt office. The sale resulted from the death of Mr Simpson. In 1894 Charles Paxton was the victualler. In 1921, the pub was owned by Sharpes of Sileby when sold to Strettons. There are no signs of the pub.

BARROWDEN
Rutland

Blencowe Brewing Company, *Exeter Arms, Main Street.*

The seventeenth century pub is named after the Marquis of Exeter of nearby Burghley House and a local landowner. The outbuildings had previously been a brewhouse. From 1835 to 1870, in addition to running the pub John Bates was a maltster, suggesting that he was brewing.

The two-barrel plant for the new brewery came from the former Scanlon's Brewery in Middlesex, and is located in the pub barn. Peter Blencowe after three years in planning, founded the brewery in June 1998. After taking a Brewlab course at Sunderland, he also received training from Rob Jones of the Dark Star Brewery and originally at the Pitfield Brewery, London.

Brewing takes place once a week, with most of the output going into the pub. The brewing liquor is mains water which has been "Burtonised". The malts used include:- Crystal, Pale, Chocolate and Cara, with some wheat for head retention. The wort is boiled with hops being added three times. The hops used being Target, Challenger and Cascade. Fermentation takes some six days.

The Exeter Arms.

Photo: Author

Initially the beer was called John Arnold, with a gravity of 3.8%, taking its name from a former vinegar factory in the village. However, the beers now available are as follows:-

| Boys | 3.6% | Big Boys | 4.5% |
| Young Boys | 4.1% | Strong Boys | 5% |

The latter beer has flavour reminiscent of another local beer from the County! There are also special brews, including Choir Boy (5.2%) made with Drambuie and mincemeat for Christmas.

The Rutland Local History Society booklet describes how once there were three "brewhouses" in the village. One was operated by William Swan on the east side of the green behind Stubbs the wheelwright (in 1979 a garage). Another one was William Dexter's at Nob Hall, down Mill Lane. The third was operated by Masons at West Farm, with maltings opposite. There are no listings for these concerns operating on a commercial basis, so one must assume that they were probably farm based operations to supply their own workforces.

BEEBY

Nuttall, Thomas, *North Leicester Brewery Company.*

In 1870, Thomas Nuttall was a landowner and farmer, living at Manor House. He was still only a farmer in 1875, when aged 40, but in that year he set up the first factory in the world for making Stilton cheese. Then in 1881 he was shown as a brewer and maker of Stilton.

BEEBY (continued)

In 1884, Thomas Nuttall of the North Leicester Brewery (F237) was also shown at 16 Southgate Street, Leicester, but this was probably only a depot (F2723). The manager was Arthur West. Nuttall owned several pubs in the town, including the following:-

>Dolphin, Lichfield Street
>Duke of Portland, Oxford Street
>Lord Rancliffe, Redcross Street
>Mechanics Arms, Alexander Street
>New Jolly Angler, Wheat Street
>Princess Charlotte, Oxford Street

In 1891, it was shown as Thomas Nathanial Nuttall of the Leicester Brewery. However, it was registered in March 1894, as the North Leicester Brewing Company Ltd, with capital of £7,000. It also had depots at Melton and Uttoxeter. The manager around this time seems to have been a Frederick Harold Pearson.

The North Leicester Brewery of Thomas Nuttall, c.1900.

From the Jack Feast collection

An article in the Leicester Drinker for August 1999 includes a description of the layout of the brewery. The boiler house is the building on the right of the photograph, hence the chimney. The mash tun, said to be some 20ft in diameter, was in a building to the rear, with the coppers downstairs, probably in the central tower. It has been suggested that the part of building on the left may have been connected with malting, although the louvres would normally be associated with a fermenting area. Another source suggests that this part of the building was actually used for the cheese factory.

Sometime around this period, Thomas Nuttall is thought to have died. Certainly in 1896, the Beeby brewery was bought by the Midland Brewery Company of Loughborough. They installed Job Facer as the manager. A photograph taken around this time shows the changed ownership and the relatively small size of the concern. It was still operating in 1899, but brewing ceased soon afterwards, possibly when the Midland was taken over by Strettons of Derby. However, it is thought to have been used as a stores until around 1913. Some of the buildings, including the hop store, are thought to be still standing at the rear of Brewery Cottages (SK 662082). In addition, a nearby farm has the old signboard on one of its sheds.

The remains of the Beeby Brewery.

Photo: Author

BELGRAVE

Billington, Thomas, *Bull's Head, 6 Bath Street.*

James Ward was the victualler at the Bull's Head in 1846 until 1855, when Mrs Louisa Bishop took over the pub. She was followed by a Mr Powell, who ran the pub from around 1867 to 1877.

In 1884, George Samuel Gask was trading at what was identified only as a beerhouse. In 1892, the Bull's Head beerhouse was shown as next to No 8. Billington was listed as the brewer in 1898. Although the pub fronted onto Loughborough Road, the back entrance was in Bath Street. It is still trading as a freehouse.

Cooke, Joseph, *The Talbot, Thurcaston Road.*

In 1835, the Talbot was kept by Thomas Kirby, who in 1848 was also listed as a maltster at the pub. From 1870 to 1877, Mrs Ann Kirby was listed as brewing and she had held the licence from at least 1855. In 1884 Joseph Cooke was the brewer to 1887, but not in 1892, when the Charity Trustees sold the Talbot to LB&M, who had been leasing it from around 1883. The Talbot is the emblem of the de Belgrave family and featured in the design of the outside lights, although they now seem to have been replaced.

The Hotel Belgrave

Fowler, Cornelius, *New Inn, 113 Loughborough Road.*

From 1855 Richard Fowler was a butcher and beer retailer, but with no mention of a pub name. Then between 1884 and 1888, William Fowler was running the pub, until Cornelius took over the licence in the October. He was listed as brewing from 1892 to 1895, as well as being a butcher and victualler, but the address may have changed to No 213. In March 1894, Joseph Thorpe took the licence, but there was no further mention of brewing and in June 1896 it was owned by Welch Brothers. The site is now the Hotel Belgrave, with an Eagle Brewery motif over the entrance.

Mason, James, *Black Lion, 4 Checkett's Road.*

In 1813, Mason was letting the pub to a Samuel Summers, who was also operating the coal and coke trade at the premises. This included a large stock of prime home brewed ale. In the 1880s All Saints Brewery were supplying at least the wines and spirits and they had bought it by at the latest 1910. The pub was later demolished.

Spence, Mrs Sarah, *Champion Inn, Leicester Road.*

In 1848, Robert Spence was a baker and beer retailer at the Champion, which was named after the horse which won the Derby and the St Leger in 1800. By 1877, Sarah was identified as brewing at the pub. She was followed by 1884 by Edward Spence as the brewer.

George Bingley was then the brewer around 1887-1888. By 1925, All Saints Brewery supplied the pub, which was mentioned as one of their managed houses four years later.

BELTON **Toone, William,** *The George, 18 Market Place.*

In 1846, the George was kept by Ann Toone, whilst William Toone was shown as a maltster. In 1870 William was a farmer, whilst Mrs Elizabeth Toone had been at the George since 1855. By 1875, he had become a maltster and farmer and two years later was shown as a maltster and brewer.

From 1881 to 1902 William Toone was listed as a brewer and maltster (F247), but in 1884 John Emerson was at the George, followed by Thomas Chesterton. It seems likely that what had started out as the pub brewhouse, may have begun to operate on a more commercial scale.

In 1904 Mrs Jane Toone was only listed as a beer retailer, but there seems to be a 1911 entry for William Toone as a brewer.

In 1944, the George was bought by Offilers for £4,000, but seems to have been sold for only £2,550 in 1964. It is still trading, with an emphasis on food. The frontage gives a date of circa 1753 and a building in the yard at the rear may be the remains of a brewhouse.

BELTON, Rutland **Rudkin, William.**

William Rudkin is listed in White's 1877 directory as a grocer, brewer and beer retailer, having previously been a draper, grocer and beer retailer. However, in 1881 he had dropped the brewing and was operating the local post office. He may have been a member of the malting family connected with the Langham brewery.

BILLESDON **Tomlin, Mr,** *The Maltster & Brewer Inn.*

In November 1809, William Webster was running the malt office owned by Mr Tomlin. The latter was shown as trading from the Maltster and Brewer. In 1811, the Lion & Lamb was for sale with details from Mr White at the Maltster and Brewer. Although Mr Tomlin was still shown there in 1813, the pub was not listed in 1835, when Thomas Penn was the only maltster in the village.

A house called "The Maltings" is still standing at 12/14 Uppingham Road. There used to be a maltings at the rear, but as yet no direct link with Mr Tomlin has been established. There were 14 pubs and beerhouses in the village in the early nineteenth century.

BIRSTALL **Porter, Mr,** *The Plough, Front Street.*

In 1811, on the death of Mr Porter, the Plough with its 50 gallon copper, etc. was for sale. In 1846, George Bishop was running the pub, but there was no mention of brewing.

In 1921, the Old Plough went with Sharpe's other property to Strettons. It would seem to have been rebuilt at some time.

BITTESWELL **Man in Moon,** *Unit L1, Elms Park Farm.*

Commenced brewing in May 1996, at Gilmorton Lodge Farm, Ashby Magna, producing some 11 barrels per week. In 1997, the brewery moved to an industrial estate on a farm to the west of Bitteswell. It now has a potential output of 15 barrels per week. The beers brewed are:-

| Harvest Moon | 3.7% | Eclipse Bitter | 4.1% |
| Ivory Stout | 4.1% | Werewolf | 5% |

It supplies some 12 local outlets.

BLABY **Burgess, Daniel,** *The Bull's Head, 22 Lutterworth Road.*

Mr Burgess was selling the pub on 21st March 1803. The sale included a truly valuable copper of 140 gallons, an 18 strike mash tub, and 10x60 gallon, 3x120 gallon and 2x240 gallon barrels. In 1809, when the proprietor Mr Corrall retired from the business, the sale included two brewing coppers.

In 1855 Samuel Bonner was at the Bull's Head, but there was no mention of brewing with this or later landlords. In November 1898, the All Saints Brewery bought the pub for

£4,000. It is still trading with beers from Carlsberg-Tetley.

BOTTESFORD

Smith, John H, *Rutland Arms Hotel, High Street.*

On a 1916 photograph of the pub the advertising states *"All ales brewed on the premises"*. At the time it was being run by John Smith. In the 1960s, it was a Shipstone's house. In addition, when the Bull Inn was included in the 1919 Adcock sale, the details mentioned a malthouse.

BROUGHTON ASTLEY

Birchnell, Mrs William, *Sutton Lodge Brewery.*

In July 1812, Sutton House, with its domestic brewhouse, was to let from Mr Boultbee. Around this time, a Mr Sutton was looking to sell a 12 quarter malt office near to the church. Robert Birchnall was a farmer, grazier and maltster in 1846.

The first mention of brewing on a large scale was in 1855, when William Birchnell was listed for Sutton Lodge, as a farmer and brewer through to 1871. However, some directories only show William Birchnall as a farmer at Sutton in Elms, with no mention of brewing. Robert Birchnall was a farmer, grazier and maltster in 1846.

In 1876, Mrs William Birchnell was shown as the brewer at Sutton Lodge, and again the following year (F809). However, White's directory for that year lists Mrs Mary Ann Burchnall as the farmer and brewer at Sutton Lodge, Broughton Astley. By 1884 William was listed only as a farmer. The farm is still standing, but with no sign of a brewhouse.

Pegg, John, *Bull's Head, Primethorpe.*

In 1848, Pegg was shown as the brewer at the pub, but in 1855 there was only a James Pegg a blacksmith. In 1884 William Cooke was at the pub, where ten years later, Jas Brookes was the victualler and baker. However, in 1890 LB&M had taken a 3 year lease on the pub, which is now an Everard's house.

BURROUGH

TH&M

The 1999 Peterborough beer festival included details of a beer called Rutland Red 4% abv from a new brewery in the village. At the time of going to press the concern was too new to obtain further information.

BURROUGH on the HILL

O' Gaunt, John, *Unit 4B Ind Estate.*

In July 1997 Celia Atton, the manager of Parish's Old Brewery Inn at Somerby, decided to set up a brewery of her own, next to the Stag. This was called the John O'Gaunt Brewery, and had originally been set up at the Hare & Hounds at Fulbeck in Lincolnshire. This was a 5 barrel plant, with one brew per week. The beers are as follows:-

    Robin a Tiptoe   3.9%   (named after local landmark)
    Cropped Oak   4.4%

At the end of 1998, the brewing was moved to share the plant with Parish at Somerby.

Parish Brewery, *Stag & Hounds, Main Street.*

In 1846, the Stag was kept by William Gee. From 1848 to 1870, George Horspool was running the pub as a victualler and cattle dealer.

Barrie Parish bought the pub from John Smiths in 1984 and set about rebuilding it. In July 1986, Barrie, with some 7 years home-brewing experience, set up as the smallest commercial brewery in the country, using a Baby Burco boiler and a barrel cut into two for the mash tun. This was based in the cellar at the pub and initially produced around 18 gallons per brew.

In total the plant produced some 72 gallons per week of Parish Special Bitter 1036°, sold at 69p per pint, and 36 gallons of Poachers Ale at a strength of 1066°. The yeast for the beers came from Hoskins & Oldfield in Leicester.

The impact of brewing meant that the proposed sale of the pub was withdrawn. Instead, the 1/2 barrel plant was replaced by a 5 barrel stainless steel brewery from Ind Coope, which was located in the stables of the pub.

The beer range was extended to include Baz's Bonce Blower at 1105° OG 13½% abv, recorded as the strongest cask beer brewed. In 1990, the Parish Brewery moved to Somerby (see entry).

BURTON OVERY **Fosberry, Mr,** *Crown Inn.*

In June 1802, Mr Fosberry was selling the pub, with brewing utensils. In 1881, the New Crown, suggesting it had been rebuilt, was an Eady & Dulley house. However, there are no signs of the pub in the village.

CASTLE DONINGTON **Heaton, William,** *Turk's Head, Bondgate.*

In 1801, the Turk's Head was for sale, with a convenient brewhouse underneath. In 1813, Thomas Oldershaw was running the pub, with James Christopher Ellingworth there by 1835, until at least 1846.

It was a CBB/Offilers pub around 1900, which was rebuilt in 1909. In 1970 Bass valued it at £15,000 and it is still trading with beers supplied by them, although there are no external signs of brewery ownership.

Lees, John, *King's Head Inn, Market Place.*

In the middle part of the nineteenth century the King's Head was run by Henry Ball, a victualler. In 1870, Henry Lees was described as a wholesale manufacturer of baby linen and ladies work baskets etc. and licensed victualler at the King's Head and brewer in the Market Place. Henry Lees was still the brewer and victualler in 1874. The Lees family were also running the Cross Keys.

In 1877 John Lees had taken over brewing and was the brewer until 1887, although the address was shown as the Bell & Crown in the Market Place, but also later shown as Apesgate, which ran into the Market Place. The following year saw George Lees as the brewer until 1894, when Edward Lees was a brewery clerk. This seems to have been the end of brewing and the pub was then owned by CBB and later closed.

Minton, James, *The New Inn, Borough or Burrow Street.*

In 1846, James Minton kept the Rawdon Hotel, but there was no mention of brewing and he was described as a farmer in 1855. The Rawdon, built in 1794, closed around 1850 and became Manor House.

In 1870 Thomas S Sharpe ran the New Inn, and also a wine & spirit vaults. However, in 1877, a James Minton was the brewer at the New Inn. He was still at the pub in 1884, but brewing seems to have ended. The pub later closed.

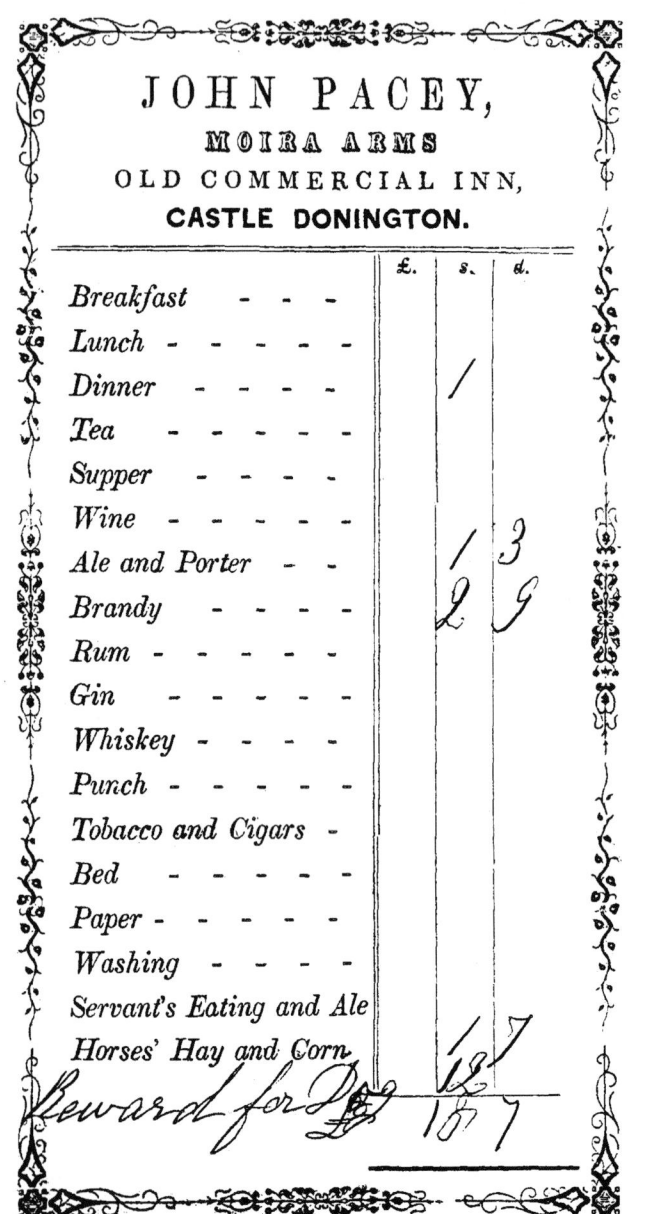

Invoice dated November 1857.

Pacey, John, *Moira Arms, High Street/Bondgate.*

In 1835, Pacey was at the pub, where he was identified as brewing in 1877. The pub is still trading, externally unaltered.

Twell, William, *Jolly Potters, 36 Hillside.*

In 1870 Joseph Beeby was at the Potter's Inn on Castle Hill, which may have been built shortly before. In 1875, Twell was running what had become the Jolly Potters on Castle Hill and sometimes Big Hill. He was listed as brewing from 1877 to 1884. The pub was being supplied by CBB/Offilers in 1911 and was later a Bass house. It is still in business.

CAVENDISH BRIDGE

Offilers' Brewery Ltd, *Cavendish Bridge Brewery.*

John Fletcher & Son established the brewery in 1815 and Fletcher & Son were listed as brewers in 1835. The Fletcher family had been brewing beer in Ripley in Derbyshire. They were shown in the 1830 poll book as John senior and John junior. George Trussell Eaton had taken over the brewery by 1840. He was born around 1821 at Sutton on Hill in Derbyshire and he seems to have been helped in the business by John, his younger brother. The Eaton family had financial connections to the brewing Fletchers of Derbyshire.

In 1846, he was listed as a brewer and maltster. His agent at 23 High Street, Castle Donington until 1855, was a William Clarke, who was also a maltster. Clarke bottled Eaton's beer at cottages in front of his home. However, in 1848 William Clarke was also shown as a maltster and farmer and ale and porter merchant at Cavendish Bridge, when Eaton was listed as a wholesale ale and porter brewer.

In 1884 Eaton was still listed, with William Hemsley the clerk at CBB. Eaton's home was shown as the Pastures. However, in June 1884, his widow Julia, née Sandford, was re-married to James Roney-Dougall. The latter had come to learn the brewing trade, but after his marriage was later ordained and became the local vicar.

In September 1896, Offilers, which had gone public in 1890, bought the Cavendish Bridge Brewery. This was financed by the issue of £20,000 preference shares and a £65,000 mortgage debenture. They doubled output at CBB, to serve the Offilers' Leicestershire pubs and to continue supplying the strong presence in Loughborough and Quorn. The main Derby brewery was still run by Henry Offiler.

Around this time, the CBB still had an agency at Ashby, then run by Mrs Ann Cox the victualler at the Waggon & Horses.

The minute books for the Offilers' Board at the turn of the century seem to devote more time to CBB than to their own Derby concern, perhaps representing the continuing management need to assimilate the two businesses. At this time, Offilers' balance sheet valued the business at £304,263, with a net profit £20,105 in 1899, paying 6% on A&B preference shares. However, in 1900 there was a call of £1 per £5 Ordinary share (£4 paid) to cover payments on the CBB debenture trust account and they were looking to issue the balance of 3,318 unissued shares. The strength of the business was shown in that these were to be issued at a £2 premium, i.e. £7. The 9th Offilers' AGM on 30th November reported that CBB was *"now moving along very nicely"*.

The trustees for the debenture were Sir Thomas Roe and Sir Henry Willmot, both from families which seem to have had other brewery connections. There was still some involvement with the previous owners e.g. transfer of debenture stock from Thomas Eaton to a Sarah Barton. Similarly, the following year a WJ Eaton offered the Old School House, Cavendish Bridge to Offilers for £300 but they declined to purchase the building. Around this time, a George Henry Eaton was at the Brickmakers in Leicester, but this was owned by Brunt Bucknall.

CAVENDISH BRIDGE (continued)

In February 1899, J Marsden, described as the Head Brewer at Offilers (actually at CBB) left to take an appointment with the Trinidad Brewery Company in the West Indies. His successor was a WA Crane from Warwicks & Richardsons at Newark. The 10th AGM on 30th November stated that the business was *"growing enormously"*, requiring further investment of some £6,000 at CBB and Derby. However, one sad note was the death of George Offiler on 3rd November.

In 1899, they were working on the water supply, and the following year saw £37 for new water mains and £24 for repairs to the chimney and new lightning conductor. The workforce at CBB presented George A Matterson, the Head Brewer at Derby, with an aneroid barometer and thermometer as a wedding present in 1900.

In March the Budget increase in duty of 1/- per barrel was passed on to the trade; however, the response from the Loughborough tenants was a circular arguing that this war tax should be abolished or divided between the parties. The Offilers' Board instructed the company secretary, Mr Brown, to respond stating that both were impossible. In September 1901, they received a letter from the Leicester & District Off-licensed Association, complaining that the tax had been charged to the tenants, but not to the free trade. Around this time Offilers had offices at Campbell Chambers, Campbell Street in town.

The 1900 AGM on 19th November saw James Cumberland, who had taken George Offiler's place as chairman, reporting an excellent year, with profits of £22,165. He stated that when the business had been founded in 1890, it had assets of £75,019 and these were now worth £321,978.

Breweries were of course still reliant on horse-drawn transport at the turn of the century; although, around this time the Brewers' Journal included articles about the growth of motor traction vehicles. Hence, a new dray for the Leicester agency cost £30, and a cart horse for CBB was £39. Old horses at CBB were sold:- a grey cart mare for £9 19s 6d, bay cart horse £21. At these prices, they were presumably for further use rather than the knackers yard!

Travellers operating from the agencies worked on commission. However, to obtain a position, they had to put down a £100 cash security on which they would receive 5% interest, with an average commission of £2 per week. Offilers were looking to expand their Leicester office and initially looked to extend the lease with the owner, Mr Winterton. The role of such agents was crucial in both developing sales, maintaining quality and acting as early forms of market research. At this time, the Burton brewers were looking to expand their trade and agents played a vital part, not least having information about the credit worthiness of local landlords. Bass had loans of some £1m at the turn of the century and the Journals were full of victuallers going bankrupt.

The new owners of CBB were also looking to upgrade the estate e.g. a proposal to give up the Lord Nelson at Loughborough for a new hotel on the Toothill estate. However, this was turned down by the licensing authorities. This did not prove too much of a difficulty, since CBB formed an agreement with the local Midland Brewery Company, not to tender for the Toothill estate, because insufficient new houses had been built. They were also offered for £2,800, the Old English Gentleman, which they seemed to be leasing and which was selling some 4 barrels per week.

To match the increased output, CBB was investing £110 in a new brewery copper from Briggs & Company. The brewhouse was of course steam powered; hence in 1901, they were ordering 100 tons of gas coal at tender between 16/3 and 19/1 per ton, as well as 300 tons of "hard" brewery coal at 14/8 from Mr Cowlishaw. The following March they also invested £290 in a new boiler, together with £42 for a second-hand one and £61 for a steam driven yeast pump and new yeast press.

However, they were obviously concerned about their distribution area, since in 1902 when Carr & Company of 178a Derby Road, Nottingham, applied for an agency to sell CBB beer, they were turned down. Offilers did not want to establish a buying agency at Nottingham. Interestingly, they also declined to supply the 26 pubs of the Derby business of Pountain, Girardot and Foreman, although they did take this contract in the 1920s. Despite this reluctance, they produced a trading profit of £21,765 for 1901.

September 1903 brought a new wooden mash tun from Messrs Buxton and Thornley for some £221, as well as new yeast backs. The emphasis on new methods of controlling brewing, particularly in terms of the yeast, can be seen in a contract with Messrs Matthews

& Lett of Burton. This was to analyse 2 samples of yeast from each brewery per week.

The assistant brewer at Derby, Mr F Allen, received an increase in salary from £150 to £175 per annum. However, brewing at CBB was not doing so well, with Henry Offiler, the joint MD reporting numerous complaints from customers and that he had to stop the beer from going out. The CBB brewer was given 3 months salary in lieu of notice and in the meantime, Henry would oversee brewing there. Henry's annual salary as joint MD was some £1,000. Mr Crane the brewer at CBB declined to offer his resignation and was dismissed. Mr JR Pick of CBB received a £5 bonus for his help whilst there was no full-time brewer. Mr George Peach also received a £5 bonus for the extra work involved with his malting on commission at Pountains. It is interesting to see the continued involvement of the Peach family in malting.

Another set-back to Offilers was the death of Mr James Cumberland in October, the Chairman of the business. He was replaced by another member of the board, James Cooper. The following year, the Company Secretary, Frank Brown, also died.

In September 1904, JR Pick's hard work was further recognised when he was appointed assistant brewer at CBB, on a salary of £3 per week. To help, W Wright, a tun room man, was appointed as working foreman on 30/- per week. Henry Offiler would continue to supervise operations at the brewery. October brought investment in a new refrigerator from Munstons for £160.

In January 1905, the problem of the brewer at CBB was resolved when Mr Guy Thompson, from the Nottingham Brewery Company, was appointed the manager. He was given a salary of £200 per annum and a cottage at the brewery. Another newcomer from Nottingham was Mr Shearer from Home Brewery, who was appointed as the Company Secretary. CBB would seem to have been operating the Burton Union brewing system, since in May 1905 they bought 24 union casks and fittings from Z Smith, their neighbours across the river at Shardlow.

From 30th September 1905, all fully licensed tenants were to be tied for wines and spirits. The Offilers' estate at the time was as follows:-

	No	Book Value	Average Barrel Trade
Freehold Fully Licensed	52	£128,210	10,488
Beer, beer & wine	30	£49,681	4,655
Beer off	17	£17,030	2,256
Short Lease Full Licence	19		2,605
Beer, beer & wine	7		1,063
Beer off	21		3,272
			24,339

The continued popularity of bottled beer, particularly from the nearby Burton brewers, led to trials with filling machines for carbonated beer. The trials were successful and two machines purchased.

In 1905 Guy Thompson the brewer was to marry and, as a result, was to take the house occupied by the CBB chief clerk, Mr Dickin, the latter presumably being single. However, in January 1906, the MD drew attention to the decrease of trade at CBB and the unsatisfactory condition of some of the beers brewed. The MD was to investigate and speak to Mr Thompson, who was to attend the mashing in the early morning and to follow through the process. Perhaps his marriage had affected his dedication to the brewing!

The Derby brewery seemed to be operating successfully, since Mr Matterson the Head Brewer received an increase in his salary to take him to £450 per annum. However, in December 1906, the assistant brewer there, Mr Allen, resigned. Amongst the 100 applicants for the post was Arthur Hill Wicks (possibly Willis), 52 Kirkstall Avenue, Leeds. This successful applicant was the son of Mr Hill Wicks previously the brewer at Cavendish Bridge. His career included one year with his father at the Exeter Brewery, a year at Russells of Gravesend and he had spent the last 15 months as assistant brewer at the Kirkstall Brewery, Leeds, producing some 1,200 barrels per week.

In 1907 they agreed a new malt contract with Pountains. Presumably this was for the Derby

CAVENDISH BRIDGE (continued)

home-brew pubs. However, in the November they were looking to sell some of their own properties. This was perhaps not unconnected with requests from the bank to reduce the overdraft on the property account, as well as its decision to raise the interest rate to 5%. The Board was also considering issuing further preference shares to raise cash.

Problems continued with brewing at CBB, when on 8th September 1908, Guy Thompson's resignation was accepted. He had been appointed Head Brewer at Smith & Company, just across the river in Shardlow. Mr HA Willmot from Sir William Dupree's brewery at Portsmouth was appointed in his place on £200 pa. Given that a Willmot was one of the CBB debenture trustees, there may have been a family connection. However, the following year, when Mr Hill Wicks (shown later as Willis), the assistant brewer requested an increase in salary, this was turned down because of the unsatisfactory trade at the time.

The trading difficulties had also caused the Chairman of the Leicester licensing committee to comment about the prevalence of the "long pull", i.e. selling over measure. He also stated that any giving away of sweets or price cuts would lead to the licence being lost. A sound economic response to poor sales! Offilers had agreed with other members of the local trade that there would be a minimum price of 4d per quart.

Licences were crucial at this time, as the authorities began to use the powers granted to them by the 1904 Compensation Act. For example CBB lost the licence for the Anchor at Thringstone, with compensation of £324, of which the tenant would receive £50.

This poor trade had led to the liquidation of another Derbyshire business, the Little Eaton Brewery. This seemed to be a small concern with about 6 pubs and an off-licence, totalling an annual trade of only £1,200. This was mainly in one gallon containers, presumably for home consumption. Offilers bought the business in April 1909, for only £525.

Whilst draught beers were still the main sales, bottled beer was continuing to grow in popularity. There was investment in the bottling department at CBB in September 1909 as follows:-

| New Kiefer Filler | £110 | Air Pump | £9 |
| Filters | £27 | Labelling Machine | £50 |

In contrast to previous directorial concern with buying horses, the year 1910 saw mention of the arrangements for Mr Offiler's motor car.

Licensing continued to exercise management attention. The increase in excise costs led to the Loughborough agency licence being dropped, whilst there was as an attempt to change that at Leicester from wholesale to retail. However, there were difficulties with the local authorities about the practicalities involved. There was also the new manufacturing tax of 12/- per barrel, leading to increased costs for CBB of £270 and Derby £476. It is difficult to translate these amounts into barrelage, since various offsets were possible. Nevertheless, they do indicate that CBB was probably only around half the size of the Derby brewery.

Nevertheless, whilst horse drawn drays limited distribution, CBB still had a role to play in supplying the southern trading area in Leicestershire. Hence, September 1910 saw investment of £150 in a new boiler and the following year £370 was spent on a new roof for the brewery.

Perhaps surprisingly, there does not seem to have been much trade in Ashby, although in the October a Mr McCarthy offered the White Hart with a trade of about £600 at 20% discount on sales. It is likely that the town was mainly supplied by Brunt's nearby Woodville brewery (see entry).

The year 1911 saw the trade gradually improving, perhaps linked to the celebrations for George V's coronation. There would be improvements at Derby to reflect the increase and the brewer there, Mr Willmot saw an increase in salary to £275. Nevertheless, the Board declined to purchase Hill's Cromford brewery.

Things were not quite so happy at CBB, where two of the travellers died within days of each other in early November. Then on 11th January 1912, Richard Finney died aged 70. He had joined the Offilers' Board at the time of the purchase of CBB. This was given as 22nd September 1896 and it seems likely that Finney had been running CBB at the time.

The Buck's Horn at Loughborough was closed and the licence transferred to a new off-licence at 31 Curzon Street. This was despite an initial objection from Marstons. Further problems arose at Leicester, where the police objected to the renewal of the licences for the

CAVENDISH BRIDGE (continued)

Warwick Arms and the Warwick Castle. The Board accepted that closure was likely, but anticipated that they could use the money received from the Compensation Fund for rebuilding the Wilmot Arms at Derby. In the event, they did not receive the anticipated £2,400, but only about £1,800.

In line with the previous tie on wines and spirits, James Gutteridge, the tenant of the Lord Nelson at Loughborough, was given notice to quit for buying his spirits elsewhere. However, the notice was subsequently withdrawn.

A sign of the times was the arrival in June 1913 of a Foden steam motor. The following year saw the purchase of another Foden and a motor car for Mr Brown, the Leicester agent. In expectation of further closures and compensation, 5 of the Loughborough houses were revalued as follows:-

The Blue Boar, Rushes	£1,600	Wheatsheaf, Bedford Square	£1,750
Green Man, Swan Street	£3,000	Old English Gent, Ashby Road	£2,210
White Swan, Wellington Street	£1,750		

In fact, most seem to have survived possible closure. Investment at Derby allowed four old fermenting vessels to be transferred to CBB. The improvements there were probably helpful in absorbing the small increase in capacity needed to cover the extra sales resulting from the eventual purchase of Hill's Cromford brewery in January 1914, for £7,250. A new second assistant brewer was H Cecil Offiler.

In July 1914, Hugh Nelthorpe Sutton, who had family links with the Pountains, died. He had replaced Richard Finney as a member of the Board. However, greater problems came when September brought the outbreak of war. The initial impact was on the workforce, as employees volunteered for the forces. The business patriotically supported them. The 4 boys who left from the bottling department were given £1 each, whilst the wives of serving men received some 5/- or 6/- per week and a coal allowance of 12/6. Mr Willis the brewer also went on active service, although he received an allowance of £5 per month.

The war does not seem to have had a major impact on the business. If anything, the minutes of the Board meetings become rather terse, with little comment on how the business was operating, nor on how the war was progressing. Still sales seemed to be reasonable and, despite increased taxes, they were also able to raise the prices. To help cover the vacancies, JH Warton, previously brewing in the Stroud area, was appointed assistant brewer at Derby.

There was also a gradual expansion of the estate e.g. 3 pubs at Spondon, but this seems to reflect increasing concern for the Derbyshire trade. However, in 1918 the Chairman James Cooper was increasingly absent from meetings because of illness. Indeed, on some occasions, the meetings were held at his house in Moseley, Birmingham.

In March 1919, FDK Willmot was to succeed J Wainwright as the maltster at CBB. The latter, aged 70 had been with the business for 48 years, which would shows he had been there from the days of George Eaton. Willmot was also to be an assistant brewer, with a salary of £200 pa.

However, the post-war period was beset with *"difficulties which the company had had to meet"*. Nevertheless, a new appointment in May 1919 as assistant MD and director, was HC Offiler, the son of the MD. He had been *"specially trained for brewery management"*.

In July, an expansion of the CBB maltings was agreed. This doubled the capacity from 35 to 70 quarters. The work cost some £5,579.

In March 1920, Mr Hill Willis left after 15 years service to become the Head Brewer at Hardy and Hanson of Kimberley. His replacement was Vivian Bailey, who came from Worksop and Retford, where he had been involved with producing some 1,500 barrels per week. Another member of the family joined the firm, when FR Offiler was appointed as motor traffic manager at £375 pa. In June the Foden 3 ton steam wagons were sold for £550 each.

On 3rd May 1921, after his lengthy illness, James Cooper died aged 78. He had been a director since the formation of the company and Chairman for 18 years. William Hart became the new Chairman.

That year GA Matterson, the Head Brewer, celebrated 25 years with the business. This shows that he had joined in 1896, suggesting that he may have started with CBB, before replacing Mr Offiler at Derby.

In June 1922, Offilers were given the opportunity to convert eight of Pountain's home brew pubs in Derby to brewery supply. However, this had to be postponed because of objections from the tenants. Nevertheless, they were supplying Pountain's other houses and this attempt to cease brewing in the pubs was to presage the events of later years.

In November, Frances Reynold was appointed as a director to fill the vacancy from James Cooper's death. However, on 28th November a further death was that of one of the founders, Henry Offiler, a director since incorporation in 1890. The AGM on the 18th December confirmed HC Offiler as the new MD, with two new directors:- Alderman JG Shields and FR Offiler, the engineering and transport manager.

This new blood immediately showed its changed view, with the directors' meeting after the AGM deciding to close CBB and transfer brewing to Derby. No doubt the introduction of motor transport, making distribution much easier, and the fight against the rating assessment for CBB, had been major factors in the decision. In 1922 HA Willmott was listed as the manager at CBB.

The 1922 Annual Report stated that whilst *"from time to time it had shown good results, owing to diminished trade it had been decided that all brewing could be done at Derby."* (BHS Journal No 48 June 1986 p7). The maltings would continue to operate. On 23rd January 1923, the Cavendish Bridge brewery closed.

The business figures for 1922 were as follows:- Trading profit of £24,103 (down from £31,143), which after interest etc. generated a surplus £10,104 (down from £15,462). This increased the P&L account to £60,012. In turn, this allowed:-

1/2 year dividend	£4,200
6% preference shares	£1,200
5% ordinary shares	£3,000

The Balance Sheet was as follows:-

4,000 A Cumulative 6% £5 Preference	20,000		
4,000 B Cumulative 6% £5 Preference	20,000		
12,000 £5 Ordinary shares	60,000		
Total	£100,000		
Mortgage debenture and interest	127,812	Freehold & long lease inc brewery	344,161
Mortgages	11,040	Plant, casks, drays etc	17,992
Sundry creditors	16,307	Stock	47,201
Reserve for income tax etc	140,453	Sundry debtors	36,356
Reserve	60,000	Cash	16,188
P&L A/C balance	57,517	Investment, war loans etc	30,580
		Short leases and goodwill	20,650
Total	£513,130	Total	£513,130

Despite the comments regarding the trading position, financially the business looked reasonably strong. Again, one might see the closure in terms of a new management team looking to the future.

In March 1923, a sale of the horses and drays yielded some £704. A Ford van was being used to transport men from CBB to the Derby brewery, to assist with its increased production. Some of the land at CBB was let. Unfortunately, there were still some problems with trade. The February figure of 3,780 barrels was some 2% down from the 3,875 barrels of February 1922. Furthermore, they had to order 100 barrels of Bass and 200 barrels of Worthington in anticipation of shortages over Whitsuntide.

Not everyone was happy with the changes. William Sherar, the company secretary, resigned after the MD asked for reports on the management structure. Still, he did get a retirement allowance of £200 pa. Stanley Brown moved up to replace him. A final change came from the death of Lord Roe, one of the trustees for the CBB debenture mortgage.

Although malting initially continued at CBB, in June the Board decided to look closely at the costings. The figures showed that 2,961 quarters could be produced at 16/3 per quarter.

Conversion to electricity would reduce this to 14/10 and if output could be raised to 3,500 quarters, to 14/5. However, Hinde & Company offered to produce 7,000 quarters at 16/6 for English barley and 14/6 for foreign. Offilers agreed a contract for 6,000 quarters and decided to close the CBB maltings. Mr Willmott would supervise until December.

Trading difficulties continued, the June 1923 sales of 4,932 barrels were 437 down from the previous year. Total sales for the twelve months were down 998 barrels. However, July's figure of 6,170 barrels, was an increase of 1,343 on the same month of the previous year and it seemed that the tide had turned, with continued growth in the following months.

In the October, Mr Abbott of the Victoria Vinegar Brewery in Sheffield looked at the CBB site, but decided that it was too large for their needs. Instead, they bought Stretton's Kedleston Road brewery in Derby. Peach & Company, the Burton maltsters also looked at leasing the CBB maltings, but this deal also fell through.

The Stenson of Loughborough (see entry) properties were on the market, but Offilers declined to purchase. And the following year they decided that Wells of Kegworth (see entry) was unlikely to be worth buying. However, they did buy some Leicestershire property, paying £1,850 for the Plough at Ashby, said to be selling some 3 to 3½ barrels per week.

AC Hinde looked at buying the malting equipment, but decided it was too dear and malting ceased. They received offers to dismantle the brewery and clear the site, but in October 1925, they were actually considering re-opening the brewery to meet improved sales. However, they decided to expand at Derby instead.

The remains of the Cavendish Bridge Maltings.

Photo: Author

In September 1931, a portion of the Cavendish Bridge Brewery, the brewery yard, malthouses, stables, garage, together with any plant and machinery, with three houses, in total some 3 acres, was sold to the Trent Navigation Company of Nottingham for £3,000. In December 1936, the Trent paid £500 for a further 7,094 square yards, with buildings. Around the same time 3 cottages at Cavendish were also sold for £275. The brewery house was demolished in 1955 for the new bridge. However, some of the maltings remain (SK448299).

Anthony Avis in his reminiscences on the brewing industry describes Offilers in the 1960s as *"one of the sleepiest brewery companies I had so far experienced, even in an era of comatose management"* (Avis p79). In the mid sixties, they were worried by the continual decline in sales from 1954 and in particular the resistance to sales of their mild in Derby. They also noted the continued rise of keg sales and were considering a 21 year agreement with Mitchells & Butlers of Birmingham to supply their houses. Instead they drew up a list of potential buyers for their business and in January 1965 they were sold to Charringtons.

Shardlow Brewery Ltd, *Ground Floor, Kiln Warehouse, British Waterways Yard.*

Representing the history of the site, previously the maltings of the CBB, the new concern uses the Eaton name for one of its beers. It opened in 1994 in the kiln house of the maltings, and moved within the site in December 1996. It is now on two floors of the former stables and supplies some 30 free trade outlets, with the current range being:-

Chancellor's Revenge	3.6%	Bitter	4.1%
Abu Derby	4.1%	New Brewery Bitter	4.1%
Reverend Eaton's Ale	4.5%	Whistle Stop	5%

COALVILLE

Shaw, James & Thomas, *Steam Engine.*

The pub dates back to at least 1813 when run by Joseph Hough, with the address shown as Donisthorpe. By 1846 James Shaw was a farmer at the Engine, which was shown as the Steam Engine in 1855.

In 1870-75 James was at the Engine Inn, whilst Thomas was shown as a beer retailer in Donington. In 1877 they were listed as brewers at the Steam Engine, but also shown under Hugglecote. By 1884 Thomas Brooks was listed at what was described only as a beerhouse, and in 1884 to 1894, James Shaw was a grocer and beer retailer at Hugglescote.

COTESBACH

Wright, Edmund.

Edmund Wright was shown as a farmer in 1875, when he appears to have been living at the Manor House. In 1880 he was described in the Brewers' Journal (p188) as a late brewer in liquidation, living at Beast Market, Lutterworth.

COTTESMORE

Cox, William.

In 1855 William Cox was a brewer and grazier, but there was no mention of him in 1863. However, in 1891 William Smeeton was then shown as a brewer, although Kelly lists him as a shopkeeper and wholesale beer seller. In 1894 William West Smeeton was a grocer and beer retailer, but in 1895 was only shown as a grocer and draper.

It is not clear whether either of these individuals was connected with the Sun, which was kept by a Francis Boulton at the time of the listing for Cox. It certainly brewed for itself at some point, since at the back there used to be maltings, until they burned down in 1909.

CROPSTON

Burchnall, Mrs Emma.

In 1846, Ann Burchnall was listed as a brewer, farmer and landowner, but two years later was only described as a farmer. In 1855, Charles Burchnall was shown as a farmer and in 1875 Emma Burchnall was listed as a farmer, and also shown as a brewer two years later.

What may have started out as only a farm brewery, at some point became a commercial concern, since in Wright's 1881 directory there was an advertisement for Mrs Emma Birchnall as a Maltster, Brewer and dealer in hops:- Casks from 4½ gallons upwards of Mild, Bitter and Porter at 1/-, 1/2, 1/4, 1/6. In 1891/2 Mrs Emma Burchnall was still listed as a commercial brewer (F1284). In 1881, William Dexter had kept a pub in the village called the Brewer's Arms, opposite the Bradgate Arms, but it is not known if there was any connection and it was owned by Pettifors, Anstey in 1896.

> **CROPSTON BREWERY,**
> NEAR LEICESTER
>
> **EMMA BURCHNALL,**
>
> **MALTSTER, BREWER AND DEALER IN HOPS.**
>
> MILD & BITTER ALES AND PORTER
>
> Supplied in Casks of 4½ gallons and upwards, at 1/-, 1/2, 1/4 and 1/6 per gallon.

From a commercial directory dated 1880.

However, there do seem to be family connections with the Burchnalls brewing at Anstey (see entry).

DESFORD

Dormer, J, *Blue Bell Inn, High Street.*

In 1848 William Newbatt was at the Blue Bell. In 1875 an advertisement in Harrod's directory mentions Home Brewed and Burton Ales. Dormer was also a plumber, glazier, painter and paper hanger. By 1884 Edward Hayes was at the pub and in 1894 William Brookes Headley was a farmer, butcher and victualler. In 1901 it was bought by Everards, who still own it.

Mansfield, Mr, *The Bull's Head, Main Street.*

In February 1811, the Bull's Head was for sale or to let, with malt office, the owner being a Mr Smith of Thurlston. Mr Mansfield was the tenant at the pub. In 1894, the victualler was a George Moore, but brewing seems to have ceased much earlier.

EARL SHILTON

Poyner, Charles, *Old Red Lion, High Street.*

In 1800, the pub was for sale with its brewing vessels. In 1894, William Gilbert was the victualler, but there was no mention of brewing. By the 1920s it was a Bass pub. It is still trading as an M&B house.

ENDERBY

Featherstone Brewery, *Unit 3 King Street Buildings, King Street.*

Initially, Kevin Featherstone was brewing at his parent's pub, the Saddle Inn at Twyford. He started in 1990 using an 18 gallon Burco plant, with guidance from Barrie Parish. Then briefly, with a 4 barrel plant, he was located at the Charnwood Industrial Estate, Vulcan Road (next to the old Eagle Brewery).

Funding from the Enterprise Allowance Scheme allowed a move to Enderby. At first he produced only Featherstone Best 1040°, then added Extra Special Bitter at 1055°. The current site with new fermenters has a capacity of 16 barrels per week. Featherstone specialises in producing house beers for pubs to sell under their own name and four local outlets are supplied on a regular basis. The beer range is as follows:-

| Hows Howler | 3.6% | Kingstone Bitter | 7.2% |
| Stage Ale | 4.8% | Best Bitter | 4.2% |

Mason, William, *The Bull's Head.*

In November 1803, the pub was for sale as a result of William Mason's death. This included a capital brewing copper. In the 1840s and 1850s it was run by Samuel Sturgess. Although he was a victualler, there was no other mention of brewing.

FLECKNEY

Deacon, Thomas, *The Crown Inn.*

The pub was built in 1797 by Thomas, before it passed to his nephew who had to sell it to creditors in 1829. This included Joseph Horton of Saddington, a maltster who had presumably been supplying the pub's brewhouse. However, it was then taken by Robert Bickley of Leicester, who was described at the time as a wholesale brewer and maltster and brewing may have ceased.

It was bought by George Hall in 1843 and although three years later, William Spokes was landlord and butcher, there was no mention of brewing. By 1921 it was a much altered Everard's house, which is still trading as the Old Crown.

Gamble, Wakelin, *Dun Cow/Golden Shield.*

The pub dated back to 1841, when it was a small beerhouse run by Sarah Perkins. From 1855 to 1876 it was run by Mrs Elizabeth Iliffe.

Wakelin "Billy" Gamble was a victualler and butcher in 1884, shown running the Dun Cow in 1888. In 1895, the pub was being run by JS Preston, whilst Gamble was operating an agency on behalf of Phipps of Northampton, who had bought the pub in 1897. Although he is listed by Friedrich as brewing in 1902, this seems only to have been as the agency.

FOXTON

Monk, Joseph, *The Black Horse.*

According to Harborough in Camera (Plate 133), the Black Horse brewed in 1870, when Monk was running the pub. Prior to this it had been run by Benjamin Goodrich from around 1846. The brewhouse was to the left of the pub. From 1884 to 1894 Mrs Henrietta Monk was running the pub, which was rebuilt in 1900 and is now supplied by Marstons.

FRISBY

Thomas, Mr, *The Black Horse.*

The 1803 sale by Mr Thomas included the brewing utensils. Around this time, a Mr Shelton was letting a malt kiln in the village. Mr Dobrey had the pub for sale or let in 1811. It was for sale again in 1813, with details available from Mr Moore at Syston. By 1894 Austin Rodwell was the victualler, but there was no identification of brewing.

The pub closed in 1974, but the building still stands towards the eastern end of the main street, opposite the village post office.

GEESTON	**(see Ketton)**
GILMORTON	**Bishop, Robert,** *The Talbot, Lutterworth Road.*

For sale in 1813, with brewhouse, with details available from Mr Bishop. In 1835, Richard Measures was the victualler, but as with other landlords, there was no clear indication of when brewing took place or not. The pub is still trading as a Banks' house and is said to be around 200 years old.

Warden, Thomas, *Red Lion, Main Street.*

The pub was for sale on 29th March 1813, the owner being either a Mrs White or possibly a Joseph Willey. In addition to the brewhouse, there was mention of an 8 quarter malt kiln being operated by John Measures.

Around 1835, Thomas Warden was the victualler and a maltster at the pub. In 1848 he was also a butcher, but in 1855 was shown only as butcher (possibly son). By 1870 Joseph Glover was at the pub and then from 1875 to 1884, Cornelius Earp. In 1890 it was an LB&M property, with James Hull the victualler in 1894. In 1898, Eady & Dulley of Market Harborough paid £4,000 for the Lion, together with the Royal Hotel at Broughton Astley. In 1956 the NBC papers show that the brewhouse building was still standing. The pub has recently been renovated, but is still trading as a Banks' house.

GLENFIELD	**Priest, William.**

In 1846 Priest was shown as a brewer and running an un-named beerhouse. However, he was only a beer retailer in 1848 and was not listed in 1855.

GREAT DALBY	**Measures, Mrs Margaret,** *Royal Oak.*

In 1848 William Measures was at the pub and was the victualler until at least 1884, although Mrs Margaret seems to have been the brewer around 1870. By 1894 Miss Lydia Measures had taken the pub. NBC seem to have bought the pub around 1935, when the brewing copper was mentioned in the inventory. The papers for 1956 mention that the brewhouse was still standing. The pub is still trading, supplied by Wards of Sheffield, until the closure of that brewery in June 1999.

GREAT GLEN	**Bland, Elias,** *Royal Oak, High Street, Upper Glen*

There was no listing before 1875. Then in 1884, Elias Bland was described as a grazier and keeping a beerhouse. In 1894 the beerhouse name was mentioned and in 1896, Bland was a beer retailer. In 1905, it was owned by Easts of Milton Malsor and then passed to NBC, when the latter took over Easts. In 1954, the brewhouse building was intact, according to the NBC papers. The pub is still trading.

Guildford, William, *Fox & Goose, Church Road.*

Friedrich suggests that Guildford was brewing between 1891 and 1895. Certainly he was a victualler at the Fox for 1884-92, but by 1895, John Egglesfield was at the pub. The pub dated back to 1719, but closed for compensation of £681 in 1909. It is now a private house next to the river.

HALLATON	**Plowright, John Simkin,** *Angel Hotel, High Street.*

In 1846, William Jones was listed as a baker and beerhouse keeper; however, he was not listed in 1863 when a John Plowright was shown as a baker. In 1877, John Simkin Plowright was listed as a baker and brewer in the village, and seven years later he was also a brickmaker. In 1898, he was still listed, but by 1900 he was shown only as a farmer, whilst Walter Plowright was shown as a baker and beer retailer.

None of the directories gives a location, nor pub name for the Plowrights, but a local history guide suggests that the Angel pub is now Old Stone Cottage, with its brewhouse now a garden on the corner of Hog Lane, next to the Post Office. It is possible that this was the location used by the Plowrights, but the name of the Angel was not listed in any of the directories, although it was trading in the mid nineteenth century.

HARBY	**Furmidge, W & Company,** *Vale Brewery Company, Langar Lane.*

In 1875, Samuel Furmidge was a coal merchant, and two years later William and Samuel Furmidge were corn cake and coal merchants. By 1881 they had started brewing, trading as W&S Furmidge. Local history books suggest that the brewery may have been located next to the canal wharf as part of the mill.

An advertisement in 1887, described W Furmidge & Co at the Vale Brewery, with stores at the Black Horse, King Street, Melton Mowbray. In 1888 they were shown as brewers and maltsters as well as corn, coal and coke merchants and farmers. They were also malting at Stathern. The Furmidge name originated as Fromagear, i.e. cheese maker.

In 1891 the business was shown as Furmidge W & Company, although the following year it was still trading as W&S Furmidge. This name was used until 1895, when shown as Furmidge and Kemp, with George Kemp as the new partner. They were shown as farmers and corn and coal merchants, as well as still malting at Stathern. The brewery was bought in 1895 by Edward Oakden, living in Nottingham. Arthur H Oakden was shown as the brewer and the following year Furmidge & Company were listed only as farmers and merchants.

However, Edward Oakden had also bought the Dolphin Brewery at North Church Street in Nottingham (F3709), although he seems to have allowed a Mr Barker to continue to operate locally there. Hence, there was a court case in 1898, at which Mr Barker argued that Oakden had broken his agreement and was poaching customers for his Harby brewery. He was offering 27½% discounts to the off-licensed trade in Nottingham, compared to the 20% given by the Dolphin. Oakden lost the case and had to pay damages of £100 plus costs and the Nottingham brewery seems to have continued under William S Barker.

In 1898 Arthur H Oakden was shown as a brewery traveller, whilst the business was trading as the Vale Brewery Company (F2011). In February 1899, the Vale was taken over by WS Davy of Newark, who had recently bought the Devon Brewery there. The following year, John Dewey was listed as a brewers traveller, but there was no mention of brewing in the village. WS Davy were themselves bought by Warwicks & Richardsons of Newark in 1919.

W. FURMIDGE & Co.,
VALE BREWERY, HARBY.

CELEBRATED
ALES STOUT & BITTER BEER
Brewed from the finest Barley, Malt, and choicest hops, delivered in 9, 12, 18, and 36 gal. casks as under:—

X mild ale	1 0	per gal.
XX "	1 2	"
XXX "	1 4	"
XXXX Strong	1 6	"
BITTER BEER	1 4	"
STOUT	1 4	"

DISCOUNT FOR CASH.

Stores: Black Horse, King Street, Melton Mowbray.

From the Melton Mowbray Times & Vale of Belvoir Gazette 1887.

HATHERN Cooper, Albert, *The Anchor, Main Street.*

The Anchor Inn as it appears in the 1990s.

Photo: Author

The Anchor dates back to at least 1799, when it was described as having a good malt office and the tenant Mr Day was looking to sell his brewing vessels. The landlord was a Nicholas Loe Smith. In 1812 it was being run by the Bellises. The following year, Thomas Bellis was looking to sell or let the spacious and convenient malt office. In 1846, William Boss was the victualler and maltster.

John Cooper was at the pub by 1848 and in 1877 was shown as a maltster, farmer and victualler. In 1894 he was a maltster and victualler, but the following year the pub was being run by Mrs Agnes Cooper. Then on 2nd February 1898, the licence was taken by Albert Cooper (F2053). On 22nd July 1936, Gertrude Elizabeth Cooper took over the licence and on 25th July 1938 she sold it for £7,500 to the Home Brewery of Nottingham. It is still signed as a Home Brewery pub on the A6 main road, although that too has closed.

Wicked Hathern Brewery, *46 Derby Road.*

Leicestershire's newest brewery is planning to produce its first trial brew in mid-November, 1999. This will be brewed on a 2½ barrel plant from Moss Brew International of Blackburn. The beers currently planned are Hawthorne Gold at around 3.8% and soar Head at around 4.8%. The brewing consultant is John Pilling.

HILMORTON

Hull, George, *The Woolpack.*

The Woolpack was for sale by auction on 11th August 1812, with brewing utensils. Mr Hull was the owner.

HINCKLEY

Bass, George, *The Queen's Head, Upper Bond Street.*

The Bass family involvement in brewing goes back to 1812, when a house and maltings were for sale near the centre of Castle Street, with Thomas Bass, a vet, one of the tenants. In 1835 Thomas Bass was a maltster and vet at the New Buildings (see Buckler entry). By 1875 George Bass was at the Queen's and was listed as brewing in 1877. The family was also involved with running the Bull's Head and the Globe.

George was still at the pub in 1884, but by 1913 he may possibly have moved to High Street, Barwell. At some point the Queen's was rebuilt, but is still trading as an M&B house.

Beardsmore, William & Thomas, *23 Stockwell Head.*

The Plough, described as an old established travellers inn, at the bottom of Market Place, was for sale in March 1810. The owner was a George Cooper, who had been there from at least 1803. The following month, there was a sale of two large coppers, two 20 strike mash tubs and various other brewing items.

Invoice used December 1897.

In 1827, William Beardsmore was at the Plough, shown as Stockwell Head and was shown as a maltster there in 1835. He was listed in 1846 as a maltster and brickmaker in Back Lane, and also kept the Plough until at least 1855. He seems to have left the pub by 1870, but between 1871 and 1877 he was still shown as a brewer and maltster in Stockwell Head. In 1867 he was also shown as a maltster in Regent Street.

In 1870, William Harrold was actually running the Plough.

However, in 1877 William Palmer was listed as brewing in Stockwell Head. Previously in 1835 William Palmer had kept the Union Inn, Borough. Shortly afterwards the executors of William Palmer were shown as running the Plough, but it remained owned by the Beardsmores. This suggests that they had moved from the pub brewhouse and set up a brewery on a more commercial scale in the area.

Thomas Beardsmore was shown as a brewer and maltster from 1877 to 1887, in both Stockwell and Trinity Lane. In 1884, Mrs Ann Palmer was at the Plough and William Beardsmore was living at 45 Regent Street. William Beardsmore died on 15th January 1888 and left the brewery to his son Thomas. In 1891 the business was still trading as Beardsmore, William & Thomas (F2133). In 1894 Thomas was living at No 45, Regent Street.

In 1894, a TB Beardsmore resigned his position at Worthington's brewery in Burton, but it is not clear if there were any family connections.

On 14th April 1896, the business was conveyed to Henry E Sugden and Alfred H Yeomans, who were running John Marston & Son Ltd of Burton. The small estate consisted of the following 7 pubs in Hinckley:-

Dog & Gun, Borough	Marquis of Granby, Regent Street
Princes Feathers, Regent Street	Plough Inn
New Inn, Castle Street	Star Inn, Stockwell Head
White Bear, Coventry Street	

HINCKLEY (continued)

The business was still trading as W&T Beardsmore in 1900. In 1913, it was operating as Marston, Thompson & Evershed, but probably ceased brewing soon afterwards, although the stores are thought to have remained open until around 1925. The buildings were later demolished for a shopping centre.

Bedford, George, *Holly Bush, Bond Street.*

The pub was not listed in 1848, but was built later on the site of the old horse pool. In 1875 Bedford was shown at the pub, where he was identified as brewing in 1884. In the same year it was shown as a beerhouse, which by 1894 was run by George junior. The pub has been rebuilt in a somewhat modernistic style and is now a Marstons house.

Blakesley, W, *Red Lion, Castle Street.*

In 1806, The Red Lion was to let with brewhouse, from W Blakesley, presumably the same individual shown the previous year as a maltster in Lichfield Street. However, it seems to have returned to the family, since in 1835 John Blakesley was listed at the pub. In 1846, he was shown as a maltster and brickmaker. This seems to be the individual shown as Blakersley at the Crown in 1848 (see Orton entry).

There are no signs of any remains of the pub and it is possible that it had taken the name of the Crown.

Buckler, Eli, *The Greyhound, New Buildings.*

Thomas Wheatley was running the Greyhound from 1835 to at least 1855. In 1876 Eli Buckler was at the pub and the following year was listed as a brewer. A possible relative may be a John Buckler of 4 Loseby Lane and Bakehouse Lane, an hotel keeper (known to be in financial difficulties around 1882).

In 1879 the address of the Greyhound was shown as Leicester Road, being run once more by a Thomas Wheatley. It was not listed in 1913, suggesting it may have been closed under a compensation scheme.

Choice, John, *Blue Boar, 33 Regent Street.*

In 1805 the Boar was shown as being in Coventry Street, when run by William Powdrell. Then between 1835-48, Job Lock was the victualler.

In 1870 John Choice was at the pub, whilst Joseph Choice was an ale and porter agent in the same street. John was listed as the brewer from 1877 to 1887 and at the pub until 1892. In 1894 Arthur Woodward was the victualler. Although trading in 1913, the pub later closed. The building is now a hi-fi shop, next to Blue Boar yard.

Clarke, John, *Lichfield Tavern, Coventry Road.*

Clarke was at the Lichfield from around 1870 to 1881 and was listed as brewing in 1877. He was still there in 1894, but it was only shown as a beerhouse. This seems to have closed by 1913.

Coltman, Edwin, *The New Inn, 108 Upper Castle Street.*

In 1848 Joseph Marshall was the victualler, and was at the New Inn until at least 1855. Edwin Coltman was at the pub by 1870 and listed as the brewer in 1877. Then Sarah Jane Coltman was brewing 1884-1895, but it was included in the Beardsmore estate in 1896. The building is now a soft furnishings shop.

Crow, Samuel, *White Bear, Coventry Street.*

The Bear, with brewing vessels was available to be let in 1813, with details from a Mr Crow. In 1849 and 1855, John Peacey was the victualler. In 1892-4 William Pratt was the victualler, but by 1896 it was owned by the Beardsmores.

Enson, John, *White Horse, Market Place.*

The pub with its brewhouse was available to be let in November 1812. Enson had been at the pub for some 30 years, which was owned by the trustees of the feoffment. The advertisement mentions its location next to the Town Hall and that it was used for many public meetings. Its ownership offered certain advantages in that it *"has privileges which Inns in general have not an opportunity of having"*.

Hall, William, *Boot Inn, 17 Coventry Road.*

In 1799, the King's Head with brewing utensils, on Coventry Street was to let from John Hicken. However, in 1802 on the death of Samuel Robinson, the sale of his property included the Boot (previously the King's Head). The sale also included the Blue Bell on Bond End, tenanted by John Deane. In 1835, George Green was at the Boot and then in 1848, a William Berridge.

The Boot continued to brew and in 1875, William Hall was listed as the brewer, after he had moved from the Prince of Wales. He was still shown as the brewer for 1877. Mrs Lydia Hall was then the victualler in 1892-94, when the address was shown as No 25. However, the pub was no longer listed by 1913, and the site is now a kebab take-away.

Hill, Willoughby, *Castle Tavern, 113 Castle Street.*

From 1835 to 1855, Thomas Dowell was at the Castle, which was given as being on Coventry Street. By 1870 John Hill was shown as a beer retailer in Castle Street and was running the Castle by 1875. In 1891-2 Willoughby Hill was the brewer, having taken the licence around 1888. The pub is still trading as a Bass house.

Ironmonger, Thomas, *Half Moon, Stockwell Head.*

Ironmonger was at the pub by 1875, where he was shown as brewing in 1877. He was still listed as the victualler in 1884. The pub was shown as a beerhouse run by Thomas Payne in 1892-4, but was later closed and demolished.

Mason, James, *Duke of Rutland, 10 Bond Street.*

In 1835 Joseph Ross was at the pub as was Samuel Kinghurst in 1870. By 1875 Mason was at the pub, where he was shown as brewing from 1877-8. He was still listed as the victualler in 1884, but Mrs Maria Mason had taken the Duke by 1892, before she moved to the Barley Sheaf. The pub then became supplied by Eadie of Burton and is now a free house.

Mason, Mark, *Barley Sheaf, Lower Bond Street.*

In 1835, Thomas Collington was running the Barley Sheaf and by 1848 William Goode had taken it over. In 1877 Mark Mason was the brewer at the Barley Sheaf, when George Mason kept the Star, Stockwell Head and William Mason was at the Crown (see Orton entry). Mark was still the victualler at the pub in 1884, but by 1894 it was being run by Mrs Maria Mason, from the Duke of Rutland. It is now a Marston's pub.

Needham, J S & Company, *Lichfield Street.*

In 1835, Thomas Needham was a brewer in Castle Street. Then in the same year JS Needham & Co were listed as brewers, coal merchants and corn dealers in Lichfield Street, with maltings in Castle Street. However, in the 1832 poll book, entries describe both John Smith Needham and Thomas Needham as gentlemen. A John Needham was malting at Preston, near Uppingham.

However, they were not listed in 1848, and it is possible that they had moved to Huncote (see entry) and later formed the firm known as Needham & Crick, maltsters of Leicester. This then became a part of Leicester Brewing & Malting.

Orton, Arthur John, *The Crown Inn, Castle Street.*

The original "Crowne" dated back to at least 1670, when it was kept by Robert Bloor. In 1848-55, the Crown was kept by John Blakesley, sometimes shown as Blakersley, who was also a maltster (see entry). Between 1870-75 the Crown was run by William Mason, also operating as a wine and spirit merchant.

In 1877, Arthur Orton was listed as brewing at the Crown and also shown as a vet. In 1884-6, he was running the Blue Bell, when he seems to have been in financial difficulties and paying off a bankruptcy. This seems to have been a family problem, in that in 1884, a William Orton was shown as a bankrupt victualler at Streets Houses, Castle Gresley. Nevertheless, by 1884 Frederick William Orton was the licensed victualler at the Marquis of Granby, Regent Street (Brewers' Journal p632).

In 1892, George Henry Rudkin was the victualler, followed by William Moore in 1894. However, brewing would seem to have stopped around this period.

Orton, William, *The George Inn, Market Place.*

In 1802 Orton was advertising to let the George. It was described as having a large brewhouse with two good coppers. However, it was for sale on 21 March 1803, because Orton was leaving the business. In 1812, The George was taken by a David Briggs from Leicester. In 1835 to 1849, William Tomlinson was the victualler. In 1892, it was trading as the George Hotel run by William Trivett (see Market Bosworth entry).

Peat, John, *The Three Tuns, 7 Stockwell Head.*

On 26 May 1801, the Three Tuns was for sale with brewhouse. Peat also occupied the nearby bakehouse. Thomas Cotton was the victualler in 1835, followed in 1849 by William Cartridge, but in 1855 it was run by Peat again.

In 1892 Frederick John Orton was at the Tuns, but it closed for compensation in 1917 and was later demolished.

Pratt, Knightley, *The Crown & Anchor, 106 Upper Castle Street, Stockwell Head.*

In 1835 Joseph Marshall was at the Crown & Anchor, but by 1848 it was being run by James Burdett and then J Hill in 1855.

In 1870 Pratt was at the pub, where he was shown as brewing in 1877. He was still at the pub in 1894 as the victualler. Then in 1894 Knightley Pratt junior was a beer retailer at 12 Stockwell Head. The Crown and Anchor building is now a hairdressing salon.

Smith, George, *Dog & Gun, 28 Borough.*

Around 1835-48 John Ayre was at the Dog and Gun, shown initially as Mansion Street and then Market Place. In 1855, it was run by Ann Ayre and by 1870 it was being run by Mrs M Ayre.

George Smith was at the pub by 1875, and was listed as brewing 1877-84. In 1894 he was described as a victualler and the pub was owned by Beardsmores by 1896. It is now owned by Marstons.

Smith, Stephen, *Prince of Wales, 34 Coventry Road.*

In 1805, the location was shown as Lichfield Street, when the pub was kept by Richard Clarke. In 1835 Benjamin Everitt was the landlord and by 1848 it had changed to John Byard.

By 1870 William Hall was at the pub, presumably before moving to the nearby Boot. By 1875, Stephen Smith was at the pub, where two years later he was identified as the brewer. He was still listed as the victualler in 1884. At some point after this the pub was rebuilt further along the road.

Tomlin, William, *Black Horse, 21 Upper Bond Street.*

In 1835, the pub was being run by John Crain and in 1848 William Wheatley. Mark Baggott was there in 1870, but by 1875 Tomlin was running the pub, where in 1877 he was listed as brewing. In 1884, it was being run by Mrs Else Tomlin and in 1894 James Crofts was described as the victualler. The Black Horse was sold for £3,100 in 1897 and was rebuilt, with the address shown as No 28.

Topp, Mrs Mary, *King's Head, 69 Castle Street.*

In September 1809, Mr Rudd, previously a dealer in Coventry porter, with a warehouse in Shamble's Lane, Leicester, advertised that he had formed a connection with a Mr Ward. This described Ward's brewery as being some six months in operation. Although in 1835 Francis Ward was running the King's Head, there was no mention of his operating as a common brewer. In 1848, it was being kept by John Sutton.

By 1870 William Topp was at the King's Head, but by 1875 his wife seems to have taken the pub. Mrs Mary Topp was the brewer until at least 1884. Then from 1887 to 1892 John Topp, presumably their son, was listed as the brewer. The buildings are now used by a locksmith and the brewhouse looks to be still standing at the rear.

HUMBERSTONE	**Underwood, John,** *The Windmill.*

In 1870 Underwood was a coal merchant, whilst the Windmill was kept by William Bent, a baker and victualler. In 1848, Joseph Bent had been a miller and maltster at the Old Windmill. Underwood then seems to have run the pub and been brewing for the period 1877-1892. In 1892 LB&M looked to buy it for £3,000, but the purchase seems to have fallen through.

It had become an NBC property by 1902 and their property books mention the pub's maltings. In 1927 it seems to have been sold for £10,000.

HUNCOTE	**Needham, Rowland & John.**

In 1846, Thomas Agar was shown as a maltster and brewer, then in 1849 James Agar was a maltster, brewer and grazier. The first individual may be the T Aggar who was a partner with J Nunneley of Market Harborough, concerning the Bull's Head at Clipstone in June 1853.

T Aggar died in May 1854 and there was no entry for Huncote in 1855, other than for William Harvey as a maltster and beer retailer. Given the similarity of name, one is tempted to wonder about a possible link with Thomas Hagger who was brewing at Northampton around this time.

The next mention of brewing was in 1870, when Rowland and John Needham were listed as brewers and maltsters. They were possibly related to the Needhams who were brewing at Hinckley prior to this. They were both still shown in 1875, but the following year only John Needham was shown as a maltster. Between 1877 and 1887, John Needham was shown as a large brewer and maltster and ale dealer. However, in 1881 John Needham was listed only as a maltster and beer retailer. Then in 1888, John Canning was listed as a brewer and maltster.

Benjamin Atkins was then listed as a beer retailer, brewer and maltster for 1891-1895. He was also a farmer and grazier at his home in Narborough. However, in 1894 Lewis or Louis Durham was listed as a beer retailer, brewer and maltster and then shown in 1896 as Mr Durham, brewer. None of the various Huncote businesses seems to have owned any tied houses, nor does there seem to have been any major commercial operation.

Harvey, Thomas, *Red Lion.*

The "Old" Red Lion dates back to at least 1849, when James Taylor senior was the victualler at the pub. He remained there until at least 1855. Then, in 1855, William Harvey was listed as a maltster and beer retailer in the village.

Although from 1894 to 1904, Mrs Eliza Williams was the victualler at the Old Red Lion, the pub was not identified as brewing its own beer. However, in 1908 to 1910, Thomas Harvey was at the pub as a brewer and brake proprietor (F2235). In 1916 it became an Everard's house, which is still trading.

HUSBANDS BOSWORTH	**Pack, Thomas Small.**

In 1848 a Thomas Pack was shown as a grocer and linen draper. The family were primarily grocers and the drapery business was something of a side-line. In 1855, another side-line was tried, when Thomas Pack was shown as a brewer, grocer and linen draper. However, by 1870 he had moved on to become a farmer.

In 1871 F Pack seems to have been running the business and in 1875 TS Pack was shown as a farmer. However, in 1876-77, TS Pack was also shown as a brewer (F2255).

IBSTOCK	**Frith, Mrs,** *Crown & Horse Shoe.*

In September 1808, the pub was for sale by Mrs Frith. The following March, there was a sale of the brewing vessels. The Crown and Horse Shoe was not listed for 1849, although Thomas Thirlby was a victualler and maltster at the Ram in Ibstock. However, there was a Crown Inn trading 1885-86, when John Baxter was the victualler.

KEGWORTH	**Crane, Thomas,** *Market Place/London Road.*

From 1828 to 1835, Thomas Crane was a brewer in London Road, whilst Charles Crane was at the Three Cranes, previously kept by Robert Crane. The latter had also stood surety for the landlords of the Board and the Horse and Groom in 1826.

Around 1843, James Birtchnell was advertising the Kegworth Ale and Porter vaults at the

Market Place in Leicester. This would suggest that the Crane family, or someone else, was operating as common brewers supplying the area.

In 1846, Thomas was shown as an ale and porter brewer, when John Crane was at the pub. Thomas was not listed for 1848 and seems to have moved to an off-licence in Carley Street, Leicester, and at some point to the Brunswick Brewery (see Flewitt entry).

From 1848 to 1855, the Old Three Cranes in the Market Place was kept by Robert Crane and then again by John Crane. The only entry in Kegworth after this date was for Richard Crane as a shopkeeper in London Road. In 1863, John Adcock was at the Cranes, but in 1884 his name would seem to be shown as Allcock.

The Cranes' brewery is thought to have stood opposite the pub in the Market Place and it seems likely that it was then bought by Sidney Wells (see below).

The Old Three Cranes, later a Sidney Wells house, was still trading in 1913. However, the licence lapsed on 5th January 1925, after it had been compensated for £855, and in the March the building was sold for £375.

Greaves, John, *The Three Tuns.*

Greaves was at the pub by 1876. Then in 1884 he was listed as a basketmaker and beerhouse keeper. In 1895 he was listed as a brewer. The pub was included in the compensation scheme in 1907 and it closed in 1913 for £400.

Osborne, Robert, *Nottingham Road.*

In 1835, Robert Osborne was a brewer and maltster, who is thought to have started around 1828. His brewery may have been extended around 1833, when Joseph Cartwright a stone mason was undertaking work on his behalf. In 1846, Mary Osborne was shown as a maltster and brewer, but she seems to have ceased by 1855. However, in 1876-77, a Joseph Osborn was at the Three Cranes previously used by the Crane family (see entry).

Smith, T & J.

John Smith was at the Crown in 1876, whilst other members of the family were involved with milling and baking and in 1884 to 1892, John Tebbutt Smith was at the Cross Keys. Then in 1891, T&J Smith were shown as brewers. However, the venture into brewing may have been short-lived, since in 1895 John Thomas Smith was a miller on Ashby Road, but only a beer retailer in Station Road.

In March 1928, the Cross Keys was a Worthington pub, suggesting that it may have come with their purchase of Wells' brewery. It was closed for compensation in 1929 and sold to a Mr Smith.

Wells, Sidney & Sons, *Market Square.*

In 1846 John Wells of Humberstone Gate in Leicester, was a porter and ale dealer, spirit and corn merchant and victualler at the Fountain on Humberstone Gate. In 1848 Sidney Wells was listed as a maltster and brewer in Kegworth, probably at the site previously used by the Cranes. In 1870, he was advertising as a mild, strong, pale ale and porter brewer and maltster at the Brewery, Market Place.

James Burgess was shown as the Leicester agent in 1870-77, at their depot, 57 Humberstone Gate. Although this was listed in Friedrich's Gazetteer (F2717), there is no evidence that commercial brewing took place at Leicester, other than possibly for the Fountain in earlier years. The address in 1896 seems to be shown as No 67, with Jas F Burgess as the agent. In 1925, it was sold to an Arthur Hawkes. The location is now a shop.

In 1877, Wells formed the Kegworth Brewery Company, which in 1891 was trading as Sidney Wells & Sons, Kegworth Brewery. The sons were Sidney Bowley and Ernest Edward, with the family home being the Lodge.

The Brewers' Journal for 1885 recorded a meeting of the Leicester & Rutland Brewers Association on 30th May at the Bell Hotel, Leicester. In the chair was W Everard, whilst S Wells (Kegworth) was the vice-chairman. The meeting discussed a resolution against the proposed increase in duty of 1s per barrel.

The 1892 directory lists a John Hall as a clerk at a brewery, but it does not state whether this was at Wells or elsewhere. In 1895 the business was listed simply as Kegworth Brewery. They were supplying the Crown in 1906, when it was closed for compensation of

£1,000. In 1913 it was shown as Wells, Sidney & Sons, with a telephone number 7!

In December 1919, a Selkirk Wells became the manager at Worthington's brewery in Burton and the following year joined the Board. That year, the Sidney Wells brewery was offered to Worthingtons at a price of £80,000; however, it is not clear whether there was any connection between the new Board member at Worthington and the chance to buy the Kegworth brewery. After considerable discussion, the Worthington Board decided that the price was too high, but stated that they were open to negotiation.

In 1925, Offilers also turned down the business. However, in the November, Worthingtons decided to purchase, paying £30,000 on 1st October, with the balance in December. The estate of 34 freehold properties, included 9 pubs in Kegworth, 13 in nearby villages, and 2 at Leicester, where they also had two off-licences. In addition, they owned the Windmill at Gotham in Nottinghamshire.

On 26th May 1926, the brewery premises were sold for £1,750 to HR Hopewell Esq. The Kegworth brewery was only demolished in recent years. Worthingtons also set out a programme of repairs and rebuilding for the estate.

Horse & Groom, Kegworth	£517	alterations
Navigation	£3,100	rebuild
Spinney Hill, Bower, Leicester	£278	alterations
Dew Drop	£330	alterations
Dog & Gun, Mount Sorrel	£300	alterations
Spade Tree, Newton Burgoland	£500	alterations

The Britannia at Kegworth was sold to the Council for £1,000, to allow the road to be widened, although it was planned to be replaced by a new pub. The Old Flying Horse in the town centre was also rebuilt.

Wilson, Hugh, *Steam Brewery, Derby Road.*

In 1826-35, Samuel Barrow was running the Flying Horse in Kegworth. Then in 1848, Richard Barrow was shown as a beer retailer, probably at the Horse and Groom which he ran in 1855, whilst Mrs Sarah Barrow was running the Flying Horse. By 1870, the Steam Brewery on Derby Road was being operated by the Barrow Brothers - East India pale and other ales, with a capacity of around 50 quarters per week. John Barrow was also a maltster at Diseworth.

However, in 1875, the brewery was trading as Peter Sullins & Company, with a depot at 5 Dover Street, Leicester, run by a William Hollis. At the time, they also seem to be have been listed for Castle Donington, but this may have been another depot.

Between 1875 and 1884, Sullins & Sons, were shown as a large brewers. In 1877, the business was listed as Peter Sullins and Son, but in 1880 Peter Sullins junior of Kegworth was in liquidation (Brewers' Journal p161) and the following year only the father was listed. They only had a small estate, of which the following have been identified:-

Prince of Wales, Shepshed	Rose & Crown, Wymeswold
Oddfellows, Kegworth	Cross Keys, Kegworth

In 1882, GH Colmore of Kegworth was mentioned in the Brewers' Journal as a brewer and shareholder in the Springwell's Brewery Company Ltd. This was registered on 20th March, worth £10,000 in £10 shares, with the initial subscribers being:-

William Nall, Southport - Brewer	WR Talmer, London - Barrister
William Nall, Manchester - Carrier	J Widdowson, Hucknall - Maltster
A Cleaver, Nottingham - Bleacher	
Francis Frederick Cleaver, Nottingham Lace - dealer	

The registered offices were at 6 Thurland Street, Nottingham. The brewery was connected with Springwell House, and the property was mortgaged to the Hemsley family.

In 1884, George Hartridge was listed as the brewing manager at the Springwells Brewery. Although a William Yeomans living in Kegworth was shown as a brewery traveller, he was more likely to have been working for the Burton concern with which his family was involved. However, at an Extraordinary General Meeting on 25th October 1884 it was decided that the business should be wound up and Henry Edward Hubbart of Nottingham was appointed as the liquidator.

KEGWORTH (continued)

On 2nd January 1885, the brewery and the other property were sold for £2,500 to Hugh Mark Wilson. However, in 1890, when he was a shareholder in Marstons, Wilson was only described as a beer merchant and brewing seems to have ceased. In the same year he conveyed to Marstons for £2,700:-

> Oddfellows (previously New Inn) Packington Hill, Kegworth
> Anchor Inn, Sutton Bonnington
> Off-Licence, Moor Lane/ Russell Street, Kegworth

Wilson was described as an ale and porter dealer. The census for the following year, states that he was a British subject, aged 35, born in Germany. Peter Sullins was living in retirement on Derby Road.

In 1894, Hugh Mark Wilson was a stout bottler and brewery agent in the High Street. In 1895, the site seems to have become a depot for Marstons, when Wilson was described as the district manager. Nevertheless, Hugh Wilson (F2306) was still listed as brewing at what had become the Springs Well or Springwell Brewery until around 1900.

At some point, John Nicholls Forsell was using the brewery premises as the Springwell Mineral Water Works, until around 1912, when it passed to his wife. The building was then used as a glue and then a hosiery factory, which later burnt down in the 1920s. However, the brewer's house is still standing at No 67.

The Brewer's House and remains of the brewery buildings.

Photo: Author

KETTON

Bean, W & Company, *Rutland Brewery, High Street, Stamford Road.*

There is some confusion because Friedrich lists 3 breweries in the area of Ketton/Geeston i.e:-

> Molesworths/Beans at Ketton (F2335)
> Ketton & King's Cliffe (F2336)
> Geeston, Rutland (F1816)

Around 1900, John Smith & Company, Oundle, bought a Ketton brewery. According to Friedrich's Gazetteer, this was supposed to be from the Ketton & King's Cliffe i.e. F2336. However, Smiths actually bought Bean & Molesworth F2335 - known as the Rutland Brewery. Hence the history of the Rutland Brewery is as follows:-

In 1861 Thomas Casswell Molesworth, born Whaplode 1821, was a brewer and maltster. The business seems to have been started in 1860 at the rear of the Northwick Arms, previously called the White Hart. It was listed in 1862 as Molesworth TC & Son. In 1870 John, or James, Goodliff was running the Northwick.

A Smith's lorry delivering to the Northwick Arms.

Photo: Courtesy Jim Irving

In 1875, Molesworths bought the Three Crowns and its attached brewery in Northgate Street, Oakham, for £510. This was still part of the estate in 1900, when it was valued at £800.

From 1871 to 1878 TC Molesworth junior was a maltster at 29 Broad Street Stamford. In 1877 TC Molesworth and his son were living at Brewery House at the side of the Northwick Arms. At this time, they started calling it the "Rutland Brewery".

TC Molesworth senior seems to have retired from brewing to concentrate on farming around 1881, when his son was listed in the census return as a maltster and brewer employing 8 men and 4 boys. In 1887 the Brewers' Journal (p516) stated that TC Molesworth & Son, Ketton & South Luffenham, common brewers, aerated water manufacturers, malt etc., had dissolved their partnership. However, they were still shown in 1888 and 1891 as TC Molesworth & Son brewers in some directories. The South Luffenham property may have been only a maltings, although they did own the Durham Ox in the village and were leasing the Railway in 1900.

The Molesworth and Bean Brewery.

Photo: Courtesy Ian P Peaty

Nevertheless, in 1887 TC Molesworth junior & William Bean owned the Windmill pub at King's Cliffe, previously the brewery tap of William Cunnington. William Bean was listed in 1889 at 59 St Martins, Stamford. They traded as Molesworth and Bean until the partnership was dissolved in 1892 and Bean took over the business; although, it was still shown as Molesworth and Bean in one 1896 directory.

At this time, Bean was living at 1 Belmont House, Duddington. He had been born in 1860 at Shooters Hill, the son of Alfred William Bean JP of Welling in Kent. Jack Feast's article in the BHS magazine says that he was an electro-mechanical engineer in 1881 and that the Molesworths may have sold up because of financial difficulties. However, TC Molesworth junior seems to have concentrated on South Luffenham, where he entered into a partnership with Thomas Springthorpe, as millers and stone merchants.

Bean's background was perhaps an odd one for brewing, the only other brewers of this name anywhere near the area were the Beans in partnership with Suttons at Brigg and they were from Hull. However, he had connections with Goole, which was only some 20 to 30 miles from Brigg. Possibly his involvement was primarily financial, with day to day business looked after by the manager. Certainly he had a town house in London, as well as his local property. Another possible link is that his wife was called Augusta Manning and there were Mannings brewing in both Northampton and Kent.

Mineral Water Bottle c.1888-89

In 1895, the business was trading as WS Bean & Company, brewers and maltsters, with a Diminic Cromin at Brewery House. Mr Bean was living at Wothorpe House, Wothorpe near Stamford. TC Molesworth senior seems to have retired to The Firs, Easton, which was later the home of William Bean. In the meantime, TC Molesworth & Sons were shown as farmers, although TC Molesworth senior died in 1895.

In 1900, the business was still trading as W Bean & Company (F2335), but the previous year, Messrs Thomas, Peyer and Miles, brewery valuers of London, had submitted a bill for work to Smiths of Oundle. This lists the miscellaneous items and is dated November, which suggests that discussions regarding the sale of the business had already taken place, In addition to the aerated water plant, the inventory included:-

Malt	£153
Casks	£495
Sugar	£15

Including the rolling and consumable stock, book debts etc., this came to a total of £3,344. The business owned 5 horses, 4 heavy horse wagons, 2 small ones and a small float. The stock of beer was as follows:-

Barrels	**Firkins**	**Beer**
42	2	XXX
16	2	XXXX
58	1	XX
37	1	X
20	1	AK
19	2	S
	2	BB
19		returns and old beer

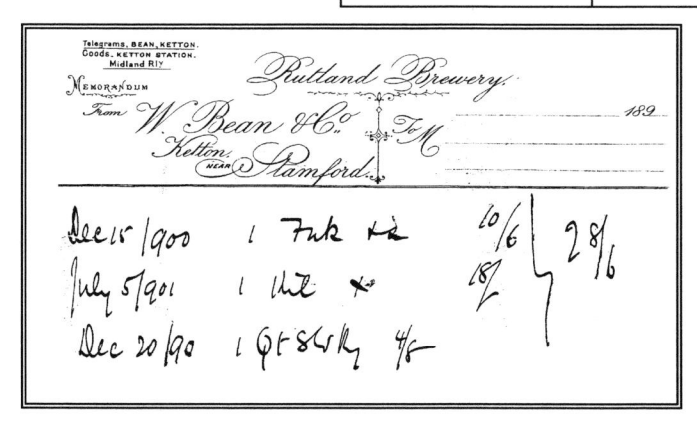

Invoice used 1899-1900.

As well as giving an indication of the product range, the stock also gives an indication of the relatively small size of the business. Smiths took over supplying some 30 freehold and 4 leased pubs and appointed T Bent Wilson as the manager.

The estate was valued at just over £20,000, of which the brewery itself was worth some £900. However, it seems that William Bean retained ownership of the actual copyholds, which were then leased to Smiths. He was the father of three daughters, which suggests that having no son to inherit might have caused him to sell up.

He was living at Easton on the Hill, and other than owning the estate, seems to have occupied his time with public service, as a local JP, Chairman of the RDC, county councillor and a governor of Brown's Hospital in Stamford. In 1910, he became the High Sheriff of Northamptonshire.

In 1904, Smiths were listed brewers and maltsters at Ketton, when Thomas Bent Wilson was living at Brewery House. They were still trading in 1908 as Smith's Ketton Brewery, but seem to have definitely stopped brewing by 1910. They may have continued with a depot as late as 1920.

Nevertheless, William Bean still owned the Windmill, King's Cliffe, and it was probably not until November 1929 that the properties were conveyed to Mrs Mary Smith after Bean's death. A valuation of the properties in October 1934, suggested that the majority was in a good and tenantable condition. However, the total sales for the 20 tied tenants were only 660 barrels and 9,000 dozen bottles, with an annual gross rental of £244. In addition, sales were falling at 6 of the pubs and the report concluded that against receipts of £1,272, there were outgoings of £1,568, giving a loss of £295.

The figures confirm both the small size of the original business and its reliance on an estate of rural pubs many of which were selling one or less barrels of beer per week. Jim Irving who was managing Smiths in the 1960s, prior to the eventual closure, suggests that even then, little had changed at many of the properties!

Mineral Water Bottle c.1888-89

The property valuation was probably linked to the changes at Smiths, consequent on the death of the MD EB Ludlow and the business being incorporated as a limited company in December 1935 (see Brewed In Northants p97). Much of the analysis in the report was concerned with whether the pubs could be upgraded and if there was space for a car-park.

The photograph on page 32 shows a lorry, presumably from Smiths, delivering bottled beer to the Northwick Arms at the time of the survey. Some of the brewery buildings remain at the rear of the pub. The entrance to the brewery site was between the pub and the brewery house, both of which are still standing. However, the brewery tower had been demolished in 1926.

Invoice used August 1903.

The Midland Hotel, previously known as Tobago Lodge, had a maltings which is still standing (SK984041). The licence from the Hotel was transferred to the Railway Inn sometime in the 1930s. When the hotel closed in 1941, it was run by a John William Goodliffe, possibly a descendant of the previous tenant at the Northwick.

Ketton Brewery Company.

In 1846, Francis Whincup was living at Geeston Lodge. He was born at Oak Hammerton in Yorkshire, the son of Henry Whincup who was running the George at Stamford. Francis was malting at King's Cliffe, Northants, in 1862 and is though to have started brewing the year before this. In 1866, Whincup & Son of the Ketton Steam Brewery were trading from Mansion House Stores in Peterborough.

In 1876, Thomas T Whincup was listed as the brewer and the following year the business was trading as Messrs Whincup, ale & porter brewers, Ketton Brewery. Francis Whincup was shown as a farmer at Geeston House, whilst Henry John Tennant Whincup ran the wine and spirit business. There seems to have been a third brother William Lawrence Whincup, who was living at Barrowden, where he was described as a brewer. Thomas W Whincup was listed in 1887, but this may be another directory error.

In 1888, William Thompson, previously at Stamford from around 1885, was shown as the brewer at the Geeston Tap, whilst Francis Whincup was listed as a private resident.

Prior to 1891 the brewery seems to have been owned by Messrs Sealy & Wilde, but that year the Ketton Brewery Company Ltd partnership was dissolved by William SW Sealy. The latter was originally from Cirencester, whilst the Wilde family was from Oldham in Lancashire, which raises an interesting question as to how they had got together to run a small brewery in the East Midlands!

In 1894, the business was trading as the Ketton Brewery Company, run by Frederick & Henry Wilde and in 1896, with William Thompson at the Geeston Tap. The 1896

KETTON (continued)

Peterborough Directory shows the Ketton Brewery Company as operating from West Street. Around this time it seems to have changed its name. The Ketton & King's Cliffe Brewery was registered as a limited company in March 1898, with a capital of £12,000 in £5 shares. The founders seem to have been one Frederick Coutts Bourne and Julia Morley, the wife of a Samuel Morley, 19 Paulton Square, Chelsea. Mrs Morley had apparently purchased King's Cliffe Manor House, the nearby Eagle Brewery and tavern, and the brewery at Ketton, including the adjoining Tap public house.

Any investors in the concern were soon disappointed, for the firm was dissolved on 26th October, 1900. After the failure of the main company, the Ketton brewery appears to have been run by a Percy Crowhurst. He was shown in 1904 as a brewer and beer retailer, until 1908. Percy Crowhurst was also shown at Geeston (F1816), but as explained, this was in fact the same concern. However, in 1908, it was bought by Claud Wyborn Gordon Walker a brewer from Gravesend, a partner in that town's Wellington Brewery. The Walker family actually owned the Wellington Brewery at this time, suggesting they were more than artisans.

In 1900 the Geeston Tap was kept by Lionel Barfield, who was also shown in the period 1922-1932 as a beer retailer.

According to the local history guide, the brewery closed when Claud Walker went off to war. However, it was listed until as late as 1933 (Coopers Directory). There was a Mr Charles William Walker from Burwash in Sussex at Papillon Hall from about 1884 to 1903, which if he was related to Claud Walker, might explain the connection with the Godfrey Keppel Papillon who owned the King's Cliffe Brewery.

In 1941 the Brewery Tap pub was run by a Sydney Jas Smith, but with no connection to the Oundle family. The pub closed in 1970, but some of the buildings are still standing as housing.

KIBWORTH BEAUCHAMP

Bolton, Charles Edward, *Coach & Horses, 2 Leicester Road.*

From 1835 to 1848, Jonathan Woodford (see below) was at the pub, which is thought to date back to the eighteenth century. Mrs Mary Woodford was at the Coach and Horses in 1855. Then in 1863, it was being run by Joseph Morris Coleman, before he moved to the Fox and Hounds. In 1870, Thomas Wilford was at the Coach and Horses until 1876, when Bolton took over. The latter was listed as the brewer in 1876-81. In 1875, he was advertising his home brewed ales in the Harrod's directory.

However, the 1891 census listed only a Georgina Bolton living on Main Street. She was described as the head of household, which suggests that her husband had died and they had left the pub. Her son, Charles Edward aged 5, had been born in Medbourne and she had a seven year-old daughter born in Surrey, all of which implies that they may have left the pub and the village some years previously.

The All Saints Brewery bought the pub in July 1897, but only sold the brewing plant in 1916, which suggests they may have continued to brew there. It was later supplied by Ansells.

Franks, Thomas.

From 1846 to 1863, Franks was shown as a maltster. In 1876 he was listed as a brewer, but this seems to be the only entry and he was not mentioned in the census of 1881.

In 1782, John Franks, previously the butler at Gumley Hall, was running the White Lion at Gumley. However, in 1797, he sold the pub for £300 and moved to Kibworth Harcourt, where he was described as an innkeeper.

Jordan, William.

In 1863, Jordan was running an un-named beerhouse. However, in 1870 he was listed as a brewer and grazier (see also Leicester).

Ward, F, *The Crown, Kibworth Harcourt.*

In 1806 an F Ward was selling the Crown, with 100 gallon copper, barrel and cooler. In 1848 William Hall was a victualler and butcher at the pub.

Ward, William, *Railway Arms Inn.*

In 1875, William Ward was at the Railway and advertising his home brewed ales. In 1886 Joseph Neath was the victualler and also at Husbands Bosworth. The pub has been completely rebuilt, but is still trading as an Ansells house. It is, of course, located near to the railway line.

Weston, John, *Red Lion, 78 Main Street, Kibworth Harcourt.*

On 14th April 1801, Weston was selling the brewing equipment, as he was going into another business. This included a 60 gallon and a 30 gallon copper, a 14 strike mash tub and 12x90 gallon barrels. The pub became a private house which still stands near the junction with Albert Street.

Woodford, Edward, *Leicester Road.*

In 1863 Mr Edward Woodford was a private resident, previously a butcher in 1855. He was born in 1826, which suggests that he had time to start on a second career. By 1870, he was a brewer and maltster in Kibworth Harcourt.

In 1876-77, Kelly's directory showed Woodford as a large brewer and maltster (F2338). However, in 1880 he was only listed as a grazier. The 1891 census shows him as a grazier, aged 75 born Kibworth, living with his son Thomas at Leicester Road.

KILBY BRIDGE

Gillam, Thomas, *Black Swan.*

In August 1812, Thomas Gillam moved from the Black Swan to the Bull's Head. As a result he put the Black Swan and its brewhouse up for sale. This included a coal merchant's business which operated from the pub. Eventually, it was taken by his brother William, previously a baker on Belgrave Gate.

However, William seems to have left the pub the following year and details were available from Thomas, who was now at the Bull's Head, Wigston. The Swan was later closed and became a private house.

KNIGHTON

Herrick, John, *Three Cranes.*

In 1801, the pub was available to let with brewhouse and bakehouse. John Herrick was the tenant, whilst William Herrick Hubberthon seems to have been the owner. It was not listed for 1855, suggesting that the pub had either closed or been re-named.

LANGHAM

Ruddle, G & Company Ltd, *Burley Road.*

Richard Westbrook Baker, originally from Cottesmore, a local farmer and substantial landowner, founded the Langham brewery in 1858. He died in February 1861 and his younger son Edward George took over the brewery. The eldest son William Henry inherited the family estates at Glaston and Exton. The executor of Baker's will was his friend Richard Thompson of Stamford, who had also provided finance for his businesses.

The Bakers employed 10 men at the time, together with a brewery agent James Edward Harris, later described as the manager. William Jones, from Stratford on Avon, was the brewer. In 1863, Edward George Baker's home was Manor House and he was the owner of much of the local land.

The directory entry for Langham also listed two brewery agents, Joseph Powell and Thomas Nettleship, but they are not though to be connected with the Baker's brewery.

The previous property division had it seems been reasonably equitable, since in 1871 E George Baker of Langham, was shown as owning 79 acres with a gross rental of £289. W Henry Baker owned 76 acres in the county, with a gross rental of £245.

EG Baker may have retired around 1875, since by 1876 George Harrison owned the brewery. He had started as a maltster in Leicester and owned a variety of breweries and maltings there (see entry). He also seems to have had an interest in a maltings on Wharf Street in Oakham, possibly through family connections with the Wingfields who owned property in the area. In 1876 Tom R Rudkin was his manager at Langham. The Rudkins were local farmers and maltsters.

By 1881, the year he died, Harrison may have sold the Langham brewery to Boys & Styles, who were also shown as brewers at 16 Southgate, Leicester, that year. An entry for 1877 seems to show Boys & Styles from the Shakespeare Brewery in Leicester (see entry). In

LANGHAM (continued)

1881, Boys and Styles were still shown at Langham, but the following year the partnership was dissolved. The Brewers' Journal in 1882 included an entry for Henry Weirs Boys, late brewer at 16 Southgate, liquidated and moved to Langham. Augustus (?) Styles was living at 13 New Walk in Leicester by that date.

Certainly, in 1884 part of George Harrison's malting business was taken over by Needham & Crick, which became a component of LB&M (see entry). By 1886, Boys & Styles seem to have passed the Langham brewery on to Harrison's nephew, Henry Harrison Parry. The Parry family may have retained some connections with Harrison's other property, in that the Duke of Bedford, an LB&M house, was mortgaged to a Joseph Henry Parry.

In 1891, John Munday was listed as the brewer to Parry. In 1894, Parry was trading from 17 Christow Street, and Langham. Henry Harrison Parry was listed as the brewer, whilst John Key was the brewery manager.

In 1896, George Ruddle became Parry's brewing manager. He had trained at Fordham's brewery in Ashwell and married Nora Fordham. The Ruddles were farmers at Netheravon, but they also ran a small brewery at Bradford-on-Avon. However, in 1846, Bart Ruddle was a boot and shoe manufacturer at Cottesmore, suggesting possible earlier family links with Rutland.

In February 1898, Parry paid LB&M £4,250 for three pubs:-

Old Greyhound, Billesdon	Queen's Head, Billesdon
Fox & Goose, Illston on Hill	

He also bought the Golden Fleece at South Croxton. LB&M had bought the Malt Shovel in that village in May 1893, in order that they could close it and concentrate trade at the Fleece, which they had leased, until they bought it in October 1893. However, LB&M had then decided on a policy of concentrating on the town trade and Parry seemed to be concentrating on the county trade. He also took the lease of the Cheney Arms at Gaddesby from LB&M as part of the deal. In contrast with the LB&M policy, they also seem to have sold him the King's Head on Abbey Street for £570.

In 1900 the business was shown at Langham and 19 Cank Street, Leicester. However, the Parrys seem to have sold off the Leicester properties around this time. An entry for the Duke of Northumberland in 1899, describes the owner as "*George Ruddell trading as HH Parry, Langham Brewery*".

In 1909, the total sales of beer wine and spirits amounted to £9,588. The bill for wages and salaries was £1,388, of which George Ruddle, as brewery manager, seems to have received £400, indicating the importance of his role. The net profit for the year was some £1,185, The estate was valued at £28,635 (Mitchell 1985).

The Staff and Brewery of H H Parry.

Photo: Courtesy Ian P Peaty

**LANGHAM
(continued)**

In 1909, Parry died, resulting in the sale the following year of the brewery with its 13 pubs, 3 beer-houses and 6 off-licences. LB&M considered buying, but decided against it. George Ruddle bought it on 20th June 1911 for £19,500, paying an initial 10% deposit and £750 each year after that (F2492). The pre-war business was mainly private trade to the "*gentry and local farmers*", but George increased the trade considerably and cleared off his debts in the 1920s. Interestingly, in 1922, the listing for the business still included the phrase "*late HH Parry*".

In 1919, Eric Munday, a great nephew of John Munday, joined the business. He was to spend fifty years with the firm as a traveller, head brewer and finally as a director.

Unfortunately in 1923, George Ruddle died aged only 48. The business was initially looked after by the executors of his will, Sidney Fordham and Ted Ruddle. The latter was George's brother and had been running the Bradford-on-Avon brewery, which the family had bought around 1906. Then in 1924, George Kenneth Fordham Ruddle, later Sir Kenneth, took over the business. He had trained at LB&M. The death also involved a stock transfer of shares in LB&M, with whom Ruddles had maintained a close working relationship.

An entry in the 1930-31 trade directory states "*high class mild and pale ales, noted for their excellence; two silver and three bronze medals and diplomas awarded; first and second prizes taken in 1929 Exhibition*".

The 1930s brought investment in a mechanised bottling plant, including metal crown corks replacing the traditional corks. There was also expansion of the estate. At the time, draught County was brewed as a mild.

In December 1945, G Ruddle & Company Ltd was formed, with Sir Kenneth as Chairman. There was further expansion in the 1940s to 38 pubs.

In 1950, County was re-introduced as a strong bitter. Langham water is similar to that of Burton and the new brew had a similarity to traditional IPAs; hence, there was an increase in its strength from the pre-war brew. In 1952 County gained a Brewex win for best cask beer. They also had a stronger ale called Old Bob. In a more innovative mode, Ruddles also made some attempts at introducing their own lager in the fifties.

In 1957, a new bottling hall was built with assistance from Whitbread as part of the latter's umbrella of holdings in country breweries. Then in 1959, Sir Kenneth's son Tony joined the company after two years training with Whitbread.

In 1963, Ruddles introduced Rutland Barley wine at 1080° to celebrate the independence of Rutland. As a result, it was initially called Victory Ale. In the 1960s, two-thirds of total output was to their own tied trade, with the rest to the local free trade. However, 1968 saw the first supply of own label beers to supermarkets, the same year that Tony Ruddle became the joint MD. A sign of later events was the decision to sell the Bewicke Arms at Hallaton to finance expansion. The old Parry family house became the offices in 1969.

In 1970 Sir Kenneth retired as MD, aged 70, and Tony Ruddle was solely running the business. In 1973, "*Ruddles Fine Ales*" were still mainly distributed within 40 miles of the brewery.

Tony Ruddle, as the new chairman, looked to expand further, including sales into the lucrative London market.

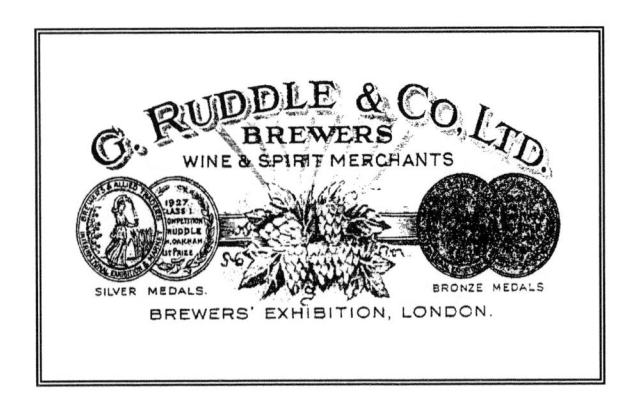

Letterhead used January 1951

In 1974-75, output was doubled, reaching 32,000 barrels pa. The products at this time were Bitter and County and the Barley Wine for Christmas. County was also available as a brewery-conditioned container beer known as Classic, and mild and bitter were also supplied in containers, which delivered the beer on a free-flow CO_2 system. They also produced "Keg", regarded as hoppier and stronger than that of many of the nationals. Perhaps surprisingly, for one of the smaller regional brewers, they now produced their own lager, called Langdorf.

The bottled range was :- Light Ale, Export, Bob Brown, County, Rutland Ale. Around this time they also introduced bottled Strong Brown, described by Frank Baillie as a full-bodied beer of 1048°.

**LANGHAM
(continued)**

Richard Boston, in his book Beer & Skittles, rated Ruddles in the top half dozen beers in 1976. In July of that year, the Sunday Mirror's first national survey scored County as 10 out of 12 and described it as *"full-bodied sweetish and strong"*. The average price was 29p per pint. Interestingly, their choice of champion beer was Tetley's brewery-conditioned Drum bitter.

In 1976 Sir Kenneth died. In June, whilst planning further expansion it was rumoured that they had considered buying Wethered's brewery at Marlow.

In 1977 they were employing 72 staff, with an estate of 39 tied houses. They produced 1,750 barrels per week or 50,000 barrels pa and that year capacity was doubled again to 100,000 barrels pa. The expansion took them to 100 workers. However, in the September, they withdrew from supplying beer to Norfolk, some 5 free houses, because of the small amounts involved.

They invested £700,000 on extending the brewery:- new silo, mash tun, copper and hop back, cask washer. This also included 5 new open fermenters - Tony Ruddle stated that he was very wary about the use of conicals *"I believe open fermenters are important to taste. Our policy is traditional techniques plus hygiene"* (What's Brewing September 1977 p6). The new plant was opened by Christopher Holmes, then chairman of CAMRA.

There was also £300,000 to expand production of bottled beer, with a new bottling hall and line. The expanded output of 2,000 barrels per week was split 40% traditional draught and 12% keg, with the rest packaged, especially in the new wide-mouthed non-returnable bottles for Sainsburys, Waitrose and Key Markets. In 1976, they were the first brewery to use wide-mouth bottles. They also developed a relationship with Wells of Bedford, as Ruddles stopped brewing their own lager in favour of kegging and packaging Kellerbrau. The production manager was Dusty Miller, previously at Phipps NBC, and who had joined Ruddles after the Watney take-over of the Northampton brewery.

In terms of draught sales, County outsold another of their ales, Blue, in a relationship of 65:35; although more Blue was brewed in total because of bottling. They were switching from own label bottling to increased use of the Ruddles name, helped by the high regard for the draught beers. Some 1,000 off-licences in the London area were being supplied.

The brewery prior to the major alterations.
Photo: Author

Tony Ruddle's view at the time was *"We are totally safe from take-over. More than 50% of the shares are owned by the family. The other aspect of our survival is producing a quality product that drinkers want"*.

The 15 months sales to March 1978 saw profits of £64,000. They had their own 36 tied houses with average prices of County at 36p per pint and Blue at 30p. However, in 1978 London prices of Blue at 36p per pint at 1032° were compared unfavourably with Bass at a strength of 1044°. It was argued that Blue was pricing itself out of market and to some extent was subsidising County which was selling at 38p. They now owned some 38 tied houses, of which 32 provided cask-conditioned beer.

However, Whitbread owned 31% of the business. This was part of the "umbrella", but unlike the earlier provision of funding for the bottling hall, Whitbread were looking to rationalise their financing arrangements. Hence, they sold their share to the Ruddle family and friends, which meant that the latter had to generate the cash to fund the purchase. They also had to consider how they would generate capital for investment in the brewery or the tied estate. Despite some internal disagreement, in June 1978, Ruddles decided to sell all but one of its 38 pubs, since they accounted for only 15% of the output. They retained the Noel Arms at Langham, but the rest were disposed of as follows:-

LANGHAM
(continued)

24 to Everards for £730,000
5 in Lincs to North Country Hull Brewery
6 in southern area as free houses

In the September, the Sunday Mirror's second national survey seemed to suggest that, although the original gravity of County had been slightly reduced from 1050.4° to 1048.9°, the alcohol content had risen from 4.64% to 5.34% abv. This may explain the change in description away from sweetness to a *"good strong powerful beer with hoppy flavour"*. Nevertheless, it still rated a score of 10, despite a price of 41p per pint.

The Sign of Quality
Phone : LANGHAM 24 and 34

WINES   SPIRITS

G. RUDDLE & Co., LTD.
LANGHAM BREWERY, OAKHAM
Winners of
CHALLENGE CUP and CHAMPIONSHIP
FOR BEST DRAUGHT BEER
Brewers' Exhibition, London, 1952
also TWO FIRST and ONE THIRD Prizes
Brewers of **"OLD BOB"**
ENQUIRIES WELCOMED

From an advertisement of 1954.

However, County did not succeed in the choice of champion beer of Britain, which was won by Thwaites' brewery-conditioned bitter, although both the keg and cask versions of the Bitter scored well in their individual classes.

The panel of 18 judges was composed of 12 members of the Incorporated Brewers Guild and 6 independent laymen representing the trade and the drinker. Roger Protz of CAMRA declared a personal interest in cask-conditioned beer and withdrew from judging in the final "drink-off" in which 3 brewery-conditioned beers were matched against 3 cask-conditioned ones.

A sign of the times was that in the Mirror's corresponding survey of lager, Grolsch was one of only two beers to score 11 out of 12. However, Scottish & Newcastle's Cavalier was rated at 12 out of 12, which may say something about the judging of the two journalists who had undertaken the survey. The average price of lager was 37p per pint, compared with 33p for bitter, despite lager being generally weaker in strength. Grolsch was the strongest lager in the survey with 5.24% abv, but it was also the most expensive at 62p per pint. Lager had grown in 13 years from 1% to 25% of the market.

In September, Ruddles withdrew from supplying about 5 pubs in the Tring area, because of distribution problems with low sales in the free trade. However, December 1978 saw them supplying British Airways with cans of County for trans-Atlantic flights.

The following March saw problems with demand outstripping supply, causing difficulties with disposing of the effluent. Indeed, they were having to tanker it off site. After cutting back on distribution to outlying areas, Ruddles stated that they would stop supplying those free houses which took less than 50 barrels per year. In May 1979, Wells bought out the Ruddle's share in the Jarvis Canning Company at the Bedford Brewery. Instead, Ruddles would concentrate on sales of beer in wide-mouth bottles.

In 1980 the business was still independent with one pub. That year saw County voted as the best cask-conditioned beer at Brewex 80 in Birmingham. June saw profits doubled, as new free trade outlets replaced the tied trade.

Dusty Miller, the former Head Brewer, became the production director. At the time, County was described as an all barley mash, with minute amounts of flaked maize to adjust the nitrogen content of the barley to prevent haze. The brew used whole hops, primarily English, but some Yugoslavian. The heavy hop rate was to balance out the sweetness which could result from the high gravity of the beer. It was now on sale in 11 British Railways station bars in London. Total output had risen as follows:-

1979 64,000 barrels   1980 74,000 barrels

Ruddle's beer production represented only 0.2% of the total UK beer trade, but 2% of the

LANGHAM
(continued)

Take Home Trade. Hence, 65% of the output was packaged. Sainsbury sales grew by 21% on the previous year and they also supplied Safeway and Waitrose.

However, in May 1981, the Hennekey (Trusthouse Forte) account for 8 bars was lost to Greene King. Tony Ruddle admitted that they had recently lost one or two other accounts because of the relatively high wholesale price. Further problems arose when the plans to expand on to a 3 acre site next to the brewery were resisted by the district council.

In May 1982, Ruddles joined the Unlisted Securities Market and on the 1st August the AGM noted profits up from £717,000 in 1981 to £833,000 for the year end to March 1982. In the October, Watney agreed to take County in 150 houses.

At the time, there was a fleet of 8 lorries for distribution:- 3 for delivering draught beer to customers within 100 miles of the brewery (agents covering anything beyond this distance), whilst the other 5 were for delivering palletised loads of packaged beer. However, in June 1983, the contract to supply about 1,000 barrels per year to BR train buffets was lost to Boddingtons. On the plus side, a further 350 pubs of Grand Metropolitan (owners of Watney) were to take draught beer. The London price was 89p pint. In November, Halls (an Allied subsidiary) signed to take County for pubs around Bristol.

In March 1984, Blue was renamed Rutland Bitter at 1032° OG and in October, the Head Brewer Tony Davies was hoping to introduce a mid-range draught beer. They already produced a 1042° Export for Sainsburys, but County still took 60% of draught sales. To cope with the changes, the brewhouse tower was rebuilt and the first conical fermenters were introduced. This was part of a 3 year expansion, to be completed by early 1986, which planned to double production to 5,000 barrels per week. In addition, the brewery tap, the Noel Arms was sold.

The Sales Director, Andrew Harter, stated that profits for the year to March 1984 were £1,021,462 on a turnover of £10m, 2/3rds of which came from Take Home Trade. This was compared to £705,087 in the previous year.

In June 1985, the Bitter was increased from 1032° to a more standard gravity of 1037°, at the same price. They were exporting some 400 barrels a year. However, County was now over £1 per pint in Watney pubs.

In July 1986, Grand Met bought the business for £14.2m, although Tony Ruddle was to continue as the chairman of what would now be a subsidiary of a major drinks company. The aim was to build a national quality brand sold in 3,000 outlets and it was felt that Ruddles would not be able to fund the advertising costs as an independent concern.

Output was now 170,000 barrels per annum of which 70% was Take Home Trade, with 20% to Watney, some 20,000 barrels for 750 outlets in London & East Anglia. Grand Met had previously closed their Norwich brewery.

Tony Ruddle: *"We'll be the Guinness of the ale world. If Bass put all their marketing behind lager, then Ruddle could become the number one premium ale"* (What's Brewing September 1986 p3). They were also looking at the possibility of the Best Bitter going national. However, ominously, the 10% which went to the free trade was declining.

In December 1986, Grand Met's Midland arm, Manns, agreed to take County in their 580 pubs, at £1.03 to £1.10 per pint. This was linked to a £5m doubling of capacity in 6 months. In 1987, the name was changed to Ruddles Brewery Ltd and in the November, Best was to go into 700 pubs of Manns & Norwich, with a £1m promotional campaign. The shortage of casks meant that the beer had to be sold in converted kegs.

However, the £1.7m "Campaign for Real Ale" used advertising which included cans and bottles and was criticised as being misleading. In January 1989, the £3m racking plant was opened, taking capacity to 250,000 barrels per year. Draught now took 70% of output of which Best now outsold County some 60:40. This switch away from bottles to draught sales took place just as the market for specialist beers was going in the opposite direction.

The 1991 Grand Met "breweries for pubs swap", meant that Ruddles became owned by Courage, who were suffering under the debt burden of their own Australian owners, Fosters. They perhaps did not need the additional capacity of nearly 300,000 barrels per year.

However, in January 1992, the second largest Dutch brewers, Grolsch, were looking to build a European collection of specialist breweries, having previously bought Wickuler.

LANGHAM (continued)

This had been the first purchase of a German brewery by a non-German concern. They now bought Ruddles. This was seen as a management strategy to fit the European open market. They were thought to have paid £20m for the business. Dermot Magee of Grolsch was to run the new business. Tony Ruddle was involved part-time with marketing and PR for a few months and then retired.

The business became Grolsch Ruddles Brewing Company, with its headquarters at Andover in Hants. They had a total staff of 140 in the UK. Tony Reynolds, who had brewed for Greenalls for 30 years until Warrington closed, would become the Technical Services Manager. They were trying to regain the quality image after Grand Met, but the perceived problem was not seen to be Langham, but the number of outlets with poorly trained staff.

They owned no tied estate. Instead they were selling beer to Courage who then sold it on to Grand Met and Inntrepreneur pubs, as part of a 7 year deal. Grolsch were looking for new markets in the growing pub chains and wholesalers, supported by freelance technical agents to maintain quality. They would also re-brand the product, with new livery, beer engines and casks. They had a 420,000 barrel capacity of which 70% was draught, in proportion 70:30 Best to County.

Tony Reynolds, the Head Brewer, aimed to improve the beers and in October 1993, their advertisement in What's Brewing used the *"We are what we brew"* motto. In terms of the brewhouse, they had 2 mash tuns, using pale and crystal malts and 10% sugar syrup. The 3 stainless steel coppers involved late hopping with whole Goldings hops for aroma. They emphasised their complex hop recipes:-

| Best | - Bramlings Cross, Fuggles, Goldings and Northern |
| County | - Challenger replaces Fuggles |

However, there was a switch to using only 18 conical fermenters, each of 350 barrels capacity. The previous yeast strain, which originated with Allied at Burton, was phased out in favour of a culture, which bottom fermented in the conicals! It has been mentioned that the local water has similarity with that of Burton and the popularity of County can be seen in terms of the IPA. The changes at Langham did not seem to take account of either the previous production strengths, nor the management comments supporting them.

Although the beers were still separate brews, under the new duty system they were shown as 3.7% and 4.9%, in each case 0.1% below the previous strength. In Grand Met they had brewed out to 1010°, but now they brewed to 1014°, with the intention of giving more body to the beer; hence the change in alcoholic strength. However, none of this quite fitted with the original 1950s County, which had made its name as a Burton style IPA.

Grand Met had brought in upright converted kegs called FBIC Fined Beer in Casks - and these were still supplied to Courage, being filled at Websters of Halifax. Alumasc developed new stainless steel casks which could be used in either traditional horizontal fashion or upright for Courage. These contained exactly 11 gallons of beer without the risk of drawing any sediment due to the Save All system. In addition, the casks used plastic rather than wooden plugs. The plugs were hinged to reduce the chances of contamination. The new beer engines to deliver the beer were effectively "swan necks", which produced a tight creamy head, unlike the previous "flatter" head, associated with this type of beer.

There was an improved delivery system based on tele-sales at Andover. There was also a TV campaign stressing the difference of the brand! The 1995 campaign which was based on taking the mickey out of the size of Rutland, was not well-received by the locals. However, they were somewhat mollified by the introduction of Independence Ale, 6.5% in 330ml bottles, to celebrate the return of the county after 21 years. Brewery tours recommenced after an absence of 3 years, but were no longer free, instead there was a charge of £10.

December 1995 figures:-

Sales	£17,578,000
Profit	£466,000
Capital Employed	£66,712,000
Net Worth	£33,954,000
85 employees	

However, in April 1994, Grolsch had been facing distribution problems in both the UK and Germany. This was resolved with joint ventures in which Bass would brew and distribute

**LANGHAM
(continued)**

Grolsch lager in UK, whilst Brau & Brunnen would distribute Wickuler in Germany. The sales and marketing staff would relocate from Andover to Langham.

In 1997, Best was an award winner at the CAMRA organised Great British Beer Festival, but they were operating at 60% of capacity and facing the end of the arrangement to supply the Courage estate; hence, Grolsch decided to sell to Morlands. The latter's intention was to use Langham for contract brews and develop the brand as a national one. However, six months later they announced the brewery was to close in October 1998. Problems with matching the brew at Abingdon delayed the closure until early 1999. The plant and equipment was sold in May 1999 and the site emptied awaiting further development (SK845110). Partly as a result of the failed investment, Morlands themselves were bought by Greene King and closed.

LEICESTER

Alford (or Halford), John, *Milk Maid, 84 Bedford Street.*

The Milk Maid dated back to at least 1848, when it was being run by Mrs Ann Nutting. In August 1867, John Staines was the victualler at the pub, on the corner of Grove Street (see Staines entry). However, it was owned by the Harrisons.

Then, in June 1882, Halford took the licence. From 1892 to 1895 John Alford or Halford was identified as brewing. However, LB&M actually leased the pub from 1882, possibly in terms of Needham & Crick supplying malt. The tenant, shown as, John or James Halford moved back here from the York Castle, and bought the Milk Maid in 1896, but it seems that brewing ceased around this time. In January the following year it was supplied by Holes of Newark. It closed in June 1938, when the licence was transferred to the Wyvern Arms, Barksby Road.

Andrews, Arthur, *Burgess Inn, 19 Burgess Street.*

In 1870 John Wesley was the victualler, but the first clearly identified brewer was Andrews, who was listed in 1877, having taken the pub in September 1873. The Brewers' Journal for 4th October 1883 mentions that Arthur Andrewshad been fined 40s for using sugar, without entering it in the brewing book (p325). He was also mentioned in the Brewers' Journal 1884 (p169) as Mr Andrews, of the Burgess Tavern, in financial difficulties, and this seems to be the end of his involvement in brewing at the pub. The pub was owned by Eliza Andrews.

In June 1886, William Darby took the licence and was listed as the brewer in 1887. In March 1890 John Allsop was the licensee, but there was no mention of brewing and on 8th September 1893 it was owned by Welch Brothers.

At some point it became an LB&M property for which they received compensation in 1925. It closed on 10th June, before it was sold in 1926, de-licensed.

Andrews, Thomas, *Turk's Head, 107/9 Welford Road.*

The Turk's Head dates back to at least 1827, when it was being run by a John Williamson, followed by Samuel Bonner around 1835.

In 1870, Mrs Eliza Wright was the victualler and then from May 1871 to October 1883, Thomas Andrews was brewing at the pub. From then until the early 1890s, the pub was run by the Dennis family, but there were no listings as brewers. However, between October 1894 and September 1902, John Dale was brewing at the Turk's Head, which was owned by the Varnham, or possibly Parnham, family. Prior to this in 1892 he was brewing at the Brewer's Arms (see Gask entry). He was followed by John Arnold, but brewing may have ceased by then.

It was still trading in 1913, when shown as 107 Welford Road.

Argyle, Frederick, *Midland Arms Hotel, 44 Upper Conduit Street.*

In 1870 Argyle was shown as the victualler, having been the licensee from December 1864. He was listed as a brewer for 1892.

In October 1897 Arthur Beardsmore took over the licence and brewing seems to have stopped. At some point it became owned by the Oswin family, who owned many licensed houses, with Harry Oswin the licensee in January 1914. The Midland was sold to Shipstones in 1914 for £5,520.

Atkin, Charles Thomas Pacey, *Painter's Arms, 2-4 Victoria Street/Clarence Street.*

In October 1845 Charles Thomas Atkin held the licence, although the address was shown as Lee Street in 1848. From 1870 Atkin was both a victualler and painter; hence the name of the pub. In 1877-87 he was listed as a brewer in Clarence Street, the pub stood on the corner of the street. Prior to this, in 1846 to 1848, a Thomas Atkins was a maltster and victualler at the Bishop Blaize, Causeway Lane/Long Causeway, but in 1871 this was owned by Ann Buttery.

The use of Pacey as a first name may suggest a possible link with the brewing family at Melton Mowbray. The pub brewed until 1887, but by 1890 it had become an LB&M property. It closed in June 1939, when the licence was transferred to the Shoulder of Mutton.

Atkins, Edward Skipwith, *Cambridge Arms, 52 Fleet Street.*

In 1870, the Cambridge was being run by John Knight, shown as a beerhouse at No 50. From 1892 to 1895 Atkins was brewing at the Cambridge.

Atkinson, George, *Cottage Inn, 20 Luke Street.*

The Cottage dated back to 1841 as a licensed property. In 1870, No 20 was a beerhouse run by William Wells, when Atkinson was running The Burlington, a beerhouse at 40 Guthlaxton Street. By 1892 Atkinson was brewing at the Cottage where he was listed until 1898. It was owned by Welch Brothers from around 1907, and was compensated and closed in January 1953.

Austin, Rowland, *Southgate Street.*

In 1827 Austin was a grocer in Belgrave Gate, but by 1835 Rowland Austin junior & Company were brewers in Southgate Street. His father continued to run the grocery. Rowland junior was listed as brewing in 1843, and also in Regent Street, to 1845.

However, in 1846-48 Rowland Austin was a porter and ale dealer in Halford Street and his own brewing would seem to have stopped. However, he was bottling Dublin porter. In 1850, he was an ale and porter dealer and commission agent. Four years later Martha Austin was at 16 Halford Street, suggesting Rowland had died and the business had passed to his wife. This was possibly the site later used by Thomas Hardy of the Kimberley brewery as an agency.

Austin, William, *Barkby Arms, 125 Bedford Street.*

The pub's name originated from its location, since in 1827, when John Maw was the landlord, the address was shown as Barkby Lane.

In 1870 Charles Wright was the victualler at the Barkby Arms on the corner of Upper George Street. In March 1871 Cock & Langmore took an interest in the property. However in May 1875, William Austin took the licence and in 1877 was shown as a pub-brewer at the Barkby Arms. Charles Wright seems to have moved very briefly to the White Swan and by 1882 Austin also seems to have moved to the White Swan (see Kilby entry). In 1891 Austin had become the victualler at the Gladstone Vaults and Concert Hall, before he subsequently seemed to have moved to London.

Between 1884 and 1887, Alfred Manship was the brewer at the Barkby, which he had taken on 13th December 1882.

In 1888, it was described as a public house, which suggests that brewing may have ceased and the short-term tenancies would support this. The address in 1892 was shown as 1 Upper George Street, Bedford Street. The pub was bought by the All Saints Brewery on 11th May 1898 and closed under compensation in 1911.

Ballard, James, *Olive Branch, 1 Willow Street.*

In July 1861 Ballard was the licensee and was listed as brewing around 1876-7. He may then have moved to the Black Lion at Thurmaston (see entry). In October 1877, the licence was taken over by Edwin Turner, described as a brewer, and who was listed as brewing at the pub 1887-1892.

In December 1893 Herbert Vickers took over the Olive Branch, which was still listed as a brewery in 1895. In 1898 Herbert Vickers was still brewing, but the address was shown as No 49. In 1906 LB&M took a seven year lease and bought it for £3,000 in December 1917. It was still trading in the 1950s.

Barber, Mrs E, *Forester's Arms, 17 Frog Island.*

In 1835 the Foresters, named after a trade society, at Frog Island was kept by George Kimber. It was possibly rebuilt around 1847.

From 1864 to 1876, James Barber was listed as the brewer. The licence was taken over by Elisabeth Barber on 16th October 1874 and in 1877 Mrs E Barber was listed as the brewer.

On 14th February 1881, Thomas Barber took over as the brewer at the pub. The Barbers also produced mineral waters. Joseph Goodwin Barber held the licence from 4th February 1893 to 25th February 1895, but brewing seems to have stopped. It then became an Everard's house, trading in 1913. It was later rebuilt and is still in business.

Barrow, William, *Old Horse Inn, 118/120 London Road.*

In July 1873 William Barrow was at the pub, which was owned by a Mr Arnold of Leamington. The 1875 Harrod's directory carries an advertisement for home brewed ales at the pub. However, Everards may have been supplying it when it was threatened with closure in 1878. In July 1880 Mary Barrow took over the pub and by 1902 Everards were the owners.

Barsby, Samuel, *East Bond Street.*

In 1813 the General Wolfe, with brewing vessels, located on Northgate Street, was to be let. This was as a result of Thomas Barsby leaving the business to become a manufacturer of worsted.

However, in 1846, Samuel Barsby was a brewer and baker in East Bond Street. He may previously have been at the Royal Oak in Barrowden. Then in 1848, he was shown as a brewer and grocer in High Cross Street. However, by 1855 Samuel Barsby was only a grocer at 71 High Cross, although William Barsby was a beer retailer in Conduit Street.

Bateman, John, *Mansfield Head Inn, 48 Mansfield Street.*

The pub dated back to at least 1827, when it was run by William Greasley, through to 1835, when it was shown as Sandacre Street. In the 1830 poll book, Joseph Ellicock was a retail brewer in Mansfield Street, but apparently not connected with the pub.

A John Bateman kept the Artilleryman, Bedford Street, in 1835, but in March 1869 John Bateman was the victualler at the Mansfield, shown as No 44. He was listed as a brewer in 1877, until October 1881 when Reuben Wakefield took the licence.

In May 1886 Thomas Blakeman was the brewer, until he moved to the Fox & Hounds in 1890. The property was leased by LB&M from 1890, when the address was shown as 2 Sandacre Street, with John Ballard still shown as the victualler. LB&M had bought the pub by September 1893. It was later sold for £175 de-licensed, after receiving £1,000 compensation.

Bateman, Hannah Jane, *Dun Cow, 11/13 Upper Charles Street.*

The Dun Cow was probably first licensed in 1861 and in 1870 Charles Mortimer was listed as a butcher and keeper of the beerhouse on the corner of Dun Cow yard. He was listed as the brewer in 1887.

Around 1892 Mrs Bateman was still shown as the brewer, but by 1903 it was owned by Everards. It closed under the compensation scheme in January 1927.

Beard, Hill & Company Ltd, *Greyfriars.*

Although Friedrich lists them as brewers in 1898, this was only an agency for their Burton brewery.

Beardsmore, John, *Marquis of Granby, 16 Castle Street.*

In 1815 Robert Orton was shown as the victualler and in 1827 Benjamin Bissell. By January 1862, John Beardsmore had taken the licence and for 1877 to 1887 was identified as the brewer.

In July 1888 William H Landall took over the licence, but there are no further indications of brewing. By June 1896, it was owned by Bell's of Burton; hence, it later became a Salt's house which was closed under the compensation scheme on 24th June 1912.

Beaumont, William Humber, *Old Axe & Square, 20 Sanvey Gate.*

From 1815 to 1827 Robert Cooke was at the pub, but in 1835 Jane Cook had taken over the licence.

LEICESTER (continued)

In February 1870, William Humber Beaumont was a cowkeeper and victualler at No 22, which was the Axe & Square, and at No 18a. The actual owner was John Johnson of Great Holme Street (see entry). Beaumont was listed as the brewer in 1877, through to 1895 (F2701).

On 20th October 1893 the Beeston Brewery Company took the licence, with Joseph Cox as their tenant. However, on 1st June 1894, Thomas Townsend took the licence and he was listed as a brewer in 1895. The pub closed on 11th July 1912, with £1,224 compensation for the owners and £148 for the tenant.

Beeby, Thomas, *Brook Street.*

Described as a brewer in the poll books from 1832 to 1847. His son does not seem to have continued in the business, since in 1857 Thomas junior was described as a butler in Friar Lane. However, in 1861, he was a victualler in High Cross Street.

Bennett, Miss Ann, *Swan & Rushes, 1 Infirmary Square.*

In 1812, the Swan & Rushes, which had been in business for over 50 years, was for sale by auction on 11th May. The address was shown as Horsepool Street and the sale details mention its very good brewhouse and that the pub had recently been re-roofed. The tenant was Ebenezer Jones.

In 1827 the address was shown as Oxford Street, with Gabriel Withers at the pub, but by 1835 Frances Withers had taken over.

In February 1869 Ann Bennett was the licensee, the owner being an Elizabeth Taylor of London Road. Miss Bennett was listed as brewing from 1870 to 1892. Then in August 1892, the licensee was Samuel Bennett, the brewer until 1898. Around 1876, they may have traded as Bennett & Bennett brewers, and there were Bennetts who were maltsters in Oakham.

At some point the pub became part of the Oswin estate. In January 1902 Edward Oswin took the licence and it was supplied by Marstons in 1902. In 1922 it was for sale, with two other pubs and in 1937 was owned by Holes of Newark. It is still trading, but has been rebuilt at some point.

Bickley, John, *Golden Lion, 26 High Cross Street.*

The Golden Lion was on the west side of High Cross, on the north corner of Thornton Lane. It was an early sixteenth century inn. In 1781, the Golden Lyon previously "The Town Seal" was run by Joseph Smith before he moved to the Crown & Thistle around 1790. The tenant in 1815 was a William Jordan (see Kibworth).

In 1827 George Loake was keeping the pub when Robert Bickley (possibly the same person also shown as Birkley) was listed as a wholesale brewer and maltster in High Cross Street. One house he seems to have owned was the Crown at Enderby (see entry). Bickley was also listed for 1835 as a brewer and spirit merchant in High Cross Street, whilst George Webb was at the pub. John Bickley was at the New Inn, High Cross Street in 1848. The 1854 sale at auction of the Lion mentioned a brewhouse and that it was the oldest remaining inn.

The Corporation sold it to John Clarke for £450, provided it was demolished by 25th March 1869 and rebuilt. Although later plans do not seem to show a brewhouse, John Bickley was the licensee in July 1870, when the owner was John Clarke of King Richard Road, and he undertook major advertising in the 1870 directories.

In 1877 John Bickley was shown as the brewer, until July 1880, when Mary J Bickley took over the licence. In August 1881, the licence passed to William Billson and there was no further listing for brewing. However, in 1881, AN Bickley was acting as an agent for the Anglo-Bavarian Brewery of Shepton Mallet at 14 Silver Street.

On 21st October 1897, TW Everard & CL Weldon bought the pub for £5,100. In 1970 it was bought by the Council for £15,950 and demolished.

Biggs, Mrs, *Nag's Head, 67 Granby Street.*

In 1794 Thomas Thornlow was keeping the Nag's Head, shown as being in High Cross. In 1805 there was mention of a malt room, when the owner of the pub was Francis Browne and the tenant Edward Burridge.

It was to let in 1806, with brewing vessels, when the owner was a Mrs Biggs (late Mrs Fever) and William Blower moved here from the Dolphin & Crown in the Market Place. In 1811

Benjamin Coleman was running the pub and in 1835 Elizabeth Bilson, who was there until around 1855. By 1870, the site was occupied by the Temperance Hall!

Biggs, William, *Boat & Engine, 20 Bath Lane.*

Chris Jenks, writing about the lost pubs of Leicester in the local CAMRA newsletter, gives a more detailed story of the Boat.

The area which had been laid out as pleasure gardens, and named Vauxhall Gardens after the London pleasure grounds, was developed in the 1790s, with the building of warehouses and wharves. In 1803 the Vauxhall on Bath Lane had a brewhouse. The Boat and Engine was first listed in 1822, but with the address shown as Vauxhall Wharf.

In 1835 to at least 1846, Elizabeth Frisby was the victualler at the Boat & Engine, whilst a Jonathan Biggs kept the Bull's Head, Oxford Street. However, in 1846, Thomas and William Frisby were porter and ale dealers 2 Market Street.

In 1870 John Orme was the victualler at the pub, whilst John Biggs was the victualler at the Crown & Anchor in Millstone Lane, but with a home in West Street.

The Boat and Engine was for sale by auction in 1873, when William Biggs was the licensee. The licence was held by William Biggs from 1873 to 1877. He was shown as the brewer at the Boat from 1877 to 1884, although, Thomas Fidler and various others were the licensees in the latter period. The pub was renamed the Bath Hotel around 1877, with the address as No 7.

From May 1887 to January 1898, the Bath was owned by the Plant family, before it was bought by Everard, Son and Welldon. From 1907, the pub was kept by Bill Sherriff, a local champion boxer, and at some point became owned by All Saints Brewery, before closing in 1958.

Bleasdale, Mrs Henrietta, *Marquis of Hastings, 65 Navigation Street.*

The Marquis traded from at least 1835, when it was kept by William Norton.

In February 1868 Henry Bleasdale was the licensee of the pub, which was actually owned by the Leicester Gas Company. In 1879 John Bleasdale was a joiner, builder and victualler at the pub, although Mrs Bleasdale was listed as the brewer 1877-84. She was still running the pub in 1892, but the licence lapsed in August 1894.

Bonner, Mrs Louisa, *Marquis of Wellington, 139 London Road.*

In 1815 The Marquis was described as being next to the Toll Gate and kept by John Gilbert. The landlord in 1827 was an Edward Blood and he was followed by Ann Blood around 1835.

By August 1865, Samuel Bonner was the victualler and licensee, although the pub was owned by a Mr Farmer. Bonner was listed as the brewer for the period 1877-84. In January 1887 George Broadley took the licence, but brewing would seem to have ended. In July LB&M considered a bid of £2,500 for the pub, but by August 1903 it was an Everard's house.

Boot, William Henry, *Freemason's Arms, 35 Burley Lane.*

In 1827 John Chamberlain was the victualler, when the address was shown as Northgate Street. In 1870 John Breedon was keeping the pub.

Then for 1877-84 Mr Boot was shown as the brewer at the pub. In 1892 it was owned by Ind Coope; however, in June 1917 the licence was refused and the pub closed.

Bostock, J, *Three Cannons, Church Gate.*

In 1810, Mr Bostock who had moved to the pub from Earl Shilton, was advertising his fine home brewed ale and London barrelled and bottled porter. He was also operating a cotton warehouse from the premises. It seems to have closed by 1827.

Bowker, James, *(King) George III, 40 Abbey Street.*

From January 1861 to 1870 John Gamble was the victualler, but by June 1875, John Brown held the licence (see entry).

In February 1876, James Bowker took over the licence and in 1877 was listed as the brewer, although by the following July the pub was being run by Henry Bowker.

The brewing plant was sold in 1891 and the George became an LB&M leased pub. It had dropped the "King" from the title by 1892. In 1898, LB&M bought it for around £7,000.

However, in 1937, the licence was transferred to the Naseby Hotel and the George was closed in the October.

Braden, John Laws, *Hatter's Arms, 38 East Bond Street.*

In 1870 William Pears was a baker and beerhouse keeper, although there was no name given to the pub. However, in 1892 John Laws Braden was listed as a baker and beerhouse keeper at the Hatters.

His name is sometimes shown as JL Bradon and he was listed as the brewer for the period 1887-1895. Then in 1898 William McCann was brewing, but there seems to be no other mention after this date.

Bray, Richard, *Forester's Arms, 27 (later 39) Dryden Street.*

In 1870 Mrs E Dorman was the victualler at the Foresters, whilst Bray was at the Lord Raglan, 55 New Bridge Street. In October 1874 John Hurley held the licence, until July of the following year when it was taken by Benjamin Walker, although Charles Scotney was the actual owner.

Bray was listed as brewing in 1877. In March 1878, William Clayton, previously brewing at the King's Head (see entry), became the victualler/owner of the Foresters and was listed as brewing there in 1881. In October 1881, Scotney himself took over the licence until December 1882, when it passed to Henry Dodger.

In June 1886, John W Morris took over the licence and was listed as the brewer at the Foresters for 1892-98. However, by 1893, it was supplied by the Nottingham Brewery Company. The pub closed as recently as 1983.

Briggs, John George, *The George Hotel, 9-13 Haymarket.*

Originally, shown as Coal Hill, in 1770-94 Thomas Robinson was running the George and then in 1798 it was run by Henry Lenton. In August 1799, Lenton was at the *"newly erected"* George and there was a mention of the brewing vessels; however, soon afterwards he was bankrupt and the pub was to let.

In 1805 it was being run by James Briggs and Jonathan Briggs was apprenticed to his father to learn brewing. This presumably was the same Briggs shown at the George in 1835. The Briggs family also seem to have been involved with the Crown and Anchor, which passed to the Brown family. Then in 1867 a J Brown was listed as a maltster at 9 Haymarket and was then shown as running the George (see Brown entry).

In 1875, Ann Maria Marston was running the George, but it was owned by Ind Coope. The site is now covered by the Haymarket shopping centre.

Brotherhood, James, *Coach & Horses, 46 Oxford Street.*

The Coach & Horses dated back to at least 1815, when it was being run by C Mallett, with the address shown as Humberstone Gate.

However, in 1870 it was only described as a beerhouse when it was being run by Charles Smith. For the period 1892-1895 Thomas Hubbard was listed as the brewer, followed in 1898 by Henry Guildford.

It was still brewing in 1902, when William Hipwell was running the pub, although he may have had connections with the All Saints Brewery. Nevertheless, for 1906-1910 James Brotherhood was still shown as the brewer, although Everards seem to have bought it around 1904.

Brown, Charles, *The Fox Hotel, 15 Humberstone Gate.*

In 1815 the Fox was being run by James Ward and in 1835 by George Phillips. In 1867, William Cooke was an innkeeper living at No 13. Then in 1870, he was operating a wine and spirit stores at the Fox and in 1871 W Cooke & Co were shown as brewers there.

However, the Cooke business did not flourish and by 1876 Charles Brown was the brewer at the pub. By 1907 it was an All Saints Brewery house and in October 1910, they were selling plant from the Fox. The following year it was included in the compensation scheme for closure. The licence was not renewed and in 1935 it was demolished for Lewis' department store.

Brown, George, *Hinckley Road Brewery, 5 Hinckley Road.*

From 1835 to 1887 the Hinckley Road Brewery site was run by the Johnson family (see entry). However, in July 1877 John George Collis had taken over the licence and he was listed as brewing from 1881 to October 1887, before he moved to the Magazine Inn.

In June 1887, the licence was taken by George Brown who was listed as the brewer in 1891 (F2703). E Brown & Sons were mineral water manufacturers at 14 London Road in 1892.

In November 1894 the owners were the Beeston Brewery Company; however, the business was still listed the following year as John Wilkinson, brewer, and he seems to have brewed until around 1902. From Beeston the pub passed to Shipstones; hence, it was later re-named the Shipstone Arms and was still trading in the 1950s, before being demolished for road improvements.

Brown, John, *Malt Shovel, 8 Lower Church Gate.*

From 1830 to 1848 John Brown was shown as a maltster in St Nicholas Street. In 1867 a J Brown was also listed as a maltster at 9 Haymarket, this being the George Hotel. In 1870 he was shown as a maltster at the George Commercial Hotel.

In January 1864, Mrs Charles Lockton was the licensee and victualler at the Malt Shovel. In 1875 a John Brown held the licence of the George III on Abbey Street; however, in the June, John Brown replaced Mrs Lockton at the Malt Shovel and was shown as a pub brewer in 1877. He was still a maltster, living in the Haymarket and in 1884, he was shown as a maltster at No 9 Haymarket.

In October 1877 Edwin Griffin, previously brewing at the Woodman's Stroke (see Griffin entry) took over the licence. He was at the Malt Shovel until December 1887, when he was followed by various members of his family.

Although it was owned by Everards in 1900, in 1914, William Moore was listed as brewing at the pub. It was later compensated and closed in November 1938.

Brown, John Stanyon, *The Crown & Anchor, 170 Belgrave Gate.*

Robert Briggs was the victualler at the Crown from 1827 to 1835, as well as being a maltster in Pasture Lane. In 1846, he was shown as a maltster and victualler at the Crown & Anchor, when John Brown was a maltster in St Nicholas Street.

From 1870 to 1877 Joseph Brown was listed at No 170, and shown as brewing in the latter year. He was also a wine & spirit merchant. In 1876 there were details of Joseph selling his copper and boiler, but he then moved to the Old Ten Bells as the brewer.

John Stanyon Brown was listed as the brewer at the Crown in 1884, suggesting that new equipment had been purchased (F2704). He may then have then moved to the Pelican (see Hughes entry).

In August 1890, Henry Bray held the licence, but by December 1895 it was held by Everards. Then in September 1897 it was run by Bell's of Burton and from them to Salt's, by 1902. It was compensated and closed in January 1954 and the building was subsequently demolished.

Brown, William, *The White Horse, 27 Belgrave Gate.*

In 1815, when William Whitehead was at the pub, the location was shown as Gallowtreegate. By May 1857 William Brown had taken the licence. He was shown as the brewer for the period 1870-77.

In December 1878 Charlotte Brown was the licensee until September 1892, when the licensee was shown as Charlotte Parkinson Brown. However, in 1884 Richard Monk was listed as the brewer. In 1907 William Stephen Brown, the executor of Charlotte, held the licence and in March of the following year Arthur Sturgess was at the pub. This was probably the end of brewing at the pub, if it had not already stopped.

The pub was still trading in the 1930s, when it was supplied by Mitchells and Butlers (M&B) of Birmingham.

Bunney, Mrs Elizabeth, *The Wool Comber's Arms, 7 Royal East Street.*

The Wool Combers was not listed in 1835, the first definite listing being in 1870, when Mrs Anne Heywood was listed as the victualler.

By March 1873 Mrs Bunney had taken the licence, although the owner was Thomas Litchfield. For the period 1877 to 1884 Mrs Bunney was listed as a brewer. However, in March 1878 John Halford had taken over the licence of the pub (see Alford entry) and by June 1882, Charles Tidd was at the pub. In July 1885 George Halford took over the licence and was listed as the brewer in

1887. Then in June 1890, it passed back to Charles Tidd, who was shown as the brewer in 1892.

In October 1894 Albert Green took over the pub and there is a possibility that in the year after, Charles Deacon was brewing here. He may then have moved to the Horn of Plenty, 14 Lower Garden Street. By January 1898, it was owned by Everards, who then gave up the licence for a new hotel on Tudor Road.

Burgess, Henry, *The Green, 37 Bath Street.*

The pub was not listed in 1870 nor 1892, unless it was re-named from the Bull's Head, although the address was also shown as Belgrave. Certainly from 2nd September 1894 to 15th September 1903, the licence was held by Henry Burgess, who was also listed as the brewer (F2705).

Then John Burgess, previously brewing at the York Castle (see Matthews entry) took over. He was the licensee until 20 February 1945 and the pub may well have been one of the last to brew in the town.

Burnhope, John, *Hat & Beaver, 60 High Cross Street.*

The Hat dates back to at least 1815, when it was kept by Richard Spencer. In 1827 William Facer was shown as the victualler, but by 1835 it was run by Edward Wright Bennett. In 1848, William Trivett was the victualler at the pub (see also Market Bosworth entry). Then in 1870 Fras Morris was listed as the victualler.

However, the first clear identification of brewing was for 1877, when John Burnhope was shown as the brewer at the pub. He was followed around 1884 by Mrs Jane Burnhope as the brewer.

In 1903, it was a Brunt Bucknall house which, with their take-over, had become a Bass pub in 1921. The CAMRA beer guide identified it as a former Bass pub, one of the few remaining traditional pubs in the town. It is still trading as an Hardy and Hanson house.

Burton, John Hunt, *Old Mitre, 1 Lower Redcross Street.*

In 1800 Elizabeth Atkins, the widow of Timothy, was at the pub, followed around 1813-15 by William Barrars and then William Burton, although this may have been the same person. From 1827 to 1835 Thomas Perkins was at the Mitre.

By 1870 Edward Dexter was the victualler, possibly before moving to the King's Head, where he was listed as brewing. In November 1874, the licence was taken by Mrs Maria Moore, who was listed as the brewer in 1875, although the owner was John Johnson of Great Holme Street (see entry). In November 1875 Josiah Langton was briefly at the pub.

John Hunt Burton took over the licence in May 1876 and was in the directories as the brewer for 1877 to 1884. However, in May 1878 Benjamin Eyley had taken the licence, and he was listed as the brewer until 1887. In March 1887, Lucy Cartwright Eyley was the licensee, but in the November Charles Newton had taken over. This may be the same individual who had been brewing at the Peacock (see entry). In June of the following year, Mrs Newton held the licence for nine months before passing it to Frederick Blockley.

In September 1890, Robert Tansley took the licence and was listed as the brewer until his death. Hence in July 1895, the licence went to Mrs Sarah Tansley, who was listed as the brewer in 1898. It then became an Everard's pub by 27th March 1906. The licence was later transferred to the Blackbird and the pub closed in August 1938.

Butler, George, *Wilton Street Brewery, 2 Wilton Street.*

The 1847 poll book lists Butler as a brewer in Wilton Street. Then in 1857 George Stafford was listed as a brewer in Wilton Street. In 1863 he was shown as running a beerhouse at 2 Wilton Street, before he moved to Newarke Street (see entry). This was later known as the Wilton Street Brewery, which in 1870 was run by Joseph Barratt. Although in 1875 Joseph Carr was at the beerhouse, Barratt was running it again 1894.

Butt, Thomas, *Crown & Cushion, 75 Belgrave Gate.*

The Crown dated back to at least 1815, when it was run by T Wilford. In 1835 Sarah Gisborn was at the pub.

In April 1872 Thomas Butt took the licence and was then listed as the brewer in 1877. However, in June 1877 Joseph Cant was the licensee (see next entry), with the owner shown as William Allen. In August 1878, it passed to Benjamin Walker.

From around the 1870s, the All Saints Brewery was supplying wine & spirits, but by 1907 it was owned by Robinsons of Burton and it closed in December 1914.

Cant, Joseph, *Shakespeare Brewery, 15 Southgate Street.*

The pub and brewery were named after local family, not the playwright. In 1827 John Payne was the victualler. In 1835, the Shakespeare's Head, 19 Southgate Street was kept by William Millson, but there was no clear mention of brewing, similarly in 1848 when run by Charles Crofts. However, in 1867 Thomas Broughton was listed as a brewer at 19 Southgate Street and advertising as the Shakespeare Head Brewery, supplying Ale, Porter and Double Stout.

In May 1869 Thomas Mayne was the licensee of the pub and in 1870, Mayne or Main was listed as an ale and porter brewer at the Shakespeare's Head on Southgate. The Shakespeare's Head was at No 19, and owned by Joseph Cant. In 1861, he had been described as a publican in Old Mill Lane. However, it is possible that a commercial brewery had been set up which was separate from the pub brewhouse, since the brewery shown at No 17 was being run by Mrs Anne Broughton, whose home was at No 12. At this time, No 15 was occupied by a sewing machine manufacturer. In 1876 they seem to have been trading as Broughton & Broughton.

In May 1875 Joseph Cant was shown as a brewer and victualler at the Shakespeare's Head, 19 Southgate. He had moved here from the Duke of Northumberland (see Clarke entry). In the December John Widdowson Tompkin took over running the pub. CW Cant was possibly listed as a brewer in 1876, as well as Joseph.

In 1877, the Shakespeare Brewery at No 15 was managed by Boys & Styles, who also seem to have been operating the Langham Brewery. Their names are given as Henry Weir Boys and Augustine Styles and both were living on the premises. In 1881, they were listed for Southgates and Langham. The Brewers' Journal in 1882 included an entry for Henry Weirs Boys, late brewer at 16 Southgate, liquidated and moved to Langham (see Ruddles entry). Augustus (?) Styles was living at 13 New Walk.

However, in 1880 the listing was for Joseph Cant of the Shakespeare Brewery & 15 Southgate Street, but he was in liquidation on 30th April 1882. Nevertheless he was still listed in 1885 as J Cant (F2702). The pub itself had several landlords over the period.

In 1884 the Beeston Brewery Company had a depot in Shakespeare's Head yard, with Styles and Gill as the agents. In 1891 the site was still being run by Beeston, but with William Burton as the manager at Shakespeare Yard. The pub passed to Shipstones in 1915 and is still trading, but has been rebuilt.

Cave, William, *Maltster's Arms, 116 Church Gate.*

Around 1870-1 John Bradshaw was a pork butcher and running an un-named beerhouse. Both he and the pub were identified in the licence for 1873. He was listed in 1884 as a maltster at No 114, but Edmund Hutt seems to have being running the pub. He was followed by 1887 by a George Butler.

In 1895 Thomas Norman took over the licence, but in 1898 he was followed by William Cave. The latter was listed as a brewer, but Everards seem to have taken the pub by 1899, with Tom Richardson as their tenant. Tom Richardson was shown as a brewer for the period 1902 to 1921 (F2706); although in 1913, the Maltsters was shown only as a beerhouse, and then Joseph Freer was briefly running the pub.

The pub was compensated and closed in December 1922 and later demolished.

Chamberlain, George, *Earl of Leicester, 30 Infirmary Square.*

The pub was first licensed in 1855. In 1864 George Burden, a beerhouse keeper, was selling his brewing vessels; however, this may have been to replace them with new ones, since he was still there in 1870.

In 1892 George C Chamberlain was the brewer, followed in 1895 by Mrs Eliza Chamberlain, who was also identified as brewing.

In 1898 Arnold Rylott was shown as the brewer. He was also a professional cricketer and beerhouse keeper. Prior to this in 1888 Harriss Rylott was a beer retailer at the George and Dragon, 25 Peel Street. By 1901 the Earl was supplied by Everards. The licence was given up for the Blackbird and the pub closed in August 1938.

Chamberlain, Thomas, *Shamrock, 24 Orchard Street.*

In November 1858, Chamberlain was the licensee of the Shamrock, which was owned by Charlotte Leay. He was shown as the brewer for the period of 1870-7. In February 1882 it was owned by Bates & Bishell and hence LB&M in 1898.

The licence was later transferred to the Board and the pub closed in April 1939.

Chapman, George, *The Blue Lion, 21 Granby Street.*

The Lion dated back to at least 1835, when it was kept by John Kingston. In 1845, the licensee was a John Whitfield, although the pub was owned by a Mrs Gibson of Rugby.

In 1848 Chapman was mentioned as the brewer at the pub. In November 1876, Frances Whitfield took over the licence, but by the following July it had passed to a George Hillery, who was there until March 1886. Very briefly, Samuel Cleaver was the licensee, before it passed to Thomas Paget (see entry). In 1898, it became part of the Orson Wright estate, which formed part of his hotel company; however, the licence was given up and the pub was closed in 1899. The site became the Jarvis Grand Hotel.

Clarke, Job, *Duke of Northumberland, 6 Northumberland Street.*

In 1870 Joseph Cant was at the Duke, which was shown as Old Mill Lane, before he moved to the Shakespeare Brewery (see entry). The pub was on the corner of Northumberland Street. In November 1873 Henry Jackson was listed at the Duke of Northumberland and was brewing for 1875-84.

In July 1875 Charles Lawton took the licence and Henry Jackson was the brewer in 1877, but he may then have moved to the Mitre & Keys by 1879 (see Lapworth entry). Around 1883 it was being run by Tom Hastings.

Then in 1892 Job Clarke took the pub and was shown as the brewer for 1892-98, with the address shown as 24 Old Mill Lane, Sanvey Gate. On 20th October 1897, the licence was taken by HH Parry and hence it became a Ruddles house in 1911. It was closed under the compensation scheme in December 1916.

Clarke, Samuel, *New Town Arms, 17 Milton Street/Bedford Street.*

By September 1867 Samuel Clarke was the licensee of the pub, where he was shown as the brewer 1870-1887. However, the pub had a series of landlords from December 1881 until October 1899, when it was bought by Salts. It closed for compensation in April 1940.

Clayton, William George, *The King's Head, 28 King Street.*

The King's Head dated back to at least 1827, when it was run by William Wragg, followed in 1835 by William Liddard Wood.

In December 1868 Clayton was the licensee and was listed as the brewer 1870-77, before he moved to the Foresters (see Bray entry)

In 1892 the address was shown as No 36, when it was being run by Ann Clayton, who had held the licence from May 1885. Joseph Cracroft Clayton was running the pub in June 1909, but brewing seems to have stopped before this. It was later owned by M&B and was still trading in the 1940s.

Clewes, John, *Freeman's Arms, 9 Aylestone Road.*

The pub was built after 1870 and shown as the Freeman's Arms run by John Clewes, with the address as Welford Road. He was also advertising Dulley's Stout from Wellingborough.

Between 1877-84 John Clewes was listed as the brewer at the Freemans, which seems to have sometimes been called the Freemasons. In 1879 a Joseph Clewes was the victualler at the Coach Maker's Arms, 13 Church Gate, whilst John, not surprisingly was a coach builder at No 15. The latter's home was shown as the Stork's Head beerhouse on Knighton Road.

In May 1877 Edward Clayton took over the licence and seems to have continued brewing until August 1891, when John Coleman was installed as the tenant. Then again in 1893 Edward Clayton took over the pub until April 1911 while William Starbuck was the licensee.

By 1913, it seems to have changed its address to No 19 Aylestone Road. It was bought in March 1921 by LB&M for £11,700, but they had possibly been supplying it from around 1900.

Clifton, Charles, *Humberstone Gate.*

In the 1847 poll book as a brewer. This may have been in connection with Thomas Clifton who ran an eating house at No 28 in 1846.

Cock & Langmore, *All Saints Brewery Company, All Saints, 21 Silver Street.*

Despite the office address, the actual brewery building was on High Cross Street. It was shown on Fowler's map of 1828, next to the new gaol, suggesting that it had been in business for some time. Later advertising by the firm suggested that the brewery dated back to 1800, and possibly as early as 1795. It was probably the site originally used by the Forresters (see entry).

The 1826 poll book lists Robert Birkley as a brewer in Northgate Street, but this seems to have been his home address. In 1832-35 he was listed on High Cross Street as a brewer, maltster and spirits merchant.

On 1st January 1843, Richard Gibbon & Company, Anchor Brewery, were advertising as previously the All Saints Brewery, some nine months in the property, late Robert Birkley. However, given the difficulties with names and entries in some of the early directories, this may be the same individual shown as Bickley (see entry). However, Gibbon also seems to have continued to run a separate business in Newarke Street (see entry).

From an advert dated January, 1843.

In 1846, Thomas Cock & Company were shown as brewers and maltsters at the Red Bull on High Cross Street. In 1815 William Gillespie had been shown at the inn as a victualler. Cock & Company were also listed as victuallers, and wine & spirit merchants; although, John Goodwin of London Road was described as the brewer in the firm. In 1832, George Goodwin, described as a brewer, was living in Wigston. In 1847, Thomas Cock, brewer, was living in Charlotte Street.

In 1848, Goodwin & Hobson (late Thomas Cock & Company) were shown as ale and porter brewers, maltsters and wine & spirit merchants in High Cross Street. This suggests that they had taken over the brewery at the Red Bull. However, in 1855 Goodwin and Hobson were also shown as brewers at the Pied Bull. The pub was called the Pyed Bull in 1805, when it was described as being near All Saints Church. They also owned the Falcon, 18 Granby Street. In 1835, the Pied Bull had been kept by John Westley Gillespie.

In 1857, Stephen James Hobson was listed in the poll book as a brewer in High Cross Street.

In 1863 the listing was for John Willis Goodwin & Company brewers, maltsters, wine & spirit merchants at 97 High Cross Street. In 1864, TG Cock was advertising in the Chronicle that he had succeeded the late JW Goodwin in High Cross and was trading as Goodwin, Cock & Company, The Brewery, All Saints Brewery. In addition to their own ale, East India Pale Ale and stouts, they were also able to supply London stout from Elliott, Watney & Company.

From the Jack Feast collection.

The confusion over name changes continued, since from 1860 to 1873 they were trading as Cock & Moon, 21 Silver Street. However, in 1867 Moon, Cock & Company were also shown as brewers in Charlotte Street. Yet in 1868, the Craven Arms was owned by Cock & Langmore.

In 1870 the business was listed as Goodwin, Cock & Company at 97 High Cross and at the Falcon Vaults. The Falcon Vaults, a wine and spirits business at 20 Granby Street was run as Goodwin, Cock & Company, suggesting this name was then used for the subsidiary. They were also in business under this name at 9 Horsefair Street, next to the Dolphin. Nevertheless, they were also still shown as Moon, Cock & Company, 103 High Cross, next to the Pied Bull run by Edward Smalley, which they owned. Thomas Godfrey Cock, the brewer at Moon, Cock & Company was living at No 97 High Cross, suggesting that brewing had ceased at this building. Frederick Greaves Moon's home was in London.

Just to confuse matters even more, in 1871 they may also have been shown as JF Moon & Company.

From the Jack Feast collection.

Nevertheless by 1871 William Langmore had certainly joined TG Cock and gone to live at the brewery house at 97 High Cross Street. Thomas Godfrey Cock, of Cock and Langmore, presumably moved out, since in 1875 his home was Shelbrook House, Humberstone Road. In November 1874, Langmore was shown as the licensee of the Britannia on Belgrave Gate. They were now trading as Cock & Langmore, All Saints Brewery. Confusion still continued in that in 1876 they were also still listed as Moon & Cock at High Cross Street.

In 1877 Cock & Langmore were shown on High Cross Street (F2707). In White's directory for that year, they were listed for 20 Granby Street, 67 Corn Exchange and the All Saints Brewery, 103 High Cross. They may have become linked with Watts & Sons around this time (see entry), but they were listed until 1882 as Cock & Langmore. Indeed, the Britannia was listed for Cock and Langmore as late as November 1896. They were renting bonded stores for £25 pa from the Midland Railway Company.

In 1881, the address was shown as 103½ High Cross, and sometime after this Samuel Nevins Bankart was in partnership with William Langmore. Samuel Nevins was the son of Samuel Stephen Bankart, who had been Chairman of the Leicester Banking Company. It is not clear whether the Bankarts were actively involved in the day to day running of the brewery. The family was living at Hallaton Hall around this time.

For the period 1884-96 the business traded as Langmore & Bankart at the All Saints Brewery, High Cross Street. Around 1892 the relationship with Watts & Sons seems to have become more formal.

The popularity of Burton beer was shown in the 1880s, when All Saints Brewery were buying beer from the Burton Brewery Company, Nunneley & Company and Marstons. They were also buying stout from Sharpes of Sileby and . soda water from Schweppes & Company of Derby. In 1882, a sign of the times was that they were buying paper labels etc. from Billing Brothers in Birmingham, some 7,000 small round labels at 3s 6d per thousand. Bottles were still corked, with corks from Thomas Peet & Sons of London. Twenty gross half-pint corks cost some £1 10s. The bottles came from Cunnington & Company of St Helens. Two gross and 11½ dozen for £1 9s 7d.

In 1893, like many other brewers they made much use of sugar in brewing, particularly from Manbres and Clarks e.g. 80 cwt for £53. They also bought caramel sugar and Caramaline from Clarkes, presumably for the dark beers, which were still the most popular. They were also buying maize around this time, possibly for its benefits in giving a good head to beer, rather than simply because it was cheap. Another more common ingredient was the June malt purchase from Long & Company of 30 quarters at 34/- each. In July they bought 205 quarters of malt, including some from Walmersleys, their prices being:- Patent 36/-, Brown 31/-, Crystal 37/-. They were also looking to buy foreign malt from Pauls, including both Californian and Chilean. Hops from Meredith & Company were at 155/-, but they were also buying Oregon hops from Morris & Company at 56/-.

The casks for the beer came from Allen Shutco, 100 strong kils at 16/- each and 4½ gallons at 6/3d. To support their wine and spirit trade, in August they were buying cider from B Wood & Sons, some 38½ gallons for £1 15s 4d. In comparison, they also bought 4 dozen pints of Bollinger at a cost of £7 14s.

The All Saints Brewery Company Ltd was registered on 30 September 1896 with offices at 21 Silver Street. It was set up to run the Langmore and Bankart brewery and Watts and Sons wine and spirits, both businesses described as having been in existence for over 100 years. However, for several years they had traded as All Saints Brewery Company and Watts and Sons. The business was financed by £100,000 in £10 shares, equally divided between ordinary and 5% cumulative preference shares, all of which had been retained by the owners. There was also a 4% First Mortgage Debenture Stock of £100,000, which was redeemable after 1st January 1916 at 110%. The brewery address was given as 103½ High Cross.

The £200,000 raised was used to pay the vendors. The profits prior to the registration had been as follows:-

1893	£10,701
1894	£9,626
1895	£10,029

In 1897, the Swan With Two Necks, where the Watts family had started their business, was on the property books at £1,800, with a 3¾% mortgage. They also seemed to have owned the Malthouse on Vine Street, which may actually have started out as a malting, but later seems to have become an off-licence. That year they bought the Cross Keys at Kings Cliffe for £2,550. This had previously brewed its own beer, but presumably the purchase led to its supply from Leicester.

In 1899 the directors were shown as William Langmore, S Nevins Bankart, H Fletcher, and Frederick Watts.

Around 1907, they were reducing their usage of the cold store at RC Allen, in which they had a part share (see entry). This may be seen as an omen of later events.

In 1908, a share issue of 1,080 new preference shares generated some £21,800, suggesting that successful trading had been reflected in a premium on their nominal value. At this time, the Nominal Share Capital of £125,000 comprised:-

5,000 £10 Preference
1,250 new Preference
6,250 Ordinary

The directors were still:- SN Bankart, living at Hallaton Hall and described as a brewer and the owner of 2,043 of the ordinary shares, Frederick Watts the other brewer was living at Kibworth, H Fletcher of East Norton Hall and FG Langmore of Manor Road in Leicester. One of the shareholders was a Walter H Goodwin, a manager in Turner Street, and presumably a descendant of the earlier brewer.

The business also included maltings at Cow Pasture, Wothorpe in Northants and property in nearby Stamford. The malting was run by BW Aldwinckle, presumably the Bartholomew William Aldwinckle brewing at the Exeter's Arms (Brewed In Northants, page p114). In 1910 they sold the High Street property at Stamford, but retained the King's Head and the Albion, later compensated and closed. They were leasing the Marquis of Exeter for 7 years in 1891. They had also owned the Cross Keys, at nearby Kings Cliffe from 1897, and it is not clear whether these properties had all come from the same purchase, but they do seem rather isolated from the rest of the estate.

The remains of the All Saints Brewery.

Photo: Author

The remains of the All Saints Brewery.

Photo: Author

In January 1909, Mr Bankart was in discussions with the Board of LB&M about a possible amalgamation, talks which presaged later events.

In 1910 the High Street property was described as the House Vaults, and they also owned the adjoining house and shop. The brewery on Silver Street may also have still been in use. The Pied Bull was still trading. Around this time, Herbert Fletcher bought Hallaton Hall from the Bankarts, who moved to Rutland. Their move may have been a factor in the previous amalgamation talks.

From a commercial directory dated 1884.

There was an investment in a new engine and hoist for the bottling department and the following January a new wort receiver for £10. In February 1911 they bought a National Cash Register machine for £50. In April there was a new bottle washing machine costing £20, and a labelling machine for £6. Then in July, there was a bottling plant from Adlams £300 and from Lumley a corking machine for £7. All these purchases show the increased sales of bottled beer at the expense of draught. To some extent this represented declining sales from the off-licensed premises, but also changes in sales in public houses as the local brewers tried to gain back some of the bottled market from the likes of Bass.

In 1911, there was an issue of 4% Preference Shares which raised £98,200. However, as a result of the 1911 Compensation Fund, the business also had to identify pubs for possible closure. In the September there was a loss on the sale of Flying Scud of some £179.

1912 saw the purchase of vehicles from Thorneycroft as the brewery switched away from horse-drawn delivery. There were also repairs to the brewery.

In 1913, the Compensation Fund was looking for the closure of the Swan with Two Necks and the Axe & Square, Countesthorpe, but they were still being supplied in 1925. The business was shown in 1913 as brewers at 103½ High Cross, where Watts & Son were also listed. The entry as maltsters was for No 103 and the offices were shown as 21 Silver Street.

As with many other businesses, profits during the First World War were quite healthy, although much was paid back e.g. 1914 War Loan of £3,000. In 1916 they issued £50,000 5% Preference shares, presumably in connection with the redemption of the debenture stock falling due. The Chairman was S Nevins Bankart, living at Marton Grange in Rutland, the other directors being:- F Watts, Francis Graham Langmore and H Fletcher.

That year, they bought the Queen's Head, Barnwell for £500. As well as investing in their estate, July saw them buy a new hop back and in September, Morris & Sons supplied new fermenting squares for £242. At this time, the brewing plant from the White Swan, Syston and the Coach & Horses, Kibworth was sold for £44, presumably for scrap. However, on Saturday 14th April 1917, FG Langmore proposed that owing to the 25% restricted output of beer at 1913 standard barrels, they should temporarily close the brewery, leaving two men to look after the maintenance. It had been agreed with Mr Turner the MD of LB&M that the latter business would supply them with beer. In May they took 330 barrels of beer and by the end of the year were taking some 5 to 600 barrels per month. However, they were still doing their own malting.

Total sales for the period were as follows:-

1912	£26,542	bottled	£9,285
1913	£26,799	bottled	£10,566
1914	£27,300	bottled	£16,104
1915	£22,096		
1916	£27,177		

The decision to buy in beer saw a profit in October 1918 of £3,598. This allowed a dividend of 6½%. In addition, director's fees were £800, £1,000 went to the reserves and £4,678 was carried forward. The following year they were averaging some 1,000 barrels a month from LB&M.

In 1919, they lost the Britannia Inn on Belgrave Gate, which was de-licensed. It had been owned by Langmore from November 1874. However, they paid £1,400 for the Chequers at Ashby Magna. On Mr Bethell's retirement, JW Whyte was appointed as Secretary and General Manager on a salary of £300 pa. That year the maltings at Wothorpe were let to Mr JG Dainton; although All Saints Brewery still seemed to be undertaking some malting until the following year.

January 1920 saw further expansion of the estate with £7,500 for the following:-

Neville Arms, Nailstone
Three Tuns, Barlestone, to be sold on for £1,250
Red Lion, Desford

From the Jack Feast collection

These were all previously LB&M properties which had been sold to WF Adams in the 1890s, as part of the LB&M policy of concentrating on the town business.

In September they sold to Everards, some 100 surplus barrels at £5 each, and 50 hogsheads at £6 each. However, they were still increasing the estate, with an off-licence at Station Street, South Wigston from LB&M for £1,600. It is still possible to make out the later markings of Ind Coope and Allsopps on this now de-licensed property in Wigston. They were also the leasing the Fox & Hounds at Skiffington.

Further property changes saw the White Swan at Syston de-licensed, and the leasing of the Half Moon and King's Arms, Nuneaton.

The 1921 Balance Sheet showed the following:-

Freehold property	£201,519
Goodwill	£33,832
Plant	£2,800
Motors	£1,750
Malt	£45
Hops	£2,891
Fox Plant	£530

In 1922, the King's Arms in the High Street, Swan with Two Necks at 58 Granby Street, and the Bowling Green on Oxford Street were all re-fitted as competition for trade grew.

They were still supplying the Albion, 22 All Saints Street, Stamford. The distance for supply, perhaps being off-set by the name of location. However, the Albion at 34 Albion Street, Leicester was de-licensed and sold at auction for £870. Another loss was the Pied Bull in High Cross Street, which was part of the origins of the business. It was compensated at £1,822.

In January 1923 they bought the Wheatsheaf and an associated baker's shop at Crick for £2,250. In the April, they bought the Plough at Sileby for £4,600. In the August, perhaps showing developing links in the trade, FG Langmore was writing to Ind Coope for advice on how they had recently handled tenant problems. The September saw a 564 increase in barrelage for the last two months compared with previous year.

In April 1924, the chilling plant in the bottling department was sold for £120 and they were also looking to sell the fermenting vessels.

From the Jack Feast collection

In 1925, the country trade consisted of some 57 pubs and 2 off-licences supplied with IPA, XXX, PA, and Guinness, Youngers and Bass in bottle. They lost the Earl Grey at Markfield and the General Sir John Moore at Sileby under the compensation scheme. Nevertheless, they continued to invest in their estate, with alterations at the Railway Tavern in Leicester, the Crown in Tur Langton, Star at Thrussington, Fox & Hounds at Syston, Greyhound at Great Glen, New Inn at Sharnford and the Queen Victoria in Leicester. They also bought the Bull's Head at Burbage for £7,250.

In March 1926, what remained of the brewing plant was sold for £300 to Smith & Sons, Coppersmiths of Leicester. They were letting part of the brewery, including the old tun room.

In 1927, the Bull Hotel at Rugby was bought for £5,500 and the Fox & Hounds Skeffington was taken on a 7 year lease. In September Mr Langmore's 30 years of service was marked. Langmore was still the MD on £1,250 pa.

In 1928 they were comparing the two months of May and June with the previous year's sales to show that they were up 49 barrels to 2,443 barrels and £353 to £16,754. That year they bought the Horse & Groom at Rearsby from Mr Moore for £5,000 and were still leasing the Albion at Stamford, which they later bought. However, the maltings at Wothorpe, previously leased out as such, were now let as a garage.

In March 1929 they arranged to withdraw the excise entries as beer dealers at 103 High Cross and as publicans at 32 High Street and 21 Silver Street. In April, the entire tied estate of 81 pubs was leased to Ind Coope for 21 years at £20,000 pa. Neale Dudley Thompson and Clement Thorley of Ind Coope replaced Samuel Nevins Bankart and Frederick Watts on the Board and the registered offices of the business were transferred to 12 Midland Chambers, Station Street, Burton on Trent.

[NB In 1895 an ND Thompson moved from being the assistant brewer at Blencowes of Brackley

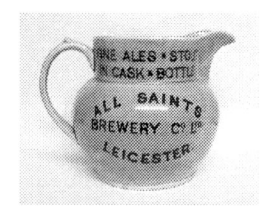

LEICESTER (continued)

to become the 2nd brewer at Kidd & Hotblack, Cannon Brewery, Brighton. In 1900 ND Thompson, 4 years at Kinnell & Hartley, Emsworth became the manager at Dover & Newsome, Thornton le Moor in Yorkshire and was to later play a crucial role in the development of Allied Breweries. One of the Ind Coope managers involved in the take-over, was a Louis E Walker. This may possibly be the same person who had previously been at the Aylesbury Brewery Company, before having a somewhat torrid time with Phipps of Northampton around the turn of the century (Brewed In Northants page 66).]

The Langmore family seem to have been the major investors, owning 5,535 of the 6,080 Preference Shares and holding £59,500 of the outstanding £98,200 debenture stock. Until 1931 FG Langmore was managing what had now become the Ind Coope depot, which operated until around 1934, when some of the Silver Street site seems to have been demolished. The brewery site, used as a bottling store, was then let. FG Langmore also became the local agent for the other Ind Coope/Allsopp subsidiaries such as Robinsons and the Lichfield Brewery Company.

Times were still difficult, and on 26th October 1931, Mr Langmore was writing to C Thorley at Ind Coope, stating that he had interviewed the manager of each managed house and that it was *"not possible to reduce the wages in many of the houses and run the same in an efficient manner"*. The managers were paid some £4 per week, whilst a barman earned from £1 to £3 and a barmaid £1 to £1 15s. Some cuts had already been made, but they managed to trim the wages bill by between 4s and 10s in four of the houses.

In the September, a letter reveals that the increase in duty was hitting sales, although sales of the 6d beer were holding up. It was noted from the manager of the Spread Eagle that the smoke room customers were grumbling at paying 5d per glass for XX and No 3 which had previously been 4½d. The White Swan manager also mentioned his smoke room customers and that those in the vaults were asking for the cheaper XX, together with a switch from bottled beer to the cheaper mild.

The workers who frequented the Railway Hotel found the 6d too dear. The Champion was £4 down, mainly from the smoke room, where there were similar complaints about 5d for No 3 and customers were trading down to the XX at 6d from the 7d. At the Hind, the XX was popular in the vault, where customers had a limited spending capacity.

In January 1932, because of the reduced takings, managers and barmen were to have their wages cut by 10½% and other staff by 5%. The old agreements were to be terminated and the staff were to sign new ones, whilst the bigger houses were to lose some staff. Langmore did his best, some reductions were made, but not as much as Ind Coope had hoped for. In May a letter from Thompson stated that *"results in many, if not most cases, are deplorable, and no doubt are primarily brought about by the general depression and consequent shortage of money"*. There was a need for further action to curtail the heavy losses, including a 10% discount off the tied list prices. They were looking at the possibility of transferring the managed houses to tenancies, but the problem was that good tenants were difficult to find. Langmore protested in response to the possible imposition of further economies.

Nevertheless, the business still operated reasonably independently. For example in 1933 they agreed to pay £20 per month to LB&M to finance extra capacity at the Charnwood Brewery, which shows that they were still obtaining beer locally rather than from Burton. In 1936 they were still expanding the estate with two off-licenses from Strettons for £1,350.

In May it was decided to standardise the prices throughout the managed houses as follows:-

Draught		**Bottled**		
XXX	3½d half-pint	Guinness	7½d half-pint	4½ or 5d per nip
No 3	7½d half-pint	NBA	4½d	8d per pint
No 1	8d per nip	No 3	7½d	4½d per nip
		PA		4½d per nip
		No 1		8d per nip
		Bass	7½d half-pint	

In June 1937 Francis Graham Langmore, described as the District Manager, was living at Wighton, Manor Road. He was also a director of Strettons Brewery in Derby. The Bankart family lived at Marton Grange Oakham. Alice Mary Watts was living at Oadby. Agnes Emily Watts, Frederick having died in 1930, was a widow living at Sheringham in Norfolk, at a house called Kibworth Lodge, perhaps evoking memories of Leicester.

In 1940, the King's Arms, 30/34 High Street and the brewery premises in Silver Street were

LEICESTER (continued)

valued at £35,000. The same year, the old boiler was sold for £30 and in 1942, building materials and scrap metal at the brewery brought £60. Finally, in October 1946, the property itself was sold. Nevertheless, the buildings remain remarkably intact.

In 1950 Elizabeth Gladys Bankart of Marton Grange, Oakham, died and the same year the business was wound up and completely liquidated in 1954. The Moon family were also still shareholders; however it is not thought that the Rev CG Moon had any connection with the Korean religious leader!

High Cross Street has some of the oldest brewing links of the town, since Nicholas Smith was a brewer there in 1664-72, with a shop near the Southgate. The All Saints Brewery is still intact, next to the church (SK585048). The High Street offices became a public house called Winstons.

Coleman, Samuel, *Cow Lane.*

In 1775 a Thomas Coleman was at the Turk's Head. Samuel was first mentioned in 1827 as a coal merchant at York Street, Welford Road. He was listed as a brewer from 1835 to around 1840. In addition, from 1815-1848 William Coleman kept the Crown & Anchor in Millstone Lane, later shown as having maltings at one side.

Collins, George, *White Bear, 28 Thornton Lane.*

Thomas Dexter was at the pub from around 1827 to 1835. Then in 1870 Mrs Mary Picken was the victualler.

In 1877 George Collins was a brewer and maltster at the pub, the owner being a Mrs Lacey of Highcross Street. Although Collins was in the directories until 1890 (F2708), in November 1879 William Ottewell was the licensee. He was the licensee until April 1881 when Jane Ottewell became the victualler.

In 1891 Jane Ottewell had financial problems, and in the June William Bentley took the licence and then in the October it became an LB&M house. It closed in 1907 for an off-licence in Hopefield Road.

Collins, John, *Lord Rancliffe, 31/33 Red Cross Street.*

In 1870, Collins was a fish salesman and victualler, who had held the licence of the Rancliffe from at least June 1868, although the pub was owned by William Neale of Southgate Street.

In 1877 Collins was listed as the brewer. However, in December 1882, Augustine Styles was the licensee. This was possibly the individual who was operating as a manager for the Harrisons (see entry). Then in February 1882 Thomas Nuttall, of the Beeby Brewery, held the licence and again from September 1885 to April 1887

In March 1890 Frederick Derbyshire took over the licence, followed by Hannah Derbyshire. Although, LB&M may have been leasing it around 1890, they gave up the lease in 1892, when the pub shown as No 33, with Frederick as the brewer. In June 1901 it was a Brunt Bucknall house, which had closed by 1913.

Collins, Richard, *Warden Arms, 61 Richard Street.*

In 1870 Samuel Moore was at the pub followed in 1875 by Thomas Cavell. In March 1877, Robert Collins took over the licence and in 1887 Richard Collins was listed as the brewer.

In February 1888 William Needham was the licensee and it then became an LB&M house by May 1891. The licence was transferred to the Rifle Butts and it closed in April 1937.

Collis, George, *Sir Thomas White, 34 Russell Square.*

In 1827 John Watts was the victualler at the pub and in 1835 it was run by Elizabeth Walton.

By 1870 Collis was at the pub, and was also running the Spinning Hill Tavern on Upper Kent Street. In October 1874 Thomas Clarke took the licence and on his death in April 1892, it passed to his wife Charlotte.

Needham and Crick were supplying malt, hence it became an LB&M leased property in 1890, when the brewing equipment was mentioned. They bought the pub for £2,625 in August 1892, presumably as a result of the death of Thomas, which may have signalled the end of brewing there. It closed for compensation in January 1956.

Collis, John, *Queen Victoria [the first], 128/130 Church Gate.*

In 1870 John Collis was the licensee at the Queen Victoria, followed in March 1872 by Oliver Grubb and then in September 1875 Thomas Mayne.

From January 1887 to 1892 John Frederick Lawrence Collis was listed as the brewer. Then in 1895 John Collis was the brewer.

In 1898 Frederick Albert Arnold was shown as brewing; however, Bells had taken the licence in July 1896. Hence, by 1900 it was supplied by Salts of Burton and closed under the compensation scheme in January 1941.

Collison, Thomas, *Old Red Lion, 47 Sanvey Gate.*

The Old Red Lion dated back to at least 1784 when it was kept by Daniel Walton. Around 1815 Robert Hertford was the victualler, followed by William Robinson in 1835.

In August 1873 Thomas Collison was at the pub and then listed as brewing 1877-1898. Photographs of the pub show his name as the licensed brewer around the turn of the century.

In February 1901 Arthur Heighton took over the licence and was shown as the brewer for the period 1902-10. The pub was closed for compensation on 24th June 1912.

Collison, Thomas Baxter, *Joiner's Arms, 73 Sanvey Gate.*

In 1815 Widow Carrett was running the Joiners, which was shown as being in Highcross Street, and in 1835 Fanny Carrett was at the pub.

Around 1873 Collison seems to have taken over the licence, but in 1875, Charles Clayton was at the beerhouse. Nevertheless, Collison seems to have been shown as the brewer in 1877.

In 1892 George Fisher was listed as brewing and then for the period 1895-98, William Shipley. In 1900 it was owned by the City Brewery of Lichfield, but in 1902 George Wright was still identified as the brewer. From 1906 to 1920 Thomas Collison was again identified as the brewer (F2712). It was later rebuilt and is now supplied by Banks.

Coltman, William, *Roebuck, 46 High Street.*

In 1809, 16 strike of malt was stolen from the store room of Mr Staples at the Roebuck Inn. In February 1811, the Roebuck was to let, with details from John D Jackson and in 1815 Charles Lewis was running the pub. By 1835 William Bull had taken the licence.

Then in 1842 William Coltman took over the Roebuck as a publican and wine and spirit merchant. From 1847, he was also a brewer and an ale and porter dealer and victualler. The following year he was listed as the brewer at the Roebuck Commercial Hotel. He also produced bottled soda water. In 1854, he was also shown as a maltster in Newark Street. From 1857 to 1863, the Roebuck was run by Daniel Brown, who was probably employed by Coltman.

In March 1874 J Meadows took over the licence, albeit only a six-day one. In 1875 the Harrod's directory carried an advertisement for the home-brewed ales and also mineral waters. He had been followed around 1881 by George Alfred Meadows.

In 1895 William Oakey was at the pub, but it was owned by Jas Sykes of Liverpool. The latter was presumably connected with the Thomas Sykes Brewery of Burton, which was used by Everards from 1898 for nearly a hundred years. The Roebuck closed in 1903.

Compton, Mrs Sarah Ellen, *Duke of Devonshire, 22 Bay Street.*

In 1870, the address was shown as No 10 and in January 1871 Mrs Compton was the licensee, although the pub was owned by George Harrison the local maltster (see entry). For the period 1877-84 she was listed as the brewer.

However, in August 1877 Charles Wilson took over the licence and in October 1881 it was held by John Flewitt (see entry). For the period 1887-1902, James Bee was shown as the brewer. On 22nd July 1896 the licence was taken by the Beeston Brewery Company and by 1928 it was a Shipstone's house.

Cook, Thomas, *The Bumper, 14 Carley Street.*

In 1835 Thomas Wilson was a brewer in Carley Street, whilst the Bumper shown in Belgrave Gate was run by Thomas Wheatley Burgess.

LEICESTER (continued)

The Bumper was for sale in 1864, with brewhouse. George Ludlam was the tenant, possibly then moving to the New Inn at Oadby (see entry). In 1870 John Wilson was running the beerhouse at No 14/16. Then in 1875 Mrs Mary Wilson took over the licence.

By 1892 Cook was at the pub, where he was shown as the brewer for the period 1895-1898. Tom Willson, who had been brewing at the Fox & Grape (see Cross entry), was then shown as brewing 1910-1914 at the Bumper (F2709). It then became an Everard's property.

Cooper, Robert, *Wool Combers Arms, 54/56 Lower Church Gate.*

In 1827 a Thomas Cooper was a retail brewer on Friars. By September 1867, Richard Cooper was the victualler at the pub, which was owned by Catherine Laxton of St Stephens Road.

In 1875 Robert Cooper had taken the pub. In 1877 he was shown as brewing and also malting in Stead's Yard on Millstone Lane. The maltings was at 29 Millstone Street near the junction with Marble Street (SK 585043). This presumably was the malting which was rebuilt by Welch Brothers in 1898 and has only been demolished in recent years.

In 1887 William Skipper was shown as the brewer until 1888, by when he had moved to the Red Lion (see Gee entry). In October 1885 William Leonard, or Lennard, had taken over the licence and was listed as the brewer until around 1895. However, in 1892 Joseph Cox was the brewer before he moved to the British Lion. In March 1895 Edward Henry Chamberlain was the licensee, although the pub was leased to T Fox on Church Gate.

In August 1897 Frederick S Wright took the pub where he was listed as the brewer in 1902. From March 1902 to 1906 Arthur Watts was brewing, although the pub was actually owned by Thomas Fox of the nearby Fish & Quart. All Saints Brewery seem to have considered buying it in February 1903 for £2,900 and they were leasing it by 1909. In 1922, they undertook major alterations, which suggests they had indeed bought it. In 1940 it was valued at £3,000.

Cooper, William, *Prince Albert, 1 Upper Conduit Street.*

William Cooper was the licensee by March 1869 and the year after was listed as the victualler. He was identified as the brewer from 1877 until January 1892, when Emily Cooper took over the licence. However in March it passed to John Kerry, suggesting that Mr Cooper may have died. In 1892 LB&M were looking to bid £4,000 for the pub. The following year the licence changed again with Walter Whiteman in the June, followed by Florence S Whiteman in the October.

However, in October 1895 it was supplied by Eadies of Burton and was trading as the Albert Hotel. In 1925 LB&M turned down its purchase at £12,000, when it was described as having sales of 7 barrels per week.

Cort, Robert, *Earl of Stamford Arms, 23 Northgate Street.*

The pub dated back to at least 1827, when Edward Bailey was the victualler at the Stamford. In November 1872 Charles Bodyatt was the licensee and in 1877 Robert Cort was shown as the brewer.

In 1892, it was trading as the Stamford Hotel, brewing having probably ceased. By November 1895, it was owned by Strettons. It was compensated and closed in June 1930.

Cotton, Mrs Sarah, *Earl of Leicester, 50 Brunswick Street.*

In April 1863 William Cotton was the licensee and victualler. Although he was listed as the brewer 1877-84, Mrs Cotton had taken the licence in June 1875. George Rice was the licensee in July 1878.

In 1887 Frederick Curtis was the brewer, having taken over the licence for the pub in July 1886. In 1898 it was supplied by Stretton's Derby Brewery when the address was shown as No 44. The licence was transferred to Beaumont Leys and the pub closed in 1954.

Coulson, Mrs Susan, *Stag's Head, 1 Augustine Friars, West Bridge Street.*

In October 1864 John Coulson was the victualler, whilst James Coulson was at the York Castle, 45 Northgate. In 1877 Susan Coulson was listed as brewing at the pub. It was still trading as a pub in 1892, but was *"pulled down"* around the turn of the century.

Cox, John Thomas, *Bower, 81 Coventry Street.*

The year 1862 seems to be when the Bower was first licensed. Around 1870-75 it was run by Matthew Needham and shown as No 31.

The first clear identification of the brewer was for 1892. when Mrs Ann Needham, as well as brewing, was also a milk dealer at the beerhouse. Then for the period 1895-96 Cox was listed as brewing. However, by 1902 it was supplied by Bass.

Cox, Thomas, *Fish & Quart, 65 Church Gate.*

In 1812, the sale by Thomas Cox of the Fish, included a malt office in Bull Lane/Church Gate. In 1866 John Stanyon (see Brown entry) of London Road, owned the pub, which was kept by Thomas Fox. The latter was later described as a beer wholesaler, who was the agent for Dulleys, Sharpes and Pettifors. He also owned the New Inn and the Travellers at Oadby, but seems to have sold up around 1899.

In 1900, the Fish & Quart and the Travellers Rest were bought by Marstons.

Cross, Charles, *Fox & Grape, 94 Belgrave Gate.*

In 1835 Jonathan Wilson was listed as a brewer in Belgrave Gate. The Fox in 1870 was run by George M King, followed in 1875 by WW Barnard. The first direct mention of the brewer was in 1895 for Charles Cross. Then, in the period 1898-1906, Tom Willson was the brewer, before moving to the Bumper in Carley Street.

Crow, John, *17 New Street.*

In 1846, John Crow was a maltster and victualler at the Nag's Head in Northgate Street, previously in 1827 having been the victualler at the Ten Bells, Sanvey Gate.. Then in 1855, he was a maltster in Northgate Street and New Street. In 1867 he was a maltster at 17 New Street and Sanvey Gate, but may also have been brewing at New Street.

Cufflin, Thomas, *Sanvey Gate Tavern, 72 Sanvey Gate.*

In October 1866 Cufflin or Cafflin was at the Tavern, whose owner was a William Moore. Prior to this Cufflin seems to have been a cowkeeper in Craven Street. He was listed as the brewer for 1870 to 1877.

Then in October 1878, the licensee was Charles Pilgrim, who was later brewing at the Fortune of War and several other pubs. In July 1880 Joseph Tate took over the pub and there were several changes of landlord until Matthew Gall took over in August 1881. He was there until it became an LB&M property in 1894. The pub was still trading in the 1970s as an Ansell's house, but is now a Burtonwood property.

The Sanvey Gate Tavern as it appears in the 1990s.

Photo: Author

Cummings, George, *Oddfellow's Arms, 25 Yeoman Street.*

Around 1870-75, the Oddfellows was shown as No 15, being run by G Cummings. George Cummings was then identified as the brewer for 1895-98. However, in 1896 LB&M were looking to bid £2,400 for the pub.

Dayman, Edward, *Crown & Thistle, 29 Northgate Street.*

The pub dated back to at least 1815, when it was being run by a John Clifton, who was followed around 1835 by William Overton.

In 1870 Matthew Hawksworth was the victualler, but in the October Edward Dayman took over the licence and in 1877 was shown as the brewer. In June 1882 it was taken by Charles Pilgrim, from the Sanvey Gate Tavern, before he moved to brewing at the Old Castle (see Stevenson entry).

In April 1883, the licence was held by M Needham and then John Draycott, who was listed as a brewer in the following year. In December 1886 Dayman returned again as he brewer, although the year after he was also shown as Dryman in at least one directory. There were then several other changes until May 1895, when it was shown as Leary & Sons to April 1915; although in 1911 Myatts of Wolverhampton seem to have been supplying the pub.

Deacon, Mrs Eliza, *Red Lion, 45 High Cross Street.*

In 1835 the Red Lion was kept by Robert Watts; however, Houlder and Deacon were listed as brewers in Archdeacon Street. John Deacon in 1846 was listed as the brewer and victualler at the Russell Tavern, Rutland Street. He also owned the Woodman's Arms, Rutland Street, where he seems to have been brewing in 1843.

In 1855 John Deacon was a beer retailer in Fleet Street and a cowkeeper at 47 Northampton Street, whilst William Deacon was a beer retailer in Bowling Green Street.

In 1870 John Cooper was the victualler at the Red Lion; however, around this time it seems to have been owned by Cock & Langmore. In August 1874 William Deacon was the licensee to June 1875, then it was taken by Mrs Eliza Deacon, who was in the 1877 directory as the brewer.

In 1891 Charles Gee was shown only as a publican at the Red Lion. It was owned by All Saints Brewery by 1905, shown as No 19, and then Ind Coope in 1925. The pub is still trading, but is now a Burtonwood house.

Denman, Thomas, *Lancastrian Castle, 27 Arthur Street.*

In 1870 Denman was the victualler and by 1876 was listed as the brewer at the pub, but then in December 1874, James Addison (or Addeson) took over the licence. This was possibly before moving to the Woodboy (see Garner entry) in 1877. By 1900 it was owned by Phipps of Northampton and hence in 1953 was an NBC property.

Dewick, George, *Salmon Inn, 15 Butt Close Lane.*

In 1870 Francis B Lewin was the victualler, followed by Francis Braithwaite. The owner was James Dewick and then Mary Dewick and in 1877 George Dewick was identified as the brewer.

In February 1882 John Collins took over the licence of the pub, before moving to the White Swan in January 1888. In turn, Thomas Foxon moved from the Swan to the Salmon! However, in October 1889, Thomas Henry Dexter took the pub and he seems to have stayed there until March 1898, when it was owned by the City Brewery of Lichfield, with the address as No 19. It featured in the CAMRA Good Beer Guide in 1998, when it was supplied by Banks.

Dexter, Edward, *King's Head/Kecks, 58 Archdeacon Lane.*

In 1835 Thomas Dexter was a maltster in Thornton Lane and by 1846 was a maltster and gardener in Narboro Road.

In 1870, Edward Dexter was at the Old Mitre, 1 Lower Redcross Street, but by 1875 he had taken over from John Mason at the King's Head. Edward was listed as the brewer in 1877, but in December of 1876 he seems to have become the brewer at 66 Burley Lane (Hitchcock). He then seems to have called that site the King's Head. Hence, it seems that at some point, this King's Head combined with the Keck's, which was next door at No 50 and adopted the latter's name.

In 1899 it was an LB&M property. In October 1939 it closed, when the licence was transferred to the Lancaster Arms on the corner of Lancaster Street.

Dicks, Thomas, *Craven Street.*

Described in the 1830 poll book as a retail brewer.

Dracott, William, *Brighton Arms, 53 Northampton Street.*

In 1846 Dracott (or Draycott) was the brewer and victualler at the Brighton Arms, which was thought to have been built some 5 years earlier. He had been listed as a brewer in 1843.

In 1855, William Weare was the licensee and victualler; however his 1875 advert placed stress on Joules Stone ales and Mander's Dublin stout. In August 1876 Samuel Weare was the licensee, but the pub was run by a Mr Parker, who was obtaining at least his wine and spirits from the All Saints Brewery.

In 1892 the Brighton Arms was kept by William Weare victualler, who was also an ale and porter merchant at 20 Gallowtreegate, as well as the manager at Chaplin & Hormer. Around this time Weare was advertising Brunt & Bucknall's celebrated Wooden Box Ales.

In September 1893 James Baskell was the victualler; however, on 12th January 1895 Ind Coope took over the pub. By 1920 it had been sold to Bass. It closed in June 1932, when the licence was transferred to the Diamond Jubilee on Belgrave Gate.

Duddle, Thomas, *Earl of Cardigan, 5 Foundry Street.*

In 1870 John Ball was the victualler; however, by October 1873 Thomas Duddle was the licensee, with the pub owned by a Mr Hancock. The Brewers' Journal for 1884, stated that on 18th December 1883, a Mr T Duddle had been taken to court for wrongly entering the amount of sugar used in a brew.

In January 1888 Henry Burgess took over the licence and in 1889, LB&M leased the pub from Ann S Hancock. In December 1917 it was bought for £3,000 by LB&M. It was closed for compensation in August 1941.

Duddle seems to have been at the George & Dragon in Freehold Street from 1890 to 1893 and it is possible that he was brewing at that pub as well.

Edgeley, Thomas, *Old Cheese, Belgrave Road.*

Friedrich lists T Edgeley as a brewer for the period 1871 to 1876. However, he seems to have retired by this time since directories list him as a gentleman at either No 301 or No 307. Nevertheless, he had been listed as the victualler at the Old Cheese in 1849.

Edwards, Mrs Susan, *Gardener's Arms, 225 Belgrave Gate.*

In 1870 John Hurley was the victualler at the Gardeners, but by 1875 William Brown had taken over, with the owner Mary Bishop March.

In 1875 it passed to William Edwards and then in the December Mrs Susan Edwards, who was shown as the brewer in 1877. From October 1878 to November 1887 James Wagg was the licensee and was listed as brewing in 1884 and 1887.

In September 1889 John Stevens took over the pub, followed in August 1890 by George Halford, who had previously been brewing at the Wool Combers. In 1892 LB&M bought the pub from Eliza Kilby. However it closed on 6th April 1905, for a new off-licence in Wilberforce Road.

Everard & Company Ltd, *Southgate Brewery, Southgate Street.*

The first potential links between brewing and the family may have been in 1800, when George Everard, previously a baker on Friar Lane, was bankrupt. The sale of his possessions included brewing vessels; however, these were probably for domestic use. In 1818 Thomas Everard was a farmer and maltster at Stoney Stanton. A Thomas Everard also owned the Elephant and Castle at Thurlaston from 1818. Thomas Hull was a maltster in Newarke Street from around 1832, and was listed as a brewer in 1843.

In terms of the background to the Southgate site, one needs to look at the involvement of the Bates family. In 1794, William Bates was listed as a victualler in High Cross. Then in 1843, John Bates was shown as a brewer on Friars Causeway, whilst William Bates was shown as a brewer and maltster on Southgate Street in 1846. Brewing on the site dated back to at least 1800. In 1801 Thomas Barry was renting a 20 quarter malt office on Southgate Street from Mr Bradley.

Although John Bates was still a brewer in 1847, William was listed as a gentleman in the poll

LEICESTER (continued)

book. In 1849 Hull and Everard's leased William Bates' brewery, suggesting he had left the brewing trade.

This was a partnership of the following:-

> Thomas Hull
> Thomas Everard, Thurlaston, William's father
> William Everard, Narborough

William Everard

They had also bought Messrs Wilmot & Company's brewing business, the latter retiring from the business. They leased the brewery site which Wilmots had used in Southgate Street (later Castle Street) from William Bates. This was presumably the Philip Mann Wilmot (mistakenly shown as Milmot in one directory) shown in 1848-49 as brewing on Southgate. Members of a Wilmot family were later to have connections with the Cavendish Bridge Brewery (see entry).

The lease was for a yearly rent of £100 in four equal quarterly instalments. The inventory included the following:- 2 coppers, 2 vats of 1,000 gallons each, as well as 136 doz quart stone bottles and 137 doz pint ones.

They started trading as Hull & Everard, ale and porter brewers, with their intention, or what might now be called their mission statement:- *"No effort shall be wanting in the production and supply of genuine ale of first rate quality."*

In 1855, Thomas & William Everard were listed on Southgate as brewers, hop merchants and maltsters. In 1863, William Everard was shown as a maltster and brewer at 45 Southgate, his home being at Narborough. His father Thomas had died in 1861.

In 1870 the Everard address was also shown as 1 Castle Street and as a hop merchant, with maltings on Calais Hill and Coventry Street. In the same year, William Everard was shown at the Rose & Crown, 31 Crab Street. It is not clear whether this was a different individual or simply the licence holder, since William Everard Esq was living at Narborough Wood.

In 1871 William Everard & Company were listed as the Southgate Brewery at 45 Southgate. Around this time they had a new brewery built, to the design of William's nephew John. The new brewery started brewing in 1875. The sales from the new plant were increasing, known outlets at the time included the Greyhound on Thames Street and the Elephant and Castle on York Street. In 1875, they were also shown as maltsters at 50 Humberstone Gate and Calais Hill. Their advertisement in Harrod's directory mentions:- Strong and Diamond Ales, Family Bitter Beer, Porter Stout and Imperial Double Stout.

By 1877, the business had become Everard, Son & Welldon at the Southgate Brewery, also maltsters. The other partner was Charles Leeds William Welldon, a local wine and spirit merchant. They were by now supplying around 100 pubs, although they owned very few. White's directory for that year gives their address as 38 Corn Exchange and the Southgate Brewery. In 1878, they appear to have supplied the Old Horse on London Road, which was threatened with closure.

The Old Horse, London Road.

Photo: Everard's booklet

In 1881 Everard's were advertising their Family Bitter Beer as well as the East India Pale, Mild, Strong and Diamond Ales. They also offered strong dark beers Porter, Stout and Imperial Double Stout. This product range represented the wide diversity of an industry at a time of major change away from traditional porters and vatted beer towards the pale ales most associated with Burton.

EVERARD, SON & WELLDON,
EAST INDIA PALE, MILD, STRONG AND DIAMOND
ALES, STOUT,
AND IMPERIAL DOUBLE STOUT.
FAMILY BITTER BEER.
SOUTHGATE BREWERY, LEICESTER.

From a commercial directory dated 1888.

In 1881 William Everard was still living at Narborough Wood House and in 1884 his son Thomas William was also living there. Interestingly, Frederick Bates was also living in the village. Although the Bates family had previously been at the Everard's site, it seems later members, including Frederick, had returned to the brewing industry (see Leicester Brewing & Malting entry).

The business traded as Everard Son & Welldon until around 1891. It had property at 45 Southgate Street, Castle Street and Great Holme Street - where Mrs Ann Johnson was listed as a brewer in 1881 - Church Gate, Bedford Street and Mansfield Street.

In 1892 William Everard died, at this time the business owned only 7 licensed houses. One of these was the Baker's Arms, 40 Friars Causeway, which although less than 20 years old, had to be demolished for the building of the Great Central Railway. Its licence was transferred to the Western Hotel.

William's son Thomas took over the business. The business was trading as Everard and Welldon, but in 1894 the name changed back to Everard, Son and Welldon, which was used when they bought the Admiral Nelson in October 1895. The business partners were Thomas William Everard & CL Weldon. They were operating maltings at 18 Calais Hill, Regent Street and Great Holme Street.

However, in 1890 they had realised that they were losing business to the increasingly popular Burton beers and so they leased the Bridge Brewery of Henry Boddington & Company. Located on an island in the middle of River Trent, this had been built in 1783 as a warehouse for the Burton Boat Company, and converted into a brewery in 1865 by Henry Eggington Whitehead.

Thomas William Everard

The Earl of Stamford, Groby, in 1929.

Photo: Courtesy of Everards

Everard's Old Bridge Brewery.

Photo: Everard's booklet

In 1869 it was operated by Henry Boddington junior, until he returned to Manchester, hence the consequent sale.

However, the plant proved too small, so Everard's leased the Trent Brewery, Anglesey Road, Burton on Trent, in February 1898 from the Trent Brewery Company, then in liquidation. The Trent Brewery in Union Street had been built in 1881 for Thomas Sykes of Liverpool. Initially, they operated both breweries until 30th June, when all operations were moved to Anglesey Road. Their output was thought to be around 20,000 barrels per year. In 1898 they were listed as Everard, Son & Welldon, Burton on Trent. They also had maltings in Wood Street.

In 1898 Charles Wood the Head Brewer died on 4th February, aged 25, from congestion of the lungs.

The Trent brewery from the air.

Photo: Everard's booklet

In November 1899, the partnership of Everard and Welldon was dissolved, when Thomas bought out Charles Welldon for £21,000.

The business then traded as W Everard & Company, but was still in a 1900 directory as Everard Son and Welldon, also Mansfield Street. In 1901 they were also using Nunneley's brewery in Burton.

The continuing popularity of Burton ales lead to the purchase of the Trent brewery in 1903 and the freehold was acquired from the Marquis of Anglesey in 1920.

In 1913 W Everard & Company were shown at 45 Southgate Street and the Trent Brewery. After the war the Crown and Dolphin was rebuilt and also renamed the Victory. The Prince Blucher on Waterloo Street was renamed the Admiral Beatty.

In 1920 they bought John Sarson's wine and spirit business and in 1922, they were also listed at Bow Bridge Street.

The Rose and Crown.

Photo: Courtesy Ian P Peaty

The Everard's Leicester Brewery from the air c.1950.

Photo: Courtesy Ian P Peaty

W Lindsay Everard

The Head Brewer was Arthur Willis (see Cavendish Bridge). In 1925 Thomas William, the son of William the founder, died and the following year the business of W Everard & Company was formed. W Lindsey Everard MP represented the continuing family involvement.

In 1931, the Leicester Brewery was closed and all production was moved to Burton. The closure was partly because of road improvements, but also because sales were down 20% as a result of the depression. A new bottling plant was installed on the Leicester site. Initially, a fleet of Sentinel steam wagons was used to transport the beer, although later these were replaced by motor lorries. The Trent brewery operated unchanged for many years. The local business was in the hands of WH and WS Hubbard and HW Lippitt.

Everard's Southgate Brewery in the 1920s.

Photo: Courtesy Ian P Peaty

At this time the major sales seem to have been the IPA and the XXXX. They also had a VB strong ale, which cost 6d per half-pint. The bottled range was:- Light Burton Ale, IPA, Barley Wine, Brown, Stout and Strong Stout.

The Braunstone Hotel on Narborough Road, opened in 1927, represented the company's investment in the new roadside pubs which were being created throughout the country. The Union Inn at Blaby was demolished and replaced by a new pub, the County Arms. Similarly the Saracen's Head on Hotel Street, which dated back to the year 1312, was rebuilt. In 1933, the Cradock Arms at Knighton was modernised inside and the following year, the Red Cow on Hinckley Road underwent the same process.

In October of 1936, the business became a public limited company trading as Everards Brewery Limited, with the address shown as Castle Street. The chairman at this time was Lindsay Everard, later knighted in 1939. In 1924 he had been made Deputy Lieutenant of the County. He was also the MP for Melton Mowbray for 21 years, as well as becoming President of the Royal Aero Club.

The County Arms.

Photo: Everard's booklet

PAWB Everard

A few months before the outbreak of the Second World War, Everards showed their vision, when they started manufacturing their own table waters, concentrated fruit squashes and cordials.

In September 1942, Offilers closed their Leicester depot because of wartime restrictions. Instead they provided 4 tons of beer per week to Everards who then provided local delivery for the duration of the war.

In 1947 Capt PAWB Everard joined the business, after war service with the Royal Horse Guards and training with Lacons of Great Yarmouth. He became the Chairman following the death of his father in 1949, a position which he held until 1978 when he became President. In the family tradition, he was also the founder of the Helicopter Club. Perhaps representing these interests, one of the new pubs opened after the war was the Airman's Rest built next to Braunston Aerodrome.

The Airman's Rest

Photo: Everard's booklet

A 1949 book celebrating one hundred years of trading gave an insight into the traditional methods of the brewery at Burton. The Morton & Company mash tuns were probably of some age and the Buxton & Thornley steam engine "Old Faithful", which was thought to date from the original brewery, provided steam heat for the coppers. It was operated by Mr Turton the foreman, who was not quite as old as the equipment, but did have 47 years service with the business. At this time Everards were still using round fermenting vessels.

Indicative of the post-war market, the 1949 book emphasised the importance and clarity of the bottled beers, which were naturally conditioned in glass lined tanks and then filtered before cold storage until they were ready to be bottled. The main bottled products were:- Light Burton, India Pale Ale, Stout, Nut Brown and a strong Barley Wine. They also manufactured soft drinks including ginger beer, lemonade and dandelion and burdock. In addition to being available in the pubs, the bottles were sold through a variety of small off-licences such as G Tomlinson & Son. The tied estate was of 150 houses requiring 100,000 miles per annum delivery from the transport fleet.

The Braunstone Hotel, Narborough Road.

Photo: Everard's booklet

The Head Brewer was AH Willis, a man of some 44 years brewing experience, 26 years of which had been at Everards. His assistant was a Mr HW Lake. Mr R Dolman, the head bottler, had been with the firm for 27 years. The Board also had similar experience, with the Managing Director, WH Hubbard, having been with the firm for 50 years. In addition to PAWB Everard, the other members of the Board were WS Hubbard, son of the MD, WB Frearson and WH Jarratt.

Continuity in the brewing industry could also be found in the retail side. For example, the landlady of Wheatsheaf at Thurcaston, had been running the pub for some 47 years and it had been run by her family for 40 years prior to that. However, the record was perhaps held by the Bricklayers at Thornton run by Mr & Mrs WAB Dilks. This pub had been in the same family hands for 450 years.

In the 1960s and 70s the company used a slogan *"Gentlemen, the Best"*, which perhaps was indicative of beer still being seen as a male drink. The estate was around 130 houses, of which 40 were in Leicester itself. The product range was:-

| Beacon Bitter | Burton Mild |
| Tiger Draught | Tiger Special Keg |

The bottled products were as follows:-

Amber Lite	Tiger Special Ale
Red Crown Bitter	Gold Medal Barley Wine
Nut Brown	Meadowsweet Stout
Bradgate Brown	

From 1970, the Burton site was known as the Tiger Brewery. The name originated from the famous Tiger Bitter, which in turn derived its name from the tiger cap badge of the Leicestershire regiment.

In 1973 Everards were introducing a dispense system in which the beer had a CO_2 covering, at low pressure, with motive power from compressed air. From the late 60s until 1976 all beer was processed at the brewery before delivery to the trade. This was fairly common throughout the industry and reflected the poor image which draught beer had acquired during the war and which had stayed with it during the fifties. This had lead to the continued growth of sales of bottled beer, with its clarity and consistency, and which also gave rise to the introduction of kegged and brewery-conditioned draught beers, including lager.

An £½m investment had been made, with beer tankered from Burton and chilling and filtering undertaken at Leicester. However, Everard's own Sabre lager was so successful that they needed the plant for it, forcing a return to traditional racking of some bitter and mild (about 15% of output).

The early seventies had seen a resurgence of interest in a wide variety of "natural" products and a number of individuals writing about beer and the brewing industry. It was at this time that the Campaign for Real Ale - CAMRA - was formed and attracted much attention.

In 1975 Old Original was introduced as a traditional cask bitter, perhaps reflecting the renewed interest in draught real ale as represented by CAMRA. The beer might be compared with the traditional Burton IPAs and the very successful local rival, Ruddles County. On 2nd June, Old Original was available at 25p per pint in 6 Leicester pubs, rising quickly to some 50 pubs and 60 barrels a week sent to the London market. The recipe was said to be based on that for the nineteenth century Diamond Ale.

The July 1976 Sunday Mirror first survey of beers, which was one of the first to provide early information on the strength of beer in terms of its original gravity, gave Old Original a score of 10 out of 12 as a *"very nice dry strong bitter"* selling at 29p per pint.

However, CAMRA's What's Brewing around this time described the business as *"an anonymous firm little known outside Leicestershire"*. The tied estate was some 160 pubs mainly within 30 miles of Leicester. Around this time, Everards considered the purchase of Shipstones, but instead the Nottingham brewery was bought by Greenalls. In 1977 Mild, Beacon and Tiger were on sale in cask-conditioned format.

In July 1978 Oliver Steel, a friend of PAWB Everard, who had been a non-executive director 1968 to 1975, became the Chairman. Prior to this Steel had been Chairman of Courage & Company, but had left as a result of the management changes there. He had joined Courage in

1946 after wartime service in the Fleet Air Arm. PAWB's nephew Richard Everard, after his Army service, was then brewing at Courage London.

The Sunday Mirror second national survey in September 1978 did not include a mention of Old Original. However, it did include details about Tiger, which rated a 10 out of 12 as a *"clean strong hoppy bitter"*. It also made mention that Tiger in London was selling for 40p per pint, which was much higher than similar beers. That year also saw the purchase of 24 pubs from Ruddles.

In September 1978, there was a CAMRA What's Brewing article on the business, perhaps trying to remedy the previous description. At this time, Duncan Bodger was the Head Brewer. Anthony Haig Morse, the Managing Director, was from one of the leading brewing families of Norwich. He had begun in the family firm of Steward & Patteson, where his father was vice-chairman. He remained there after the Watney's take-over in 1963 before moving to Northampton until 1971. When the Phipps NBC brewery closed for the construction of Carlsberg, he joined Everards.

In 1979 there was a major investment for the future, with the purchase of a new greenfield site of 134 acres to the south of Leicester near the motorway junction. This proved to be a bargain at £500,000 and initially was for the offices, which were to be moved out of Castle Street. Hence the site was named Castle Acres.

The July 1980 half year results showed profits of £629,300 on sales of £5.93m. Despite the previous disparaging comment, the CAMRA branch in Peterborough voted the Bull Hotel at Market Deeping as their Pub of the Year.

In July 1981 profits had risen slightly to £651,200. In the August Everards gained a contract to supply Tiger to Aylesbury Brewery Company, an Allied Breweries subsidiary, for a dozen or so pubs. That year, Tuborg replaced Sabre as the brewery's lager. In December 1981 Sarson's off-licence Queen's Road, Clarendon Park was advertising Everards on draught, showing the continued interest away from bottled beer.

In 1982 annual profits were up to £1.6m. On 16th March 1982 the 45th AGM passed a special resolution not to be registered as a public company. The Chairman R Steel, noted that barrelage was up 6.8% compared to a national decline of 5.5%. Output exceeded 100,000 barrels for the first time and they were developing the new site. This included a £6.5m move of packaging of keg and cask. The fall in profits from £1.6m to £1.32m was put down to the cost of the move and the general economic recession.

In June 1982 there was a £800,000 six week campaign on Central Television, in the run up to the World Cup. The campaign focused on Old Original and featured the television actor Bill Maynard. November 1982 saw the second TV advert. The advertising was backed up by a motorised barrel on a 1961 Morris J chassis from the British Leyland Transport Museum.

In September 1982 there were plans to open a small brewery on East Falkland - Penguin Ale. The brewery at Port Stanley opened in March of the following year, with the 1040° OG beer available in 11 gallon casks or 4½ gallon polypins. It employed Philip Middleton as the manager with 3 staff.

In August 1984 it was announced that the Burton Brewery was to close, with Old Original to be brewed at Castle Acres. The Tiger Brewery was closed and sold in 1985 for a museum. The attempt to preserve the Burton site as an active brewery museum initially included a 5 year contract to supply Everards with Tiger and Mild. Geoff Calderbank production brewer would remain at Burton to run the brewery on behalf of the Trust.

The new brewery at Narborough was opened by the then Chancellor of the Exchequer, Nigel Lawson. The plant was set up to brew Old Original and expected to produce 15,000 to 75,000 barrels per year. However, capacity could be raised to 150,000 barrels in a very modern brewery which had a mash vessel, described as multi-duty, since it was re-used after the lauter tun and sugar tank stage of the brewing process. Three days fermentation was then followed by three days cooling to racking temperature.

Whitbread's brewery at Samlesbury in Lancashire was to brew a Bitter at 1033° to replace Beacon at 1036°, Anthony Morse was quoted as saying "*I'd say 98% of drinkers are more than happy with it. Our market research showed that people wanted a lighter beer, one that was less filling. We have reduced the chloride content, roughly to that of other brewers, making the beer lighter and so more quaffable*". However, the beer was not liked by CAMRA, members regarded it as a poor replacement for Beacon and sales were lower than Beacon despite the strength being increased by 2°. Ind Coope at Burton trial brewed Tiger, but Everard's Head Brewer John Peacock was not prepared to risk their reputation on it.

In 1984, they were part of the group which formed Brewers' Dray to deliver within the area bounded by the M25. The other members being Adnams, Godsons and Ruddles.

In July 1985, they bought Rutland Vintners (now a wholly owned subsidiary of John Sarson & Son). In the October, they arranged a "beer-swap" with Camerons in which Old Original was supplied in return for Lion Bitter.

However, things were not going well in the Falklands and it was reported in December 1985 that there were difficulties with selling draught Penguin because it could not compete with the sale of canned beer through NAAFI. It closed in April 1986, because the manager had moved to England. On the plus side the month saw the launch in the UK of Old Bill, a 1068° winter warmer.

In November 1986, Everards owned some 142 houses. They were also taking Sam Smith's Old Brewery Bitter as part of their guest beer policy, which included Adnams as well as Camerons. The following year the estate had risen to 150 pubs, of which 95 provided real ale.

On 5th November 1987, Beacon bitter was brought back, after an increase in the capacity at Castle Acres, with two extra fermenting vessels costing £70,000.

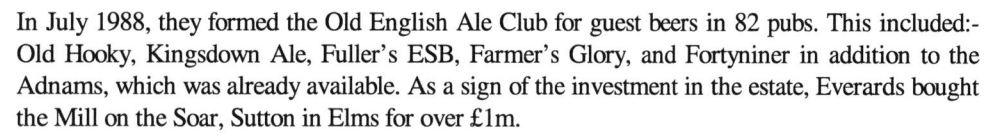

In July 1988, they formed the Old English Ale Club for guest beers in 82 pubs. This included:- Old Hooky, Kingsdown Ale, Fuller's ESB, Farmer's Glory, and Fortyniner in addition to the Adnams, which was already available. As a sign of the investment in the estate, Everards bought the Mill on the Soar, Sutton in Elms for over £1m.

In September 1988, there was some estate rationalisation, with a pub swap with Banks, the Wolverhampton Brewery. This involved the Racehorse in Warwick, plus £1m in exchange for 9 smaller pubs in Leicestershire and Derbyshire:-

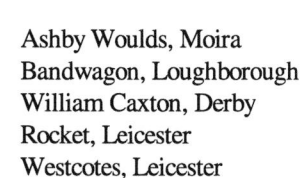

Ashby Woulds, Moira	Balloon, Lutterworth
Bandwagon, Loughborough	Shakespeare, Repton
William Caxton, Derby	Forester's Arms, Leicester
Rocket, Leicester	Sportsman, Leicester
Westcotes, Leicester	

This took them to a total of 131 pubs of which 111 were in the county. Nevertheless, they were looking to expand into the West Midlands, with £500,000 to be spent on the Racehorse. In October 1988, the strong winter brew Old Bill was on sale again, with a gravity of 1080°. Brewers' Dray became an Adnams' subsidiary, but was still used for delivery by Everards.

In February 1989 the estate of 135 pubs was to receive a £3m investment programme, with an emphasis on pubs as locals. This included the Original Inns concept for 20 pubs. Some 60% of the spending would be on the 44 managed pubs e.g. £200,000 on the Crown at Uppingham. They had already spent £336,000 on the Cradock Arms at Knighton. To cope with this, the brewery capacity was doubled, split evenly between cask and bright beer.

In March 1990, they bought the last batch of Tiger from Burton. The same year, the beer was a gold medallist at the Brewing Industry International Awards.

In 1992, the management team was as follows:-

- PAWB Everard, President
- RAS Everard, (Chairman) Directors
- JN Lloyd
- MA Newman, Managing Director
- Mrs SA Richards, non-exec Finance Director and Company Secretary
- AR West, non-exec
- CM Faircliffe
- AO Norman, Managing Director Training

The Cradock Arms, Knighton.

Photo: Everard's booklet

The Head Brewer was RJ Butler and part of his work included reformulating the Mild, with a higher gravity of 3.1% abv. The Old Original won a silver medal at BIIA. Their faith in cask-conditioned beer was backed by an investment in a new cask-washing machine, which was regarded as most useful given the dry-hopping of full casks.

August 1993 saw the formation of the Independent Family Brewers of Britain, of which Everards are a member. The following year they hosted a meeting of IFBB to discuss the problems from duty on beer and the rising tide of legal and smuggled imports.

In August 1994 Beacon was voted the winner of the bitter category at the Great British Beer Festival. The win resulted in an article in the November What's Brewing. This emphasised that family ownership was the key to survival, with Richard Everard and his sister Serena Richards on the Board. The article contrasted the traditional nature of a family brewer with its very modern brewery with its *"unusual brewhouse"*. Head Brewer Graham Giblett accepted that the design and space-saving layout was unique. The compact nature of the pair of dual purpose vessels was achieved through their usage both, before and after, the wort went through the lauter tun. This allowed two brews to be handled at the same time. However, they were using conical fermenters.

The throughput was doubled to 66,000 barrels pa, including Labatt Lager. A new beer, Daredevil at 7.1% abv, replaced Old Bill and was also available in bottle. This was seen as part of the drive to recruit new drinkers to the ale market.

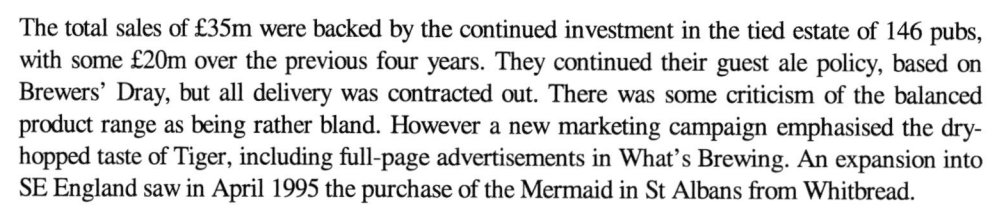

The total sales of £35m were backed by the continued investment in the tied estate of 146 pubs, with some £20m over the previous four years. They continued their guest ale policy, based on Brewers' Dray, but all delivery was contracted out. There was some criticism of the balanced product range as being rather bland. However a new marketing campaign emphasised the dry-hopped taste of Tiger, including full-page advertisements in What's Brewing. An expansion into SE England saw in April 1995 the purchase of the Mermaid in St Albans from Whitbread.

The September 1996 figures were:-

	£,000
Sales	39,564
Profits	4,952
Capital Employed	37,549
Net Worth	36,421

The Chairman was Richard Everard, with PAWB Everard as the President. The Head Brewer was GF Giblett. The £3m capital was made up of £1 ordinary shares, 90% owned by Richard Everard and his sister Serena. The output was 52,000 barrels. The business had 1,100 employees and 154 retail outlets, 39 managed houses and 115 tenancies. They were gradually expanding as well as supplying around 500 free trade outlets with national distribution. The products were:-

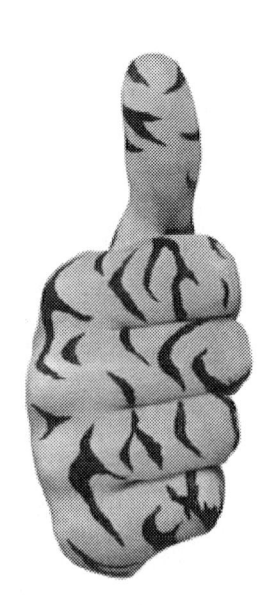

Beacon Bitter	3.8%
Tiger Best	4.2%
Old Original	5.2%

The latter was to be re-named Original, with new pump clips and advertising to back a new campaign. They also brewed Nutcracker Winter Ale 5% which had replaced Daredevil, and a variety of seasonal specials, as well as Chester's Best Mild for Whitbread. To celebrate the 150th anniversary they brewed Tiger Triple Gold 5%.

Findley, John, *7 Infirmary Square.*

In 1887 Findley or Finlay, was listed as a brewer. However, before and after this entry he was shown as a pawnbroker at 6 Taylor Street then No 9.

Findley, Mr, *The Antelope, 16 Silver Street.*

In 1809, when the Antelope "*now in full business*" was for sale it included a brewhouse and malt chamber. Interested parties could apply to Mr Findley on the premises. The latter had been there since at least 1791. The 1826 poll book lists Henry Findley as a brewer "*near All Saints Church*", but this may well have been in connection with what was to become the All Saints Brewery (see entry).

In 1874 the Antelope was run by Thomas Rowley and then in August 1879, John Smith. By February 1903 it had been bought by Everards who may have leased it from around 1888.

Flavell, John, *Belvoir Castle, 125 Northampton Street.*

From 1835 to 1846 Edward Glover kept the Belvoir Castle (see Glover entry). By 1870 Joseph Goode was the victualler.

In December 1872, John Gardiner was the licensee and in 1875, was listed as the brewer. In October 1875, Flavell took over the pub where he was shown as brewing for the period 1877-87, James Moore, a brewer's assistant, was living at No 126 in 1870.

In March 1887 Mary Flavell took over the licence, which she held until April 1889 when it passed to Henry Olorenshaw. He was listed as a brewer in 1892; however, the pub was pulled down on 18th January 1892.

Flavell, Joseph Kilbourn, *Britannia, 10/12 Castle Street.*

The Britannia dated back to at least 1815, when it was run by T Farrer. For the period 1827-1835, it was kept by Joseph Mitchell Gardener.

JK Flavell took over the licence by April 1866 and was in the 1877 listing as a brewer. The owner of the pub was a Joseph Williams. In March 1878 Ellen Flavell took over the licence, followed in November 1882 by Alf Priestley. He did not stay long, since in January 1883, Jasper Toon was the licensee.

In August 1887, Alfred Tilley took over the pub and was listed as the brewer in 1892, although in 1891 Joseph Toone had taken the licence. There were several other landlords until March 1906 when it was owned by Everards. In 1912, the licence was surrendered for an off-licence at 1 Paget Road.

Fletcher, James, *Holly Bush, 211 Belgrave Gate.*

By 1870 James Fletcher was at the pub, where he was shown as the brewer in 1877. For the period 1884-87 Henry Whitworth was shown as the brewer. In 1887, it was included in the list of properties of the NBC Debenture, and described as being on the corner of George Street. NBC were trying to sell it in 1956 and it was later demolished for construction of the Haymarket shopping centre.

Flewitt, John, *Brunswick Brewery, 24 Upper Brunswick Street.*

The public house and brewery are thought to have been built in 1859 by Thomas Crane, who had moved here from Kegworth (see entry). He had briefly run an off-licence in Carley Street, but was shown as a maltster in Brunswick Street in 1861. Crane died in 1866 and was succeeded by Samuel Flewitt and then Mrs Louisa Flewitt around 1869. Around this time, Christow Street was built parallel to Upper Brunswick Street; hence the change in address for the brewery, whilst the pub's remained the same.

Thus, in April 1870, John Flewitt was shown at the Upper Brunswick Brewery and was also shown as a maltster (F2713). Additionally, in 1871 a Mrs Louisa Flewitt was a maltster at

Huncote.

Until 1877, John was at the Brunswick Brewery, and described as such by All Saints Brewery who were supplying the wines and spirits. In 1877, he was also listed for Christow Street. Occasionally his name may be mistakenly shown as Fletcher.

In 1881, John Flewitt was shown as the brewer and victualler at the Brunswick Brewery; however, his address was also shown as 17 Christow Street. He was still also a maltster. He then seems to have moved to the Duke of Devonshire until the following year.

In January 1887 Johnson Gibbins was shown as the brewer at the Brunswick, but he seems to have held the licence for only a few months, since John Sharp took the pub in the April.

Around 1888, the brewery was shown as owned by George Harrison, when described as the Brunswick Brewery, Christow Street (see LB&M entry). However, Harrison had died around 1881. In 1891, Harrison's nephew, Henry Harrison Parry, was shown at the Brunswick Brewery, 17 Christow Street, and also at 99 Humberstone Road and Langham. He had been listed there from at least 1888, but had most likely taken over on the death of his uncle. He was still operating in 1892 as the Brunswick Brewery to 1895.

In August 1896, John Flewitt, who in the intervening years had been a milk dealer, returned. However, on 25th April 1898, the pub and brewery were sold to the Nottingham Brewery Company.

Brewing ceased, and a new business, The Brunswick Bottling Company, was established at the Christow Street premises, although the address was later shown as No 15a. Edward John Neale was the manager of the new concern which bottled various products from the Nottingham Brewery Company, until it closed in 1922.

The Brunswick pub was closed on 29th April 1914, with the owners receiving compensation of £1,379 and the tenant some £160. It was demolished soon afterwards and the Saint Matthew's housing was built on the site.

Flower, Charles, *Black Horse, 191 Belgrave Gate.*

In 1815 W Freer was at the Black Horse, followed in 1835 by William Taylor. In 1870 John Swift was the victualler.

In 1877 Charles Flower was shown as the brewer at the pub. He had previously been at the Pointsman beerhouse, 121 Northampton Street, before moving here by 1875.

In 1894 it was supplied by the Manchester Brewery Company, but by 1910 the Frank Myatt brewery of Wolverhampton was the owner. In 1931 the licence was transferred to the Telegraph on Belgrave Gate and it closed in the March.

Flude, William, *New Leicester Arms, 56 Upper Brunswick Street.*

In October 1867, Joseph Lawton was at the pub, which was owned by Mrs Little. In 1877 Flude was listed as the brewer, in joint ownership with Joseph Lawton. Before this, William Flude was a greengrocer and beerhouse keeper at the Freemason's Arms, 54 Braunstone Gate, and a John Flude was the victualler at the Britannia, 247 Belgrave Gate, although this was owned by Langmores. The family was also involved with running the Vine, 17 Devonshire Street and the Lion and Lamb (see White entry). They were also coal and corn merchants at the public wharf, Belgrave Gate from at least 1847.

In April 1882, Richard Crafts Harriman was the victualler, followed by a series of landlords. However, it had become an LB&M house by October 1891.

Forrester & Son, *High Cross Street South.*

Around 1791-4 Forrester & Son were brewers and brandy merchants, and in 1794 Alexander Forrester was a maltster in High Cross. In the 1800 poll book, Alexander was a brewer in High Cross, whilst William was the maltster.

From 1805 to 1815 William Forrester was a brewer in High Cross Street and his address in 1818 was shown as the Brewery. However, in the 1826 poll book, there was no mention of Alexander and William was described as a gentleman. The latter was no longer in the 1830 poll book.

A Robert Birkley married Ann Forrester in 1818, which suggests that he may have taken over the business of his father-in-law, Alexander. This site then later became used by the All Saints Brewery (see entry).

Fosbery, Henry, *Royal Standard, 21/23 Charles Street.*

In January 1869, Fosbery was the landlord at the pub and was shown as the brewer 1870-1877. In June 1882 George Stevens took the pub until November 1883 when it passed to Edward Dayman, who had possibly been brewing previously at the Crown & Thistle (see entry).

In August 1888 J Rylott was the licensee. In May 1892 Ind Coope supplied the pub, although in 1898 Harriss Rylott seems to have held the licence and by the turn of the century it was supplied by Brunt Bucknall. It was later owned by Bass. It is still trading, although it has been rebuilt.

Foster, Charles, *7 Silver Street.*

Listed in 1892 with Richard Foster as ale and porter agents and also shown as brewers. However, in 1895 William & Charles Foster were again only ale and porter agents.

Fox, Charles Oliver, *Black Boy, 33/35 Albion Street.*

In 1835 Daniel Winterton was the victualler at the Black Boy. In March 1870, Charles Oliver Fox took over the licence, with the address shown as No 35. Fox was identified as the brewer in 1877. On 14th August 1912 it was leased to Brunt Bucknall, who later bought it. Hence, with their take-over it went to Bass by 1926. At some point the Black Boy was completely rebuilt.

The pub was for a while a free house and the home of the local CAMRA branch, but has now reverted to beers from Bass.

Foxon, Thomas, *White Swan, 17 Market Place.*

The Swan dated back to at least 1560 and in 1794 William Wood was running the pub, which was shown at No 15. In 1796 James Fenton was the victualler.

In 1802 it was advertised that the Misses Wood had rebuilt it. There was no mention of brewing, but there was a wine & spirit warehouse. By 1804 Mr Rickards a bank hosier and liquor merchant was at the pub, but in 1806 it was still for sale. In 1815 William Richardson was shown as the occupant, and by 1835 Edward Sharples.

In December 1868 Thomas Foxon was at the pub, when a Thomas Liggins Foxon was at the Keck's Arms (see Rawlings entry). The Swan was owned by William Winter. Around this time, Thomas Foxon also owned the British Lion, Russell Square. He was listed as a brewer in 1877 at the Swan. In 1889 a Thomas Foxon also owned the Anchor, 43 Charles Street.

In June 1888, John Collins took the Swan, possibly having moved from the Lord Rancliffe (see entry). Then in February 1893, it was run by William Thomas Wright. By May 1895 Ind Coope were supplying the Swan and they bought it at auction on 23rd September 1924 for £23,600. Hence in 1931 it was an All Saints Brewery managed house.

Frearson, Samuel, *Griffin, 89 Belgrave Gate.*

In 1827 Samuel was listed as a retail brewer, presumably at the Griffin, which he was running in 1815. However, the actual brewing may have been undertaken by John Frearson, possibly his son, living on Humberstone Road.

In September 1868 James Smart held the licence, but there was no indication of brewing. In October 1891 Ind Coope were supplying the pub; although, John Hurley then owned the pub from 1895 to 1904. By 1912 it was owned by Hansons of the Kimberley Brewery.

Gamble, Henry, *Lord Durham, 41 Albion Street.*

The Lord Durham dated back to at least 1835, when John Haddon was shown as the landlord. In 1870 Richard Gray was the licensee, but it then passed to Henry Thomas Gamble. Gamble and Gilbert were operating as wine & spirit merchants at 25 High Street, and in 1875 were also hop merchants. Around 1870-75 Joseph Gamble was the agent for Nunneleys at 14 Silver Street.

In 1877 Henry Gamble was listed as the brewer at the Lord Durham. However, the Brewers' Journal for 1883 states that the Gamble & Gilbert wine & spirit merchants' partnership had been dissolved.

In February 1879 Job Clarke was the licensee at the Lord Durham until October 1883. He was later brewing at the Duke of Northumberland (see entry).

However, there were then eight landlords of the Lord Durham over the next ten years or so. Then by December 1899 it was supplied by the Nottingham Brewery Company. It closed under the compensation scheme on 31st December 1913.

Garner, Mrs Mary, *Woodboy, 8 Woodboy Street.*

In 1808 Mr Watts was retiring from the business, and there was a sale of coppers and vessels, including 100 gallon and 36 gallon coppers and 8x180 gallon barrels. In 1835 John Smittheman was the victualler.

By January 1855, Mary Garner was at the pub, where she was shown as the brewer in 1877. In December 1877 James Addison took the licence, possibly having moved from the Lancastrian Castle (see Denman entry), but he may have died in December 1882, when Elizabeth Addison took over the pub. She was the licence holder until October 1887, when Albert Holland took over. However, by June 1893, the pub was owned by Welch Brothers.

It closed under the compensation scheme in June 1935.

Gask, George, *Brewer's Arms, 128 Belgrave Gate.*

In 1870 Thomas Bailey was running the beerhouse. By 1884 George Gask was the brewer, before moving to 6 Harcourt Street in 1888, where he was shown only as a beer retailer.

In 1887 John Wren was listed as the brewer. Then in 1892 the brewer was John Dale, before he moved to the Turk's Head (see Andrews entry). The address was shown as 128-130. Then from 1895 to 1898, George Samuel Gask was listed as the brewer. The building seems to be intact, albeit now used as a shop selling telephones.

Geary, William, *Town Arms, 18 Pocklington's Walk.*

In 1870 John Sheffield was the brewer, at what then seems to have been called the Crown. He had been a victualler in Pocklington Walk from at least 1859. Although in January 1875 Mrs Ann Adelaide Sewell took over the licence, there was a suggestion that Sheffield was still the brewer in 1876. However, he was actually shown as an accountant and manager of the Town Arms Loan Office, 22 Pocklington Walk.

The pub was run by William Geary, from at least February 1876, and he was shown as the brewer in 1877. Prior to this, a William Geary had been at the Bow Bridge in 1874, when it was owned by Watts & Son. The Brewers' Journal for 1882 includes mention of W Geary at the Town Arms Hotel in debt. However, in 1896 a Nicholas Geary of 153 Cranbourne Street was described as a jobbing brewer.

In June 1882, Matilda M Perkins took over the licence, which she held until April 1889 when Annie Levers took over, but brewing seems to have ceased around this time. It was for sale at auction in 1898.

The pub is still trading, with beers from M&B.

Gee, Charles, *Red Lion, 110 Wellington Street.*

The Red Lion seems to have first been licensed in 1855. In 1870 Barnard Hyde was keeping the beerhouse. The first listing for the brewer was in 1887, for Charles Gee.

For the period 1888-95, William Skipper was listed as brewing. He seems to have moved from the Wool Combers (see Cooper entry). However, by 1897 it was owned by the City Brewery of Lichfield.

Gibbon, Richard, *Newarke Street.*

In 1846. Gibbon was a brewer and maltster in Newarke Street, his home was in Humberstone Road. Although he had become involved with the All Saints Brewery (see Cock & Longmore), he also seems to have continued with this separate site. Prior to this in 1794, a Mr Gibbon was a victualler in Market Place.

Gilling, Robert Charles, *Old Black Horse, 20 Abbey Gate.*

In 1870 Thomas Hassall was a cowkeeper and victualler, with the address shown as No 22. In 1877 Robert Charles Gilling was brewing at the pub, which he ran with William Christopher Gilling, who had been the licensee from around March 1872.

In June 1878 William Potter was the licensee until June 1888 when Henry Freer took over; however, there were no listings as brewers.

The pub was closed on 12th February 1895 and demolished, when shown at No 64, for the construction of the Great Central Railway. At the time it was owned by Welch Brothers, who built a new pub on Harrison Street as a replacement.

Glover, Henry, *Sailor's Return, 20 West Bridge Street.*

In 1815 John Hargraves was at the Sailors and by 1835 William Southey. Then in 1870, George Glover was the licensee, with the address initially shown as 20b and later 16/18. The pub was owned by the Hospital Trustees.

Prior to this, a George Glover was the licensee of the Angel in 1866. Also in 1835 and 1846, Edward Glover kept the Belvoir Castle (see Flavell entry) and in 1817 W Glover had been at the Green Dragon, Market Place.

Henry Glover was listed as the brewer in 1877, when the pub was described as being on the corner of Duns Lane. In January 1892 Katherine Ann Glover took over the licence, but by the July it had passed to William Harrison.

It has been suggested that the Sailors and the nearby Reindeer were demolished in the 1890s as part of the railway building. However, the pub was sold in 1897, when it may have been owned by the Illstons (see entry) and it was still trading in 1907, when owned by Everards; although the address was shown as No 16.

Goodman, William, *West End Inn, 42 Duns Lane.*

In 1870 William White was the victualler at the West End.

In 1871 Goodman & Company were brewers in High Cross Street, but with no indication of their location. In June 1873, Eli Shuttlewood was at the pub, with the address initially shown as Braunstone Gate.

By August 1875 William Goodman was at the West End and was listed as brewing in 1877. However, in December 1881, the licence passed to Emma Ball and after she left the following April, there was a series of landlords, until the Carrs took the pub in November 1885. In 1891 it was still in business, but around this time James Carr may have died and the pub became leased by LB&M. They bought it the following year for £1,250.

It was later closed and demolished. It then seems to have been rebuilt and was trading in the 1970s as an Ansell's pub.

Goodrich, Henry, *Wharf Street.*

Listed in the 1830 poll book as a brewer, whilst Thomas Cooper Goodrich was a wine merchant in Newark Street.

Goodwin & Hobson, *Pied Bull, 105 High Cross Street.*

See All Saints Brewery entry. The pub dated back to at least 1799, when John Millwood was running it. From 1815 to 1835, it was kept by John Westley Gillispie. Then from 1848 to 1855, Goodwin & Hobson were listed as brewers. In the 1847 poll book, John Willis Goodwin was a brewer, living in Princes Street and in 1857 in High Cross Street.

In October 1866, the licence was held by Edward Smalley, with the owners of the pub being Cock & Langmore. In May 1883 Thomas Carver was at the pub, but it is not clear if he had any links with the Thomas Carver of LB&M.

The Pied Bull was shown as an All Saints Brewery property in 1898. It was compensated for £1,822 and closed in April 1924.

Goodyer, Thomas, *26 Nelson Street, London Road.*

In 1843-46, Thomas Goodyer was a brewer in Nelson Street and then in 1848 Henry Goodger (presumably a mis-print) was described as a retail brewer in Nelson Street.

Thomas Odams was then shown as the brewer in Nelson Street in 1855 and in 1863 shown as No 26.

Granger, William, *Braunstone Gate Brewery, 64/66 Braunstone Gate.*

This seems to have previously been the Freemason's Arms which was sold at auction for £1,275 in 1889. It was listed in 1892 as the Braunstone at No 54. It was described as a brewery in 1900 when being run by Granger. However, he was also a mop manufacturer, which may explain why this seems to have been a somewhat short-lived concern. In March 1900, Granger sold the pub for £6,050 to LB&M, who planned to rebuild it two years later. In fact it was not until 1925 before the work was done.

Greasley, Mr, *Bull's Head, 25 Market Place.*

For sale with brewing vessels in November 1812, with the retirement of Mr Greasley. By March 1865, Matthew A Cooke was the licensee until April 1891, but there was no listing for brewing. In 1898 it was owned by Worthingtons, and was still trading in 1900.

Green, Thomas, *Green Man Inn, 78 Wharf Street.*

In October 1874 Thomas Green was the licensee of the pub, which may well have been named after him. In 1875 a directory advertisement mentioned the home brewed ales. Green seems to have moved here from the Theatre Royal and Rifle Volunteer Hotel, which was also on Wharf Street.

However, in June 1879 William Barnard held the licence, and then it returned to Green in July 1883, before he passed it on to the Jones family. There were then several landlords, including some members of the Toone family (see entries).

By April 1895, it was a Welch Brothers' house and then LB&M in 1914. It was compensated for closure in July 1933.

Greenwood, Edwin, *Jolly Angler, 122a Wharf Street.*

The Jolly Angler dated back to at least 1835, when it was kept by William Bailey. In 1870 John Greenwood was at the pub and Edwin was a greengrocer at no 124. In March of the following year Edwin was at the pub and listed as a brewer in 1877.

In December 1882 it was transferred to Mary A Greenwood, who kept it until November 1887, when it passed to Thomas Henry May. However, by December 1888, it was supplied by the Manchester Brewery Company. It then went to Myatts of Wolverhampton and through them to Ansells. It was demolished in the 1970s.

In 1889, a Francis Greenwood was a beer agent at the Clowe's Arms, possibly in connection with a Lutterworth brewery. John Greenwood died around 1903, when he was living at 190 Belgrave Road and was the owner of the Craven Arms.

Gregory, William, *Russell Tavern, 6 Rutland Street.*

In 1846, John Deacon was the brewer and victualler at the Russell Tavern, and was also shown there in 1835. However, in 1855 T Allen was only shown as a victualler at the pub.

In July 1868 Gregory took over the pub, where he was listed as the brewer for 1870-77. In December 1880 the licence went to Claude Hampton, who was in the directories as the brewer 1884-87.

In June 1889 George Duxbury was running what had become the Queen Hotel and brewing had probably ceased. By 1895 it was an Ind Coope house.

Griffin, Edward, *Woodman's Stroke, 19 then 23 Wellington Street.*

In 1870 Val Harris was a tripe dresser and victualler, but also a cooper at the Woodman's; hence the name, though the address was shown as 15½ Chatham Street. In March 1872 the licence was taken by Edward or Edwin Griffin and he was listed as the brewer in the period 1875-77. He then seems to have moved to the Malt Shovel, where he was also listed as brewing (see Brown entry).

In October 1877 John Gilbert took over the licence, but there was no mention of him as a brewer. In August 1888 it passed to Hannah George and had become the De Montfort Hotel. In January 1898 it was owned by Warwicks & Richardsons of Newark.

Grimes, James, *Crown & Dolphin, 1 Holybones.*

In 1835, the Crown & Dolphin in Holy Bone was kept by Ann Wilkinson. In 1870 John Moore was shown as the victualler.

By July 1874, Grimes was at the pub, which was owned by John Brown of Rutland Street. Grimes was listed as brewing from 1877 to 1882, when the licence was taken by Elizabeth Reddel in the October. James Grimes, previously a victualler, was in liquidation in 1880.

In April 1890 Everards seem to have taken over the licence. It was rebuilt after the First World War and became the Hotel Victory, which was demolished in 1967.

In 1908, one of the travellers for CBB was a Mr Grimes.

Groocock, Samuel, *Belvoir Street.*

Samuel was listed as a brewer in 1835 in Belvoir Street, whilst George Groocock was a cooper at Great Claybrooke. The only other mention of the family was in 1848, when Joseph Groocock was the victualler at the Crown & Dolphin.

Gurden, Cornelius, *Highcross Brewery, 86 High Cross Street.*

In 1846 William Gurden was an auctioneer, porter and India Pale Ale dealer in Rutland Street, with his home in New Bridge Street and may have brewed in Newarke Street in 1842. James Watson seems to have been the brewer at the Highcross site from 1849 to 1863, but was not shown in 1865. In addition, a John Watson kept the Old Robin Hood on Abbey Gate.

By 1863 Gurden Cornelius had moved to the brewery. In 1867, his prices were as follows:-

	per gallon		
IPA	1s 8d	Best Bitter	1s 6d
XXXX A	1s 10d	XXXX B	1s 6d
XXX	1s 4d	XX	1s 1d
X	1s 1d	Stout	1s 4d
Table Ale	9d		

In 1876 he was listed as a brewer and maltster and had been a maltster at Thames Street wharf from around 1870. That year he was again advertising in the Kelly's directory.

In 1877 Cornelius was described as a large brewer, also with malt offices at Vauxhall Street. In 1880, he was advertising as the Highcross brewery supplying:- Fine Family Ale, Mild & Strong, Table, Porter and Stout.

From 1881 Gurden was listed at 86 High Cross (F2714). His 1892 advertisement stated that *"The Ale is noted for being Fine and Sound. The Porter and Stout can be had Ripe all the year round at 86 High Street".*

However, in 1894 Gurden was shown only as a maltster at No 86 and at Vauxhall Street. From around 1890, Henry Heys was brewing at what then became the High Cross Brewery Company. He seems to have stopped brewing around 1904.

In the 1950s the building was the Rail & Road Transport Workers Club, which was supplied by Offilers. The building was later demolished.

Gutteridge, Henry, *Wharf Street.*

Gutteridge was listed as a retail brewer in 1827, but in 1830 was described simply as a brewer in the poll book.

Hack, Richard Thomas, *Old King's Arms, 100 Sanvey Gate.*

In 1794 James Abel was the victualler at the pub, but by 1815 it had passed to Catherine Abel. In 1835 Henry Simpson ran the pub.

By March 1864 Richard Thomas Hack was at the pub, where he was listed as brewing in 1877. The pub was owned by a James Lines.

Although in 1882 LB&M leased the pub and in the June, Henry Walker was the licensee, from July 1884 Mrs Eliza Walker was listed as the brewer until 1898. In 1904 it was owned by LB&M, who gave up the licence in 1909 when it closed for compensation.

Haddon, Samuel, *Talbot, 57/59 Denman Street.*

In 1835 Samuel Haddon was listed as a brewer in Denman Street and in 1846 was described as a brewer and victualler. In 1855 he was still at the pub, but there was no mention of brewing.

In December 1863, Thomas Cole took over the licence. He remained as the owner, although from June 1875 to August 1881, Richard Vann was actually running the pub and looking after the brewing, before he moved to the Prince of Wales (see entry).

The licence was then taken by John Carr, followed in January 1894 by Alfred Carr, who was listed as the brewer for the period 1895-98. On 21st July 1897, John Carr sold it for £5,600 to LB&M.

Handford, Mrs Catherine Kidney, *Sun Inn, 96 Church Gate.*

In 1815 Joseph Pegg was at the Sun, which dated back to at least 1763 when it was kept by Edward Worrall. In 1835 it was kept by John Stringer.

In May 1866 Thomas Handford was the licensee at the pub, which was owned by the Trustees of Trinity Hospital. Then in May 1876 Mrs Handford took over and was listed as the brewer from the following year until 1884.

In May 1885, James Samuel Allsop took the licence and was shown as the brewer at the Sun from 1887 to 1895; however, William Leonard was also listed as brewing here around this time. In the January 1895, Edwin Heath Wortley took over the licence, but there was no further listing for brewing. By 1901 it was an Everard's house, which later closed in April 1927.

Hannam, Mary, *15 Northampton Street.*

In 1815, John Hannam was the victualler at the Black Horse, London Road. By 1827 he was shown as a wholesale brewer in Northampton Street. In 1835 Mary and William Hannam were listed as brewers and John Hannam was listed as a maltster, all in Northampton Street.

In the 1840s Mrs Mary Hannam was a brewer and maltster in Northampton Street, whilst John Hannam was a maltster at No 15. James Hannam was a baker and victualler at the Woolstapler's Arms, Charles Street, and Thomas Hannam was a corn & flour merchant in Bridge Street West.

In 1855, Mrs Hannam was a brewer at 15 Northampton Street and also a maltster. However, in 1863, Mrs Mary Hannam was living at 100 London Road, with no mention of brewing. In 1873 Mrs Hannam was the owner of the Rainbow and Dove at No 13 and the brewery presumably grew out of supplying the pub.

In 1864, TC Carver advertised that he had taken the Northampton Street Brewery (see LB&M entry).

Harriman, John, *Bowling Green, 21 St Peter's Lane.*

The Bowling Green was built around 1733. In 1812 it was kept by a William Hester and in 1815, Joseph Spencer. In 1800, a John Spencer was an innkeeper at Welford, together with William Spencer a maltster. By 1820 John Knight was at the Inn and also a wholesale and retail wine & spirit merchant.

In 1835 it was kept by Ralph Kirk, previously involved in wine & spirits and also a hop and porter agent in Cank Street, and also with Henry Soar in Silver Street.

In 1870 Thomas Cooper was at the pub until July 1874, when John Harriman took over the licence. He was listed as the brewer in 1877, with the pub owned by Richard Wright. In October 1888 the licence passed to John Taylor, but there was no listing for him as a brewer.

By 1897 it was owned by the Nottingham Brewery Company. It was compensated and closed in December 1939.

Harrison, George, *Haymarket.*

The papers in the Leicester Record Office for Harrisons, the local seed merchants, include documents relating to the Lion and Dolphin, which had its own brewhouse (see Moore entry). These provide the first links between the family, which was primarily concerned with the malting side of the business and the brewing/retailing aspects. They also suggest links with the Bates family (see All Saints Brewery entry).

In 1813, a John Harrison of Stocking Farm had a new 30 quarter malt office next to the North Bridge for sale or to be let and in 1826 William Harrison was a maltster in Belgrave Gate. In 1835, Isaac Harrison was a maltster at 2 Haymarket and a gardener in Bedford Street, where he also malted in 1848 (Harrisons Nursery off Barkby Lane on Fowler's map of 1828). Previously, a William Harrison kept the Blue Boar on Southgate.

In 1859-63, his son George Harrison was listed as a maltster at 2 Haymarket, which in 1870 was shown as his home. He seems also to have been farming at Belgrave. In 1870 he also owned the following:-

- 9 Wanlip Street maltings, later used by Henry Harrison Parry then sold to Everards and then Showells
- 82a Syston Street maltings, the site later used for the Clubs Brewery
- Gresham Street (sometimes shown as Graham Street) off Belgrave Road used by

LB&M. There also seem to have been premises at 59 Corn Exchange.

He supplied malt to many of the local small home-brew pubs, including the following:-

    Cricket Players, 9 Church Gate   1874
    Dixie Arms, 1 St Peter's Lane   1868

But then by 1876, he seems to have bought the Langham Brewery (see entry). Initially, Tom Rudkin was his manager at Langham, but at some point it seems to have been operated by Boys & Styles, who may also have been his managers. In 1877, he had offices at Church Gate, with his home address still shown as 2 Haymarket. By 1881, the year of his death, he may actually have sold Langham to Boys & Styles, who were also shown as brewers there and at 16 Southgate that year. The latter was a site used by Thomas Nuttall in 1884 (see Beeby entry).

The Blue Boar on Southgate Street. It is rumoured that Richard III slept here before the Battle of Bosworth Field.

Photo: Everard's booklet

In 1884 George Harrison's malting business was taken over by Needham & Crick. They were shown with offices at Tower Buildings on Church Gate and maltings at Syston Street and 153 Gresham Street.

However, the Harrison family seems to have retained the Brunswick Brewery, Christow Street (see Flewitt entry) as well as 99 Humberstone Road and 19 Cank Street (see Moore entry). In 1891, Harrison's nephew, Henry Harrison Parry, was shown at the Brunswick Brewery, 17 Christow Street, and also at 99 Humberstone Road and Langham. In 1873, a George Parry was the licensee of the Curzon Arms, which like much of the Harrison estate became a Beeston Brewery property. They had established a depot, at what had previously been the Shakespeare Brewery, operated by the Harrisons or at least their managers (see Cant entry).

In 1892, LB&M were considering a bid, when the Brunswick Brewery was shown at 24 Upper Brunswick, but as 17 Christow Street in 1894. Parry was also running a maltings in Wanlip Street. In September 1896, he seems to have put the following up for sale:-

    Dog & Hedgehog, Dadlington   Wheatsheaf, Melton Mowbray
    Dolphin, High Cross Street   St Leger, Leicester

The following year, he was in discussions with LB&M regarding pubs at Croxton. In 1900 Parry was the owner of shares in LB&M, buying 200 preference at £13. He seems to have died early in 1909. His descendants seem to have taken the name Parry Wingfield, in honour of an uncle Maurice Edward Wingfield of Tickencote Hall, and the family was living at Hereford.

Hayler, Charles, *Dolphin, Burley's Lane/2 Lichfield Street.*

From around 1870 Mrs E Hollingworth was running the pub until April 1874, when it passed to William Kington, who was shown as the brewer in 1875.

In May 1876, the licence went to Hayler, who was listed in 1877 as the brewer. In July 1886 John Glover was the licensee, but around this time it was owned by Nuttall's Beeby Brewery. However, after the take-over of Nuttall's brewery, the pub had become run by Thompsons of Burton and hence in 1901 it was a Marston's house. The licence was transferred to the Speedway Hotel and the Dolphin closed in February 1937.

85

Healey, Thomas, *Wharf Street.*

Listed as a retail brewer in 1827, but with no other listings or details.

Herbert, Thomas, *George & Dragon, 11 Kent Street/Newbridge Street.*

In 1870 Charles Sawbridge was a joiner and victualler at No 11/13. Then in August 1874 Thomas Herbert took over the licence and was listed as the brewer in 1877, although the actual owner was a Mrs Coleman. In October 1877, Millicent Herbert was the licensee.

In August 1881 Henry Bodycote took over the pub until December 1886, when it passed to Richard Clarke, then there was a series of annual tenancies. However, in May 1894, Andrew Birtles took over the pub and was listed as the brewer in 1898. Then in January 1900, it went to his widow Jane. In November 1910, an Andrew Birtles was at the pub, presumably this was their son, and around this time it became an LB&M house.

Hicklin, William, *58 Noble Street.*

Hicklin was listed as a practical brewer in the 1890s, but with no indication of where he was brewing. Possibly, like the Norths at Loughborough, he worked at various small pub breweries.

Hitchcock, Henry, *King's Head Inn, 66 Burley Lane.*

The first mention seems to be in December 1876, when Edward Dexter moved here from the King's Head on Archdeacon Lane, presumably bringing the pub name with him. He was listed as the brewer in 1884.

In July 1886, William Kirby took over as the brewer until 1892. Then in July 1892, Hitchcock took over the pub and was listed for 1895. In May 1897 it was supplied by Everards. It was compensated and closed in June 1935.

Hitchcock, Robert Wells, *Red Cow, Hinckley Road, Forest East.*

Hitchcock was at the pub in 1870 and listed as a brewer in 1877, although he was only shown as a victualler in 1881. The pub is still trading as an Everard's house, described as one of Leicester's most historic inns, dating back to at least 1660.

The Red Cow, Hinckley Road.

Photo: Everard's booklet

Holland, Thomas, *Sand/Sandacre Street.*

In the 1826 poll book, Holland's occupation was shown as brewer. However, in 1830 he was described as a gentleman and living on London Road, yet two years later was shown as a brewer in Sandacre Street. He was still there in 1835. In addition, Charles Holland was a brewer in Church Gate.

Holt, John, *White Hart, 105 then 93 Wharf Street.*

Thomas Shipman was at the pub by 1870, and shown as the brewer for the period 1877-87. It was owned by Robert Briggs.

In March 1888, John Alfred Holt took over the pub and was in the directories as a brewer around 1894-5. Harry Burley seems to have taken the licence in April 1895, but was possibly being

LEICESTER (continued)

supplied by LB&M. It was an Everard's house in 1901 and closed under the compensation scheme in July 1933.

Tom Hoskins Brewery plc, *Beaumanor Brewery, 133 Beaumanor Road.*

Some time before 1877, Jabez Penn, a former blacksmith (born 1843 Warwickshire), set up a general store supplying, amongst other items, beer for the workforce involved in building the Great Central Railway. His shop was on what was then called Beaumont Road and it seems that he started brewing in the cottage; hence the initial name was the Hope Cottage Brewery. In 1877, he constructed a brewhouse measuring 32 feet long, 12 feet wide, 18 feet high and containing a copper and a coalhouse.

In 1895 he built a traditional tower brewery, now the oldest Victorian tower brewery in the county. In 1896, the name of the road was changed to Beaumanor Road. Over the next 15 years the brewery was extended 3 times, doubling the capacity.

Jabez's daughter Elizabeth was thought to have been carrying out the brewing. In 1901, Thomas Hoskins, from Worcestershire, married Elizabeth, joined the business and in 1904 became a partner. The business was trading as J Penn & Co, but Tom took full control in 1906 and in 1909 the name was changed to Tom Hoskins Brewery.

In 1913, new fermenting vessels were installed, further increasing the capacity. However, quality was not forgotten in the drive for quantity. There were medals at the Brewers' Exhibition in 1922, 1926, 1932 and 1936.

Tom Hoskins was listed as the brewer in 1925 and in 1932 it became identified as the Beaumanor Brewery. In 1930 Tom also installed a bottling plant.

The brewery continued to be well-regarded. In 1938, they received the Diploma of Excellence and Gold Plate for the IPA and strong ale at the Brewers' Exhibition.

In June 1947, the business was registered as a Private Limited Company, with one pub and one off-licence. In 1952 Tom died and his son George took over the brewing. However, the Fifties was not a healthy time for small breweries and in the latter part of the decade, Hoskins considered a merger with Ruddles. However, they struggled on and were probably too small to attract interest during the merger and take-over boom of the 1960s.

Excellence was rewarded again in 1968 when the IPA was graded first in its class and the strong ale won second in its.

In 1973, they were still advertising *"have a drink at home"*, with draught beer available from the off-licence at the brewery. Even the one tied pub, the Red Lion did not carry the brewery name. They supplied the free trade in Leicester and delivered to private houses. The off-licence in Twycross Street, Highfields, did not however supply draught. Their slogan was matched by the product range, in that they brewed only a draught bitter and a mild. However, the bottled range was much wider:-

Home Brewed - pale ale	Strong - dark ale
IPA Bitter - the draught bitter bottled	Best Mild - mild in bottle
Nut Brown - stronger version of mild	

The bitter and mild were also available in 7 pint cans (readers of a certain age may remember the "Party Seven") and 9 gallon kegs were also available. They may have been ahead of their time if one considers how many of the current generation of craft brewers see their future in sales of bottled beer.

In 1974, they were brewing only some 10 barrels per week. The brewery was still run by four members of the family. This included Nellie at the off-licence and Phil (aged 26, Nellie's nephew) as brewer in 1976. In 1978, after the death of Phil's father George, there was some family disagreement as to whether to continue. However, he continued, ably assisted by Andrew "Pat" Paterson, aged 70, some 11 years at Hoskins, and previously the Head Brewer at the Midland Clubs Brewery and with experience at Home in Nottingham.

They were producing a Bitter 1039° OG and a Mild 1033° OG. However, the latter sold only some 12 barrels per month. They were supplying some 5 outlets, but gradually increasing. The bottled range was:- Home Brew (light mild), Best Mild, Nut Brown, IPA and Strong Ale. The latter was a darker version of the bitter, occasionally in cask as Old Ale. In 1979, draught beer at the off-licence cost only 27p per pint.

LEICESTER (continued)

In 1982 Pat Paterson retired, Phil Hoskins was keen to continue brewing, but he was not a shareholder. In May 1983 the business was for sale, Nellie had broken her leg and retired, leaving Betty Branson as the only active member of the six family shareholders. The production was 20-40 barrels per week.

In the August, the Hoskins family sold the business to TRD Estates Ltd, which also ran an English vineyard and orchard. This was a business owned by Barrie & Robert Hoar of the Saffron Waldon Vineyard Company. They had considered setting up a brew pub in Thaxted and had previously tried to buy the Three Tuns at Bishops Castle. They were helped by Tony Diebel, a former Truman district manager, who became the MD. On the brewing side they had assistance from Geoff Sharp, former Head Brewer at Hardy & Hanson, and Bill Urquhart of Litchborough.

The brewery was renovated with a new wider range of draught beers such as Penn's Ale at 1045°, new beer mats and polypins, although bottling ceased and Holdens contract bottled for them. There was a £70,000 investment in the Red Lion and plans for a brewery tap in the old offices. The Crown & Cushion at Whitwick was bought from Ind Coope.

In May 1984, they opened the Tom Hoskins' pub, created from what was once the family living room. At first there was just a "spit and sawdust" basic public bar, a later "Grist Room" with carpets became a slightly more up-market lounge created from what had previously been the old office, malt store and grist mill. The old brewery well remains in the garden.

In February 1984, they bought an 8% stake in Midsummer Inns, formerly CAMRA Investments, to become the second largest investor in the concern. By April they had raised their stake to 24.3%. In June 1984 Swithland Leisure, having bought the Hoar's 24.7% share in Midsummer bid £1.88m for the latter.

In August 1985 Hoskins bought the Rainbow & Dove, Charles Street, from Allied, and were planning to build an estate in London. In the October they bought the Waterside Inn. Then in November, Hoskins Brewery plc was formed, with 3 pubs including the tap. There was a BES share issue, through Oceana Investment Management Ltd, to raise between £1.2m and £2.1m. This consisted of 3½m shares of 50p at 60p, with the money being needed to repay loans.

In February 1987 they opened the Clock Warehouse at Shardlow, near the old Smiths and CBB brewery sites. This had previously been a small museum and became Hoskins Wharf and later the Canal Tavern. In July, Premium at 1050° was launched to replace Old Nigel during summer.

Elsewhere, financial issues were growing. In April 1985, Netherton Ales had been set up to buy Ma Pardoes, based at a famous old home-brew pub at Netherton in the West Midlands, but losses of £60,000 led to Hoskins buying the Old Swan for £250,000. The intention was to continue brewing, with sales through Hoskins' 5 pubs. The brewing would be supervised by Hoskins' Head Brewer Nigel Burdett, and returned to its 1034° OG, with an intended 28 barrels per week.

They had also considered buying Simpkiss, another small scale brewer in the West Midlands, but were beaten by Greenalls who promptly closed it.

The Leicester capacity was 60 barrels per week, with production averaging some 40 barrels. They owned 6 pubs, together with the Waterside hotel and a country club in Warwickshire, and had plans for further pubs. The business was valued at £2.5m and they were looking to raise a further £1m to finance the expansion.

The Waterside was sold to Whitbread, but in turn Hoskins bought 6 pubs from Allied plus the Bradgate Arms free house at Cropston. The purchase included:-

Mash Tub, Melton Mowbray	Ray's Arms, Heanor, Derbyshire
Golden Fleece, Leicester Street	Black Lion, Loughborough
Albert, Tamworth	

However, at Netherton, the Ma Pardoe brewer George Cooksey and his assistant were sacked because of the sales decline and quality problems. In the October Nigel Burdett, the Hoskins brewer, also brewed at the Old Swan. Despite these problems, Hoskins sales were up to £1,494,000 from £899,000.

In March 1989, Ma Pardoe's was sold to Wiltshire Brewing Company for £304,125, including Hoskins 10% of Netherton Ales. However in August 1990, there were problems with the BES buy-back of Netherton Ales shares which lead to a High Court writ on behalf of Mercia Venture Capital. Hoskins now had an estate of 11 pubs and were considering joining the Unlisted Securities Market, together with the possibility of increasing the brewing capacity by 50%.

**LEICESTER
(continued)**

However, in September 1991 the AGM reported a £167,000 loss in the year to March, and the shares were at 40p compared to the high of 120p. They also failed to buy 18 pubs from Bass.

A new business, T Hoskins Ltd, was formed in 1992, with BJ (Barrie) Hoar as the Chairman, the other director being Adrian Robert Hoar. The brewer was ND Burdett. The Annual Report in March 1992 stated, *"this year has been, on the whole, the most testing ever experienced by your board of directors, and it has contained all the economic ingredients for a commercial calamity."* However, they had managed a profit of £83,060 and the 3 houses were all profitable. They had also bought a small managed house in Burton on Trent and two tenancies in Nottingham, but felt that it was not a viable proposition to expand the licensed house estate and it would be prudent to reduce debt instead.

At the time, Hoskins employed some 4 people in manufacturing, 5 in administration and 87 in distribution. The tangible fixed assets were some £4m.

In August 1992, Elizabeth Ryan Holdings, an East Anglian pubs and hotels group business, took a 3% stake; although the Hoars still owned 30%. In November the Ryan share had risen to 13%; however Richard Cattermole of the company pulled his proposed resolution for management change, one week before the EGM on 18th November. Hoskins sold 8 of their 15 pubs to Wolverhampton & Dudley Breweries for £2.45m to reduce debts.

In April 1993 there was a further threat as Richard Holman acquired some 2.25% of the business, causing shares to rise to 55p, the highest price since 1991. In July 1993, there was news of a planned reverse take-over by the Fatty Arbuckle chain run by ex-Midsummer Leisure chief Adam Page for £4.3m, based on £2.1m cash and 4m new shares. The Hoars would step down and Page would become Chairman and Chief Executive. However on the due date of 16th July, the relevant shareholder notifications had failed to materialise. Non-executive director David Shaw MP called for the Department of Trade and Industry to investigate.

In August 1993, Holman's share had increased to 7.4% and he was calling for a special meeting, particularly as the company results had not been issued. In the meantime, the Page deal had lapsed. In October, the Hoars sold the business to Howard Hodgson who had made his money in the family funeral business, and some thought this might be a message for the future of the brewery. Robert Hoar stood down from the board, but Barrie remained as a non-executive director.

The new owners intended to increase from 1,300 barrels to 5,000 barrel per annum. They brought in a former Scottish & Newcastle account director Philip Thistlewaite to run the business. They also planned to expand from 6 back to 15 pubs and gain free trade accounts to reach the capacity of around 130 barrels per week.

They hoped to push Hoskins' Premium as a free trade and guest ale brand, possibly at the expense of some of the other brews. They also considered bottling Premium. However, Nigel Burdett the Head Brewer commented on the previous lack of investment in the brewing plant, citing £23,000 on fermenters and £5,000 on a cask washer, with the rest of the equipment dating back to the foundation of the brewery. There were no filters or chilling, but they were looking at the possibility of a small centrifuge to help get consistency.

The Tom Hoskins Brewery.

Photo: Author

The Tom Hoskins Brewery.

Photo: Author

Despite the good intentions, the business lost £830,000 in the six months to September 1993. It was renamed Halkin Holding, with more plans to expand. At an EGM on 12th January 1994 it was agreed to buy the Ronson luxury goods business for £10m and LGW, the duty-free trader at Gatwick, for £9.5m. September 1994 saw half year profits of £50,000 from the 6 pubs.

On 9th January 1995, there was a management buyout costing some £1.7m, followed by the doubling of production to 80 barrels per week to supply the 5 pubs and the free trade. The business was renamed Tom Hoskins Brewery plc, but was in receivership soon afterwards.

In March 1996, the Cherryhawk pub chain, based in Northampton, bought the brewery and its two pubs and then in May made a reverse take-over of Hoskins Inns plc. The business was re-named Tom Hoskins. They retained the brewer Andy Allen, with some 11 years experience of the business.

The beer range would be all malt, mainly Marris Otter, but with some crystal and wheat malts. They would use amber malt for colouring, instead of the previous use of caramel. Challenger hops were brought back, to give the characteristic bitterness and the Bitter would be dry hopped with East Kent Goldings.

They were still using the original mash tun and copper and one of the fermenting vats from 1913. However, they intended to re-line the others with stainless steel and bring them back into use to create a working museum. They were looking to raise capacity to 7,000 barrels, compared with the actual production of 2,000 barrels per annum. National distribution would be through Beer Seller and there was also a contract to supply Mansfield Brewery with Churchill's Pride.

The business now owns 14 pubs, mainly in Northamptonshire, plus the brewery tap and the Fountain in Leicester. Old Nigel was brought back, albeit at a lower gravity of 5.5% abv. The emphasis would be on: *"A Truly Satisfying Pint"*. As well as producing Hoskins' Bitter and Tom's Gold, available all year round, Hoskins also re-launched Churchill's Pride as a premium beer. This would be available not only in cask, but also in bottle conditioned form, with a 5.1% abv, in time for the millennium. In addition, Double Zero was their exclusive millennium ale and they developed a range of Brewer's Choice beers, with a different beer for each and every month of the year. They also produce Old Nigel as 5.5% abv winter warmer, described by the brewer as *"russet in colour with an explosion of roasted malt"*.

The business is now listed on the AIM as Tom Hoskins plc, with a head office at Navigation House, 149-151 Bridge Street, Northampton. The Chairman is R Ellert and Chief Executive is DL Clarke. The current output is 2,200 barrels per annum. The business has 87 employees, 14 pubs, 2 disco-bars and a night club. These represent assets of £2.7m, but the turnover in 1997 produced a loss on ordinary activities before tax of £66,254.

The business is now listed on the AIM as Tom Hoskins plc, with a head office at Navigation House, 149-151 Bridge Street, Northampton. The Chief Executive is Clive Watson, with David Clarke as Deputy Chairman. The business now owns 17 pubs, with

LEICESTER (continued)

approximately 300 employees and an output of 2,200 barrels per annum.

In August 1998, Hoskins had bought the award winning Olde Coach House at Ashby St Ledgers and were looking to develop the restaurant and accommodation. The intention is an estate of 50 houses "The Tom Hoskins Traditional Ale and Food Houses".

The emphasis would be on: "A Truly Satisfying Pint". As well as producing Hoskins Bitter and Tom's Gold, available all year round, Hoskins also re-launched Churchill's Pride as a premium beer. This would be available not only in cask, but also in bottle conditioned form, with a 5.1% abv, in time for the Millennium. In addition, Double Zero was their exclusive Millennium ale and they developed a range of Brewer's Choice beers, with a different beer for each and every month of the year. They also produce Old Nigel as 5.5% abv winter warmer, described by the brewer as *"russet in colour with an explosion of roasted malt"*.

The Tom Hoskins Brewery 1999.

The workforce at the brewery increased by some 50%, with Head Brewer Andy Allen also being joined by assistant brewer Steve Gamble. In addition to their own beers, they allow guest beers as well as keg and lager. They were also investing in a new 12 barrel fermenter/ racking tank, to boost output beyond 40 barrels per week to keep up with the increased demand. They were also planning a three to five year programme to re-line the old fermenters with stainless steel.

As well as dealing with increased sales of both beer and brewery related merchandising, such as clothing, the business staff organised their first, of a proposed annual, beer festival in September 1999. In addition to this commercial success, the brewery was being developed as a working museum, to be fully open to the public in the year 2000.

Hoskins & Oldfield, *North Mills, Frog Island.*

On the sale of the Hoskins brewery in October 1984, brothers Phillip & Stephen Hoskins with accountant Simon Oldfield formed a new brewery. They used plant from Hawthorne of Gloucester, to produce 5-10 barrels per week of HOB Bitter at 1041° OG. They had a capacity of 20 barrels. Initially the beers were available at Cotes Mill and the Albion, both in Loughborough.

In December 1987 they introduced Christmas Noggin at 1100° OG, and this was followed by Tom Kelly Stout at 1043°.

In 1994, they introduced White Dolphin, a wheat beer, in response to the growing sales of imported bottled wheat. They were also selling Ginger Tom, a 5.2% ginger beer. That year also saw a win at CAMRA's Great British Beer Festival for the Mild. This was followed by a celebratory brew called Ten Years After and a new Christmas brew, Tom Kelly's Christmas Pudding Porter at 5% abv.

With a normal brew length of 10 barrels, they are currently brewing 20-30 barrels a week for a scattered free trade, including the nearby North Bridge Tavern.

Phillip having been the Head Brewer at Hoskins before the family sale looks after the brewing side, whilst Stephen looks after the sales.

The current range of beers is as follows:-

HOB Mild	3.5%	Tom Kelly Stout	4.2%
IPA	4.2%	HOB Bitter	4%
Supreme	4.4%	Little Matty	4%
White Dolphin	4%	Porter	4.8%
04 Ale	5.2%	Ginger Tom	5.2%
Brigadier Bitter	3.6%	EXS Bitter	5%
Old Navigation Ale	7%		

The Hoskins & Oldfield Brewery.

Photo: Author

Christmas Noggin at 10% is available all year and is also bottled. They also brew specials e.g. for the 1999 Newark beer festival, they brewed a cask-conditioned lager called Shenanigans at 5%. They currently supply some 15 outlets, including their first pub called The Ale Wagon in Charles Street.

Hotel Inn, *Fair Street.*

In 1810, the Hotel Inn was advertised for sale with a large brewing copper of 190 gallons and one of 36 gallons. The whole was *"nearly new and in high preservation"*.

Hubbard, Samuel, *Waggon & Horses, 61 Granby Street.*

In 1827 Thomas Hubbard was a retail brewer, possibly in Archdeacon Lane, where William Hubbard was a victualler in 1830. Thomas was also a victualler at the Black Horse in Granby Street. At this time, a Samuel Hubbard was a maltster on Freeschool Lane. In addition, there were Hubbards at four pubs in the city.

In 1835, the Waggon & Horses was kept by John Peberdy, whilst Sarah Hubbard was a maltster in Sanvey Gate. Samuel Hubbard was listed as a brewer at the pub in 1870-77, although its owner was a Francis Thompson. In December 1887, Thomas Farrer took the licence, but with no mention of brewing. By July 1895 it was owned by Everards.

Hughes, Henry, *Pelican, 49 Gallowtreegate.*

Around 1815-35 Solomon Bray was at the Pelican. In 1848 John Clarke was the victualler.

Henry Hughes had taken the licence by August 1862 and was identified as the brewer at the pub for the period 1877-84. In August 1890, the licensee was John S Brown (see entry) who held it until September 1893. In 1896 it was supplied by Everards. The pub, which stood next to the Lion and Lamb, closed in 1968.

Hunt, Samuel, *Wheatsheaf, 39 Gallowtreegate.*

In 1835 Thomas Fardell was at the Wheatsheaf. By 1870 it was being kept by a Mrs M Cave, with the owner being Mr Sharpe in Waterloo Street. However, in the September Samuel Hunt was at the pub, where he was listed as the brewer in 1875-77.

In May 1887 William Toone took over the licence and in February 1898 it was supplied by Everards. The licence was not renewed and the pub closed on 10th October 1901.

Hutt, Edmund, *Duke of Cumberland, 39 Cumberland Street.*

The Duke of Cumberland was built around 1814, when it seems to have been run by a Mr Daws. In 1835 it was kept by John Peel.

By August 1859, Sarah Smart was the licensee, but the pub was owned by John H Taylor, the maltster (see entry). In July 1878, it was taken by John Smart, possibly the same individual later

**LEICESTER
(continued)**

brewing at the Talbot. In August 1883 Edmund Hutt took over the pub and was listed as a brewer in 1892-95.

On 29th September 1898, LB&M bought it for £4,700 from the late Edward Butt, probably another example of a mistake in spelling. In 1919 a half-timbered frontage was added and the pub was still trading as an Ansell's house in the 1980s.

Illsley, Henry, *Black Lion, 64 Belgrave Gate.*

In 1794 Thomas Wheatley was the victualler at the Black Lion and when he retired in April 1806, the sale details of the pub included the malt office and brewing vessels. His retirement proved to be short-lived, since he died in the August. The pub was for sale again in August 1809 after the bankruptcy of John Judd, the victualler, who was also a framework knitter. This sale described the valuable brewing vessels, coppers etc. as being in excellent condition, with a 150 and a 50 gallon copper.

In 1812, James Mason was selling the pub and its brewing vessels. He operated from the maltings on Church Gate, which he had presumably bought from the creditors of Mr Brombley, after the bankruptcy of the latter. By 1835 Arthur Johnson was at the pub.

From October 1869 John Woollereton was the victualler, the pub being owned by a Mary Hinten. By September 1875 Henry Illsley owned the pub and brewed there. He had previously been at the Spital House Inn. This may also be the Henry Illsay shown as brewing at the Red Cow, 142 Belgrave Gate, the year after.

In June 1886, Alexander Ross took over the Black Lion until March 1889, when Joseph Hiller took the licence. However, there was no further identification of brewing and on 27th January 1893 it was an Everard's house, which closed in 1916. The site is now "Hartleys" bar.

In October 1893, LB&M bought the nearby Old Black Lion, at No 169, from Arthur Newton for £4,000 and this later became The Pickwick, and then "Skandles"!

Illston, John, *Nag's Head, 2 Northgate Street.*

Kept in 1815 by Edward Bailey, in 1835 John Crow was at the pub (see entry). He was shown as a maltster in 1855 in New Street and Northgate Street. However, in 1870 Mrs Maria Brice was running the Nag's Head, whilst Crow seems to have been concentrating on the New Street business.

In October 1871, John Illston was the holder of the licence, but the pub seems to have been owned by Cock & Langmore. In 1875 Illston was also listed as a cab proprietor and victualler at the Orange Tree, 55 Northgate Street, before being listed at the Nag's Head as a brewer by 1877. His son John junior was then shown as brewing at the Orange Tree. The latter pub dated back to at least 1835, when it was kept by William Spencer. In July 1886, George Joseph Illston was at the Nag's Head.

Around 1890, a George Flude Illston was at the Angel on Oxford Street, suggesting a link with another local family involved with several home-brew pubs (see Flude entry).

In March 1897, a sale of three properties reported the following prices:-

Nag's Head	£5,500
Orange Tree	£4,050
Sailor's Return	£7,400

This suggests that all three pubs may have been owned by the family and that Cock & Langmore had previously sold their interest. Everards were the owners by March 1898 and after the building of the new railway, the Nag's Head was renamed the Great Central Hotel in 1899. The Orange Tree was bought by Holes of Newark.

Johnson, Edward, *Durham Ox, 239/241 Belgrave Gate.*

In 1815 James Hutchinson was the victualler and in 1835 William Tacey.

From July 1869 to 1875 it was run by Henry Sketchley, although the Ox was owned by George Shipley Matts (see Pettifor entry). Then in August 1875, the licence was taken over by Joseph Stacey, who was joined in November 1876 by Edward Johnson, shown as the brewer for 1877-84.

In March 1885 Robert Shaw took the pub, and was presumably brewing, but was not covered by any of the directories. However, he was not at the pub for very long since in

LEICESTER (continued)

December 1885, Samuel Henry Roper took over and was listed as the brewer in 1887. When he died around May 1890, his wife Annie took over the pub, but only until September 1891 when Nathaniel Mawby took the licence.

In 1892, the address was shown as 241 and around this time it became an LB&M house. In 1919 LB&M sold the de-licensed premises for £750.

Johnson, James, *Prince Regent, 56 Granby Street.*

From 1835 to 1846, James Johnson was the victualler at the Prince Regent, shown as 6 Granby Street. This was on the corner of Albert Place and in 1855, the address was shown as No 56.

During this period, Richard Johnson was the victualler at the Wellington Castle, 36 Granby Street.

For the period 1876-84, James Johnson was shown as the brewer at the pub. In August 1889, John Johnson took the licence, but he died the following year. As a result WF Bramley became the owner of the pub, which was rebuilt and in May was leased to LB&M. It closed in June 1900 and the licence was transferred to the Uppingham Road Hotel.

Johnson, John, *90 Great Holme Street.*

In 1794, the Johnsons were maltsters in Northamptongate. Then in 1835 to 1848 John Johnson was listed as the victualler at the Birmingham Tavern, Hinckley Road (see Brown entry), where he was also shown as a maltster in 1876.

In 1835 and 1846 Thomas Johnson was shown as a brewer and maltster in Southgate Street. Thomas also seems to have bottled beer. From 1848 to 1855 the address was more clearly given as 47 Southgate. From 1835 to 1848 Joseph Johnson was also a maltster in Oxford Street.

The Johnson family was involved with some 7 pubs during this period. For example in 1835, Arthur Johnson kept the Black Lion (see Illsley entry) and from 1835 to 1846 Thomas Johnson kept the Admiral Rodney, High Cross Street previously run by the Coltmans. In 1870, they also owned the Axe & Square, Sanvey Gate.

However, the 1867 directory lists John Johnson as a maltster in Great Holme Street, but also still the brewer at 5 Hinckley Road. whilst T Johnson was a maltster in Mansfield Street. In 1875 John Johnson was shown as a brewer at Great Holme Street and a maltster at 4 Harvey Lane and Hinckley Road, where the following year he was again shown as brewing.

In April 1871 the licensee was James Robert Johnson and he was listed as the brewer for the period 1876-87, until the site became owned by the Browns (see entry).

Mrs Ann Johnson was then listed as a brewer and maltster at Stanley House in Great Holme Street in 1881-84. Henry Earny, a maltster's foreman was living at No 88. This site then possibly became used by Everards.

Jones, John Evans, *Royal Oak, 6 George Street.*

In 1870 Robert Dicks was running the Royal Oak beerhouse, followed in 1875 by John Benson. John Jones was listed for the period 1877-84, brewing at an un-named beerhouse, which by 1892 was again called The Royal Oak. Its rebuilding may account for the gap.

Jordan, William, *Butcher's Arms, 40 Church Gate.*

In 1870 John Woolman was running an un-named beerhouse, whilst a William Murdy was a butcher at No 38. Then in 1875 William Murdy was a butcher and beerhouse keeper at No 38/40, possibly resulting in the pub's name.

In 1886 John William Morris was at the pub, whilst William Jordan was shown as an hairdresser. In 1887 Jordan was shown as the brewer, although the following year he was shown only as a beer retailer at No 40 and the pub was not named, (see also Kibworth).

Juba, James, *Welford Road.*

Described in the 1847 poll book as a brewer. However, this seems to have been the only entry, although later members of his family may have been running a pub in Oadby. In 1875, a Henry Juba was at the Dun Cow in Infirmary Square.

Kegworth Brewery Company, *Wells, Sidney & Sons, 57 Humberstone Road.*

Originally the Fountain pub, this became a depot (see Kegworth entry).

Kell, Walter, *Odd Fellows, 79 Gladstone Street.*

The pub was first licensed around 1867 and in 1870 Francis Hill was running the beerhouse. In 1875 he was described as a machinist and beerhouse keeper.

In 1886 Charles Tallis was at the pub, before moving to the George III, whilst Walter Kell was a shopkeeper at No 67. In 1888 Kell was a beer retailer at No 79, but was listed as a brewer for the period 1892-5. In the latter year, Eadies of Burton took the pub.

Kellam, William, *The Engine Inn, 12 Queen Street.*

In 1870 Edward Wilkinson was running the Engine, whilst William Kellam was the victualler at the Full Moon (see Knapp entry). He was also a maltster in Mansfield Street. By March 1875, he was at the Engine as the victualler, and also a maltster and corn and flour dealer at 164 Highcross Street and a maltster at 31 Mansfield Street.

In 1877-87 William was listed as the brewer at the Engine, with maltings in Rutland Street and 31 Mansfield Street. He died around July 1891 and in 1892 Mrs Mary Kellam was shown as the brewer, until her own death in March 1895. Albert Edward Kellam, possibly their son, then ran the pub, but by June 1896, it was supplied by Robinsons of Burton.

Kilby, William, *White Swan, 77 Belgrave Street.*

The White Swan was run in 1815 by Joseph Staines and in 1835 by Henry Staines. In September 1870, Charles Hayler was running the pub and also a wine & spirit business at No 77, before he moved to the Dolphin (see entry).

In May 1876 Charles Wright took the licence, but in June it passed to William Kilby, who was shown as the brewer in 1877. However, from June 1879 to 1882 it was run by Bates & Sons, before William Kilby took back the licence and installed William Austin as the tenant. Both William Austin and Charles Wright had previously been at the Barkby Arms (see Austin entry).

In May 1886, Walter Hugh Goodwin took the pub, before Kilby returned yet again in July 1889. From October 1890 to July 1891 Goodwin was briefly back at the pub, and perhaps the absences were due to illness. However, it was sold, with brewhouse, in 1890 and by 1894 was being supplied by Worthingtons. The licence was transferred to the Broadway and the pub closed in July 1930.

King, Mrs Anne, *Royal Lancer, 47 Asylum Street.*

In 1892 Mrs King was brewing at this address, but this seems to be the only mention. However, in 1883 the All Saints Brewery had bought a small amount of stout from a King in Leicester, but it is not known if this was the same family. In 1894, it was an Everard's house.

Kingston, Mrs Ann, *Vine Tavern, 14 Vine Street.*

In 1835 Joseph Musson was at the pub. By 1870 the pub was being run by Jas Kingston who was shown as the brewer around 1875-77. However, in November 1876 Ann Kingston had taken the pub, the owner of which was an Elizabeth Case. At some point William Goodwin seems to have been involved with the pub.

In January 1895, David Richards was the licensee of the pub, which was then owned by John Henry Taylor the local maltster (see entry). By 1902 LB&M had bought it, with the address shown as No 38, on the corner of Elbow Lane. The pub was closed for compensation in December 1936.

Kingston, Daniel, *Coach & Horses, 34 Humberstone Gate.*

In 1835 Benjamin Meres was at the pub, when John Kingston kept the Blue Lion, 21 Granby Street.

In 1870 Edward Rutt was at the Coach and Horses, whilst Daniel Kingston was at the Admiral Rodney, 82 High Street, before moving here by May 1873. For the period 1877-84 he was listed as the brewer.

In August 1879 George Illife was the licensee and in June 1891, it was Thomas Richard Johnson; however, there were no listings for brewing and by 1905 it was supplied by Eadies of Burton. The licence was later transferred and the pub closed in August 1925.

Kirchin, Robert, *Leicester Volunteer, 2 Watling Street.*

Friedrich gives an entry for Robert Birchin as a brewer in 1892; however, this seems to be Mr Kirchin who had taken over from John Tow at the Leicester Volunteer beerhouse by 1894. In 1895, it was run by a Samuel Dawson Jackson, who was only described as a beer retailer.

Kisby, William, *Bowling Green, 44 Oxford Street.*

In April 1865 William Kisby took the licence of the pub, which in 1870 was shown as the Old Bowling Green, although Cock & Langmore would seem to have had an interest in the property. Previously in 1848, a Thomas Kisby had been a maltster at the Talbot on Belgrave Gate. William Kisby was listed as brewing in the 1877 directory through to 1892 (F2718).

From December 1892 to around 1902 Thomas Orton was the brewer. Then in January 1904, the licence was taken by Thomas Luck, but he died in the May, and the pub went to Charles Luck. He was listed as brewing to 1920, but he was shown as a tenant of the All Saints Brewery, which had bought the pub around 1904. The property was re-fitted in 1922, and valued at £5,000 in 1940. It is now the Fullback and Firkin.

Knapp, John, *Full Moon, 16 East Bond Street.*

Around 1760-70 the Full Moon was run by John Wright, in 1815 by James Wilson and in 1835 it was kept by Samuel Bull.

By 1870 William Kellam had taken over the pub, before he moved to the Engine Inn (see entry). In December 1872 John Knapp took over the licence and was listed as the brewer for 1875-77. In July 1878 Joseph Wilson was the licensee until October 1882, then it went to Thomas King, who was shown as the brewer in 1884. In April 1888 James Toon was at the pub, but there was no indication of brewing.

In July 1904, it was run by Sharpes of Sileby, and went with some of their other property to Strettons in 1910. The licence was transferred to the new Full Moon on Green Lane Road and the original pub closed on 27th August 1938.

Lant, Thomas, *British Lion, 14 Russell Street.*

In 1870 Hiram Richards was at the pub. In March 1875 Lant took over the licence, although the pub was owned by Thomas Foxon (see entry). However, on 30th August 1877, William Lenton then appears to have become the licensee and it seems to have become owned by Frederick Bates, brewer (see LB&M entry). Nevertheless, Lant was listed as brewing for that year and the plans for the building show the brewhouse (Pyrah p16).

In 1892, the address was shown as Russell Square. It was an LB&M property in July 1894. It closed for compensation in July 1933 and the building became a cafe.

Lapworth, Henry, *Mitre & Keys, 26 Applegate Street.*

The pub dated back to 1560. The earliest clear evidence of brewing was in 1763 when John Nutt moved from the Red Lion, Hinckley, to the Blue Boar. Then in 1772 he moved to Blue Bell, followed by a further move in 1778 to the Swan with Two Necks (see Watts entry). Finally in 1793, together with his son Thomas he arrived at the Mitre, where the latter married Mrs Stafford, the widow of the late landlord. In 1781, Dorothy Watts had been shown at the Mitre & Keys. The following year, Thomas was shown as the victualler at the Inn.

In November 1799, Nutt was looking to let the Mitre. It was described as being free of tie and with brewing vessels *"second to none"*. In March 1800, Mr Hunt was selling his brewing vessels at the Fox and Goose on Humberstone Gate, before he moved to the Mitre and Keys, but shortly afterwards it was again to let.

In 1800, James Nutt, at the Castle on Humberstone Gate, was advertising bottled London porter at 4s 6d per dozen *"ale at this time being very indifferent and consequently not a wholesome liquor"*. The following year he advertised having a large quantity of his incomparable bottled porter and brown stout. However, in 1802 he seems to have overstretched himself in that he was bankrupt. He was described as a grocer and dealer, which suggest that the family no longer brewed. In 1808 he retired completely and his business as a liquor merchant was taken over by Thomas Eyre.

Perhaps Mr Nutt had been badly affected by the budget and competition. Mr Richards on the corner of Humberstone Gate was advertising that he had 36 gallon barrels at 48s and 18 gallons

LEICESTER (continued)

at 25s. These had been laid in before the new duty of 6s per barrel. Samuel Bradley on High Cross was also selling at pre-budget prices. Possibly their descendants are now driving white vans across to France for cheap beer!

In 1801, the Mitre and Keys was taken by Richard Poole, who moved there from the White Bear. He was still at the pub in 1812. It continued to brew throughout the nineteenth century, in 1835 John Nokes and in 1870 William Whatton were the respective victuallers.

Henry Lapworth seems to have taken the Mitre by December 1873, although it was owned by Mary Whatton of Spinney Hills. He was still brewing in 1877, but in the December, it passed to Charlotte Lapworth. She was the licensee until May 1879, when it was taken by Henry Jackson, from the Duke of Northumberland. He was followed by Elizabeth Jackson from August 1881 to March 1884.

Although Henry was still listed at the pub in 1892, brewing seems to have ceased by then and ownership may have returned to the Whattons. It was certainly leased by Everards in January 1896. The pub was rebuilt towards the end of the nineteenth century, and was owned by Everard Son and Welldon around 1900. The licence was transferred to the Rocket on Stephenson Road and the pub closed in April 1956.

In 1908, an Arthur Lapworth was the local sub-agent for CBB.

Lawrence, Mrs Mary, *Rising Sun, 120 Wharf Street.*

In January 1870, John Collis was at the pub, which was owned by the maltster George Harrison. In September 1875, Mary Lawrence took the licence and was listed as the brewer there to 1886. In 1895 she was brewing at 33 Cross Street.

From June 1889 to around 1895, James Mirrall/Merrall was the victualler, but in July 1894 it was run by the Beeston Brewery Company. It closed for compensation on 23rd December 1905.

Leake, John, *King Richard III, 70 Highcross Street.*

In 1870 John Foxon was the victualler, but by 1875 Leake was at the pub. He was listed as brewing in 1877, although supplied with wines and spirits by the All Saints Brewery. By 1901 it was an Everard's house.

It is not clear whether there were any family connections with the Leake Brothers brewing at Mount Sorrel soon afterwards.

Lee, George, *Duke of Wellington, 74 Wellington Street.*

In 1835 Frances Shilcock was the victualler. In 1870 it was run by William Sutton. By December 1873, Lee was at the pub, where he was listed as a brewer for 1877. It was owned by Mrs Moore of Syston.

In December 1881, the licence passed to Maria Lee, who ran the pub until September 1884, when it was taken by Thomas Jarvis. Then in June 1887, Charles Woodford bought the pub and became the licensee. By October 1894, it was owned by Bells of Burton and then in 1902 Salts. It closed under compensation in February 1929.

Leicester Brewing & Malting, *Eagle Brewery, 51 Upper Charnwood Street.*

In 1791, a Mr Bates was listed as a victualler in High Cross Street and prior to this a William Fancote had been operating a malt office on the street.

In 1812, the Pack Horse with its brewhouse was available on a 22 year lease. There was also a sale of the previous tenant's goods, one John Bates. In addition, in 1827, Henry Bates was at the Rainbow and Dove in Northampton Square, which was linked with the Hannam's brewing interests (see entry).

Then in 1846, John Bates was a brewer in Friar's Causeway, whilst William Bates was a brewer and maltster in Southgate Street. William Bates may have been using the site which was later used by Everards. Prior to this a James Bates was letting the Nag's Head and malt office at Mount Sorrel.

In 1864, TC Carver was advertising in the Chronicle, that he had left JW Goodwin in order to operate the Northampton Street Brewery as TC Carver & Company. His move seems to have been a result of TG Cock taking a role at Goodwins (see All Saints Brewery entry).

Letterhead used July 1895.

Around 1867, Carver & Bates were shown at the Eagle Brewery, Northampton Square. This was originally the Northampton Square brewhouse owned by the Hannam family (see entry). Thomas Cave Carver was at 15 Northampton Street, next to the Rainbow and Dove. They were advertising the availability of their Mild at 10d per gallon and their *"Very Strong Old Ale"*.

In 1870, the Charnwood Street area was developed. Prior to this date, the street was not shown in the directories. However, it is not clear if this was when Carver and Bates built their new brewery there. In the same year, Carver and Bates were also shown as maltsters at Syston, but this may possibly be a mistake for Syston Street, which was a site shown later in their property books.

Despite the new building, in 1870 and 1871, Carver and Bates were still shown as brewers and maltsters at 15 Northampton Street. Frederick Ernest Bates was shown as the brewer, living at 6 Stockdale Terrace on London Road. A John Bates was shown as an ale and porter agent at 95 Palmerston Street and a William H Bates was a similar agent at 75 Willow Street. Despite all the seeming family connections, Frederick seems to have been the son of a hosier, also called Frederick.

In 1875 Frederick Bates was still shown at the Eagle Brewery, 15 Northampton Street, but with his home at 4 Fosse Road Terrace. In 1876 the Charnwood site was extended; however the same year they were still shown as TC Carver & Company, brewers in Northampton Street, which suggests that this was still the offices if not the main brewery.

In 1877 Frederick Bates was shown as a brewer at 15 Northampton Street and also operating from 73 Corn Exchange, the latter address presumably being offices. Around this time, he was also shown at Lower Kent Street, possibly where he was a maltster, and the Eagle Brewery, Upper Charnwood Street. The Kent Street site may be that used in 1870 by Charles Sawbridge, who was a joiner and victualler at the George & Dragon, No 11/13.

Frederick's advertising stated that he was an ale and stout brewer. His speciality was *"a pure bitter ale warranted thoroughly sound at all seasons"*. This was presumably the Diamond Pale Ale which retailed at 1/2d per gallon.

By 1880 Frederick Bates had become Bates, Son & Bishell (F2700), Northampton and Lower Charnwood Streets. The following year, Bates, Son & Bishell were listed as ale and stout brewers, 15 Northampton Street and both Upper and Lower Charnwood. They were also shown at the Queen's Head,, 12 Town Hall Lane.

In 1884 both Northampton Street and Upper Charnwood were still listed, whilst Frederick Bates was shown as a brewer in Townhall Lane. In 1886, the Brewers' Journal reported that Bates, Son & Bishell had agreed to have brewery work done by Briggs & Company of Burton (p291).

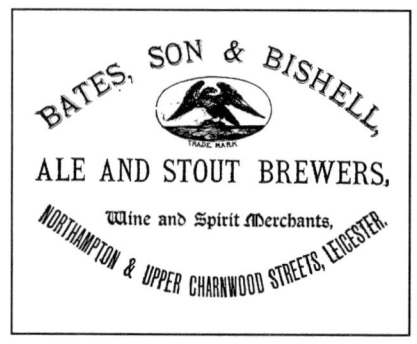

From a commercial directory dated 1888.

On 30th June 1890, Bates Son & Bishell registered the Leicester Brewing & Malting Company Ltd. This was together with Needham and Crick maltsters, Tower Buildings, Church Gate. The background to Needham and Crick is somewhat confused, with links to several different sites, but in particular the Harrison family (see entry). It would seem that their business was in supplying the many small brew-pubs which were still in existence and these seem to have been inherited by LB&M. This caused numerous changes of ownership during the next few years as the emphasis switched from supplying malt for brewing to actually supplying beer from a single central plant. A later analysis of the "goodwill" of the business, placed a value of £10,000 on BS&B and £5,000 on N&C, giving an indication of their respective contributions.

LEICESTER (continued)

Needhams may also have been operating the maltings at the Rutland Brewery in Oakham, and previously malting at Hinckley and Huncote. Needham & Company of Norfolk also supplied malt to the All Saints Brewery in Leicester, in some cases via Syston. Interestingly, a William Bates and William Needham were millers together at Thrussington in 1884.

The new company owned 50 freehold licensed houses, numerous shops and cottages, 84 leasehold, mortgaged and other houses. The total value of the business was £112,104. This was payable to the vendors for the properties, goodwill and plant, made up of £50,000 in ordinary shares and the balance in preference shares and cash. The share capital was:-

>   5,000 x £10 Ordinary Shares
>   5,000 x £10 Cumulative Preference

There was also a £50,000 debenture mortgage, of which £47,200 had been issued to cover property. The first meeting of the new Board had taken place on 1st June. Major Frederick Carne Rasch MP was the Chairman and the other directors were:-

- Richard Turner, vice-chairman, Cliftonville, Northants
- Frederick Bates, Elmstead, Kirby Musloe
- Ernest Frederick Bates, Managing Director, Claremont Villa, Humberstone Road
- Joseph Bishell, Northampton Square, Leicester
- Throne Crick, Clydesdale, Stoneygate
- Henry Woodcock Needham, Syston
- William J Crick, Company Secretary, Northampton Square

Major Rasch also became a director of the newly-formed Birmingham Breweries Ltd in 1896. Another link was Robert Longman, who was both a director of LB&M and the brewer for, and son-in-law of, William Blencowe at Brackley. Perhaps somewhat ominously, Major Rasch, who lived at Danbury in Essex, was also a director of the Birmingham Vinegar Brewing Company.

Throne Crick, the son of a William Throne Crick a commercial traveller, seems to have been a shoe manufacturer. Hence, his connection with Needhams may have been purely financial.

The company employed 3 agents, 5 travellers and 9 clerks. The brewer was Charles Edward Saunders, with Walter George Turner as the under-brewer. The brewery employed 21 men and there were 6 carters for delivery.

In addition to the brewery, the business was renting an office and stores next to the Dove, with a yearly lease of £180 going back to 1882. This expired on 1st April 1892 and was given up. There were two 75 quarter malthouses on Gresham Street, valued at £4,400. The two 45 quarter malthouses on Syston Street were valued at £4,050, but were sold for £3,600 in September 1892 to John Taylor (see entry). Malting was clearly still a major part of the business in its own right. For example they were prepared to allow Langtons of Melton to supply beer to the Princess Charlotte for £83 pa if they took 300 quarters of malt. Langtons agreed the deal at 250 quarters.

However, the minute books show that there were initial problems with the Birmingham houses, which the company had inherited. One of the first steps was the dismissal of the local agent, a Falkoner Morgan, and his replacement by JL Needham. The warehouse and office at 33 Albert Street, which was rented for £60 pa, was given up and the fixtures removed to Leicester. They had also inherited a contract with Marstons for the supply of beer to the houses, but they were able to re-negotiate this from 8 barrels of pale ale per week to 6 barrels.

In November 1890, the Board decided that the Birmingham houses, which were not paying, should be advertised as brewing houses. The following month it was decided:-

- Hands to Pump, Stourbridge - tenant to be allowed to put in her own brewing vessels, 1889 agreement to take 2 barrels of Marstons per week
- Old Station - structural alterations
- George & Dragon, Oldbury - to try Leicester beer for another month
- White Lion, Bilston - accept best offer over £50
- Jolly Sailor, Bilston - keep trying
- Three Crowns, Lye - tenant to put in plant and take fittings
- Dog & Partridge - 5 month's notice to give up
- Flag Tavern - sell with licence for at least £750
- Seven Stars, Willenhall - tenant to put in plant

LEICESTER (continued)

Nevertheless, despite these problems, they managed 5% on the debenture and an interim 6% dividend on the ordinary shares.

The following year, the problems with the share issue were resolved with a re-allocation as follows:-

Frederick Bates	1-650
Ernest F Bates	651-1,150
Joseph Bishell	1,151-2,650
Throne Crick	2,651-3,375
Henry W Needham	3,376-4,100
Richard Turner	4,101-4,300
Walter G Turner	4,301-4,600
Everard & de Peyer	4,601-4,900
CE Saunders	4,901-5,000

Problems continued with, in June 1891, the Board instigating a scheme to investigate whether salaries and wages could be reduced. Possibly related to these discussions, the following month, Mr Saunders the brewer resigned. WG Turner's salary was increased by £50 pa, so presumably he had taken on Saunder's role. They considered buying the properties of the Whissendine Brewery, but continuing problems with the Birmingham houses were probably sufficient to stop them so doing. They were prepared to accept any offer over £1,500 for the outright purchase of the Birmingham properties, or a separate offer of £150 if tied for malt. This shows a hangover from the malting business and it is of interest to note, that the 6 Black Country houses seem to have been bought separately by Mr Needham.

The continuing difficulties were probably why they rejected the offer of the Church Hill Tavern, Wednesbury, available for £800 to £900 and the British Lion at Digbeth.

Problems were still continuing from the work at the brewery and the change in focus of the business, as shown in the following notice to the workforce from R Turner:-

"To impress upon the management the necessity of economy in every department and endeavour to counteract as much as possible the serious loss which must inevitably follow the sale of the inferior article we have been for some months supplying to our customers."

No doubt they needed a management consultant, a mission statement and focus groups!

The complicated nature of property ownership can be seen in the loan of £12,000 to Orson Wright to buy properties, which were then tied to LB&M. Similarly, many of the properties were owned by the holders of the debenture mortgage, rather than LB&M. The three properties in Grantham seem to have been owned by J Bishell.

The year 1892 saw the extensions to the brewery and new offices completed, financed by the sale of the Syston Street maltings, representing the switch from malt to beer supply. This allowed the move from the other properties. However, they also leased offices at 76 Upper Charles Street until 1896, when they are also shown at No 74, the latter possibly being the beerhouse which James Hannam had owned. For a brief period around 1892, they also leased offices at 7 Abbey Street, Nuneaton. The brewery address seems to have changed from 73 to 51 Charwood Street, presumably as a result of the re-building.

In the January, they considered buying HH Parry's brewery, but it is not clear if this was at Langham or Leicester (see Harrison entry). They did buy the Rainbow and Dove, which they had previously leased and this represented part of a continuing rationalisation of the estate. This involved a move away from leasehold and country properties to town pubs, to which they owned the freehold. These property deals were linked in several cases to Orton Wright and a WF Adams. The latter individual seems to have bought the houses in the Nuneaton area, but may well have continued to purchase beer from Leicester. They seem to have turned down the Sir Thomas Whyte with its brewing plant at £2,625 and it remained owned by Needham and Crick.

In May 1892, WG Turner was still described as the under-brewer, so it is not clear who was regarded as the Head Brewer, whose salary was £300. Turner was also the secretary, assistant manager and inspector of houses, which seems a wide range of duties for his £170 pa salary. However, around this time they were also having problems with bad beer. The following year EW Beale was mentioned as the brewer and it is possible that he had replaced one of the Bates family.

In the September, they finally managed to dispose of the Birmingham properties. In October

LEICESTER (continued)

1892, they sold three houses to HH Parry as part of the continuing programme of estate rationalisation.

In December 1893, they declined a Stamford brewery. This was probably the St Martin's brewery of Phillips which had been on sale in the July, but had failed to reach its reserve price. They had previously turned down a brewery at Spalding with 11 houses and also Bannisters at Lutterworth.

In March 1894, they were looking to increase the private trade by offering more discount for prompt payment. In September there was discussion regarding the payment of bonuses linked to the shareholder dividends, which caused some disagreement within the Board. Indeed, JC Rasch stated that he would resign unless his fee was fixed at 100 guineas, independent of the dividend.

In December 1895, WG Turner was to have a pupil brewer, which suggests that he had become the Head Brewer by this time. Perhaps linked to this, in June 1896 EF Bates was relinquishing some of his duties as MD and secretary. Turner was to become the general manager at an extra £60 pa. Although, the Wright's directories of 1894 and 1896 identify a GE Bates as the MD, this name does not fit with those shown in the minute books. In June 1896, some property was sold to Brunt Bucknall.

The town office at Northampton Street was to close, leaving their directory entry as 51 Charnwood Street and 74 Upper Charles Street.

In July 1897 HW Needham who had been living at Syston, died, shortly after having bought the Victoria Inn in the village. Perhaps as a mark of his growing importance to the business, WG Turner was on a salary of £40 per month.

January 1898 saw discussions regarding the possibility of investing £1,000 in a proposed business to bottle beer and mineral waters. This was a classic example of how local brewers often worked together. This was the business of RC Allen (see entry).

In 1898, there was further work at the brewery, with £2,000 for a new boiler house and chimney. This also provided steam heating for the premises. They also spent £46 on re-painting the exterior. The brewer, who by this date may have been EW Beale was paid £5 per week, with a £50 bonus if an annual dividend of at least 8% could be achieved. There would be an additional £50 if 10% was achieved, a clear example of performance related pay.

In May 1898 a decline in sales was noted and this was presumably related to the decision to sell the outlying country houses. The only director to vote against this was Mr Bishell, which was not surprising given his ownership of the three Grantham pubs. He was living at Baldock around this time, which may explain his ownership of properties so far from the brewery.

The property disposals included two houses to Eady & Dulley. They also sold some 7 pubs to WF Adams for £13,000, presumably with some tie on beer. In the December, although the cost of raw materials was rising, they decided not to reduce the strength of their beer, after comparing it with the other local brews. However, they did decide, if necessary, to engage a detective to monitor if their tenants were buying spirits elsewhere!

In 1899, they were reporting a gross profit on trading of £45,253 against a capital value for the estate, goodwill and plant of £179,500. The bill for wages and salaries was £6,765. They also owned 400 shares in RC Allen (see entry). The July AGM agreed a 10% dividend, making 15% for the year. They were also able to add £9,000 to the reserves, taking them to £42,000. In the October an EGM was held which increased the capital of the business to £150,000 by the issue of 5,000 £10 shares. This was linked to a proposal to pay off the debentures.

In September, they were noting that the sales for the three months were up by 700 barrels. As a result of the increased beer tax, the strength of the beers was examined once more, and this time the strength was to be reduced as follows:-

XXX and XXXX by 1½lbs each
X and XX by 2 lbs

The weights were presumably related to those of the raw materials i.e. malt being used in the brews.

In consideration of the financial situation, they decided to sell the five remaining country houses, with provisional values as follows:-

Oadby	£1,300
Blaby off-licence	£500
Earl Stamford, Ratby	£2,400

Yew Trees, Ratby	£3,000
New Inn, Cosby	£2,400

The latter two properties were bought by the Lichfield Brewery Company. However, they were prepared to invest £1,000 on new machinery for the maltings. EW Beale, the brewer who was also responsible for barley and malt purchasing, also joined the Board. The managing director's salary was raised to £50 per month.

As a result of the death in 1897 of HW Needham, some of his shares went to the Crisp family. The latter family is of course a famous malting one and it may be that this is evidence of the connections common in the industry. Mrs Crisp then disposed of some shares to the Marstons and the Ruddles. Close links can also be seen with the opening of a joint bank account with Everards. This was to handle monies arising from the licensing and de-licensing of properties.

In 1900, they seem to have resolved their property ownership in the town and they were only shown at Upper Charnwood Street. The 1900 AGM on 28th June, saw a 15% dividend and a further £8,000 to reserves. However, the following year the March trade was some 314 barrels down.

In 1903 Thomas Buffey was appointed as the secretary on £4 per week and WG Turner, some 11 years in office, was presumably able to reduce some of his workload as a result. Further change came from the death of Frederick Bates in the October, with T Crick taking his place as vice-chairman.

In 1904, the Board considered its relative position in terms of the excise paid for the year end in April:-

Everards	£30,671	Sharpes	£11,702
LB&M	£24,551	Welch Brothers	£ 7,458
All Saints Brewery	£12,600		

The amounts were presumably based on the barrelage which each of the local brewers was selling and give a handy guide to their differing levels of output.

Sir Carne Rasch died in 1908 and WG Turner, the MD, became the chairman. Nevertheless, the year end for the twelve months to 31st May showed a profit of £20,989, giving a 10% dividend and £10,409 to the reserves. The following year brought the death of Edgar W Beale, the brewer.

In 1909, they were brewing IPA, probably to counteract the popularity of Burton beers, which had already caused Everards to move their brewing to the town. They were also paying commission to Bass, presumably for bottling their beer.

In 1912 wages at the brewery were increased to 18s per week and the following year, they set a minimum of 20s per week. January 1914 saw the investment of £2,500 on further alterations at the brewery. Despite this investment, they were still facing competition, but they decided to hold the gravity of their beers and to try brewing a stout at 27lbs. The latter decision was presumably to counteract growing sales of Guinness. In May Mr Bishell retired; unfortunately his retirement was short-lived, since he died in the October. In December, as a result of the impact of wartime restrictions, the gravity of the beers was again reduced. The following year, a sign of the times was the consideration of using CO_2 with the bottled beer.

In March 1916 there were more problems with the wartime restrictions on output and in May Mr Barrett the brewer was called up. October saw further restrictions on barley. Then on 14th April 1917, the All Saints Brewery directors decided to close their own brewery and to buy their beer in from LB&M. In addition, Welch Brothers had also decided to have their supplies brewed by LB&M (see entry). This resolved any capacity problems at the Eagle Brewery. At the same time, the gravity of the beers was reduced from 40 to 30 i.e. 1040° to 1030°.

The end of the war brought hopes of a return to prosperity, which were somewhat tempered by the death of Mr Bishell. In 1919, as an indicator of the previous policy regarding the pubs, the freehold properties were valued at £207,000, with a mortgage of £15,000. The price of the beer was raised from 102/- to 108/-. In terms of the raw materials, like most British breweries, they were buying raw materials from abroad, e.g. 1,000 quarters of Californian barley at 96/- per quarter. This was linked not simply to price, but the need to brew different styles of beer for bottling.

In 1920, £75,000 of the reserve funds was capitalised by the issue of 15,000 £5 shares, on the basis of 1 for every £10 ordinary share held. The ordinary share capital was increased to £100,000, by the creation of 20,000 £5 shares. The EGM on 23rd February meant that the

LEICESTER (continued)

business was now valued at £300,000. This was linked to the purchase of Welch Brothers' houses and casks. HR Welch, living at Oadby, received 3,200 ordinary shares and became a director, whilst Arthur received 1800. In line with previous policy, Welch's five country houses were sold for £5,450.

No doubt as a result of the changes to the capital and the previous discussions, an amalgamation with the All Saints Brewery was discussed. Tantalisingly, the July minutes state that Mr Ruddle's scheme was explained, but there is no clarification of what this probable further rationalisation entailed! The following year, there was mention of a 25% discount to Ruddles, so presumably the scheme may have involved the planned closure of the Langham brewery. On the plus side, the October meeting approved the introduction of stronger beer, as the wartime limitations were put to one side.

In the November, there were further alterations to the brewery and maltings, including the construction of a garage. Earlier in the year they had sold all their horses and carts. A sadder construction was that of a memorial to the three men killed in the war, Messrs Bryan, Hood and Matthews.

In 1921 they were trying light beer in bottle, but the September meeting noted that the bottled trade was bad. However around this time, even the Burton brewers were having difficulty with their product.

Despite the worries, 1922 saw the purchase of the Old Cheese on Abbey Street for £3,000, this was in-line with the policy of concentrating on a local trade. This meant that the company now owned 100 houses. There was additional investment in the form of a yeast press for £2,500, refrigerator at £220 and a cask injector for £34.

In 1923 EF Bates died and Thomas Buffey became a director, joined by HH Bates. The following year Thomas Irwin Bishell also joined the Board. In October they were looking at tenders for rebuilding the new brewery, they also sold off their stock of 9 gallon casks. The Board voted £6,700 for work at the brewery, which was expected to be completed the following year. This was partly financed by All Saints Brewery, who agreed to pay another £20 per month.

In 1925 the extension was completed but £1,009 over budget. WG Turner was the Chairman and MD, with T Buffey as the Company Secretary. Captain AFJ Roberts-George, the son-in-law of Mr Turner, was attending meetings. They were turning to imports again, with 2,000 quarters of Californian barley; not surprising given the price had fallen to 47/-.

In the April, Bass & Company were selling 19 country houses, but none were bought, in line with previous policy. They also decided against buying any of the properties of the Brackley Brewery which were available.

In June 1926 AE Barratt was the brewer on a salary initially of £360 pa rising to £420, with commission on the profits. In September 1927 Throne Crick died. Two years later, CE Saunders, previously the brewer, died.

The friendly nature of the industry could be seen in the donation of £100 to help with WL Everard's aeroplane. In October 1930 they gave £13 12s 6d for a wedding present for Ken Ruddle. However, the money did come from the charity account, which might unintentionally give an insight into how they viewed their rivals.

In 1931, the Board were looking at the estate in terms of the previous policy of rationalisation. In 1890, they had started with 49 freehold and 63 leasehold, giving a total of 112 properties. Now

**LEICESTER
(continued)**

they had 103 houses, of which only 3 were country properties. These were made up of 25 of the original freeholds and 7 leaseholds, together with 71 which were entirely new to the business. Around this time, Roberts-George was running the business.

The 1936 listing shows the address as 51 Charnwood Street. HR Welch was the chairman, AFJ Roberts-George the MD and T Buffey the Secretary. There was further work on the brewery in 1938.

The war years saw mixed benefits for the business. In 1941 Major TI Bishell was the Chairman, whilst Roberts-George was the MD. The following year, Lt Col Bishell was away on active service and Herbert Henry Bates was the Chairman. The latter was an engineer living at Teddington. However, the war provided increased sales to servicemen. The June Profit & Loss account showed £46,848, of which £10,788 was carried forward. There was also a large credit at the bank. Nevertheless, the business paid a price, when RL Martin, the Company Secretary was injured in a flying accident in March 1943. Worse was to follow, when Mr Bishell was killed in action in October 1944.

The 1945 investment, in a duplicate bottling line from Messrs Worrsam for £8,500 and a new washing machine for the mineral water stores at £600, represented the changing times and markets. However, the year after, they also bought a new cask washer and had the fermenting vessels copper-lined. RL Martin was able to re-join the business.

In March 1947, they were advertising for the post of assistant brewer. There were 20 applicants and G Noble was appointed on an initial salary of £900, rising to £1,000 in the second year. The Head Brewer at this time received just under £2,000, with a commission related to profits. That year they were paying 20% dividend on the ordinary shares. This was in addition to £20,000 to the reserves, £18,500 for deferred repairs and £15,800 carried forward. They had come out of the war in a relatively healthy financial position, allowing further investment of £5,291 for new plant in the bottling stores.

In October 1948, there was concern at the general fall in trade, although they were still making 20% dividends. In June 1949, there were still problems with trade, but these were put down to the continuing high levels of duty. Unfortunately, things worsened with the death of the Head Brewer Mr Barrett in the October and a heavy decrease in trade. It seems that Mr Noble moved up to become the Head Brewer. Still, the Board were optimistic for the future, as evidenced by the purchase of a 120 barrel pressure copper for £2,875, plus £1,550 buildings costs and for four fermenting vessels to be copper-lined at a cost of £1,237. However, there were delays with installing the new copper, because of problems with obtaining a building licence and it was May 1950 before the licence was granted. At least by this time, there had been some improvement in trade, although profits were down at £46,896. RL Martin was forced to retire as a result of his wartime injuries.

In March 1951, the Board decided to take a close look at the costings. Nevertheless, the following month they approved a new colour scheme for all their houses and in May the new copper was said to be working well. Profits for the year were up slightly at £47,076, although one director voted against the payment of a 13% dividend, and there was slight improvement in trade in July. There were still staffing problems on the brewing side, with a re-application for the position of assistant brewer. Eventually, a G Bodger from Worcester was appointed. His salary was £650, rising to £700 and the initial appointment was for six months. Both the amount and the contract were down from the appointment of four years previously, which did not bode well for the future.

In November 1951, the Board was looking to buy new mineral water plant and also to sell mineral waters to the free trade. However, "*draught beer still showed a decline*" and they were also considering dropping out of the Brewers' Society.

The following year saw profits down at £43,639 and an EGM on 22nd July 1952 agreed the sale of the business to Ansells and the payments to the directors for their loss of office. Ansells in looking at the business produced an adverse report on the barley and malt. The MD stated that he had previously told the Head Brewer, that he was not to buy Kenyan barley, nor home farm dried. In fact 75% of the UK purchases had been home dried, with consequent problems for germination. The Board interviewed Mr Noble and suggested that he was a good brewer but a poor judge of barley. He received £2,500 compensation for loss of office.

Ansells had bought 140 licensed premises, but perhaps because of the problems with the beer, they promptly closed the brewhouse, although they used the bottling plant and store until the early 1960s. One of the simpler changes was that, from the take-over, the minutes were typed rather than hand-written, perhaps showing the different style of the new management.

AE Wiley replaced HH Bates as the Chairman and W Scott became a Director in place of Captain AFJ Roberts-George. They were joined by AE Norris and JA Gopsill joint Secretaries, presumably Ansell nominees. Geoffrey M Barnett remained as a consultant to the new owners.

In September 1956, the freehold properties were sold to Ansells for £888,882, with the money left as an unsecured loan to them. The last entry in the minute books was for 12th January 1959, and the business was wound up soon after this date.

The brewery buildings on Upper Charnwood Street remain, with the dates of various extensions on the wall and an Eagle over the Vulcan Road entrance. They are now occupied by motor engineers. The Eagle motif can also be found on the Belgrave Hotel on Loughborough Road. The rebuilt Rainbow and Dove is still trading.

Letts, George, *Crown & Cushion, 32 Church Gate.*

The Crown dated back to at least 1815, when it was being run by Samuel Ward. In 1835 Charles Hawkins was shown as the victualler.

By October 1864 George Letts was the licensee and he was listed as the brewer in 1877. In 1888, Mr Letts leased the fully licensed pub to J Eadie of Burton; however, when he died his executors conveyed the pub to the Beeston Brewery Company. This ended in a court case after the licence was lost in 1897, because of the pub being used for immoral purposes. LB&M had considered buying the pub that year, but the convictions for allowing prostitution and use as a brothel were sufficient to close the pub on the 25th May.

Lomath, John, *King & Crown, 37 Town Hall Lane.*

Samuel Ross was running the pub in 1835. By 1870, John Lomath was the licensee at the Inn and identified as the brewer. However, in 1871 Charles Flewitt was at the pub and possibly it was then supplied by the Brunswick Brewery (see Flewitt entry).

In August 1878 Edwin Fox was the tenant, with the pub owned by John Foxon of Hinckley Road. There then followed a variety of tenants, with an average stay of about two years each, supporting the probability that brewing on the site had ceased. In the 1890s, it was owned by Ratcliffe and Jeffrey of Northampton, and then went to Phipps when they bought the former. Its address was then shown as No 33 and it was closed for compensation in January 1925.

Long, John, *Albion, 34 Albion Hill.*

By 1870 Long was at the pub, where he was listed as a brewer in 1877. In July 1880, the licence was passed to Sarah Long, but the pub was owned by William Langmore, brewer (see All Saints Brewery entry), and the following year Richard Hughes was at the pub.

In 1892 the address was shown as No 35 and it then became an All Saints Brewery house. The property was to be de-licensed in 1922 and sold for £870 and it finally closed in April 1923.

Lord, Mark, *St Nicholas Street.*

The 1826 poll book describes Lord as a brewer. He was still shown in 1835, but with the address as St Nicholas Square.

Lowe, William, *Pack Horse, 246 Belgrave Gate.*

In 1835 George Hunt was at the original Pack Horse, which had been on the site from 1539. In July 1868, William Lowe was the licensee, although the pub was owned by the Webster family. In 1870 Lowe was listed as a victualler, but was more clearly identified as the brewer for the period 1887-95.

In January 1897 it passed to his widow Ann and in the March, Richard Pick took over the licence and was in the directories as the brewer until 1902. However, it had been sold to Bass by 1916.

Manton, John, *Duke of York, 10 Southgate.*

In 1794 Charles Cramp was the victualler at the Duke, which in 1835 was run by Ann Yates.

In September 1844, Edward Kilbourn took over the licence, although the owner was a Mrs Martin or possibly Manton. Kilbourn was there until November 1875, when Mrs Elizabeth West took over the pub.

In March 1877 John Manton took over the pub and was listed as the brewer in 1887. In March 1888 Mrs Manton, possibly John's widow, took over and she held the licence until around 1901,

LEICESTER (continued)

when it went to a William Walter Starbuck. It may have been supplied around this time by Everards, who owned it in 1904. The licence was refused at the Brewster sessions and it was closed in May 1917.

Markham, Betsy, *Pine Apple, 16 Archdeacon Lane.*

In 1835 Matthew Green was the victualler at the pub. In August 1869 the licence was held by Joseph Markham, who was listed as the brewer for 1877 to 1887. However, in February 1884, the licence was transferred to Mrs Betsy Markham and she was identified as the brewer for 1892-1906 (F2719).

In May 1906, it was transferred to Joseph T Markham who was in the 1910 directory as the brewer. However, in February 1913, the licence went to Julia Sybilla Markham. There is a suggestion that in 1913 it was sold by LB&M, one assumes that they had bought it from the family, but then sold it on. There also seems to have been some involvement with Holes of Newark.

Nevertheless, in July 1914, it then went to John J Hull, who was recorded as brewing until 1920. When it closed in 1939 for a new pub on the corner of Grafton Place, Burley's Lane, it was owned by Holes.

Markham, William, *Brickmaker's Arms, 3/5 St George Street.*

In 1835 Thomas Palmer was at the pub. By 1861 William Markham was the licensee and property deals in Queniborough and Great Easton describe Markham as a licensed victualler from 1868 to 1882. He was listed as the brewer at the Brickmakers for the period 1877-84. However, in March 1877, Thomas Caswell actually took over the licence until 1886, when it passed to Charles Bond. He was there until June 1891, when John Talbot took over the pub. However, there is no clear indication that any of these individuals was brewing and by 1901 it was owned by Brunt Bucknall.

Matthews, Frederick, *York Castle, 45 Northgate Street.*

In 1835, the landlord was a John York, who may have given his name to the pub. From around 1870 to 1875 it was run by James Coulson, until John Goodwin took over for two years.

In 1877 Frederick Matthews was at the pub and was shown as the brewer from then until 1887. In September 1890 William Skipper was the licensee, possibly having moved there from the Wool Combers (see Cooper entry), before moving on to the Red Lion (see Gee entry). He was certainly at the York until September 1891, when it passed to Henry Burgess. In 1892 John Burgess was listed as brewing, before moving to brewing at The Green (see entry). Then in July 1893, John or James Halford seems to have been brewing here, after moving from the Milk Maid (see Alford entry). It closed for compensation in June 1895. The York was demolished sometime afterwards for the building of the Great Central. Halford then seems to have gone back to the Milk Maid, which he bought in 1896.

Mawby, William, *Prince of Wales, 56 Church Gate.*

The first mention seems to be in 1870, when Charles Bateman was running the beerhouse. For the period 1895-98 William Mawby was the brewer and the Mawby name crops up at various other pubs.

Midland Brewery, *44 Humberstone Gate.*

Although Friedrich lists this as a brewery site, it was probably never more than a depot. In 1865 it was a store for the brewery at Loughborough and in 1870 to 1881, John Meadows was advertising as a distiller and importer of wines, spirits and liqueurs.

In 1895, the advertisement for the Midland Brewery describes this as late John Meadows. After the take-over of 1902, Strettons continued to use the depot (F2720).

From a commercial directory dated 1895.

> **MIDLAND BREWERY CO., LIM.,**
> **BREWERS,**
> MALTSTERS, WINE AND SPIRIT MERCHANTS,
> Importers and Bonders, British Wine and Aerated Water Manufacturers,
> BOTTLERS OF ALES AND STOUTS,
> **LOUGHBOROUGH,**
> AND
> **44, HUMBERSTONE GATE** (JOHN Late MEADOWS), **LEICESTER.**
> Bonded Warehouse—No. 1, (L. & N. W. Rly.), Leicester.
> Ales and Stouts in splendid condition in Cask and Bottle.
> Fine Old Ports and Sherries. Purest Home-made Wines. Finest Old Whiskies and Brandies well matured in Bond.
> Burgundies, Champagnes, etc., of the Best Brands.
> Orders sent to the Brewery, Loughborough; or to 44, Humberstone Gate (LATE JOHN MEADOWS), Leicester, will receive prompt attention.

Miller, Thomas & Son, *Loseby Lane.*

In 1815, Thomas Miller Esq of London Road, was in partnership (from around 1811) with Henry Peach of Talbot Lane, as brewers in the High Street (see Watts entry). Thomas was Mayor in 1816, when he was described as a banker and brewer. His background was not known, but he was thought to have been born around 1766. He had two sons and in 1827, Miller, Son & Watts were shown as brewers and maltsters in Silver Street.

In 1835 the business was shown as Thomas & Son, also hop merchants and maltsters. In 1843, the business was listed as Miller and Son and in 1846 they were brewers and maltsters in Loseby Lane, with a home in London Road. However, the poll book for the following year lists Thomas as a gentleman living in London Road, whilst his son, Thomas junior, was described only as a maltster. Thomas senior died on 26th March 1849, although in 1855 Thomas Miller was a maltster in Calis Street. In 1867 William Everard was malting at 10 Calais Hill.

The brewery site in Loseby Lane may possibly be that which was then used by Welch Brothers. In 1870 John Miller was shown only as a corn and flour dealer at 31 Wharf Street.

Mitchell, Henry, *County Arms, 42 Chester Street.*

In 1864, the newly erected County Arms with its brewhouse was for sale, the occupant being an Henry Mitchell. Its location was described as being on the corner of Chester and Rodney Streets. It was later an LB&M house by 1900, which was compensated and closed in December 1930.

Moore, Methuselah, *19 Cank Street.*

In 1794, an E Moore was a victualler in the High Street, and in 1799 Francis Moore was at the Lion & Dolphin in the Market Place, which was for sale in 1802, with its new brewhouse. The latter was still at the Dolphin in 1810, but he died soon afterwards and the Dolphin was being run by his widow Ruth in 1812-15. However, the ownership of the pub seems to have included the Bates family of Halifax (see All Saints Brewery entry). It later became the Royal.

In 1827 Methuselah Moore was a wine and spirits merchant and also a dealer in hops, malt etc. in Cank Street and William Moore was a brewer in St Nicholas Street. Methuselah Moore was then listed as a brewer and maltster in 1835, through to around 1843. In 1846, Joseph Cooper Moore was shown as a brewer and maltster in Cank Street (see Boat, Thurmaston entry). However, in the following year's poll book, both he and William Moore were described as brewers in Silver Street. In 1855 Joseph Moore was listed only as a beer retailer in Peel Street.

Around this time, various members of the Moore family seemed to be running some 6 pubs. In 1870 John Moore was the victualler at the Crown and Dolphin, whilst Jas Moore was listed as a brewer's assistant, living at 126 Northampton Street. Samuel Moore was brewing at the Warden Arms.

The Cank Street site seems to have become owned by George Harrison soon after this (see LB&M entry). In 1898-1900, his nephew Henry Harrison Parry was listed as a brewer at 19 Cank Street as well as at Langham (see Ruddles entry). As with most central locations, the site is now used for shops, but Dolphin Square in the Market Place at least retains some memories.

Moseby, William, *Full Moon, 20 Russell Square.*

The pub dated back to at least 1835, when it was run by Charles Craythorn and in 1870 he was listed as a brewer at 25 Russell Square. He was also listed as the brewer for the period 1875-87, although the pub may have traded briefly as the Half Moon in 1875. However, one directory shows Christopher Cowper Craythorn at the Full Moon in 1875.

In March 1878 Joseph Palmer took over the licence, but he only held it until May 1879 when it was transferred to Harry Booth. However, in 1888 Harry Booth, was described as a bankrupt innkeeper/victuallers manager. He seems to have been involved with several properties, including the Nottingham Arms, Belgrave Gate and the Duke of Rutland, Oxford Street. The latter was owned by Cock & Langmore and closed in 1892.

However, in July 1883 the Full Moon was run by John Smart, who may have later brewed at the Talbot. Then in June 1885, it reverted to a Charles Craythorne, still shown as a brewer in 1895. On 1st October 1896, he sold it for £5,800 to LB&M, who may have already been leasing it. It was closed for compensation, £3,540 to the owners and £820 to the tenant, in January 1953.

Mosedale, Mr, *Crown & Thistle, 16 Loseby Lane.*

In 1781 Joseph Smith moved from the Golden Lyon to the Crown & Thistle, Loseby Lane, then in 1790 to the Lion & Dolphin in the Market Place. The latter was for sale in 1802 with its brewhouse.

The Crown and Thistle was for sale by auction on 24th July 1811, when Mr Mosedale was the owner. The Crown was described as having been in business for over 100 years. It had a roomy brewhouse, with the brewing vessels, coppers etc. recently bought in.

It seems to have been taken by a T Kirk, who as well as supplying the pub, also advertised his sales to local households. His advertisement also mentioned that he was selling tripe. He was clearly an enterprising salesman, since two years later he was advertising the availability of oysters, including a room at the pub for those gentlemen who wished to eat them on the premises. He may have been related to the Richard Kirk who had been a partner in Kirk & Soar, hop and porter merchants in Silver Street, before he set up on his own in Cank Street.

In October 1872 Julia Lee was the licensee, until in March 1892 it was taken over by Joseph Simpson. However, there was no mention of brewing and in June 1897 the licence was held by Orson Wright.

The pub was sold at auction in 1898. The auction also included the Magazine and the Town Arms, possibly all three being owned by the same individual. In 1907, it was owned by the Leicester Hotel Company, in which Wright was a major player.

Neal, Richard, *Rose & Crown, 31 Crab Street (later St Mark Street).*

In 1835 Francis Hubbard kept the Crown, which was shown as 31 Crab Street. However, in 1870 William Everard was shown at the pub, but it is not clear whether this was in connection with the brewery. Certainly, in September 1874 it was held by Richard Neal who was listed as brewing for 1875-87. Despite these listings, the licence in March 1877, went to Joseph Stacey and in February 1882, to William Needham.

The pub was shown as 31 St Mark Street in 1895 and shortly afterwards was supplied by the Cardington Brewery of Bedfordshire. Hence, with their sale in 1901, it was supplied by the Nottingham Brewery Company. The licence was transferred to the Salutation in October 1936 and the pub closed.

Needham, William, *County Arms, 97 Denman Street.*

In 1870, the property was being run by Thomas George Wilford, as an un-named beerhouse. It seems to have received its name in 1875, when Jas William White was the licensee.

In 1884 James Clark was the licensee until 1888 when it passed to Henry Heath. However, the latter was only shown as a beer retailer, but in 1895 Needham was shown as the brewer here. Prior to this a Matthew Needham was at the Bower in 1870 (see Cox entry) and from 1882 to 1888, possibly at the Rose and Crown (see entry).

In 1898 William Stretton was shown as the brewer, but by 1902 it was an All Saints Brewery house. However, the licence was refused in 1915 and the pub closed in the December.

Newton, Charles, *Peacock, 2 or 20 Belgrave Road.*

The Peacock dated back to at least 1700 and in 1835 Catherine Taft was running the pub shown as in Belgrave. In 1870 Mrs Elizabeth Hunt was at the pub.

In April 1874 Charles Newton took the licence; although the pub was owned by the Earl of Dysart. In 1875 Charles' advertisement mentions the home brewed ales. He also seems to have had a connection with the nearby New Inn at the time. The Peacock was described as off Belgrave Gate, on the corner of Syston Street.

He then seems to have briefly run the Old Mitre (see Burton entry). In 1883 Charles Newton a manager, previously at the New Inn, Belgrave Gate, was the victualler at the Haunch of Venison, 99 High Street, but apparently with financial problems.

It was supplied by Salts in 1898, but the licence was refused and the Peacock and the New Inn were demolished for the Great Northern Hotel.

Newton, John, *Sir Robert Peel, 50 Jarrom Street.*

In 1870 Joseph Mee was running the pub, whilst Newton seems to have been at the Bricklayer's Arms, 64b Welford Road. Then in August 1874, John took the licence for the pub, where he was listed as the brewer (F2721) in 1877 and 1887. The pub was owned by a Mrs Higgs, from whom Newton bought it. However, in 1892 Everards may have been supplying; although, from 1894 to 1897 John Newton was back as the licensee. It was run by Everards in 1912, but was later demolished.

Nichols, Thomas, *New Inn, 290 Belgrave Gate.*

In 1870 the address was shown as Wood Street. In November 1868 the licence was held by Nichols. He was brewing 1877-84 at the pub, which was owned by George Harrison.

Then in June 1878 Charles Newton (see entry) took over until February 1882, when it passed to Alfred Jesson. In December 1888 Edward Mason was the licensee, followed briefly by William Peck and Thomas Wright.

In April 1894 it was owned by the Beeston Brewery Company, with Nathaniel Mawby as their tenant. Together with the Peacock, the New Inn was demolished for the Great Northern Hotel, built at No 292.

Northants & Leicestershire Clubs' Co-operative Brewery Ltd, *Syston Street Brewery, 82 Syston St.*

The growth of the licensed clubs movement, was partly a reflection of the post 1869 control of licences and later restrictions on opening houses, together with the general growth of the labour movement. Although the Leeds & District Clubs Brewery had existed since the early 1900s, the real development of clubs' breweries did not take place until after the end of the First World War. The brewers had, out of restrictions on production, met the needs of their own houses first and left the clubs short of supplies. In addition, there was a link with the wider political view on the profits made by the brewers. Hence, growth was as follows:-

   1904 6,589 registered clubs
   1919 8,994 registered clubs

The Northants Clubs Brewery Union Scheme dated back until at least 1900, when AA Vince was the Secretary. At this time they were setting up to produce mineral water and may have been bottling beer soon afterwards (see Irthlingborough entry in Brewed In Northants).

In 1919 the Leicester branch was founded with the support of clubs with a total membership of 50,000, at £2 per member. In July 1920 the business was formed as the Northants & Leicestershire Clubs' Company-operative Brewery Limited (F2722). The brewery opened in 1921 and was listed the following year.

The brewhouse was in what had been the Syston Street maltings of John Henry Taylor (see Taylor entry), previously George Harrison in 1876, and shown in 1913 as No 84. Later they also had a transport department at 118 Gypsy Lane.

From the Jack Feast collection.

TRADE PRICE LIST

CASK BEERS			BOTTLED BEERS		
		BARREL		PINTS	HALF-PINTS
S.A. Strong Ale	8d.	132/-	PALE ALE	4/9 per doz.	2/6 per doz.
B.A. Bitter Ale	7d.	116/-	NUT BROWN	5/3 ,, ,,	2/9 ,, ,,
XXXX Best Mild Ale	7d.	116/-	I.P.A.	—	3/6 ,, ,,
XXX Mild, Light, Medium, Dark	6d.	100/-	STRONG	—	3/9 ,, ,,
XX Mild, Light, Medium, Dark	5d.	76/-	"CLUB SIX"	4/- per doz.	—

The above prices are NETT CASH at one month but are subject to a BONUS declared annually.
Returns must be sent back within one month from delivery or Credit will not be given.

Unfortunately, little has been discovered about the brewery's operations, other than a 1935 price list which exists in the LRO. In 1957 the name changed to the Midlands Clubs Brewery Ltd (or 1960 according to one House of Commons Report).

In February 1961, the product range was as follows:-

Golden Brown	Club Light
Royal Brown Ale	Club Six
IPA	Strong Ale (1055)

To **NORTHANTS & LEICESTERSHIRE CLUBS CO-OPERATIVE BREWERY LTD**
SYSTON STREET BREWERY, LEICESTER
M _Wellingboro' Labour Club_ Feb 1 1961

In addition to Guinness, they also wholesaled Double Diamond, John Bull, Artic and Graham's Lager. The latter brews were from Allied Breweries, perhaps representing the strength of their sales in Leicester. The brewery closed on the 24th January 1969 and the House of Commons Report on the Supply of Beer in April 1969 stated that the Monopolies Commission had been informed that *"due to poor trading, we have been forced to close our Brewery, and are now in the hands of a Receiver and Manager"*.

The remains of the Midland Clubs Brewery buildings.

Photo: Author

Their clubs became supplied by United Clubs Brewery of Pontyclun, which too later closed. Some of the buildings remain.

Oakland, Emanuel, *[Old] White Hart, 24 Metcalf Street.*

By November 1868, Oakland was at the pub, and for the period 1877-84 was listed as the brewer. However, in July 1876 Edward Weston took the licence and in November 1886 it went to Tom Orson. He was there for less than two years, since in August 1888 it passed to Sam Smith.

In 1899 it was owned by HH Parry of Langham. In 1900 JW Laxton the victualler was bankrupt, perhaps not surprisingly the pub was closed under compensation on 13th July 1907. The owners received £867 and the tenant £162.

Olphin, Mrs Mary Parker, *Generous Briton, 105 Wharf Street.*

The Briton was built in 1820 and in 1835 John Bushnell was at the pub. In July 1865, the licence passed to Mrs Mary Parker and she was listed as the brewer in 1877.

In August 1881 Charles H Olphin was the licensee and he was shown as the brewer for 1884-87. In February 1890 Alfred Blanch took over and he ran it until May 1894, when the licence was taken by Edward Henry Craythorne. By September 1895 it was owned by Brunt, Bucknall & Company.

Original Brewery, *Hollywood Bowl, Meridian Leisure Park.*

A Bass concept was launched with this brew-pub at Braunston in June 1995. The micro-brewery is housed in a ten-pin bowling alley, located at a leisure facility on the southern outskirts of the town.

The Head Brewer is Matthew Cook, with Assistant Brewer Dave Wood. Brewing Design Services provided the 5 barrel plant and 3 fermenters, giving a weekly through-put of 15 barrels. Full mash beers are then kept under CO_2 in casks and cellar tanks. The product range includes 2 bitters and 2 lagers plus an occasional special brew.

It is now part of a chain of 10 similar outlets throughout the UK, which are owned by Bass Leisure Entertainment.

The Original Brewery Company   Photo: Author

Orton, Samuel Thomas, *Fox & Hounds, 158 Humberstone Road.*

In 1835, the pub was run by William Mossendue. In 1870 John Orton was the licensee and in July 1873 it passed to Samuel Thomas Orton. He was listed as the brewer for the period 1875-84, the pub being owned by Jane Beckett. In July 1880 Christianne Orton took over the licence, perhaps on the death of her husband. A Thomas Orton, possibly their son, was later brewing at the Bowling Green from 1895 to 1902 (F2718).

In July 1883 Silas Oakland took over the pub and was listed as the brewer in 1887, when Martyn Collis took the licence. Thomas Blakeman, who had previously been brewing at the Mansfield Head (see entry), was brewing here between January 1890 and 1898. However, on 15th September 1898, he sold the pub for £9,300 to LB&M. At this time the address was shown as No 184. The pub was later demolished for Lewis' department store.

Pacey, T, *6 Southgate.*

The only entry for Pacey was for 1867, when he was listed as a brewer and maltster (however, see also Melton). However, he was not listed in 1870 and may only have operated as a maltster.

Paget, Thomas, *9 King Street.*

In 1911, Paget was described as a *"British wine brewer"*, living at Grace Road. He was listed as a brewer in 1913, but this may not have included beer, since he was shown as producing British wines until 1932. However, he may have previously been at the Blue Lion and before that at the Marlborough Head.

The business was for sale in 1936, when the address was shown as Saffron Lane. It was described as having 6,000 private customers and 240 wine clubs with 8,000 members. Thomas was living on Grace Road, Aylestone Park.

Paul, George, *British Arms, 83 Asylum Street.*

On 3rd August 1867, the pub was first licensed, when owned by George Smith, who may have been brewing and producing mineral waters. George Paul was at the pub in 1870 and the brewer until 1st June 1876, when it was taken by Tom Snow. Paul also produced bottled mineral waters such as ginger beer.

For the period 1887-92, John Snow was listed as the brewer. On 27th January 1892, Henry Earp took the pub and was identified as brewing until 1898. On 12th February 1901, it passed to Marstons, but then by 1906 it was in the hands of John Henry Taylor, malting in Syston Street (see entry). He later sold it to Bass by 1931.

Pegg, Samuel, *Stirling Castle, 41 Ruding Street/Charlotte Street.*

In 1827 Widow Hubbard was at the Stirling Castle in the Friars. In 1835 John Rogers was running the pub. By February 1841 Samuel Pegg had become the licensee.

In 1870 Pegg was running an iron and brass foundry, castle foundry and victualler. He was shown as brewing 1877-84, at the pub, with the name perhaps linked to that of the foundry. However, in August 1886 the licence passed to Sarah Jane Pegg.

In March 1888 Charles Bowler took over running the pub, but there seems to be no listing for him as a brewer. In January 1891, the licensee was a William Bates, but it is not clear whether he was linked with the local brewers.

In January 1896, it was owned by Brunt Bucknall, when the address was shown as 20 Ruding Street. It was closed under the compensation scheme in March 1927.

The nearby John Barleycorn, with brewhouse, was demolished in the 1890s as part of the railway construction. There was also a malting on Charlotte Street which was demolished before 1892.

Perberdy, William, *Woolpack, 1 West Bond Street.*

In 1815 Daniel Webb was at the Woolpack and in 1835 William Hopkins. In November 1868, William Perberdy took the licence, when the address was No 1 St Peters, the owner being a Mrs Handley. Perberdy was listed as brewing for 1877-84. The pub was later demolished.

Pilgrim, Charles, *Fortune of War, 14 Northgate Street.*

The pub dated back to at least 1835, when kept by William Howgill, with the address shown as North Street. However, it may have been called the Tiger in 1870, before reverting to the Fortune again by 1875.

**LEICESTER
(continued)**

In March 1867, Charles Pilgrim was the owner and brewing in 1877, before he was shown as brewing at the Sanvey Gate Tavern the following year. Pilgrim was later shown brewing at the Old Castle, Castle View from 1885 to 1898 (see Stevenson entry).

In December 1877 James Bentham took over the Fortune, but after this there was quite a turnover in landlords, many only staying for a year.

The licence expired in October 1896 and when the pub was demolished for construction of the Great Central, it was owned by Ind Coope, but the brewhouse may have still been in use.

Pougher, Thomas, *Willow Tree, 91 Willow Street.*

The Willow Tree is thought to date back to the 1850s. In February 1864 Thomas was the licensee at pub and shown as the brewer in 1877. In February 1879, the licence went to Sarah Grace Pougher, but in the August to Charles Cox, which suggests that Mr Pougher may have died.

In March 1883 James Brindsley (possibly Bindley in some directories) took over and was listed as the brewer in 1884. Then in July 1886, Charles Hampton Burrows took over as the brewer. On his death, the pub went to George White in September 1893.

In 1898 it was a freehold beerhouse for sale at £3,950 and by 1901 it was an Everard's house, at No 151, on the corner of Syston Street.

Preston, Nathaniel, *Cross Keys, 107 High Cross Street.*

In 1835 Isaac Gray was at the pub and in 1864 the Cross Keys was described as an old licensed inn. It was for sale by Mrs Deacon with its brewhouse in 1864.

In 1870 Mrs Sarah Hawley was running the pub until December 1874, when the licence was taken by Preston, who was then shown as the brewer for 1877-84.

In June 1885 it was taken by Henry Cotton, who was there until March 1887 when it went to William Mosley, conceivably the same person shown as William Moseby connected with the Full Moon. However in the October it went to William Henry Robinson. By 1896, it was supplied by Allsopps. The licence was refused and the pub was closed on 30th April 1924.

Preston, Samuel, *Rutland Arms, 180/2 Belgrave Gate.*

The first licence for the Rutland seems to have been in 1871. Preston was listed as the brewer for 1887-98. However, in 1888 he was described only as a beer retailer at 180, which in 1892 was shown as the Rutland. In 1898 it was sold as a free beerhouse for £2,850, with the annual rent of £35. By 1904 it was owned by the Nottingham Brewery Company. The licence was refused and it closed in May 1917.

Rawlings, Richard, *Keck's Arms, 50 Archdeacon Lane.*

In 1848 George Bishop was running the pub and in 1870 Thomas Liggins Foxon (see Foxon entry).

In September 1873, it was taken by Richard Rawlings, previously a leather worker, and he was shown as brewing in 1877. The pub was probably named after Anthony Keck, elected for the borough in the late eighteenth century.

In August 1877 the licence went to Mrs Maria Rawlings who for the period 1884-92 was shown at Burley Lane, but was actually brewing at the Keck's. Around this time Reuben Rawlings was running the Dixie, but with no mention of where his beer came from. In January 1889 the Keck's was an LB&M house.

In 1892 the address was shown as No 58. It may then have been combined with the nearby King's Head.

Read, Alfred, *George IV, 67 Wharf Street.*

The George IV dated back to around 1835, when Charles Palmer was at the pub. By 1870 it was simply called the George.

In May 1869, Read was the owner and listed as the brewer for 1877-87. However, in April 1886 the licence passed to Alfred Ewing, but only until the following February and this was followed by a series of yearly or six monthly stays. This suggests that brewing had probably stopped and by 1903 it was owned by Salts. It closed for compensation in January 1956.

Reynolds, John, *White Lion, 20 Market Place.*

In 1794 John Reynolds was at the pub and in 1804, the Leicester Journal mentions a Mr Reynold's malt office near St Nicholas Church. John Reynolds died in 1808 and the Lion was to let with an *"extensive brewhouse with mash tub to brew 4 quarters, copper to correspond... the whole well adapted to lessen manual labour"*.

The pub was taken by Thomas Hose, previously a butler. However, the following year, he had to retire because of ill health. The Lion then seems to have been used by John Messenger, who also seems to have been a confectioner on Belgrave Gate. John Reynolds' son, also called John, was at the pub in 1812.

In 1906 it was being run by W Elizabeth Bailey, but seems to have been owned by Peter Walkers of Warrington. Since this was their only pub in Leicester, it was presumably supplied from their brewery at Burton. However, at some point it was sold to Brunt Bucknall, before it was closed for compensation in May 1922.

In 1870 Watts & Sons had malt rooms at 70 Bedford Street, which were described as being next to the White Lion.

Richards, George, *Bowl Turner's Arms, 156-158 Belgrave Gate.*

Originally a beerhouse, the Bowl Turners was first licensed in 1855. In the 1870s several neighbours were still in the carpentry trade from which the pub's name derived. In 1870 Thomas Cattell was shown at the Bowl Makers, 156 Belgrave Gate.

In 1888 William Baynard at the beerhouse was bankrupt. In February 1891, the licence went to George Richards, who was listed as the brewer until 1920 (F2724). In November 1919, the licence went to Robert Hill, but the following January, W Thomas from the Brighton Arms had taken over and brewing had probably stopped. By 1931, the pub was supplied by Shipstones of Nottingham.

The pub is still trading, albeit somewhat refurbished The pub featured in the CAMRA guide selling "Shipstones" beer, although these are to be discontinued, the brewery having closed several years ago.

Robinson, William, *Duke of Cambridge, 1 Grape Street.*

In 1835 Lane & Robinson were porter dealers in High Cross and in 1835, a William Robinson kept the Black Horse, Granby Street. Then in November 1864, William Robinson took the licence of the Duke, which was owned by Edward Newton. For the period 1875-7 Robinson was listed as the brewer.

In August 1879, William Walker was the licensee, with the pub now owned by Joseph Sharp and others. The Brewers' Journal for 1882 mentions William Robinson of the Duke of Cambridge as a victualler; however, in the same year, William Walker was in liquidation at the pub and had moved to 25 Wigstone Street (now Welford Road).

In October 1882 Joseph Carter was the licensee, and the following year Edward Wheeldon. On 2nd October 1907 it was taken over by the Beeston Brewery Company, before going to the Nottingham Brewery Company later that year. In 1956 the licence was transferred to the Goodwood and the pub closed.

Roper, Charles, *Horse & Jockey, 46 Humberstone Gate.*

The pub dated back to 1835, when it was run by William Ball. In 1870 it was run by Henry Lamb, whilst Roper was a clerk. He was at the pub by November 1874 and was shown as brewing in 1877.

The pub was owned by the Hospital Trustees. Charles Coltman followed as the licensee, before the pub was run by the Goddards. By April 1903, it was a Beeston Brewery pub, but with the address as 212 Dorset Street.

Scott, John, *Horse & Jockey, 10 Northgate Street.*

In 1835 Thomas Thompson was at the pub. In 1870 it was run by John Wildbore, but in June 1874, James Coulson took over the licence. This may be the same person who had been brewing at the York Castle (see Matthews entry).

In February 1876, it went to John James Cooper Scott, who may well have owned it already. In 1877 Scott was listed as the brewer, but he was followed by a series of short-term tenancies and brewing may have stopped.

LB&M leased the pub in the 1890s, when it was briefly owned by the Manchester, Sheffield and Lincoln Railway Company. However, it was included in the 1899 Debenture Mortgage for the Midland Brewery of Loughborough and hence later owned by Strettons. It was closed under the compensation scheme in January 1956.

Seale, Richard, *38 Burgess Street.*

Seale was listed in Wright's 1894 and 1896 directories as a jobbing brewer. He presumably operated at the remaining brew-pubs when the landlord had neither the time nor the skill (see North, Loughborough entry).

Shelton, William, *Porter's Lodge, 36 New Bond Street.*

In April 1808, Shelton was advertising the sale of the Porters, which was on the corner of Swines Market. The sale included:- a 160 and a 36 gallon copper, 18 strike mash vat and 180 gallon cooler. The whole was described as suitable for any person going into the public line. The following year the pub was being run by W Forrester, possibly the William Forrester who was listed as a brewer on High Cross at this time (see entry).

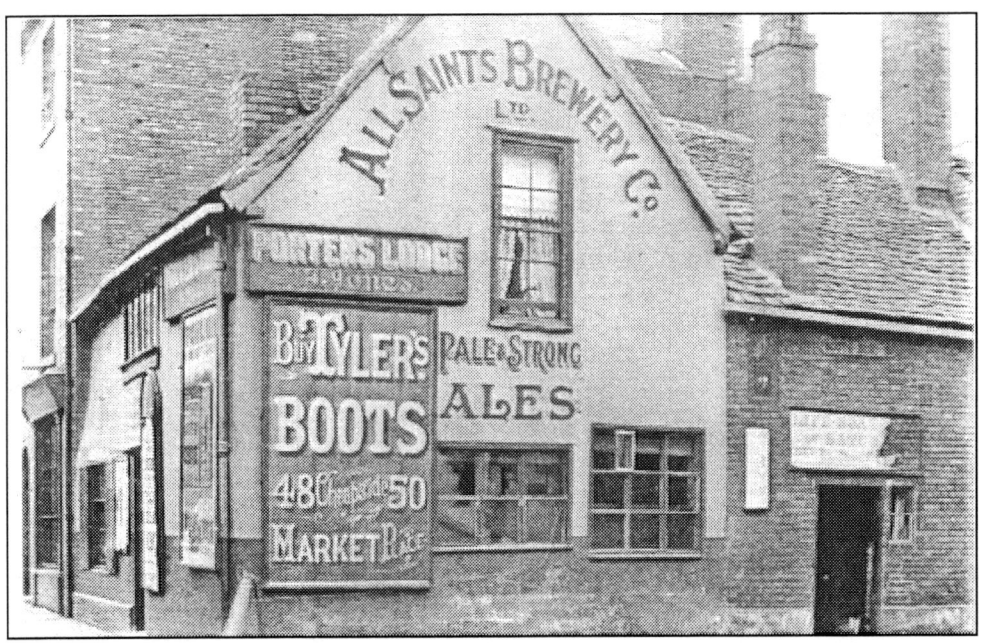

The Porter's Lodge c.1890 located at South and East Bond Street.

In 1835, Isaac Noon was running the pub. In 1874 it was owned by Cock & Langmore. The pub was supplied by All Saints Brewery in 1890, when J Jones was running it and they had ownership by 1910. It closed for compensation on 13th July 1907.

Siddons, John, *Northgate Street.*

Described as a brewer in the 1830 poll book.

Smart, John, *Talbot, 62 Applegate.*

From around 1835 to 1864, the Talbot was run by George Evans. In 1870, it was run by Joseph Glover and advertising "*Home brewed and Burton ales*".

In 1884 John Smart was a beer retailer and greengrocer, shown as at No 62. However, he was listed as a brewer for 1895-98 at the Talbot, 19 St Nicholas Square, on the corner of Applegate. Unfortunately, there was also an entry for 1887, which shows ownership by All Saints Brewery, with the tenant being William Henry Ganney so there may be some confusion with names and locations.

In 1933 it was agreed that the licence should be transferred for the new Coronation Hotel and the Talbot closed in January 1937. It was later demolished.

Smith, Charles, *Lord Raglan, 55 New Bridge Street.*

In 1870 John Bray was at the pub, but in November 1874 Smith took over the licence and was shown as the brewer in 1877. He had previously been at the Coach & Horses, 46 Oxford Street. The owner of the Raglan was one Betsy Bray of Humberstone Road.

In November 1879 Alfred Orton took the pub until 1881, when it went to his wife Mary Ann. In September 1895, it was owned by Brunt Bucknall and shown as No 35.

Smith, James, *King George III, 22 Wharf Street.*

In 1835 William Taylor Laughton was at the pub, whilst a William Smith kept the Hind Inn on London Road. Other Smith family involvement around this time included the following:-

- John Smith was a maltster in Freeschool Lane, previously in 1815 at Newark Street
- Richard Smith, maltster in Church Gate, and in 1846 a maltster and beerhouse keeper who also owned the Boat and the Black Horse, Thurmaston
- William Smith, maltster, miller and flour dealer at 35 Belgrave Gate, possibly in connection with Fleur de Lys which was next door

In 1870 James Lee was running the pub, which in October 1872 was taken by James Smith, although the pub was owned by Mrs Lee. In 1877 Smith was listed as the brewer.

In September 1886, the licence was taken by Charles Tallis and he was shown as the brewer here in 1892 (also shown as Challis in some directories). He had previously been brewing at the Oddfellows (see Kell entry). On 19th October 1898, he sold the pub to LB&M for £7,000. The following year William Tallis was the brewery's tenant.

The licence was transferred to the Shoulder of Mutton Hotel and the George closed in June 1939.

Smith, Thomas, *Old Black Lion, 71/73 Humberstone Gate.*

In 1855, despite the "Old", the Black Lion was first licensed only as a beerhouse. In 1884 Thomas Smith was at the pub, where he was shown as the brewer in 1887-88. In the 1890s it was owned by LB&M, who were still supplying it in 1948.

Spence, Thomas, *The Queen, 13 Blackfriars Street.*

Around 1892-95, a Thomas Spence was brewing at the Queen beerhouse. The Queen was described as having a brewhouse when demolished in the 1890s.

In the 1818 poll book, a Robert Lenton, shown as Linton in 1830, had been described as a brewer on Black Friars, but no other details have been forthcoming.

Spring, James, *Erskine, 6 Erskine Street.*

In 1864, the newly erected Erskine in Erskine Street, together with its brewhouse, was available from Mrs Harmer the owner, who was living on the premises.

In 1870, George Green was an artist and painter who was also listed as a brewer in Kelly's 1881 Directory. In 1884 it was kept by James Spring, described also as a porter brewer.

Stafford, George, *26 Newarke Street.*

In 1835 a Thomas Hull was a maltster and porter dealer in Newark Street and around 1846 to 1849, he was shown as a brewer and maltster and dealer. Then in 1849 he was a partner with the Everards. However, he seems to have continued to operate in his own right since he was still listed as a brewer in 1855. Two years later he was shown only as a maltster. In 1863 his address was shown as 26 Newarke Street, but in some directory entries for the early 1870s he may be listed as Thomas Hill.

In 1855 George Stafford was a brewer in Wilton Street (see Butler entry), but by 1867, Cook & Stafford had moved to the premises which had previously been used by Hull and were listed as brewers at 26 Newarke Street. They may have continued to supply the Wilton Street beerhouse. From 1870 to 1880, George Stafford was shown as brewing on his own and in 1877 was shown as a large or wholesale brewer (F2725).

However, from 1880 to 1884, Edward Masters was an ale and porter brewer, described as *"the Newark Street Brewery (late George Stafford)."* He advertised his Family Ale in 6 gallons upwards at:- 10d; 1/-; 1/2; 1/4.

He seems to have died around 1886, when the business was run by his executors. In 1888 the business had become Masters, E & Company, shown at 26 Newarke Street, but the following year the brewery at 2 Wilton Street was still listed, suggesting that the first address was being used as the office. The business was actually being run by Mrs F Masters.

From 1887 to 1896, the business was listed as Masters & Allen brewers. George Allen was

LEICESTER (continued)

Master's partner. The background to the Allen family involvement in the trade can be seen in 1870, when John Allen was a wine & spirit merchant and victualler at the Grapes, 2 Gallowtreegate and Thomas Allen was an innkeeper in Red Cross Street. Then in 1875, Southam & Allen were mineral water manufacturers on the corner of Yeoman Lane and Charles Street. Allen & Company were also wine and spirit merchants at 1 Humberstone Gate, previously run by Matthew Henry Allen who also had premises at 2 Gallowtreegate.

In July 1896, the partnership of Richard Charles Allen and Fanny Ann Masters was dissolved. This was not the end of the business, since in April 1898, RC Allen was floated as a limited company. This had 1,500 shares, held equally by AW Dymock, HR Welch and WG Turner, the latter then sold 400 of his shares to LB&M, where he was a director. It was set up to *"bottle beer other than that of Bass, Allsopp and Guinness"*. It was effectively a joint venture between three of the local breweries:- Everards, LB&M and Welch Brothers.

It presumably inherited some licensed houses from the previous business, since in September 1899, Allens were involved in the sale of the Gladstone Arms, 21 Thomas Street to LB&M. The pub was described as the property of the late John Masters. They also offered other services to the local breweries. For example in 1902 the cold store was being used for LB&M's hops. In 1907, the All Saints Brewery cold store space was shared between Everards and LB&M. The actual brewhouse is thought to have been demolished around 1904.

In 1913, the business was trading from 16 Oxford Street. RC Allen died in July 1918, but the business continued to operate under his name.

All Saints Brewery were supplying Allens with bottled beer in 1912 and Smiths of Oundle were also a supplier, in the 1930s. In 1942, when Offilers closed their Leicester depot because of wartime restrictions, they were looking to supply their local houses with mineral waters from RC Allen. The business was taken over by Praeds in 1951, possibly as part of the take-over of LB&M by Ansells (Brewed In Northants page 143) and the premises sold for £38,000.

Staines, Albert, *Waggon & Horses, 67/69 Belgrave Gate.*

In 1835 Charles Staines was at the pub, when Thomas Staynes was shown as a maltster in High Cross Street. The latter was shown as a cooper in St Nicholas Square in 1847. In 1870, Miss Charlotte Marie Staines was at the pub, which was owned by a Mrs Goddard.

In July 1873 Albert, previously a pork butcher at No 71 in 1870, moved here and was shown as the brewer for 1877-84. By October 1886 Staines was at the George and Dragon, Freehold Street, where he may have continued brewing. However, Elizabeth Staines took the licence for the George in 1887.

From July 1885 to 1892, James Lander was then brewing at the Waggon & Horses, which was shown as No 69. George Almey took over the licence in August 1893, but LB&M leased it from June 1894, when the inventory included the brewing vessels. On 24th June 1897, LB&M bought the pub for £4,500 from a Joseph Goddard. It was closed for compensation in December 1916.

Stanyon, Joseph, *Ship, 11 Soar Lane.*

In 1835 Edward Ward was at the pub, which by 1870 was being run by Joseph Catlow. In February of that year, Joseph Stanyon took over the licence and was listed as brewing for the period 1875-84.

In April 1882, Thomas Ward held the licence, and presumably he was a member of the family previously involved. In November 1883 it passed to Joseph Wilson who was there until June 1888, when William Potter took over the pub. However, the latter was only described as a publican, which suggests that brewing had already ceased. In 1895, it was supplied by the Beeston Brewery Company, when shown as No 13.

Stevens, Enoch, *Golden Ball, 21 Bakehouse Lane.*

In 1835 Richard Finch was running the pub. By 1870 Mrs Lucy Topp was the victualler. In December 1874 Enoch Stevens, previously a greengrocer, took over the licence and was listed as the brewer for 1877 to 1884.

In February 1878, the licence went to George Tompkin, but then there was a series of short-term landlords, until around the end of the century, when it became owned by Phipps of Northampton. One of these short-term licences was for one year from July 1880 by a George Ruddel, but it is not known if there was any connection with the later brewers at Langham.

It was closed for compensation of £1,739, and £239 to the tenant, on 13th July 1907.

Stevenson, Mrs Elizabeth, *Old Castle Inn, 12 Castle View, The Newarke.*

In 1835, when kept by Daniel Christian the address was shown as Newark. However, in 1861 T Addison was shown at what seems to have been trading as the Castle View pub. In December 1863 Mrs Stevenson was at the pub and was listed as the brewer 1877-84, although the pub was owned by the Duchy of Lancaster. However, the licensee in April 1882 was a Benjamin Walker.

In August 1885, the licence was transferred to Charles Pilgrim, previously brewing at the Fortune of War. He was shown as brewing here for the period 1887-92. In January 1898 the licence went to Jas Cooper Beaumont; although for 1895-98, John R Dean was listed as the brewer.

In August 1901 it was owned by Brunt Bucknall, but by 1936 it was owned by Everards and was still trading in 1964. The property seems to have been extensively re-built at some time and is now used by a conservation group.

Stonehall, George Henry, *Admiral Rodney, 82 High Cross Street.*

In 1814 a Mr Coltman was running the pub, which was built around this time. In 1835 Thomas Johnson was at the pub.

In 1870 Stonehall was at the Ram, 13 St Nicholas Street, when the Rodney was run by Daniel Kingston (see entry). Stonehall was at the Rodney by March 1872 and listed as the brewer in 1877.

In August 1876 William Billson took the licence, which he held until August 1881; however, in the 1880s it was owned by Mr Seckham and hence from 1901-1908 it was leased by NBC, the brewery which he owned. In 1909 it was a Brunt Bucknall property. It closed on 20th August 1910.

Tarry, Isaac, *Dover Castle, 34 Dover Street.*

In 1835 the victualler was Thomas Inchley Spawton. By 1870 Tarrey was at the pub and shown as the brewer for 1877-84, although the pub was owned by a Mr Powell of Newport Pagnell.

In March 1890, William Baker was the licensee, but with no mention of brewing. In December 1891, it was an LB&M property. The pub is still in business, with beer from Burtonwood.

The Dover Castle as it appears in the 1990s.

Photo: Author

Taylor, Adam, *Cherry Tree Inn, 43 East Bond Street.*

From 1796 to 1835 John Fossett was running the Cherry Tree, whilst in 1795 John Taylor was the victualler at the White Horse. Then at some point the Cherry Tree was transferred to the Taylor family.

In March 1869 Adam Taylor took over the licence and in 1877 was shown as the brewer. However, in March 1876, the licence was passed to Elizabeth Taylor. In May 1878 the licence was held by Arthur William Watts, possibly linked to the local brewery.

In April 1897 it was supplied by Eadies.

Taylor, John Henry, *109 Belgrave Gate and Syston Street.*

Although the Taylor family were primarily involved with malting, it is important to take note of them because of their links with the pub breweries of the town, including some which they seem to have operated themselves.

In 1794, William Taylor was a victualler at the Three Cranes on Humberstone Gate (now site of Boots). In that year, James Taylor was a maltster on Sanvey Gate and in 1815 Joseph Taylor was a maltster at Belgrave Gate. Then for 1835-48 John Taylor was shown as a maltster at 109 Belgrave Gate. For 1867-70 John Henry Taylor was the maltster at 109 Belgrave Gate.

In 1835 John Taylor was at the Prince Blucher, 136 Wellington Street and in 1846 Jas Taylor junior, was a maltster and victualler at the pub.

Also in 1835, William Taylor kept the Black Horse, Belgrave Gate, whilst also shown as a maltster in Bedford Street. Then around 1870, a W Taylor was listed as a maltster at 189 Belgrave, presumably the same site being used by John Henry Taylor.

In October 1891, John Henry Taylor bought the Syston Street maltings from LB&M, for the sum of £3,600. This suggests that his main business was in supplying malt to the numerous small brew-pubs which were still operating and which are mentioned elsewhere in the text.

John Henry Taylor was still malting in 1913 at 84 Syston Street. However, in 1922 his property was for sale and most seems to have been bought by Everards, though the British Arms on Asylum Street went to Bass. The maltings had already gone to the Clubs brewery (see entry).

Taylor, Mrs Sarah, *Queen's Head, 12 Town Hall Lane.*

In 1815 John Hurst was at the Queen's Head and in 1835 William Leman kept the pub. In March 1853, Mrs Sarah Taylor was at the Queen's Head, and also the owner. She was listed as the brewer in 1877.

In August 1879, the licence went to John Moore, but in April 1881 it was owned by Bates & Bishell. In 1892 the Queen's Head was trading as The Opera Hotel and it closed in January 1914, when it was supplied by Coopers of Burton.

Thompson, James, *Royal Oak, 7 West Bridge Street.*

In 1806 William Harrison moved from the Royal Oak to the Blue Boar on Southgate and Henry Hall took the Oak. In 1815 it was run by John Mudford and then in 1835 Robert Gardner. For 1846 George Johnson was listed as the victualler at the Royal Oak, shown as Bridge Street.

By 1870 John Thompson was at the Oak, shown as 7 Bridge Street. In November 1874 James took over at the pub, which was still owned by John, and was listed as the brewer in 1877.

In May 1883, the licence went to Mrs Sarah Thompson and she was shown as the brewer in the following year. She presumably continued to brew until October 1891, when the licence went to Martin Collis. It was owned by Thomas William Goddard and brewing may have ceased. It closed on 10th October 1897, when the licence was transferred to the new Balmoral Hotel on Belgrave Road.

Tompkin, William H, *Earl of Lancaster, 11 Goswell Street.*

The pub seems to have been first licensed in 1864 and in 1870 Johnson Tompkin was running the beerhouse. In October 1873, it was owned by Harriett S Tompkin, possibly his wife. William H Tompkin was listed as the brewer for the period 1892-98.

In 1921, it was an Everard's house, with the tenant Samuel J Tompkin. However, on 1st November 1922 it was for sale at public auction and went for £2,500.

Townsend, Fred, *Lord Byron, 14 Gravel Street.*

In March 1852 William Townsend was at the Lord Byron, which was shown as a small pub brewery in 1877. For the period 1884-1887 Henry Townsend was shown as the brewer.

William Townsend was then listed as brewing from 1892 to 1902 (F2726). In 1904, the licence was held by the Executors of Edward Townsend, but on the 12th February, Fred Townsend took over the pub. The last mention being for Fred in 1923, when the pub ceased brewing.

There were alterations in 1927, when it was supplied by M&B. In October 1939, the pub was closed and the licence transferred to the Huntsman.

Townsend, James, *Swan with Two Necks, 46 Granby Street.*

A pub dating back to 1777, the Swan had been kept by the Nutt family from 1778 to 1793 (see Lapworth entry), although it seems to have been owned by Thomas Peach in 1787. In 1794, William Watts took the Swan with Two Necks on Granby Street, where he was also shown as a maltster and brewer. Around this time a branch of the Watts family seems to have been partners of the Peaches. Francis Braithwaite, a dealer and chapman, seems to have undertaken a speculative building project which lead to the building of properties on Granby Street. This led to his bankruptcy in 1801 when the Swan and its brewhouse were included in the sale of 19 lots of his property. The pub was described as newly-built, which seems to be stretching the point a little.

At the time, there was no tenant at the Swan, although the year before William Watts was still the occupant and he was running the pub again in 1806. At this time he was advertising his purchase of porter and stout from Loughborough. Nevertheless, the pub may still have been owned by the Nutt family, until at least 1809. However, in 1808, Watts was again advertising the sale of excellent Loughborough porter and brown stout. He seems to have run the pub until around 1820.

In 1835 Jas Townsend kept the Swan, shown as 46 Granby Street/London Road, to the south of the town. In September 1865, William Watts was again at the pub, whose owner was Henry Brown. This seems to suggest that William may not have been directly involved in running the Watts' brewery on the High Street.

In August 1876, James Pole was the licensee, but there do not seem to be any directory inclusions for him as a brewer. Certainly in March 1897 it was owned by Cock & Langmore; hence in 1902 it was an All Saints Brewery house, with the address of 58 Granby Street.

Townsend, James, *North Bridge Inn, 1 Frog Island.*

In November 1872, George Collis was the licensee, with William Bowmar the owner. In July 1877 it went to William Leonard, but the following month it went to Thomas Holmes. Leonard seems to have later been involved with the brewing at the Sun (see Handford entry).

In December 1880 Reuben Thomas Cramp was the licensee, until November 1884, when William Tone took over the pub. He was followed in May by 1887 Harry Bray; however, there are no directory entries for these individuals brewing.

In August 1890, James Townsend took over the licence and was listed as brewing for the period 1892-95. However, LB&M leased it from at least September 1893 and bought it for £3,000 at auction, on 31st December 1894. It is now a free house, which takes Hoskins & Oldfield beers.

Tyler, William, *Admiral Duncan, 24 Fleet Street.*

In 1846 John Winterton was the victualler at the pub; however in February 1870 Tyler was at the pub and was listed as the brewer for 1877-84. The owner was George Harrison and later it went to HH Parry.

In July 1883, Wallace Phillips took over the licence and was shown as the brewer in 1887. However, in 1892 William Tyler returned as the licence holder. In December 1895 it was a Beeston Brewery house. It closed on 13th July 1909, when the owners received £1,593 compensation and the tenant £200.

Vann, Mrs Elizabeth, *Prince of Wales, 2 Crafton Street/Wharf Street.*

In 1870 John Millington was the victualler, but in December 1871 the licence was transferred to William Atkins, although the owner was Mrs Millington in Crafton Street.

In August 1876, Joseph Raven took over the licence and was listed as the brewer in 1877.

LEICESTER (continued)

However, in January 1879, it passed to William Henry Smith, but he seems to have missed the directory entries.

From August 1881 to 1886, it was run by Richard Vann who was listed as the brewer. He died on 24th March 1887, aged 44. Prior to this he had been at the Talbot, another small brew-pub (see Haddon entry). His son, also called Richard, was manufacturing mineral waters at 30a Crafton Street.

Hence in 1888, his wife Mrs Elizabeth Vann was running the pub, but Bass seem to have had an interest from May 1887. In 1892 Mrs Vann was the brewer, living at No 30. The son Richard junior died on the 16th June 1895, aged 30, and this may have been the end of family links with brewing. In 1901 it was a Bass house. It was due to close in late 1999.

Veasey, Samuel, *The Star, 30 Lower Church Gate.*

In 1884-86 Samuel Veasey was brewing at the beerhouse. Although the family business was listed as painters, they were involved with several pubs and prior to this a Samuel Veasey ran the Magazine Inn from around 1864 to 1876.

Voss, Henry, *Woodman's Arms, 18 then 22 Rutland Street.*

In 1835, the Woodman's was run by Samuel Freer. By November 1867, Henry Voss was at the pub and listed as the brewer in 1877.

In May 1878 the licence was passed to James Tabberer and then Edwin Charles Tabberer in August 1894, but neither of them seems to have been listed as brewers. In November 1905, it was an Everard's house. It closed for compensation on 13th July 1907, with the owners receiving £1,120, the lessee some £200 and the tenant £465.

Wainwright, Thomas, *10 King Richard's Road.*

In 1876 Thomas Wainwright was listed as a brewer, but not for the previous year. In 1880 Mrs Mary Wainwright was living at No 10, but in 1884 Thomas was again shown at the address. Since he was not described as a jobbing brewer, one can only assume that he was employed elsewhere.

Wakeling, James, *Old Ten Bells, 33 Sanvey Gate.*

In 1815 William Barnes was running Ten Bells and in 1835 William Cook was at the pub. By October 1864, James Wakeling was at the pub, which was owned by Thomas Johnson. Wakeling was listed as the brewer for 1877-84.

However in November 1883, it was transferred to Joseph Brown who was shown as the brewer in 1887. Given the names of the owners and the dates, this would seem to suggest a connection with the Hinckley Road brewery (see Brown entry). From 1889 to September 1892, the LB&M were leasing the pub, possibly due to changes at the Hinckley Road business.

However for 1892-1895 Mrs Emma Anne Brown was shown as the brewer. In September 1895, William Robert Barker took over the licence and was the brewer at the pub in 1898, whilst the owner was an H Oldershaw of Highcross Street. In April 1899 it was owned by Brunt, Bucknall & Company.

Ward, Frederick, *Marquis of Granby, 51 Welford Street.*

In 1835 Richard Pilcher was the victualler at the pub. In 1864 the Marquis of Granby, with an address on London Road, was for sale with brewhouse. There was also a 10 quarter malt kiln at the rear, in the occupation of SC Spencer.

In 1870-75, the address was shown as No 61 and the pub was kept by Thomas Toone. For the period 1895-98 Frederick Ward was the brewer, with the address shown as Welford Road. In 1898 Frederick Ward then seems to have moved to the Dog & Gun, Balby Gardens.

Although in 1901, Everards seem to have become involved with the pub, for the years 1902-1910, Jesse Chaplin was listed as brewing. Then for the period 1914-1921, William Marshall was brewing (F2727). However, it actually closed for compensation in December 1919 and was later demolished.

Watts & Son, *30/34 High Street.*

In 1791 to 1794, the partnership of Watts & Peach was shown as brewers in the High Street, and wine and brandy merchants in Loseby Lane. In the Universal Directory of 1794, the entry shows Watts, William, brewer and maltster in the High Street. He was also listed as a brandy merchant. He may be related to the William Watts who was running the Swan with Two Necks at this time. Thomas Peach was listed separately as a brewer in Saint Martins and also seems to have been a wine merchant on Loseby Lane. He was the eldest son of Robert Peach, who was a member of the malting and brewing family of Northampton (see Brewed in Northants for details).

In 1805 Thomas Peach, having recently been Mayor, was shown as a brandy merchant and brewer in the High Street and there then seems to have been a new partnership with the Millers (see entry). In 1815 Henry Peach Esq of Talbot Lane was in partnership with Thomas Miller, as brewers in the High Street (from around 1811). A Samuel Peach was also shown as the victualler at the Ram, St Nicholas Street. However, the Peach family interest in brewing at both Leicester and Northampton seems to have ceased around this time, although it is possible that their interests in malting continued. Thomas Peach had retired from business by 1820, living at Scraptoft Hall until his death in May 1823. However in 1848, a Joseph Peach ran a wine, spirit, ale and porter merchants at Butchers Row, Melton Mowbray.

Then in 1826, Miller, Son & Watts were listed for Silver Street and in 1827, Thomas Watts was a wholesale and retail, wine spirit and hop merchant in the High Street. William Watts was a liquor merchant, High Street, but in 1830 was described as a maltster and in 1835 as a brewer.

In that same year Watts, Thomas & Son were shown in the High Street as brewers, wine & spirit merchants, maltsters, hop merchants, porter dealers. However, William Watts was also listed as a brewer at Silver Street. In 1840, the business was still trading as Thomas Watts & Son in the High Street.

They were still shown in 1846-49, but as Watts & Son, brewers and maltsters in the High Street, with William Watts a maltster, home address London Road. In addition, Robert Watts was shown as a victualler at the Red Lion, High Cross. In 1848, the Red Lion was being run by Mrs Elizabeth Watts, with Henry Watts at the Old Peacock, 1 High Cross. Henry Watts kept the pub (previously kept by Thomas Sharp) until 1863. In 1803 the pub had been owned by Ald Oldham and the brewhouse was mentioned when Mr Moxon was the tenant.

In 1855, the business was again shown as Watts, Thomas & Son brewers, hop merchant and maltsters, High Street, also Silver Street. In 1861 the address was more clearly identified as 32/34 High Street. Two years later William Watts was listed as the brewer and a wine & spirits merchant at No 32, with his home being at Oadby. William junior was a brewer at No 34, and in 1870 was a corn factor there.

In 1870 Watts & Sons were shown as wine & spirit merchants at No 32 High Street and brewers and maltsters at 19-23 Silver Street. This suggests that all brewing had been transferred to the latter site. They also operated malt rooms at 70 Bedford Street, next to the White Lion.

In 1875 Alfred Edward Watts, of Watts & Sons, had his home at Flavell House, 1 Lincoln Street. William Watts had retired to the Isle of Wight, whilst Henry Watts was a corn factor at 21 Silver Street, with his home in Birstall. William Watts died in 1875.

In 1877, they were still shown as 30/34 High Street and the Silver Street Brewery, with offices at 16 Corn Exchange and the Gladstone Vaults, 27a Wharf Street. They seem to have taken the latter property around March 1874; it was previously the property of HB & AF Westbrook, wine and spirit merchants, but then became owned by a Mr Smith. This site later became the New Empire Theatre around 1893, but was closed for compensation in 1907. The High Street site, which became the wine vaults, was the location of the Royal or King's Arms. In 1656, this had been run by a William Lash, when the location was known as Swinesmarket.

Around 1877, possibly as a result of William's death, they had become linked with Cock and Langmore (see entry), certainly there were transfers of stocks in the February.

In 1877, an Edward Watts was shown as brewing at a pub in Atherstone, Warwickshire which in 1910 was owned by Watts & Son. However, it is not clear if there were any family connections. Interestingly, this brew-pub was run by an Augustine J Trivett in 1923 (see Market Bosworth entry).

In 1880 Alfred Watts of Watts & Sons was living at Wigston. In 1881, they were listed for 32 High Street and Silver Street, with maltings in Bedford Street. Then in 1882, the Watts & Sons,

LEICESTER (continued)

High Street and Silver Street, wine & spirits, hop merchants, maltsters and brewers partnership was dissolved (Brewers' Journal p383).

In 1890, the business was officially merged with Langmore and Bankart to form the All Saints Brewery Company, Watts & Son (F2728). They were trading at 30-34 High Street, 19-21 Silver Street and High Cross Street.

In 1891, Frederick Watts, aged 37 was living at Kibworth, together with his wife Agnes and two servants. However, there was also an AW Watts at 39a Humberstone Gate, the agent for James Eadie.

In 1896 with Langmore & Bankart they formed a limited company, where Frederick Watts was shown as the brewer. His sons seem to have become solicitors, but were also shareholders in the new company. Another shareholder was William Watts, described as a gentleman and living at St Albans, to where presumably he had retired.

The High Street site is now shops; however, Silver Street retains some connections with the industry. Although a modern building, the premises are still licensed as Spencers, an Ansells property.

Webb, Henry, *Nag's Head, 26 Millstone Lane.*

In 1870, Webb was a hay dealer and victualler at the Nag's Head, 19 High Cross Street. However, in March 1875, Webb was at 26 Millstone Lane and seems to have taken the name of his old pub, with him. George Green was malting in Steads yard next to the pub. In 1877 Webb was shown as a brewer.

In January 1885 Isaac Stanton took the licence, but he was only there for a year and there was a series of short-lasting owners until the Jelly family took the pub in 1889. In 1892, the address was shown as No 40.

In December 1896, it was owned by Bells and by 1905 Salts. It later become a Bass house, with their purchase of Salts. It was demolished in 1960 and rebuilt, and is now owned by Hardy and Hanson.

Welch Brothers, *St Martin's Brewery, 10/12 Loseby Lane.*

In 1843 Samuel Else was a brewer, maltster and wine & spirit merchants at 43 Humberstone Gate. He possibly moved to the Loseby Lane site used by the Millers (see entry) after 1849, since his brewery was thought to date from the late eighteenth century. In 1847, Richard Pepper Froane was an auctioneer in Bond Street East, but in the 1857 poll book was shown as a brewer in Loseby Lane.

In 1855, the business had become Else & Froane, shown in Loseby Lane as brewers, hop merchants and maltsters. In 1863 Else & Froane were listed as maltsters and brewers at 14 Loseby Lane, next to the Crown and Thistle, and at 50 Humberstone Gate. However, Alfred Else was an architect and surveyor at 12 Loseby Lane, his home being at 5 de Montfort Square. This would suggest that the Froanes had become the more active members of the brewing partnership.

The premises were rebuilt as a tower brewery around 1863 and in 1867 the address was shown as 12/14 Loseby Lane. In 1870, the Else & Froane brewery was listed at 12 Loseby Lane, ale and porter merchants etc., with No 10 being used by a bookbinder. Alfred Else, of Else & Froane, was living at 4 de Montfort, with Mrs Mary Else at No 5.

The maltings at 50 Humberstone Gate, were on the corner of Upper Hill Street. Richard Pepper Froane was described as the maltster in the business, living at 45 Waterloo Street. However, he died in 1870. Charles Henry Orton, manager at the brewery, was living at 56 Southgate Street. In 1875 William Salmon, at Else & Froane, was living at this address. Around 1871, the business may possibly have been trading as Alfred Else & Company as well.

White's directory for 1877 lists them at 10 Loseby Lane and Friar's Road. The Friar's Road maltings were built in 1872, but later demolished for the construction of the Great Central Railway in the mid 1890s. They were replaced by a building on Millstone Lane, which seems to have been bought from Coopers (see entry).

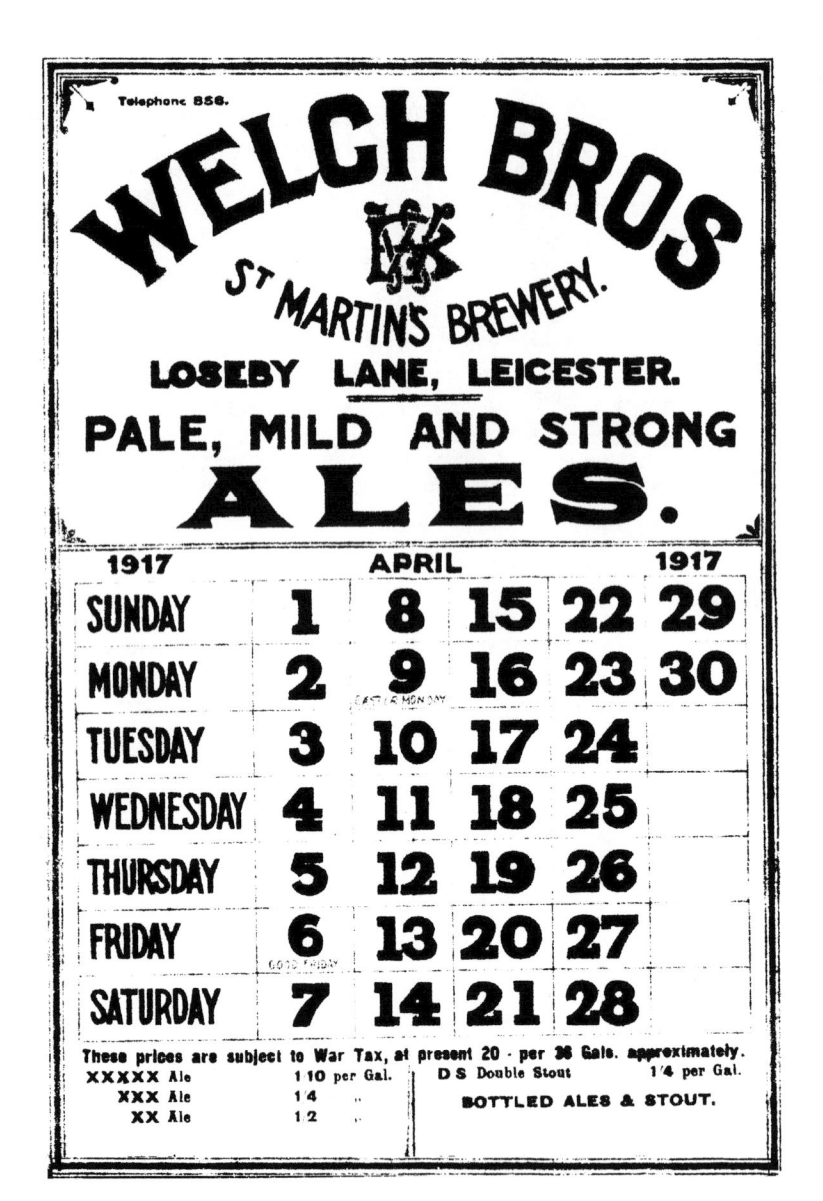

WELCH BROS
ST MARTIN'S BREWERY.
LOSEBY LANE, LEICESTER.
PALE, MILD AND STRONG ALES.

1917	APRIL				1917
SUNDAY	1	8	15	22	29
MONDAY	2	9	16	23	30
TUESDAY	3	10	17	24	
WEDNESDAY	4	11	18	25	
THURSDAY	5	12	19	26	
FRIDAY	6	13	20	27	
SATURDAY	7	14	21	28	

These prices are subject to War Tax, at present 20 - per 36 Gals. approximately.
XXXXX Ale   1 10 per Gal.   D S Double Stout   1 4 per Gal.
XXX Ale   1 4   "
XX Ale   1 2   "   BOTTLED ALES & STOUT.

Wright's 1881 Directory shows Else & Froane at 12 Loseby Lane and maltsters in Friar's Road selling - Pale Ale, Bitter Beer and Double Stout. Bennett's directory for 1888 shows the business as Else and Thorne; however, this series of directories was prone to errors and this was probably another one.

In 1888, the Brewers' Journal stated that Else & Froane had been taken over by Welch Brothers; however, the business was still shown in 1891 as Else & Froane (F2710). Nevertheless that year, Welch Brothers were listed for 10/12 Loseby Lane and in 1894 were also shown as maltsters.

In October 1897, Welch Brothers bought the Light Hussars, 142 Stoughton Street from LB&M. However, the following year the partnership of J Welch, HR Welch and A Welch was dissolved. There was investment in the business, with new maltings built at Millstone Lane.

In 1913, 43 Humberstone Gate was used by Warwicks & Richardsons, the Newark brewers. The following year the New Inn was sold to LB&M. Then in April 1917, partly as a result of the wartime restrictions on output, but also because of the close links between the local brewers, Welch Brothers arranged for their beer to be brewed by LB&M. In December 1919, they offered their houses, but not the brewery site to LB&M.

To finance the purchase, LB&M had increased their ordinary capital by £100,000. However, the LB&M minute books show a figure of £700 for the Welch Brothers houses and casks, which seems rather an understatement and at least £7,000 seems more likely. Henry Robert Welch became a director of LB&M. In line with LB&M's estate policy, the country pubs were sold and these seem to have included the following:-

Barley Sheaf, Whetstone   Shoulder of Mutton, Anstey
Fox, Barrow   Cock, Peatling

The sale included an off-licence, but no location was given. The sale was finalised in February 1923 and it seems that Ansells bought the properties for around £5,000.

From the Michael Jones collection.

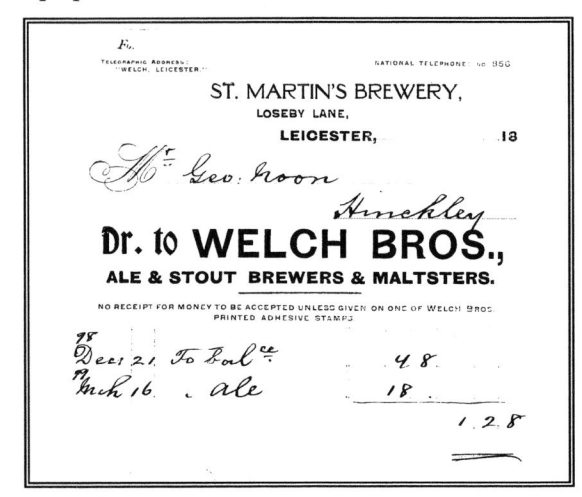

LEICESTER
(continued)

Arthur Welch seems to have moved to Farnham, where he died in 1940. He was described as a brewer, suggesting that he was still employed in the trade. His brother HR died three years later.

The brewery is a listed building, next to the old Crown & Thistle, and is now used as offices.

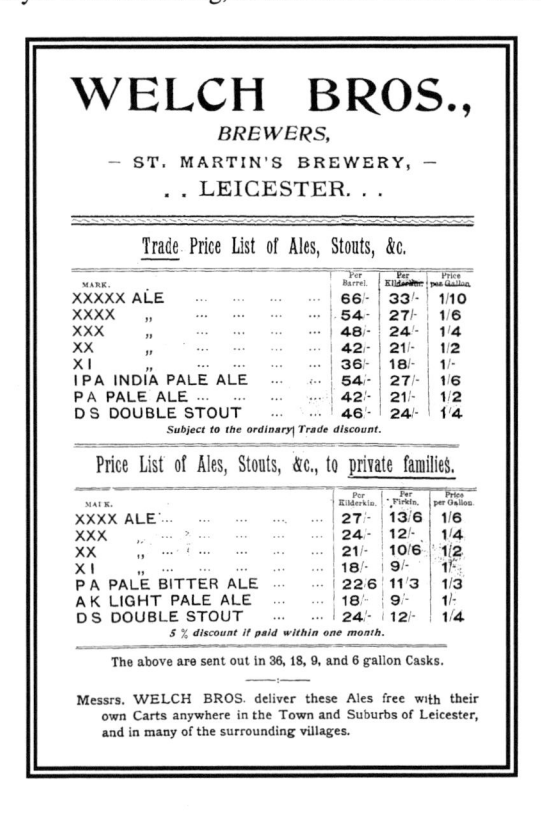

```
WELCH BROS.,
BREWERS,
— ST. MARTIN'S BREWERY, —
. . LEICESTER. . .

Trade Price List of Ales, Stouts, &c.

                                    Per      Per      Price
MARK.                              Barrel.  Kilderkin. per Gallon.
XXXXX ALE        ...  ...  ...  ...  66/-   33/-     1/10
XXXX    "        ...  ...  ...  ...  54/-   27/-     1/6
XXX     "        ...  ...  ...  ...  48/-   24/-     1/4
XX      "        ...  ...  ...  ...  42/-   21/-     1/2
X I     "        ...  ...  ...  ...  36/-   18/-     1/-
I P A INDIA PALE ALE ...  ...  ...  54/-   27/-     1/6
P A PALE ALE    ...  ...  ...  ...  42/-   21/-     1/2
D S DOUBLE STOUT ...  ...  ...  ...  46/-   24/-     1/4
            Subject to the ordinary Trade discount.

Price List of Ales, Stouts, &c., to private families.

                                    Per       Per      Price
MARK.                              Kilderkin. Firkin.  per Gallon.
XXXX ALE        ...  ...  ...  ...   27/-    13/6     1/6
XXX    "        ...  ...  ...  ...   24/-    12/-     1/4
XX     "        ...  ...  ...  ...   21/-    10/6     1/2
X I    "        ...  ...  ...  ...   18/-     9/-     1/-
P A PALE BITTER ALE ...  ...  ...   22/6    11/3     1/3
A K LIGHT PALE ALE  ...  ...  ...   18/-     9/-     1/-
D S DOUBLE STOUT    ...  ...  ...   24/-    12/-     1/4
            5 % discount if paid within one month.

The above are sent out in 36, 18, 9, and 6 gallon Casks.

Messrs. WELCH BROS. deliver these Ales free with their
own Carts anywhere in the Town and Suburbs of Leicester,
and in many of the surrounding villages.
```

Wells, Frank, *Stockdale Arms, 27 East Street.*

In 1870 Thomas Butt was at the pub and in February 1877 it was taken by Frank Wells, who was shown as a brewer with William Pears from April 1873 to around 1875. From February 1877 to April 1883, Frank Wells then seems to have been operating on his own. He was followed by Edward Hughes until October 1885, when the licence passed to Eli Hall. However, neither of these two seems to have been listed as brewers.

All Saints Brewery leased the pub from November 1889 and bought it in June 1899. It was valued at £3,508 in 1940. However, in 1956 the licence was transferred to the John O' Gaunt and the Stockdale closed in the December.

Wells, William Henry, *The New Plough, 2 Lower Church Gate.*

In 1799 the Plow and Crown on Humberstone Gate, together with its brewing vessels was to let, by Mr Harrapath. William Kealing moved to what seems to have become the Plough, from the King's Arms. However, this seems to have been closed and replaced by the nearby Crystal Palace, which was re-named the Plough.

Hence, the name of the New Plough, which in 1875, was operated by Goulding & Son at No 2, with Richard Goulding living at No 3.

Then in 1884, Thomas Wells was listed as the brewer. He was followed in 1895, by William Henry Wells as the brewer (F2729).

In 1898 John Knight was the brewer and then for the period 1921-23 John Sharpe was listed. In the 1960s it was trading as a Worthington house, but was later demolished.

White, Mr, *Lion & Lamb, 57 Gallowtreegate.*

The pub dated back to at least 1790, when it was kept by Joseph Atwell. In 1794 Richard Glover was at the Lion & Lamb, shown as the Market Place. On 29th July 1811, it was for sale with excellent brewhouse. It was later owned by the Foxton and then the Flude families and run by

Henry Flude in 1873 (see entry). It was later demolished for Central Building.

White, Jonathan, *Chelsea Pensioners, 46 Southgate Street.*

In 1835 Jas Taylor kept the Chelsea Pensioners (see Taylor entry). By 1870 it had passed to John Hubbard.

In April 1874, the licence went to Jonathan White, listed as the brewer until 1884. The owner of the pub was John Lang. In December 1886, Benjamin Charles Robertson took over the pub and was shown as the brewer in the following year. In May 1888 William Preston was at the pub, but with no mention of brewing.

In January 1897, it was run by Sharpes of Sileby. The pub was closed on 13th July 1907, with compensation of £1,087 to the owners and £250 to the tenant.

Whitwell, Henry, *Jolly Tar, 121/123 Wharf Street.*

For the period 1870-75 William Lenton was running the beerhouse. Around 1877 Whitwell took over from Lenton and was listed as the brewer.

In the 1890s, it was run by LB&M and in addition to the Jolly Anglers at No 122a (see Greenwood entry), they also had a New Jolly Anglers on Wharf Street! Leicester's location at the centre of the country obviously was not a problem for those naming local pubs.

Wildbore, William, *Cape of Good Hope, 34 Carley Street.*

Wildbore was at the pub in November 1869 and shown as the brewer in 1877, although the owner was a Miss Glover. Wildbore may also have been running the Hare & Hounds from around 1875 to 1877.

In February 1889, Thomas Burdett took over the licence and was there until March 1891 when it passed to Henry Hendrick. However in the June it went to James Harrison and in 1897 was owned by Sharpes of Sileby, with William Harrison as their tenant.

In 1921 it was included in the estate of Sharpes, although its supply may have been transferred to Strettons as early as 1902. It was closed in June 1955.

Wilkinson, Samuel, *Earl Grey, 26 Ashwell Street.*

Wilkinson was at the pub by November 1866 and was shown as the brewer in 1877. In August 1881 Joseph Fox took the licence; however, in 1897 this was a Sharpe's house which they exchanged for the LB&M's White Lion at Sileby. It may then have been included in the Oswin family's estate. The Earl Grey closed in April 1956, when the licence was transferred to the Mayflower.

Wilkinson, William, *Daniel Lambert, 54 Dover Street.*

The pub dated back to at least 1835, when it was kept by George Toone. Wilkinson was the licensee by 1870 and was listed as brewing for the period 1877-84.

However, the directories were again rather out of date, since in May 1877 the licence was transferred to Joseph Moore, but there seem to be no entries for him as a brewer. By December 1895 it was owned by Thompsons of Burton.

The pub stood on the corner of Albion Street; hence, around the turn of the century, the address was also shown as 1 Albion Hill. At the time, it became supplied by the Nottingham Brewery. It closed in June 1956.

Wilson Thomas, *Belgrave Gate.*

Described in the 1830 poll book as a retail brewer, but in 1832 simply as a brewer.

Windram, H, *Spitalhouse Brewery, 252 Belgrave Gate.*

In 1870, it was described as the Spitalhouse Inn, which was run by Henry Illsley (see entry). By March 1875, Windram had taken the licence and was listed as the brewer in 1877. In the July of that year William Green held the licence, but there do not seem to be any entries for him as a brewer.

In May 1889, the licence went to Walter Elton and he held it until his death in July 1891. Mary Ann Bella, his widow, took the licence for the pub, but the following year it went to William Pickering and the property became the Spitalhouse Hotel. On 5th October 1897, James Muddiman sold it to the Lichfield Brewery Company. It was still trading in the 1950s.

Woolman, John, *Welcome Inn, 23 Canning Place.*

In 1870 William Barratt was the victualler until July 1873, when John Woolman owned the pub, having previously been at the Butcher's Arms, 40 Church Gate. For the period, 1877-84 Woolman was the brewer and some tokens exist. However, in February 1878, the licence was transferred to Sarah A Woolman, suggesting that John may have died.

Then in August 1881 Arthur Riley took over the licence, until November 1883, when it passed to Walter Creasey. The latter was described as a victualler in 1886. In the June of that year it went to Thomas Henry Bickley, described as a brewer (see entry) and in 1888 H Bickley seems to have been the brewer. However, in October 1887 it seems to have gone to Oliver Wilson.

In March 1889, the licence was taken by Samuel Hopkins, but in May 1890 it went to Mrs Martha Mills Hopkins, who was listed as the brewer in 1892. In July 1894 William Mossendue was the licensee, but there do not seem to be any listings for him as a brewer and by March 1901, it was supplied by Robinsons of Burton.

Wright, Charles, *Rifle Butt, 16 New Bridge Street.*

In 1870 John Gardiner was running the Rifle Butt, whilst Wright was at the Barkby Arms, 1 Upper George Street. He moved to the Rifle Butt in November 1872 and was listed as the brewer in 1877.

In July 1887 John Pick was at the pub, but there does not seem to be any direct mention of brewing. By December 1904, it was an Harry Oswin property and supplied by the Beeston Brewery that year. It then went to Bass around 1914.

York, Arthur, *21½ New Bridge Street.*

Described as a jobbing brewer in 1894 and 1896, but with no further details.

LONG CLAWSON

Coleman Brothers, *Belvoir Hunt Brewery.*

In 1896, William Coleman was a farmer living at The Hall in the village. Then two years later, William and Thomas Coleman were shown as partners in the Vale of Belvoir Hunt Brewery (F3076). However, this was a very short-lived affair since the Coleman Brothers' business was wound up in 1900.

It is possible that this was an attempt to turn a farm brewhouse into a commercial concern by the sons of the family.

LOUGHBOROUGH

Abbey, John, *The Ram, 23 The Rushes, Derby Road.*

The Ram dated back to around 1799, when it was kept by David Farrow. Mrs Farrow bought it for £400 in 1809, when the tenant was Edward Gilbert. In 1835 Matthew Wild was the landlord and in 1870 Joseph Marsh was at the pub.

However, the first distinct mention of brewing was in 1877, when John Abbey was listed (F3091). For the period 1884-98, Mrs Anne Abbey was the brewer.

From 1922 to 1925, William G Green was starred in the directories as the brewer of beer retailed. On 6th December 1928, the local Midland Brewery bought the Ram from William Arthur Thompson. It was renumbered and rebuilt as the Swan, now a popular freehouse with a wide choice of beers.

Allen, Edward Thomas, *Wellington Brewery, Wellington Street.*

The first mention of brewing was in 1835, when John Mitchell was listed as a brewer in Wellington Street, until around 1840. Allen was listed as a brewer in 1876 and the following year, he was listed as at the Wellington Brewery, with offices at 53 Church Gate. Allen's home was in Park Street. However, there is some confusion, since entries in the Brewers' Journal for 1881 and 1884 mention Edwin Allen as a brewer's foreman, Burton Street or Burton on Trent, now Loughborough. The brewery was located near to the White Swan, which had previously been a brew-pub, and it is possible that the two had initially been connected.

Nevertheless, he was identified as a brewer living in Burton Street in an 1884 directory (F3092). The Journal entries suggest that he was in financial difficulties, which perhaps led to the sale of the brewery. Certainly, in 1894 an Henry Allen was the brewery foreman at Oldershaws, who seem to have taken over the site.

Barrs, William, *Nottingham Road.*

Freidrich has an entry for Barrs as a brewer in 1884; however, he does not feature in the local directories.

Berrington, William, *Old Pack Horse, 4 Woodgate.*

```
OLD PACK HORSE INN,
Wood Gate, Loughborough.
─────
SPIRITS OF THE FINEST QUALITY.
BASS'S BOTTLED ALE & STOUT.
FINE HOME-BREWED ALE.
Cigars of the Finest Brand.
GOOD STABLING.
H. BERRINGTON, PROPRIETOR.
```

From the Loughborough Almanac 1887.

In 1809, the pub was bought for £370 by a Mr Paget, with the tenant being a John Bates. This was a busy main road inn until 1820, when the coach road was straightened leaving the pub up a side street. At the time it was run by John Bales and then in 1835, by John Summerfield.

The Pack Horse was run by William Yates in 1870, but the first identification of the brewer was in 1877, when William Berrington was listed. For the period 1884-95, Mrs Harriet Berrington was the brewer. In 1888 she was advertising her home brewed mild beer.

In 1980, the Pack Horse was owned by Hardy & Hanson. The pub is still in business, on the corner of Pack Horse Lane. Externally, it looks unchanged and there is no brewery signing.

Birkin, Elijah, *Derby Road.*

In 1848-49, Joseph Birkin was running a beer shop and blacksmiths in Ward's End. Then in 1870 John Birkin was a beer retailer in Wellington Street and Luke Birkin was brewing at what seems to have become the Blacksmith's Arms, perhaps representing the family's previous trade (see Holmes entry).

In 1877, Elijah Birkin was brewing in Derby Road, but there was no entry for 1884.

Brotherton, John David, *White Lion, 9 Swan Street.*

In 1812, John Messenger moved from here to the Bull's Head and in 1835 Thomas Tyler was running the pub, possibly before moving to the nearby Saracen's Head where he was later brewing (see Tyler entry).

By 1870 John Brotherton was at the pub, where he was listed as the brewer in 1877. Then in 1884, Mrs John David Brotherton was the brewer, also shown as Mrs Jane Ann in some directories.

```
MARQUIS OF GRANBY,
Wood Gate, Loughboro'.
─────
S. BURTON, Proprietor.
─────
DEALER IN ALL KINDS OF
Foreign Spirits of the best qualities.
─────
HOME-BREWED, MILD, STRONG AND
BITTER ALES,
WHOLESALE AND RETAIL.
```

From the Loughborough Almanac 1887.

In 1888, the Lion was back with the Tyler family, when the licence was held by Henry Tyler junior (see entry). In 1894 William Kennington, the victualler, was bankrupt and James Harris took the pub. It probably stopped brewing around this time. It was later closed and demolished, and the site now seems to be a car showroom.

Burton, Samuel, *Marquis of Granby, 5 Woodgate.*

In 1809, the Marquis was bought for £610 by a Joseph Ball, with the tenant being Amy Capp. The pub was kept by Thomas Yateman in 1835. In 1870 William Faulks was at the pub, but the first distinct indication of brewing was in 1877, with the listing for Samuel Burton. He was still brewing as late as 1902. The pub was later closed under the compensation scheme in 1917 and was later demolished.

Cook, William, *Angel, 44 Baxtergate.*

In 1809, the Angel, with an associated malting, was described as being in the Market Place, when S Peck paid £410 for it. The tenant was a Thomas Andrews. However, the site later became the Midland Counties Bank. The Angel in 1835 was run by Elizabeth Hudson and in 1848 by Thomas Greensmith. In 1870 Emmanuel Dyball was at the pub, but again as a victualler.

LOUGHBOROUGH (continued)

William Cook was identified as the brewer for the period 1877-84, although the street was renumbered. By 1899 the Angel was owned by the Midland Brewery. The pub was not listed in 1913, suggesting that it may have closed under the compensation scheme. The building remains, now used as a dental centre.

Cooper, Henry, *Green Man, 12 Swan Street.*

In 1835, Hannah Bailey was running the Green Man, followed in 1848 by Samuel Bailey. The pub had previously been run by the Harleys (see Midland entry).

Henry Cooper was at the pub by 1870 and in 1877 was described as a brewer and maltster. He was listed until 1884, then in 1888 James Scotton was the victualler, but brewing may have stopped by then. In 1896, George Offiler, brewer in Derby, was listed in Green Man Yard.

By 1900 it was a CBB/Offilers property, which in 1913 was described as an Hotel run by J Knights and a target for compensation, at an anticipated £3,000. In 1963 ownership was transferred to Bass, who in 1970 valued it at £18,344, but it was demolished in 1971.

Cooper, Samuel, *Old Castle Inn, 54 Baxtergate.*

The Old Castle was bought for £385 in 1809 by William Polkey. In 1835 it was run by John Slater. In 1870 George Swan was a victualler at the pub.

Samuel Cooper was listed as the brewer for the period 1877-1884 (F3093). However, the site then seems to have been used as a brushmakers, next to Castle yard, and was certainly no longer listed as a pub by 1888. The site would now seem to be occupied by the health information centre.

Cooper, William, *Boat Inn, Canal Bank, Meadow Lane.*

In 1835, the address seems to have been Stamford Road, when the Boat was run by Bridget Turner.

In 1870, William Cooper was shown as being at the Boot, presumably a misprint, on Canal Bank, since the Boot was in Fish Pool Head. It was identified as the Boat in 1884. William Cooper, was shown as the brewer 1892-95. Prior to this, in 1809, a William Cooper was running the old established Grey Horse, which he had bought with its brewhouse for £600. The latter pub stood on the corner of Sparrow Hill and Baxter Gate and was later trading as the Mundy Arms.

The Boat is still trading and featuring in CAMRA guides.

Coup, William, *Royal George, Freehold Street, 23 Nottingham Road.*

In 1809, the Royal George seems to have been located in the Rushes, when a Mr Darker (possibly the same individual who bought the Windmill - see North entry) bought it for £230. The tenant at the time was a John Hopewell. However, in 1835, the George was shown as on Sparrow Hill and kept by Samuel Kirby. In 1848 Edward Gilbert was the victualler at the pub.

William Coup, shown sometimes as Coupe, was the brewer for 1877-87, but George Coupe seems to have run the pub in 1884. Mrs Ann Coup was then the brewer for 1892-95.

From 1898 to 1906, Samuel Coup was the brewer, with the address shown as Nottingham Road. Around 1922-5, Charles E Limbert was starred in the directory as the brewer of beer retailed, but not in 1932.

The pub, which has external signing for Ansells, is still trading, but has been rebuilt, possibly in the 1920-30s judging by the architecture.

Dakin, Charles, *Druid's Arms, 14 Pinfold Gate.*

From 1877 to 1887, William Webster was brewing at the pub, which was named after The Druid's Sick Club, for local stocking makers. The address at this time was shown as No 72. The pub seems to have been rebuilt around 1888, when the licence was transferred. In 1913, the brewer was listed as Arthur Webster, but he was actually running the pub between 1892 and 1914.

Around 1921-22, Charles Dakin was the brewer (F3104), but by 1924 the Druids was owned by Stensons (see entry), although Dakin was still listed as the brewer for the following year. In the 1950s, it was rebuilt and by 1980 was a Shipstone's house. It is now called the Bitter End and still carries Shipstone's sign, although the brewery in Nottingham closed several years ago.

Diggle, Samuel, *Hare & Hounds, 53 Ward's End.*

In 1835 William Martin was running the pub. In 1870 Samuel Diggle, linked with Claypole, Diggle and Hardy, who were coal merchants and bleachers in Ward's End, was the brewer. He was the brewer to 1884. He was followed around 1887-88 by Johnson Diggle as the brewer.

From 1894 to 1898 Mrs Mary L Diggle was brewing at the pub (F3094). For 1902-04, Henry Murcott was identified as the pub brewer. Then for 1906-1921, Thomas Webster was brewing; however, at some point it became owned by Sharpes of Sileby and was closed for compensation in 1926. It was later demolished for shops.

Farrers, Thomas, *Britannia, Castle Street.*

As a result of his debts, Farrers put the Britannia up for sale by auction on 19th October 1812. The sale included a 16 strike mash vat, 140 gallon copper and a 36 gallon one.

Fisher, John Thomas, *Crown & Cushion, 45 Ashby Square.*

In 1870, John Thomas Fisher was at what was then the Cap & Stocking, Ashby Place. In 1888, he was an hay and straw dealer and victualler with the re-named pub until 1894. He was listed as the brewer 1892-95. The pub is still in business with beers from Hardy & Hanson.

Fowler, Edward & Son, *King's Head, High Street.*

In 1810, the Talbot, described as being at the top of the Market Place, was for sale. Applications should be made to Mr Edward Fowler in the High Street, who also had a quantity of fine old malt to sell. Two years later he was advertising in the Leicester Journal that for sale at the brewery was *"fine strong ale at 2s 4d per gallon, in cask not less than four gallons"*. He also had fine bottled ale at 7s per dozen. There was clearly some competition in the town, with W Barlow, an ironmonger, selling brown stout and mild porter in 9, 18 and 36 gallon casks.

In 1835, John and George Fowler were running the King's Head. Although listed as maltsters, there was no mention of brewing. By 1846, only John Fowler was shown as a maltster. The Fowler family was one of the oldest in the town, with John Fowler a mercer/grocer recorded in 1665. The King's Head was rebuilt in 1927.

Gadd, Septimus, *Fox & Hounds, 20 Wellington Street.*

From 1884 to 1887 Gadd was listed as a brewer and maltster, but he also seems to have been trading as Wilcocks and Gadd in Hume Street (see entry). In 1888 James Harphan was at the beerhouse, but with no mention of brewing.

Gale, Jonathan, *Generous Briton, 51 Ashby Road.*

The pub dates back to at least 1835, when it was kept by George Green. In 1870 when run by Joseph Chester, it was shown as the Generous Burton, presumably a mis-print not an indication of the supply of IPAs. Jonathan Gale was listed as the brewer for the period 1877-87, but by 1899 it was a Midland Brewery property.

In 1894 to 1913, when kept by RB Squire, the address was shown as No 85 and later as No 81. The pub, which has been rebuilt, is still trading.

Giles, William, *The Wheatsheaf, 10 Ward's End.*

In 1835 John Humber was at the Wheatsheaf. Giles was at the pub from around 1884 to 1888 and he was listed as the brewer in 1887.

By 1900, it was owned by CBB/Offilers, with the address shown as Bedford Square. In 1970 it was transferred from Offilers to Bass, when valued at £15,250. This may be the building which trades as the Orange Tree, a somewhat peculiar shade of colour, presumably aiming at the passing student trade.

Grey, Frederick, *The Unicorn, 1 Church Gate.*

In 1835, the address for the Unicorn was Biggin Street, and it was kept by Elizabeth Goff, with Arthur Ball at 1 Biggin Street a hop merchant.

In 1870 John Parkinson was running the pub, when the address was also shown as Church Gate. In 1877 Frederick Grey was the brewer, but by 1884 it was kept by John McDowell who was only described as a victualler.

The Bass pub, which has been rebuilt, stands on Biggin Street at the entrance to Church Gate.

Harvey, Joseph, *The White Swan, 80 Wellington Street.*

In 1848 James Harris was at the White Swan, but by 1870 Matthew Gall was at the pub. However, the first clear listing of the brewer was in 1877 for Joseph Harvey.

In 1884, John Tom Gamble the victualler was bankrupt, receiving his debtor discharge application in 1892. The pub must have been continuing to have poor sales, because in 1893, William James the victualler was also declared bankrupt. By 1900 it was owned by CBB/Offilers, and it was valued for compensation of £1,750 in 1913. By 1967 the pub had been demolished, since the land was sold in that year.

Holmes, Herbert, *The Blacksmiths, 47 Ward's End.*

The pub was previously run by the Birkin family and known as the Black Boy Inn, Forest Road. By 1877, when it was run by Luke Birkin, the name had changed and in 1884 Thomas Thompson was running the pub and soon afterwards John Thompson seems to have been brewing there.

Kelly's directory for 1877 shows William Holmes as a brewer at the Nelson Vaults, 35 Market Place (NB Admiral Nelson 1815-1970, Everards 1895).

In 1888 S Pashley was the victualler at the Blacksmiths, but from 1892 to 1921 the Blacksmiths was run by Herbert Holmes, although in 1894 the address was shown as No 46. In 1904-14 he was identified as the brewer (F3095). Sydney Holmes was shown as the brewer in 1922-25, but not in 1932. However, the pub had been completely rebuilt in 1931.

It was a Home Brewery pub in 1973, when the address was shown as Bedford Square.

Hopkins, George, *The New Inn, 59 Baxtergate.*

In 1809, the New Inn was bought by Mr Marsden for £510, with the tenant being Edward Ratcliffe. In 1835 Charles Garret was the victualler at the New Inn, which by 1848 was being kept by James Gore.

George Hopkins was the first identified brewer for the period 1877-84. Prior to this in 1835, Thomas Hopkins was a maltster in Church Gate. The Albion on the Canal Bank, which beer guides describe as an old brew-pub, was being run by William Hopkins. Then from 1835 to 1846 Thomas Hopkins was a coal merchant, maltster, wharfinger and victualler at the Greyhound in Thames Street, Leicester. Thomas Hopkins junior was at the Cooper's Arms, Barrow Street, as a beerhouse keeper in 1882.

In 1882 Adams Arthur, the victualler of the New Inn was in liquidation. By 1884 George Blant was the victualler and four years later Albert Holland. In 1888, the owner, JO Hargreaves, applied to transfer the licence to a property in Oxford Street. The turnover in landlords suggests that the pub was not trading very well and brewing had probably ceased. The pub which was next to the Infirmary, was later owned by Shipstones and was still trading in 1980, but now has been closed and demolished.

James, Henry, *12/13 Market Place.*

Listed in 1884 as a brewer in the George yard and also at 5 Derby Road. He was also a wine and spirit merchant. The George yard had been a wine & spirit merchants as far back as 1835 for Thomas Capp. James at some stage was in partnership with Thomas Bryen. The trade-mark of a sailing ship represented the town's position as the furthest inland port!

However, by 1888 he was shown only as an ale and stout merchant, grocer and wine & spirit merchant. By 1894, he was only a merchant and he died on 27th January 1900. The Market Place has been very re-developed and no traces of the old site remain.

Lamb, Henry, *Old Talbot Inn, 9 Mill Street.*

In 1810, the Talbot was for sale by Mr Fowler who was using the maltings (see entry) and by 1835 was kept by Richard Cox. The address was originally shown as Fish Pool Head.

In 1835, Carter and Bird were listed as brewers in Mill Street, but no further details have been forthcoming.

For the period 1877-84, Henry Lamb was the brewer, but then Richard Cox seems to have taken over again. Charles Clarke was the victualler in 1884, but with no indication of brewing. The site was later that of the Golden Fleece.

A. HUTCHINSON,
DOG AND GUN INN,
59, Ward's End, Loughborough.

BASS'S BOTTLED ALE AND STOUT.
Home-Brewed, Mild, Strong & Bitter Ales
LEMONADE, PEPPERMINT,
Lime Juice, Ginger Ale, Ginger Beer, &c.
CIGARS OF THE FINEST BRAND.

GOOD STABLING.

From the Loughborough Almanac 1887.

JAMES LORD,
EAGLE INN,
CHURCH GATE, LOUGHBOROUGH.

WINES & SPIRITS
OF THE BEST QUALITY.
HOME-BREWED & BASS'S ALE
AND
Guinness's Dublin Stout.

A MARKET DINNER
Provided every Thursday at Two o'clock.

A QUANTITY OF STABLING AND LOOSE BOXES.
EVERY ACCOMMODATION FOR CONVEYANCES

PRIVATE QUOIT GROUND.

From the Loughborough Almanac 1887.

Lewis, Samuel, *Dog & Gun, 59 Ward's End.*

Samuel Lewis was brewing 1884-87 at the pub, but the following year was only shown as a beer retailer. Advertisements in the local almanac show that A Hutchinson had previously been brewing at the pub. From 1889, J Collins was there until it closed in 1913, when it was thought to have become a confectioners. However, the site seems to have been occupied by George Hall's wine merchants, trading in 1909, and is now shops.

Lord, James, *The Eagle, 30 Church Gate.*

In 1616, the pub was known as the Three Tuns. In 1809, it was bought for £325 by William Henson.

In 1870 Harry Harridge was at the pub which seems to have been re-named by then. James Lord was then listed as brewing 1877-84. However, in 1885 he was described as an innkeeper, who was bankrupt and paying a 4s dividend. In 1888 William Webster was the victualler, but in 1894, it was only a beerhouse run by Joseph Collin.

In 1953, it was bought by Everards and three years later, the name was changed to the Three Nuns, perhaps a pun on its original one.

Midland Brewery Company Ltd, *20/21 (later 12) Derby Road.*

The 1791 directory listed Messrs Harleys as brewers, one of only 3 such businesses in the whole of the county. This would seem to have been the business operated by two brothers, William (1755-1817) and Francis (1756-1821) of the Harley family, which originally came from Osgathorpe. In March 1804, W&F Harley were advertising the sale of a 400 gallon copper, made by Mr Richard of Burton. It was described as being very little worse for wear, having only been used for boiling worts.

This seems to imply that Harleys had replaced their equipment and extended their business. Local history books suggest that what became the Midland Brewery had indeed been built in 1801. Interestingly, in November 1804, there was an advertisement for a brewhouse, malt office stores etc. for carrying out the business of a wholesale brewer. This was to be let for a term of years and entered into immediately or at Christmas next, application to Mr Hardy who was leaving the business or to Mr Kirkman. Possibly he had been influenced by the investment at Harleys.

Certainly in 1806, William Watts at the Swan with Two Necks in Leicester was advertising that he had Loughborough porter and brown stout from a particular brewery. He emphasised that the previous year he had run out of supplies and his customers should take note.

In 1809, William and Francis Harley were operating a malting room in the Rushes. This was the site which was used by Robert Oldershaw in 1902. The Harleys also ran the Old Green Man and its maltings in Swan Street.

Edward Harley was shown on Derby Road as a brewer, maltster and cooper from 1835 to 1855. In 1855, the only entry was for Mrs Elizabeth Harley with no mention of brewing. Edward Harley, born 23rd March 1795, died on 29th August 1861, suggesting that he may have retired from the business. His wife, Elizabeth, was the daughter of Ambrose Brewin, a local maltster. However, neither of their sons, Edward Ambrose Harley and William Harley, seems to have joined the business. Their daughter Caroline married a John N Smith, possibly from the family of maltsters on Derby Road.

LOUGHBOROUGH
(continued)

In 1855, George Redrup was shown as a brewer in Derby Road and he seems to have taken over the Harley's business. On 7th February 1863, George Redrup, brewer, took out a patent for a machine for cutting shives, bungs etc. Around this time, the business seems to have been trading as G & JA Redrup.

In September 1865, the Midland Brewery Company was registered to acquire the Loughborough brewery and the stores in Humberstone Gate, Leicester. In 1870, John Sworder was listed as the manager, but between 1871 and 1876 Redrup was still shown as the brewer. However, in 1876 George Trease was listed as the brewer and the following year was also shown as the secretary and manager. In 1884, he was living at No 22, next to the brewery, and described as both the manager and secretary at the business.

In 1876, the Midland agency at 90 High Street, Leicester, was being operated by Charles Brunt Bowmar & Son (see Woodville entry).

In 1888, the brewery was described as being on the corner of Broad Street, with George Trease as the manager. Their price list was as follows:-

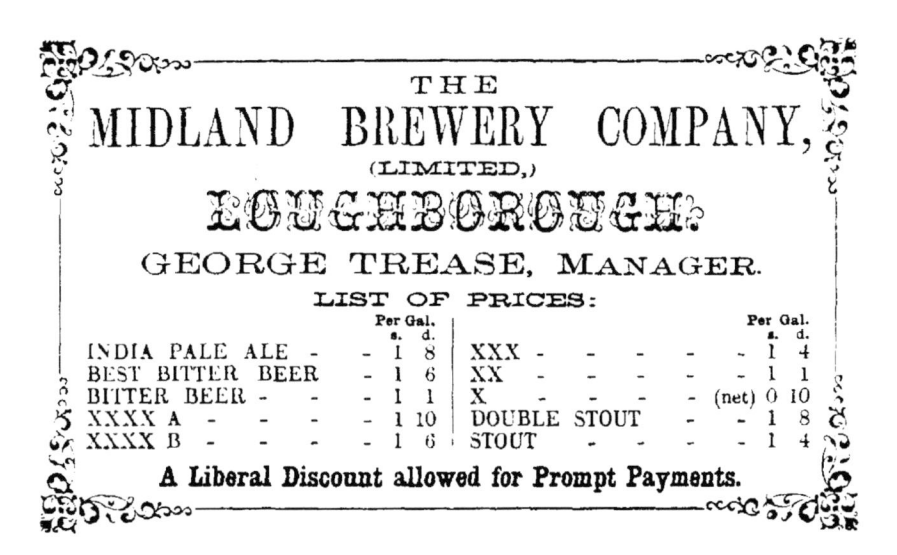

```
                THE
    MIDLAND BREWERY COMPANY,
              (LIMITED,)
            LOUGHBOROUGH.
        GEORGE TREASE, MANAGER.
            LIST OF PRICES:
                    Per Gal.              Per Gal.
                     s.  d.                s.  d.
  INDIA PALE ALE  -  1   8    XXX  -  -  -  1   4
  BEST BITTER BEER -  1  6    XX   -  -  -  1   1
  BITTER BEER  -   -  1  1    X    -  - (net) 0  10
  XXXX A  -  -  -  1  10   DOUBLE STOUT -  1   8
  XXXX B  -  -  -  1   6   STOUT  -  -  -  1   4
     A Liberal Discount allowed for Prompt Payments.
```

From a commercial directory dated 1885.

In 1891, it was listed as the Midland Brewery Company Ltd, with Benjamin Fisk shown as the secretary and manager (F3096). However, at the 26th Annual Meeting on 30th October, Alderman Griggs, the Chairman, was apologising for the fall in trade and the large quantity of bad beer in stock which had caused a loss. Despite income for the year of £29,000, they had shown a debt of £5355 on the Profit and Loss Account.

To remedy this, the former manager and brewer had been sacked and they were undertaking repairs to the brewery and the licensed houses. One of the shareholders, a Mr Clifford, proposed a committee of inquiry, but after some *"warm discussion"* the Annual Report was carried.

However, at the following year's AGM, Alderman Griggs was able to report a decided improvement in business, with a profit of £1,911 allowing a 4% dividend. He stressed that two things were essential for prosperity:- good reliable beer and access to a remunerative market. They had invested £830 in a new mineral water plant and all their houses were now tenanted rather than managed. A call to shareholders had raised £8,861, which as well as providing scope for investment, had helped to reduce bank balances by £6,000.

The 1892 entry for the local trade guide mentioned that the brewhouse contained a mash tub of more than 2,000 gallons. It also described the 72 unions which were being used for fermentation. They also undertook their own bottling.

Nevertheless, problems continued, since at the 1894 AGM, Henry Deane the Chairman explained the business and social reasons why his predecessor had left. However, he was able to report a profit of £2,261 on sales of £29,643, compared with a loss in the previous year. He stated that they had now recovered from the low of 1891 when net sales had fallen to £22,588, down £7,000 from the previous five years average. He praised the manager Mr Edn J Collins, who had put the business back on its feet. Nevertheless, the shareholders at the meeting were clearly still unhappy, since one proposal was to reduce the number of directors to three and another was to limit their remuneration to £25 rather than the expected £50. Both proposals failed to gain sufficient votes.

LOUGHBOROUGH (continued)

Henry Deane had retained the chair at the 1895 AGM and was able to report a considerable increase in profit to a gross £8,068 on net sales after discounts of £37,657. This would allow payment of a 5% dividend. The sales had been helped by the construction of the new railways, which had brought many thirsty workers. Mr Collins was praised for his efforts once more.

The brewery, plant and maltings were valued at £20,000, a large sum for the period, together with a small mineral water plant at £493. They also owned freehold pubs to the value of £31,858 and had leaseholds worth some £3,601. Salaries and wages for the year were some £3,393 in total. It was decided to carry forward money to the reserves, partly because of the need for new boilers, but also because payment would be due on the debentures. The agency at Leicester had moved to Highcross Street.

However, in 1896, an alternative use for the funds was found when the Midland bought Nuttall's brewery at Beeby (see entry). This was valued at £3,318, compared with the Loughborough brewery, and maltings. Nevertheless, the relatively small size was supporting an estate valued at £66,390. The nett sales of ales wines and spirits for the year end 31st August 1898 totalled some £44,516. The Loughborough brewery was in the books at £25,697 in 1898, suggesting some investment had taken place.

The 1896 AGM reported a steady growth of trade and the year as the most satisfying yet, with debts at the bank reduced from £5,000 to £518. The gross profit for the eleven months to 31st August was £9,803, allowing a 10% dividend. The property was in thoroughly good repair and full allowance had been made for depreciation. However, the following year 30 Midland shares, up for sale by auction, were withdrawn at £12 2s 6d.

January 1897 saw the recruitment of a new brewer. This was RG Percival who came from Marshall Brothers at Huntingdon. The annual dinner on 29th January was attended by some 50 employees. Mr Collins was in the chair, supported by JH Bennett, J Randle, JW Sculthorpe and Percival H Taylor. These were presumably the managers of the business.

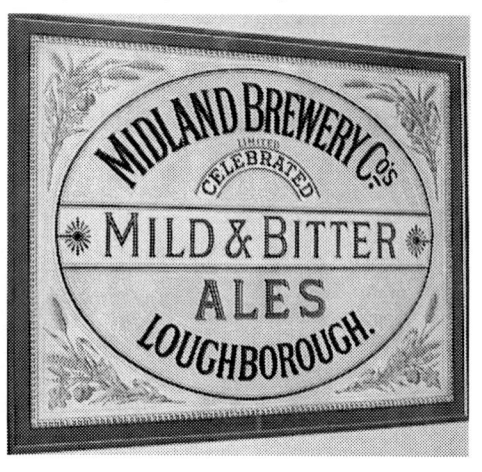

From the Jack Feast collection.

On 15th March 1899, there was a £75,000 debenture mortgage on the properties, the trustees being Thomas Hill and Charles Henry Aldridge. The money from the mortgage probably helped further growth in the estate, with the purchase of the Three Tuns, Melton Mowbray and the Salutation, Keyworth. They also moved their Leicester depot to 44 Humberstone Gate, where James A Hartopp was the manager.

In September 1900, the AGM reported gross profits £10,489, net £6,457. This allowed £3,000 to be added to the reserves, taking them to £10,000. Henry Deane was still the Chairman of the Company. The other directors were William Porter, John Sharkey, Charles Keightley and JA Saunders. EJ Collins the manager and secretary was taken on to the Board.

A further purchase in 1901 was the Royal Hotel, Long Eaton. However, in 1902 the Midland, together with 22 licensed houses and 11 off-licensed properties, was bought by Strettons Derby Brewery Ltd. Although the registered office became the Wardwick Brewery at Derby, the Midland continued to trade in its own right, for example buying the Britannia Inn, Queniborough and the Three Crowns, Barrow upon Soar in 1920, the latter from the 1899 trust.

In 1927 Allsopps bought Strettons, but seem to have kept the Midland site open, despite closing the Derby brewery, which became a mineral water manufactory for Burroughs & Sturgess. However, the Loughborough brewery was closed in 1932, when sales seem to have been handled from a depot in the High Street. In 1934, the debenture mortgage, which had been reduced to £36,000 was transferred to the General Investors and Trustees Ltd, and the brewing business was

**LOUGHBOROUGH
(continued)**

liquidated on 1st November 1935. The site was then developed as a chemical plant, which is currently being demolished.

North, Herbert, *Queen's Head, 4 Barrow Street.*

In 1870 when shown as being on Forest Road, the pub was being run by Mrs Caroline Hopkins (see entry). However in 1884 George Willett was the brewer, until in 1888 George Wilcocks moved here from Hume Street.

However, Willett seems to have taken the pub back again by 1894 and he was listed as brewing here in 1906. From 1910 to 1914 Henry Willett was listed as the brewer (F3105), although in 1910 it was leased by Sidney Wells of Kegworth (see entry). Sometime after, it was taken by Herbert North who was listed as the brewer 1921-23.

Around the turn of the century North had been the brewer for a local firm, then travelled around the district on his bicycle as a freelance brewer for home-brew pubs.

The Queen's Head closed for compensation in 1923, when the family moved to the Britannia. The Queen's Head was later demolished.

HERBERT NORTH, Licensed Brewer For Sale
LICENSED TO RETAIL BEER, WINES & SPIRITS FOR CONSUMPTION ON OR OFF THE PREMISES
LICENSED DEALER IN TOBACCO

North, Herbert, *Britannia Inn, 29 Pinfold Gate.*

In 1870, Charles Hutchinson was at the Britannia; however, sometime after 1877 William Russell moved here from the Half Moon, 21 Pinfold Street, where he had been brewing from around 1870. By 1884 William Russell was shown at the Britannia Inn, but almost immediately Charles Hutchinson took over and was there until 1888.

From 1892 to 1898, Mrs Eliza Hutchinson was described as running the Britannia Inn Brewery. Then in 1902-10 William James Hutchinson was the brewer.

Thomas Dakin (see Dakin entry) was then brewing here for a brief period in 1913. Then for 1914 to 1921 Walter George Dowding was brewing at the pub.

In 1923, the North family moved here from the Queen's Head and William North was listed as the brewer at the Britannia (F3099). The previous family occupation of brewing at other home-brew pubs died out as the free trade was bought up by the local breweries

The Britannia Inn as it appears in the 1990s.

Photo: Author

135

LOUGHBOROUGH (continued)

In 1935 Herbert North was listed as the brewer and around 1940, he took over the business, after his father and mother died. Frank Baillie's description mentions that unlike many concerns, no sugar was used in the brewing process and that Herbert North was extremely skilful at getting the most from his malt. The beer's natural ability to retain its head was also stressed. Baillie also described how the whole family of two sisters and four brothers worked towards the success of the business (Baillie pp73-74).

On 28 May 1972 Herbert North died, aged 64. His brother Harry took over the running of pub, but with supplies from outside, rather than the home brewed mild and best. The pub was sold to T Hoskins Ltd and in 1977 was a free house supplied by Ruddles; although, it now seems to be supplied by Bass and trading under the name "Peggy's Bar".

North, Isaiah, *Windmill, 62 Sparrow Hill.*

In 1809, the pub and brewhouse were bought for £540 by a Mr Darken of Nottingham. At the time, John Cleaver was the tenant. In 1848 Christopher Cleaver was a maltster at the pub, which he had kept from at least 1835. By 1870 Robert Speed was at the pub.

In 1877, Isaiah North was listed as brewing at the Windmill. In 1884, a Henry North was operating as an aerated water manufacturer at 37/38 Church Gate, on the corner of Sparrowhill, but also as an haberdasher at No 52. Benjamin Sharpe became the victualler until around 1888, with Mrs Emma Sharpe the victualler in 1894. Brewing seems to have ceased around then, although Luke Birkin was running the pub around 1900 (see entry).

In the 1970s it was owned by Ind Coope and later Ansells. The 1998 Good Beer Guide suggested that it was the oldest inn in the town.

Oldershaw, Robert W, *Wellington Brewery, Wellington Street.*

As early as 1812, a Mr Oldershaw ran the Turk's Head at Castle Donington and there were individuals with this surname at various pubs in the county throughout the century. However, the first useful mention was for 1877, when Robert Oldershaw was shown as a maltster in Pinfold Gate.

Then in 1881 Oldershaw Brothers were shown as brewers and maltsters at 34 High Street and the Wellington Brewery. Three years later, J&R Olderhaw were listed as brewers, and from then until 1888, they were trading as Oldershaw Brothers (F3097), with a brewery located at the end of Wellington Street. The brewery and maltings seem to have been located next to the White Swan. This was presumably the site previously used by ET Allen (see entry). Robert Watson Oldershaw was also a seed and cake merchant at 34 High Street, next to the Bull's Head, and a maltster on Sparrow Hill on the corner of Pinfold. The High street address was also his home.

In 1891 Robert Watson Oldershaw was shown as running the Wellington Brewery (F3098). The following year he was also listed as at a brewery in the High Street, which operated until 1898; however, as mentioned, this was probably only his home and office.

OLDERSHAW BROTHERS,
Brewers and Maltsters,
34, HIGH STREET, LOUGHBOROUGH.

LIST OF PRICES.

	PER GALL.		PER GALL.
X, Mild Ale	1/1	Bitter Beer	1/4
XX, do.	1/2	Best Bitter Beer	1/8
XXX, do.	1/4	Porter	1/2
XXXX, Strong Ale	1/6	Stout	1/4
XXXX B, do.	1/8	Extra Stout	1/6
XXXX A, do.	2/-		

A Liberal Discount allowed if paid within the Month.

From a commercial directory dated 1881.

LOUGHBOROUGH (continued)

In 1894, Henry Allen was the brewery foreman, with an address of 4a The Rushes, also shown as the address for RW Oldershaw.

In September 1900, Oldershaws bought an off-licence at Park Road, Blaby, from LB&M for £600, but few details of their estate and beers have been forthcoming. In 1915 RW Oldershaw was still shown at the Wellington Brewery, but by 1922 it had closed; however, he was still listed as a brewer at The Rushes.

Prior, Alfred.

Friedrich lists Prior as a brewer in 1871 and also at Sileby, but there are no other entries.

Roberts, John, *White Hart, 27 Church Gate.*

In 1809, Samuel Stevenson paid £425 for the pub and its brewhouse. It was later occupied by Hensons the coopers. In 1870 Roberts was at the pub and was also a stone and marble mason. He was listed as the brewer from 1877 to 1887. However, in 1894, Frederick Ellis was running the White Hart, but with no mention of brewing. By 1899, the pub was a Midland Brewery property. The pub is now a Forshaw's Quality Ale House, presumably supplied by the Burtonwood Brewery.

Robey, Samuel, *King William IV, 40 Pinfold Gate.*

The King William in 1835 was shown as being on Aldgate and kept by William Green. In 1870 John Bennet was the victualler. However, by 1877, Robey was shown as the brewer.

Mrs Sarah Ellis was the victualler by 1884 and in 1886 George Blunt, the victualler, was in financial problems, and brewing had probably already ceased prior to these difficulties.

By 1900 it was owned by CBB/Offilers, who later sold it to a Mrs Moore. The building, which now seems to be an Indian take-away, unless the street has been re-numbered, has probably been rebuilt.

Smith, George, *Peacock, 26/27 Factory Street.*

When in 1835 the Peacock was kept by Thomas Hudson, the address was given as Factory Lane. By 1870 George Smith was at the pub and between 1877-84 was listed as brewing. It was then taken by Samuel Clements, but there was no further mention of brewing.

The pub was a CBB/Offiler house at the turn of the century. It was valued at £8,000 in 1970 when transferred to the Bass property books. It seems to have been rebuilt around 1980.

Smith, Samuel, *Three Crowns, 16 Nottingham Road.*

In 1870 Samuel was at the pub, where he was shown as brewing in 1877. This may have been linked with Smith, John & Son, maltsters in Derby Road, where John Smith had been malting from at least 1835.

By 1884 William Perkins was at the pub, located at No 16, and was shown as the brewer in 1887. However, in 1888 William Derry Perkins, a victualler bankrupt at the Three Crowns, moved to Nottingham.

Arthur Dunkley was listed as the brewer for the period 1892-95, but the address was shown as No 36. Israel Smith was then brewing 1898 to 1902, when the address had changed again to No 56. Edward Arthur Hitherley was the next brewer for 1904-1921 (F3100).

In 1922, Miss A Brooks was listed as brewing, this time at No 36 and in 1925 Redfern W Hart was identified as the brewer of beer retailed, still for once at No 36. However, this seems to have been the end of brewing at the pub.

The pub is now a freehouse called the Tap & Mallet, although it has been rebuilt at some time.

Spencer, Henry, *Three Horse Shoes, 13 Nottingham Road.*

Henry was listed as a horse dealer in 1870, which perhaps explains the name of the pub which he seems to have opened soon afterwards. He was listed as a brewer in 1877.

For the period 1884 to 1887, John Riseam was shown as brewing. Although he was at the pub the following year, brewing would seem to have stopped. It was still trading in 1913, but the pub was closed in 1924 for £2,297 compensation and the site later became a motorcycle shop.

> THREE HORSE SHOES'
> Wine & Spirit Vaults,
> Nottingham Road, Loughborough.
>
> HENRY SPENCER, Proprietor.
>
> WINES & SPIRITS
> OF THE FINEST QUALITY.
> GOOD HOME BREWED ALE.
> CIGARS OF THE CHOICEST BRAND

From the Loughborough Almanac 1887.

Stenson, Frederick Alan, *Steam Brewery, King Edward Road.*

Although not shown in 1911, Frederick Allen Stenson was listed as a brewer the following year on King Edward Road (F3101), which was newly built. He is thought to have started originally as an ale and porter merchant around 1910. Certainly, a Rowland Stenson was a beer retailer at 44 Moor Lane in 1908, and the family involvement in beer retailing may go back some twenty to thirty years before this date. FA Stenson had married into the Sharpe brewing family of Sileby.

> TO THOSE WHO APPRECIATE A GLASS
> OF GOOD AND PURE ALE.
>
> **F. A. STENSON**
> **BREWER**
>
> **KING EDWARD ROAD, Loughboro'**
>
> Invites anyone to come and SEE THE ALE MADE
> FROM MALT AND HOPS ONLY.
> In Six and Nine Gallon Casks and Bottles.
> Guinness' Stout, Bass's Ale and Scotch Ale all in
> perfect condition.
> ORDER DIRECT FROM THE BREWERY
> **Wine and Spirit Department—SWAN STREET**

From the Loughborough Almanac 1939.

In 1922 the business was listed as King Street. However, as early as January 1924, Stenson was trying to sell the business to Offilers of Derby (see Cavendish Bridge entry). The business included a detached villa and brewery on King Edward Road, together with the following estate:-

Druid's Arms, Pinfold Gate, Loughborough	Blackamoor's Head, Loughborough, Market Place
Bull's Head, Diseworth	Navigation, Barrow upon Soar
Albion, Canal Bank, Loughborough	Old Plough, Sutton Bonnington

Together with an off-licence at Hall Croft, Shepshed and plant and machinery, stock and goodwill, the whole was available for £30,000. After an inspection by their MD, Offilers declined to purchase the business. Stensons' advertisements of the period state that not only could people visit the brewery to see how the beer was made, but that they could taste it "*free of charge*"! He also stressed that the beer was sold at pre-war prices, with the exception of Government duties, a novel marketing campaign.

> *Laugh more—Worry less—Live longer!*
>
> # F.A.S. HOME BREWED ALE WILL HELP YOU
>
> 6/- & 7/- per doz. Pint Bottles
>
> *Order Office:*
> **F. A. STENSON,**
> **SWAN STREET, LOUGHBOROUGH ∴ 'PHONE 242**
>
> *We stock everything in the Fluid line, and shall be glad of your enquiries!*

> *From* **KING WILLIAM IV.**, Retail Dept.,
> **QUORN,** .... 193......
>
> M ....
>
> *Bought of* **F. A. STENSON,**
> **BREWER AND WINE MERCHANT,**
> **LOUGHBOROUGH.**
>
> BREWERY—KING EDWARD ROAD.   Telephone No. 649.
> WINE & SPIRIT DEPT.: SWAN ST.   Telephone No. 242.

Despite the previous attempted sale, there may have been some extension to the brewery around 1930. In 1933, Stenson bought the King William IV at Quorn, which had been supplied by Offilers. However, in April 1935, the business was offered and rejected again at £12,000, but this time the estate included only the brewery, and the following pubs:-

Bishop Blaize, Woodgate, Loughborough   King William IV, Quorn
Falcon, Long Whatton

There was also a wine and spirit business on Main Street and the following February, Stenson was looking to sell this as a separate concern, but Offilers were still not interested and the brewery was still listed for the following year.

Yet again, on 22nd June 1948, the business was put to the board at Offilers for £50 to £60,000. The accounts showed a net profit for 1947 of £9,729, but Offilers suggested that this was more likely to be around £4,874, giving a value of £45,450. The properties were examined by HC Offiler and John Shields and found to be very poor and in need of spending. They declined the opportunity to purchase the business.

The brewery closed in 1951, but Stensons may have bottled until 1958. However, FA Stenson died in 1956, aged 79, the same year that the King William at Quorn was demolished. The brewhouse at Loughborough, which stood between Nos 10 and 18, may have remained standing into the 1970s, but nothing now remains.

Stretton, German, *Forester's Arms, Bedford Square, 7 Ward's End.*

Stretton was brewing at the Foresters in 1884, which by 1888 was run by William Hall. Little is known of the subsequent history.

Street, Frederick, *Stag & Pheasant, 11 Nottingham Street.*

In 1835 James John was at the pub, when the address was shown as North Street. George Tansley was brewing at the pub in 1870.

LOUGHBOROUGH (continued)

In 1884 Frederick Street was listed as the brewer, but he may then have moved to the White Horse. The Stag was then renumbered to No 24, probably when it was rebuilt in 1887, and was later supplied by the Home Brewery of Nottingham. Although it is now a hairdressers, the Home Brewery and pub names are still visible.

Tansley, William, *White Horse, 17 Bedford Street.*

In 1803 Nicholas Martin was a bankrupt innkeeper and the sale of his property at the pub included a good copper, 8 hogsheads and various other brewing items. By 1848 Thomas Glover was listed as the victualler.

In 1870 George Tansley was brewing at the Stag & Pheasant (see entry), whilst Joseph Tansley was running the Blue Boar. William Tansley was running the White Horse at the time and he was listed as a brewer from 1877 to 1887.

In 1888, the pub was kept by William Kennington, but he was only shown as a licensed victualler. The pub may have become the Garton Inn, which is the only licensed property remaining on the street.

Truman, Thomas, *Nottingham Road.*

The only mention of Truman as a brewer was a listing for 1877.

Tyler, Henry, *Black Lion, 6 The Rushes.*

In 1877 Mrs Mary Ann Bentley was brewing at the Black Lion, with the address shown as 6 West Street, Derby Road. In 1884 James Johnson was running the pub, with the address now shown as 6 The Rushes.

In 1888, John Henry Tyler was a maltster and farmer living at 5 The Rushes, with a malting in Meadow Lane, whilst Henry Tyler junior was at the White Lion, 9 Swan Street. Then from 1892 to 1914 Henry Tyler was the brewer at the Black Lion (F3102). The pub is now owned by the Wychwood Brewery and trades under their Hobgoblin name.

Underwood, William, *Fox Inn, 19-20 Baxtergate.*

By 1870, Underwood was at the pub and was shown as the brewer from 1877 to 1884. From 1884 to 1888, the address was shown as 17/18 when it was kept by Thomas Tyler, although Kelly's directories for 1877-87 also show Thomas Tyler as the brewer at the Saracen's Head, 21 Swan Street.

In 1894 John Henry Tyler was running what had become the Fox Hotel, which by 1899 was a Midland Brewery property. The site is now occupied by offices.

Walley, Leonard, *Bishop Blaize, 46 Woodgate.*

In 1835 John Shepherd was at the pub, on the corner of South Street. For the period 1884-1892 Samuel Walley was shown as the brewer.

Then for 1895-1921 John Henry Walley (F3103) was starred in the directories as the brewer of the beer retailed at the pub. From 1922 to 1930 Leonard Walley was the brewer. He was still at the pub in 1932, but no longer brewing. In 1935 it was owned by Stensons, but was bought by Everards in 1953.

Walls, Richard, *Duke of York, 58 Nottingham Road.*

In 1813, the Duke of York was for sale from a Mr Black. It was described as having a large brewhouse and being situated near to the canal bridge.

From 1835 to 1848, Joseph Henson was a timber merchant and maltster at the pub, whilst Ann Henson kept the Plough Inn, Market Place. In the 1840s John Henson was a cooper at the Three Tuns in Church Gate. This would seem to suggest that brewing continued to take place in the earlier period on at least one of these sites, probably the Duke. Certainly in 1877, Richard Walls was brewing at the Duke of York.

In 1888, when the address was shown as No 53, Thomas Barsby was the victualler, but with no mention of brewing. By 1894 the address seems to have changed to No 112.

Whitby, John, *George IV, 67 Regent Street.*

The George IV dated back to at least 1835, its name suggesting that it had been built shortly beforehand, when it was kept by John Copp.

LOUGHBOROUGH (continued)

By 1870 William Abel was running the pub, where from 1877 to 1884 John Whitby was then listed as the brewer. The next brewer to be identified was Elijah Cooke for the period 1884-98. However, in 1913, the landlord was only listed as a publican, suggesting brewing had probably stopped some years before. The pub was later closed and demolished.

Willcocks, George, *Cherry Tree Steam Brewery, 2 Hume Street.*

In 1884 George was listed as a partner in Willcocks and Gadd (see entry); however, he was also a victualler in his own right at the Cherry Tree. In 1888, he seems to have moved to the Queen's Head (see North entry) and William Cooke had taken the Cherry Tree, which is still in business.

Williams, Thomas, *Barley Mow, 38 Mill Street.*

In 1877, Thomas Williams was brewing at the pub, which seems to have been opened shortly beforehand. He was listed until 1895. The pub was later rebuilt. The address was then shown as Market Street and the pub was supplied by Home Brewery in 1980.

Withers, George, *The Griffin, 67 Ashby Place.*

In 1809, the address of the Griffin was shown as Bear Place, when it was bought for £600 by a Mr Cradock, with John Kiddier as the tenant. However, in 1811, the old Griffin was for sale having closed. This was followed by the sale of its brewing vessels. William Bryan was the owner at the time. On 16th March 1812, the new Griffin at the bottom of Mill Street on Ashby Road was for sale. The sale, which included the brewhouse, was a result of the tenant John Kidger leaving the business, possibly because of bankruptcy. Details were available from a Richard Attenborough, a maltster on Baxtergate.

By 1870 George Withers was at the pub and was identified as the brewer for the period 1877-87. The windows are etched with Marston's Horninglow Brewery and since they moved to the Albion Brewery in 1902, this gives both an indication of by when they had bought the pub and the possible rarity of the windows. It is still a Marston's house.

Woodward, Mrs Emma, *Cross Keys/Phantom & Firkin, 1-2 Leicester Road.*

In 1809, the Cross Keys was described as *"lately built"*. The tenant, John Sugden, bought the pub and brewhouse for £600. In 1848, when Henry Dougherty was the victualler, it was described as being on the corner of Pinfold.

By 1870 Joseph Woodward was running the Cross Keys, where in 1877 Mrs Emma Woodward was listed as the brewer. By 1884 it was run by the Harford family, but with no mention of brewing.

The Cross Keys then became an Allied-Domecq brew-pub, called the Phantom & Firkin. This opened in 1994 and also supplies the following Firkins:-

Fuzzock, Leicester Fourpence, Leicester
Fraternity, Oadby Fullback, Leicester
Physio, Leicester

THE FIRKIN BREWERY™

ALLIED DOMECQ HOUSE, 2 WATERLOO STREET, LEEDS. LS10 1JL
Telephone: 0113-200 2000 Fax: 0113-200 2041

The Head Brewer is Steve Jones, using a ten barrel plant with a maximum output of some fifty barrels per week. The three core beers are Best Bitter 3.8%, House Bitter 4.3% and Dogbolter 5.6%, together with a monthly guest beer. The beers are brewed from a full mash and English cone hops.

However, an earlier Cross Keys had famous connections. According to Colin Owen's book on Bass, in 1766 William Bass bought the assets of John Farrow of the "Cross Keys Inn" at Loughborough. This was presumably to extend his business as a carrier, since he did not enter the brewing industry until 1777.

Wootton, William Henry, *Volunteer, 13 Devonshire Square.*

The Volunteer was a late eighteenth century building, dating from the period of Napoleonic recruiting. In 1835, it was kept by David Ramsey. By 1870 Mrs Juda Wootton was running the pub. William Henry was identified as the brewer for the period 1877-84. In 1888, he was shown as a brass founder and victualler at 13 Cattle Market.

In 1891 Edward Brindley was the victualler at pub, although there was no mention of brewing. He had previously been at the Albion Hotel in Whitby, and after financial difficulties at the Volunteer, he then moved to Derby.

Around 1913 it seems to have been renamed the Volunteer Hotel, and supplied by Eadies of Burton. In 1978 the Bass plans to demolish and sell the site were fought by the local CAMRA branch. A preservation order was placed on the building, but subsequently it seems to have been converted to a bank rather than the shop which was the original intent.

Wright, Mrs Ann, *Old English Gentleman, 23 Ashby Road.*

In 1870 there was no mention of the pub, suggesting that it was either built or re-named shortly afterwards. Certainly by 1877 Mrs Wright was shown as the brewer, being listed until 1884. That year Tom Cooper was at the pub, but by 1888 he had moved to the King William IV, Pinfold and Tom Thurma had taken the Old English Gentleman, which was then shown as No 26. In 1894, A Thurma was the victualler, with the address shown as No 104.

In 1900, CBB/Offilers leased it from Mr Lyatt or Lycitt. In 1970 Bass valued it at £12,500 and it is still trading, with a brewer's Tudor black and white frontage.

LUTTERWORTH

Buck, Thomas Palmer, *George Street.*

The first mention of the Buck family involvement with the beer trade may be in the 1860s when William Kelsey had an ale stores and butchers in Oxford Street. This was property owned by a Mrs Buck. He was the agent for the Burton Brewery Company.

From 1884 to 1892 Arthur Bannister (F3158) was brewing in the High Street. Originally from London, he had previously been working in Loughborough, but it is not known whether or not he had been at one of the breweries. Although known as Bannister's Brewery, it was also called the Steam Brewery, with the address shown as Beast Market. In 1887 Bannister was described as a steam brewer and wine merchant in Beast Market and wine and spirit, hop and ale and porter merchant in the High Street. In 1892-94, he was also shown as victualler and brewer at the Board. The Board may have been no more than a small lodging house and his own home was at The Elms. However, it was presumably not a very successful enterprise, since the previous year it had been offered to LB&M who declined to purchase it.

In 1895 the address was shown as Beast Market, but by 1900 it had been bought by Buck. He was then shown as brewing in George Street (F3159) from 1902 to 1926. He had moved from Walton, where he had been brewing at the Windmill (see entry); although the family seem to have been bakers in Lutterworth from the 1840s.

In 1906 he applied for a licence to sell in smaller quantities from the brewery. Previously, he had been limited to a minimum of 4½ gallons or two dozen quarts. In future, he would be allowed to deal in quantities of 2 gallons, one dozen pints or two dozen half pints. The family trade was very important to small scale brewers such as Buck.

> # THOS. P. BUCK,
> ## BREWER AND — —
> ## SPIRIT MERCHANT.
>
> ✻ FAMOUS PURE ✻
> ## HOME-BREWED ALES,
>
> In Casks of 6 Gals. and upwards.
> In Bottle Pints, 3/6 per doz.
> " " Half-Pints, 4/- per 2 doz
> " Quarts, 3/- per half-doz.
>
> ## Xmas Strong Ale 4/- Per Doz Pints.
> A TRIAL SOLICITED.
> *Malt and Hops at lowest Market Prices.*
> HIGH-CLASS SPIRITS DIRECT FROM THE MOST FAMOUS DISTILLERIES.
> ☞ PRICE LIST ON APPLICATION.
>
> ## THE BREWERY, LUTTERWORTH.

From Bottrill's Almanac 1915.

The brewery was behind Buck's off-licence (SP545845). In 1914 it was described as an half-tower brewery, with 4 tied houses:-

- Royal Oak, Bitteswell, later sold to Thornley of Leamington
- Cock Inn, Peatling Magna, later sold to Holes of Newark
- Shoulder of Mutton, later sold to M&B then de-licensed
- Windmill, Walton, at some point became a Banks' pub

The Royal Oak, Valley Lane, Bitteswell c.1910.

LUTTERWORTH (continued)

He also had malt and hops at the lowest market prices. He may also have been supplying the Old Cock at Arnesby, which was sold to a Mr Adams for £700 in 1920. At some point he also owned the Barley Sheaf at Whetstone.

Mr Buck was still listed as brewing in 1922, but in February 1923, there was a sale at auction of the following properties:-

Windmill, Walton	£1,000	Shoulder of Mutton, Arnesby	£ 900
Hat & Beaver, Atherstone	£ 750	Off-licence, Portland Street, Cosby	

The sale fell through and the prices are those quoted for the properties to Offilers of Derby. The Cosby off-licence was on sale again in 1925 at £1,000.

In 1931, three of TP Buck & Son's properties were mortgaged to Elworthy's of Kettering for £2,500 at 5%. Elworthy's were supplying some 970 barrels of beer to Bucks, who in turn bottled the equivalent of some 360 barrels, which were then re-sold back to them. Elworthys were also supplying some 122 gallons of wines and spirits and this with the beer would probably have been sufficient to supply the whole of Buck's estate. Elworthys were also supplying a Mr Buck at the High Street in Husbands Bosworth.

Although the purchase had fallen to 539 barrels the following year, this may have been caused by the closure of the Kettering brewery and its sale to Marstons, which operated a different year end for its accounting. Although Bucks were still listed as brewers in 1932, in 1936 and 1941 they were only shown as bottlers.

The firm continued as bottlers and brewer's agents. It seems that the pubs were finally sold in 1945-46. This was probably linked to when Robert Buck succeeded to the business in 1946 (What's Brewing June 1985 p13).

They continued to bottle Guinness for Marstons until about 1960. Although bottling ceased in the early 1970s, they continued as agents and operated a beer at home service. When Mr Buck retired in 1982, the business closed. In 1985 the buildings were demolished for a new Co-op.

Childs, George, *Rose & Crown, Baker Street/Regent Street.*

The Rose & Crown dated back to at least 1835, when it was kept by Joseph Williams. George Childs was at the pub in 1870, when the address was shown as the Wood Market. For the period 1877-87 he was listed as brewing. Although Mrs Hannah Childs was the victualler in 1894, with the address as Regent Street, brewing had probably ceased when her husband had died.

The pub later closed and the rebuilt building is now the Rice Bowl restaurant.

Church, Thomas, *The Peacock, Regent Street/High Street.*

The Peacock was trading in 1835, with Moses Shellard the landlord. In 1848, the Peacock was kept by William Wormleighton and he was still there in 1855. By 1870 Thomas Church was at the pub, where he was listed as a brewer for the period 1877-84. In 1894, William Harris was listed as the victualler, but with no mention of brewing. In 1901, Phillips & Marriott of Coventry, who were supplying the pub, allowed the lease of the Peacock to lapse.

Fox, Samuel, *The Fox, London Road.*

The pub is thought to have been named after Samuel who died in 1830, when he was described as a brewer. In 1848 it was kept by John Holman. However, from 1855 to 1870, it was being run by Edward Voss. At this time a Charles Fox was at the King's Head, Ely Lane, Town Hall Street, and Kelly's 1877 directory lists Fox as the brewer there.

The Fox Inn in 1894, tenanted by William Henry Blunt victualler, was leased by Phillips & Marriott for 7 years at £30 per annum from JH Watson, The Hill. However, in 1901 the lease was allowed to lapse. In 1985 it was being supplied by Whitbreads.

Hirons, John, *Stag & Pheasant, Beast Market.*

In 1848 John Scrimshaw was running the Stag. The owner was shown in 1870 as John Heron, but in 1877, John Hirons was listed as the brewer. This was probably the same individual and there seems to be no other mentions of brewing. The pub was later closed and demolished.

Lavender, Egbert William, *Station Road.*

Lavender started around 1894 as a grocer in the High Street. Then in 1904, he was shown as an agricultural engineer etc. in Station Road. However, in 1928 he seems to have briefly added brewing to his list of trades and he may also have been running an agency for NBC. By 1932, there was no further mention of him in the directories. Given the dates, one is tempted to consider the possibility that he may have been trying to follow on from the Buck's brewery, which seems to have stopped brewing around this time.

Mash, William, *Greyhound, Beast Market.*

The Greyhound dated to at least 1794, when Charles Ward was at the pub. In 1806, the pub with its large brewhouse was to let, with details from the appropriately named Mr William Mash at the Denbigh Arms. Although for example, in the 1830s the Nutt family were victuallers at the pub, there were no references to brewing.

It was owned by NBC in 1923, to at least 1956, and is still trading on the main road through the town.

Mawby, Ellen, *Queen's Head, Regent Street.*

In 1791 Charles Neale was the victualler at the pub. By 1848 Allen Mawby was running the pub, where he was still listed for 1870. Ellen was listed as the brewer for 1877-84. It was bought by Phipps of Northampton for £710 in 1887. It was still open in 1956, but sometime after this it closed.

Muddiman, Mrs Elizabeth, *Coach & Horses, Church Street.*

In 1835, the Coach & Horses was already owned by the Muddiman family. In 1870 Thomas Muddiman was at the pub, Mrs Elizabeth Muddiman was listed as the brewer in 1877, but was also running an agency for Bindley & Company.

In 1884 Thomas Osborne was the brewer and then in 1887 Mrs Emma Osborne was brewing, but this was the last entry. This was possibly the site where Frank Buswell was an ale and porter merchant in 1912.

Needham, *Lutterworth Brewery.*

Listed only in 1881, possibly the brewery used by Bannisters and Bucks.

Oram, Thomas, *Unicorn, Church Street.*

Jeremiah Cotton was the victualler at the Unicorn in 1791. Then in 1835 it was kept by Thomas Coleman, but with no mention of brewing. It remained with the Coleman family until the 1870s, with various members acting as the licensee.

For example in 1867, the pub was run by Miss Coleman and owned by William Coleman. Thomas Oram was shown as the brewer here from around 1877 until 1884 (F3160).

George Moulds then took over the pub, and sometime afterwards it was rebuilt and brewing seems to have ceased. At some point it was run by Jimmy Cave who then moved to the Ram. It is now an M&B house.

Payne, Charles, *Ram, Beast Market.*

The pub dates back to at least 1791, when it was kept by William Roe. By 1835, Thomas Leader was the victualler, until around 1855. Charles Payne was at the pub in 1870 and, as well as being a plumber, he was also shown as brewing 1877-87. However, in 1894 Charles C Payne was at the pub, when Phillips & Marriott bought the premises for £823 12s. The pub is now the Cavalier.

Veres, George junior, *White Hart, Ely Lane, Town Hall Street.*

From around 1791 to 1855, William Leason owned the Hart, although in 1835 Elizabeth Shepherd was running the pub. In the latter year William Vears kept the Denbigh Arms, High Street, but by 1848 he was at the White Hart

In 1877 George Veres junior was identified as the brewer at the White Hart, previously run by William Line. However, in 1880 George Vears, victualler in Ely Lane, was in financial difficulties. The pub was later closed and demolished

MARKET BOSWORTH

Trivett, William Henry, *Red Lion, 1 Park Street.*

William Trivett was running the Red Lion in 1835, followed by John Trivett in 1848 and it remained with the family for over a century to 1942. However, the earliest mention was in 1696 when a document describes the foundations of a malthouse which seems to have been constructed by Henry Cantrell, a carpenter.

In 1870 William Trivett was a butcher at the Red Lion, whilst his father, also called William, had been at the Dixie Arms from at least 1855. Then in 1884, a John Trivett was a butcher and victualler at the Lion, where in 1904 he was identified as the brewer. The outer facade of the pub was re-modelled around 1896.

He was followed as the brewer in 1910 by Henry Trivett. In 1913 William Henry Trivett was listed as a brewer in Park Street (F3318), when Mrs Rose Trivett was running the Old Red Lion Commercial Hotel, although the pub's address was shown as Main Street. The Trivetts are thought to have stopped brewing in the late 1920s, although there was a directory entry for 1932 which starred the pub as brewing. The brewhouse, which was at the rear of the pub was then demolished and the bricks used for Long's slaughter house in Back Lane (Foss 1983). At some point the Red Lion became the whole of the Hoskins' tied estate!

The Trivetts may have also brewed at the Gate, Osbaston, which they appear to have run and which was described as a an old brew-pub in a local beer guide.

MARKET HARBOROUGH

Aldwinckle, Mrs Louisa, *Windmill, Fox Yard, Adam & Eve Street.*

In 1848, Joseph Aldwinckle was running the Windmill and was also a lace agent on Mill Hill. However, in 1857 Jonathan Deacon was shown at the pub.

In 1870 Joseph Aldwinckle was listed as an innkeeper on Windmill Hill, with Mrs Louisa Aldwinckle identified as the brewer in 1877. By 1884, Henry Aldwinckle had taken over the brewing. Around this time, a family with the same name was brewing at Stamford.

In 1883, the property became owned by Mr Seckham of NBC, to whom it was transferred in 1887. Around 1914, NBC appear to have sold the Windmill, possibly to Eady & Dulley who had already owned the Fox from 1895. The Windmill was on the corner of Mill Hill and Fox Yard and was demolished in 1920 for the extension to Symington's factory.

Baum, John, *Coach & Horses, High Street.*

In the 1770s Elizabeth Oswin was the victualler at the Coach & Horses. She was possibly the mother of Ann Oswin who married Samuel Smith in 1773, he being a cooper at the Angel in the High Street and later a victualler at the Fox Inn, Tripe Alley. Elizabeth had previously been at the Queen's Head. Her son David was also a victualler. By 1822 Ann Rodgers was at the pub.

The first clear mention of brewing was for 1877, when John Baum was listed. He was the brewer until around 1884, when shown only as a victualler. In 1901, Messrs Flint, Wine & Spirit merchants (previously also maltsters and porter, hop and seed merchants at the Angel) closed the pub, which was then demolished with the construction of Abbey Street. The name was then transferred to what had previously been the White Swan.

Bland, John, *Dolphin, Church Square.*

In 1848, when the Dolphin was being run by Mrs Sophia Branston, the address was shown as New Street. She seems to have run the pub until at least 1857. Bland had taken the pub by 1870, and was listed as brewing in 1877. In 1880 it became an Eady & Dulley property which closed in 1929, with compensation of £250, before being sold for £1,500. The pub was demolished in 1935 for further extensions to the Symington factory.

Bosworth, William, *King William, St Mary's Road.*

The King William in 1848 to 1855, was run by Titus Bosworth, who was also a tailor. William Bosworth had taken the pub by 1870, where he was listed as a brewer in 1877. The plant was for sale in 1881, although William was still there in 1884. The pub stood on the corner of Mill Hill and was later owned by Everards. It closed for £2,850 compensation in 1922.

Burditt, John, *Union Inn, Leicester Road.*

The Inn was built around 1810, by the Union Canal Company, with the first tenant being a Thomas Munton. He was advertising the sale of home brewed beer as well as London

MARKET HARBOROUGH (continued)

porter. The latter was important for custom, since around this time Thomas Bull junior was advertising Capital London Porter at his grocers and tea dealers near the Angel Inn. He stressed that he had a large quantity of Meux's Capital Brown Stout in 18 or 36 gallon casks.

In 1822, George Furnival was at the pub, but by 1835 it had been taken by Rebecca Furnival.

In 1870 John Burditt was the tenant and in 1877 he was listed as brewing. Although Burditt was still at pub in 1913, it had been bought by Eady & Dulley in 1895. In 1929 with the sale of the local brewery, it too went to NBC. It was later called the Six Packs, but after renovation in 1997 it re-opened as a hotel and regained its old name.

Garner, Thomas, *Red Cow, High Street.*

The Red Cow dates back to at least 1793, when the owner was an M Bayley. In 1837, mention was made of the brewhouse at the rear, when owned by Thomas Garner, previously it had been owned by Catherine Bailey.

In 1848 William Jarvis, also a lace dealer, was at the pub. By 1870 it was being run by Ann Jarvis, but there was no mention of brewing. In 1905, when John Smith was running the pub, which had been rebuilt, All Saints Brewery bought it for £2,940. In 1924, they were looking to buy the property next door at No 58. The pub is still trading as a Marston's property.

Hudson, Henry, *Duke of Wellington, High Street.*

In 1822, the pub was run by J Taylor and in 1848 by a Thomas Taylor. By 1870, Thomas Hall was running the Duke, where seven years later, Hudson was listed as the brewer. It was later closed, but the building is still standing.

Letts, Joseph, *Rose & Crown, Church Street.*

From 1822 to 1848 Charles Gibbs was at the pub, followed by R Eames around 1855. By 1870 Letts had taken over the licence and he was listed as the brewer in 1877. The pub closed under the compensation scheme in 1907.

Monk, Joseph, *Bell Inn, Coventry Street.*

The Bell Inn dated back to the seventeenth century when it was owned by a Henry Smith; however, at that time it was called the Three Bells. In 1791 Thomas Hill was the victualler.

In 1822 it had returned to the Smith family, when William Smith was at the Bell Inn, shown as being in Coventry Road. However, in 1848 when Stephen Branston was running the pub and also operating as a blacksmith, the address seems to be Lubenham Lane.

From 1877 to 1887 Joseph Monk was brewing at the Bell Inn, possibly before moving to the Sun. The NBC papers mention the brewhouse, when they inherited the property from Eady & Dulley in 1929. However, the pub was later demolished and the licence transferred for a new building, with the same name.

Monk, Robert, *Sun Inn, Church Square.*

The Sun Inn dated back to at least 1791, when it was being run by Thomas Sheppard. Joseph Tirrell, in 1822, and Simeon White, 1835 to 1848, were early landlords. In 1870 Mrs Ann Branstone was running the pub.

Then in 1877 Robert Monk was the brewer, and his advertising mentions home brewed ales until 1887, although John Mutton may have been at the pub by 1884.

George Mutton was then brewing from 1892 to 1895, followed by William Plant in 1898. The last mention of brewing seems to be in 1913, for Joseph William Monk, presumably having moved from the Bell. The Sun which stood on the corner of the square was demolished for the construction of Roman Road.

Nunneley & Eady, *Little Bowden Brewery.*

In February 1799, John Smith was advertising his new brewery at Little Bowden, in the Leicester Journal. The advertisement mentioned his long experience in the business, presumably a reference to his brewing at Oundle (see Brewed In Northants). In 1804, another series of advertisements marked the transfer of the brewery to his son William.

MARKET HARBOROUGH (continued)

The Nunneley family had lived in the Kettering and Market Harborough area since the eighteenth century. In 1808, Joseph Nunneley of Humberstone Gate in Leicester was advertising for an apprentice for a liquor and grocery trade a few miles from Leicester. The following year he bought the wholesale grocers business of Samuel Bradley at the top of the High Street. At some point he bought a wholesale grocery in Harborough from John Byng. In 1835, a John Byng had been listed as a brewer at Kegworth.

In 1837 John Nunneley was listed as a grocer in the town (probably from around 1811) and in 1846 Joseph Nunneley was shown as a brewer on the High Street. The Smith's brewery was on Northampton Road, where Nunneley owned property opposite and by 1848 the brewery was trading as Joseph Nunneley & Company. However, in 1855 Joseph Nunneley & Company were shown as grocers, bacon factors, wine & spirit merchants and brewers in the High Street. Around 1862-77 Joseph Nunneley's location was also shown as Sheep Market, possibly his home address.

On 1st June 1865, Nunneley formed a partnership with Joseph Chamberlain Eady (born 1838 Leicester). In White's 1877 directory the entry shows Nunneley and Eady as brewers in St Mary's Road. However, there was also an entry for Joseph Nunneley showing 14½ Silver Street and Burton, with Joseph Gamble as the manager at the first address. The Joseph Nunneley who was brewing in Burton around this time was also from Leicester and they were at least related, if not even the same individual!

The brewery was transferred to JC Eady in 1880, with the Nunneley & Eady partnership dissolved in November 1881, In 1882, Eady formed a new partnership with James Dulley of the Wellingborough brewing family, running the business as Eady & Dulley (F3325). In 1888, J Nunneley & Company were still trading as wholesale grocers and wine merchants and in the same year, Little Bowden moved from Northamptonshire to Leicestershire as part of the boundary re-organisation. In 1895, Joseph C Eady Esq JP County Councillor 1888 was living in St Mary's Road. The full story of the Little Bowden Brewery can be found in "Brewed in Northants".

Salt, William, *Talbot, High Street.*

In May 1810, the sale of William Salt's possessions at the Talbot included both domestic and commercial brewing vessels. He was a bankrupt innholder at the time, so it seems likely that he was actually running the Talbot. The Talbot was then taken by Richard Fox, who moved there from the Queen's Head. The latter, with brewhouse, was for sale, with details from Mr Ford on the premises.

The Talbot was an Eady & Dulley property included in the sale to NBC in 1929, and was still an NBC house in 1956. It is still trading, but most of the outbuildings have been demolished.

Smith, Thomas, *Lamb, Sheep Street.*

From 1791 to 1799, the Lamb was being run by a Joseph Bayley. It was for sale, with brewhouse, on 6th April 1813, when owned by a Thomas Smith.

Wells, John, *King's Head, High Street.*

In 1628, when John Wells was the innkeeper at what is thought to be the King's Head, his inventory listed the following brewing equipment:- *"2 coppers, 1 mashing fatt, 1 yeiling fatt, certen brewing vessells, 1 little garner & other implements"*. The total value was £6, with a cellar with 10 hogsheads i.e. 500 gallons ale (Davies p174).

The King's Head was reputedly used by Charles I before the Battle of Naseby in 1645. A new pub was built in 1828, on the corner of Church Street, opposite the Talbot. This later became the Grapes and then the Harborough Lounge. Closed at one time and used for shops, it has now re-opened as a pub.

MARKFIELD

Hoball, Mr, *Coach & Horses.*

Advertised to let in April 1811, with *"a 9 strike mash tub, 50 gallon coppper etc. Details from Mr Hoball"*.

MELTON MOWBRAY

Adcock, Pacey & Company, *Egerton Brewery, Bentley Street.*

In September 1808, there was an advertisement in the Leicester Journal for the Prior's Close Wharf with warehouse. This stated that the premises were suitable for a common brewer *"much wanted in that part of the country"*. Hence, one can assume that the majority of pubs were brewing for themselves, rather than buying from a common brewer.

In 1812, the Three Horse Shoes in Burton End was for sale as a result of the death of George Adcock. The sale included the brewing utensils. It later became a private house. In 1830, William Adcock was described as an innkeeper and in 1835 was listed as a maltster at Little London, whilst Thomas Pickering Adcock ran a wine and spirit business in Sherrard Street. In 1846, George Adcock was a spirit merchant in Burton End; however, in 1848, they seem to have combined the businesses, since they were shown as Thomas Pickard Adcock and George Adcock, wine and spirit and ale and porter merchants in Sherrard Street. Around this time, a John Adcock was running the Blue Cow at nearby Buckminster; although in 1846 he had sold some of the brewing equipment, including a 12 strike brewing copper.

Then in 1855, Adcock W&G were shown as running the Egerton Brewery and as maltsters. This further linking of the family businesses would seem to be supported by an indenture of 1860 on the Noel Arms. The indenture mentions George Adcock the elder, Thomas Pickard Adcock and William Adcock.

Three years later, the business was more clearly identified as Adcock, William & George, Egerton Brewery and Sherrard Street on Tuesdays. Thomas Rowland was the agent at Nottingham Street, this was later shown as offices at No 7. However, there seems to have been a family dispute around this time, since whilst the Egerton Brewery remained in the hands of William, George Adcock appears to have set up in business on his own (see entry). Meanwhile, Thomas Pickard Adcock was brewing at Whissendine around this time with a Mr Fast (see entry) and with separate stores in Melton.

Hence the Egerton Brewery was shown as William Adcock in 1867 and in 1870 William Adcock was advertising himself as:- mild, strong and East India pale ale and porter brewer and maltster wine and spirits, Egerton Brewery and stores in Market Place.

In 1871, the business was trading as W Adcock Egerton Brewery (F3359). In 1874 some of the property was mortgaged, probably to raise cash for the purchase of additional pubs. In 1876, the mortgage was added to, with the business operating as W Adcock, Market Place. In 1877 they were also shown as maltsters.

However, in 1877 it was trading as Adcock, Pacey & Company Egerton Brewery Nottingham Street, with William Adcock living at North Lodge in Bentley Street. In 1880, William Adcock and James Pacey were in partnership running the brewery.

In 1884 Adcock, Pacey & Company were maltsters and brewers at the Egerton Brewery, which was shown as being in Bentley Street. William Adcock was living at North Lodge, whilst William Darman, a jobbing brewer was at No 11. James Pacey, brewer, was living at Morecambe Villa, 8 Asfordy Road. The brewery offices were still at 7 Nottingham Street and the business operated as wine and spirit merchants at 19 Market Place.

On 24th July 1885, a J Pacey of Leicestershire took out a patent for *"Improvements in finings making machines"*. In 1890, William Adcock and William Pacey were the partners and it is not clear whether at this point James was simply employed by the business or was included in the ownership. The Adcock, Pacey & Company partnership was dissolved and this may have been the end of James' involvement.

The following year the business was still trading as Adcock, Pacey & Coat at 7 Nottingham Street. They continued to be shown in 1894 and 1900 as wine & spirit merchants at 19 Market Place. The Adcock involvement also seems to have ended around this time.

After James Pacey retired the business passed to his brother, but was being run by John and Walker Pacey, presumably his nephews, who were living at Morecambe Villa. Nevertheless, the following year there was still a directory entry for Adcock, Pacey at Bentley Street.

In 1903, William Walker Pacey, originally from the nearby village of Saxby, died on 13th August. His sons, Walker and John, were his executors and trustees and they carried on the

From the Jack Feast collection

MELTON MOWBRAY (continued)

brewery, although John seems to have sold his share in 1914 for £24,500. James Pacey JP, born 1846 at Garthrope and presumably the uncle, was still involved with owning the business.

In 1915, the business was still trading at 7 Nottingham Street as Adcock, Pacey & Company. However, on 22nd December 1919, Bindley & Company bought it for £63,000. The estate included 32 pubs, one of which was de-licensed, and an off-licence, although there was no mention of the brewery in the conveyance document. Bindleys had themselves been taken over by Ind Coope in 1914, but were still operating independently.

The brewery (SK754195) was demolished in the early 1990s.

Allen, George, *Ram.*

In 1799, the Ram with its excellent coppers was for sale, details from Mr Allen. He was moving to the Granby Inn at Grantham.

Angus, Mrs Mary, *Half Moon, 36 Nottingham Street.*

The pub dated back to at least 1848, when Matthew Fardell was the victualler. Mrs Angus was listed as the brewer in 1884. The pub, now a Bass house, is still trading next to the famous town pork pie shop. However, the street would seem to have been re-numbered at some time.

Bailey, Mrs Mildred, *Black Horse, 16 King Street.*

The Black Horse was kept by George Rushby in 1835, until around 1848 when John Watson took over the pub.

Mrs Bailey was shown as the brewer for the period 1877 to 1884, and the pub was then taken by Thomas Holman, victualler. In 1887, W Furmidge & Company of the Vale Brewery at Harby were advertising their stores at the pub, suggesting it may have ceased brewing. The pub was part of the Thorpe End sale of 1910 and was still trading in 1913, but was later closed and demolished.

Ballets.

Friedrich lists this firm for 1876, but no other details have been found and it may be a mistake. The only similar name is that for the previous entry.

Bolderson, J, *King's Head, 26 Nottingham Street.*

The Bolderson family ran the pub from at least 1835. J Bolderson (probably James) was running the pub in 1870, and was listed as brewing in 1877.

From 1884 to 1913, when described as an Hotel, John Coulston was the victualler and proprietor, and brewing had presumably stopped. It was rebuilt around 1920, when it was supplied by the Home Brewery of Nottingham. It is now owned by Mansfield Brewery.

Childs, Alfred, *George Hotel, High Street.*

In 1791 Robert Skerrit was the innkeeper, at what had originally been the George & Talbot. It has a "Georgian" frontage, with older buildings at the rear. It was run by the Watson family in the first half of the nineteenth century.

John Selby was running the pub from 1870 to 1884, although in 1877 Alfred Childs was listed as the brewer. In 1899 T Eady was a bankrupt hotel proprietor, which suggests that brewing had already ceased. It is now a free house with beer from Banks.

Cotton, Mrs Hannah, *Generous Briton, 11 King Street.*

From 1835 to 1848 Richard Hubbard was running the pub as a victualler. By 1870, Henry Cotton had taken the Briton, where in 1877, Mrs Hannah Cotton was listed as the brewer. Brewing seems to have stopped soon afterwards.

The pub is now a Mansfield house.

Dale, Alfred, *Harborough Hotel, 49 Burton Street.*

Around 1835, William Hubbard was the victualler at the Harborough, Then in 1846, William Mason was the licensee, followed by Mrs Lucy Mason. It was bought in 1864 by a Mr W Shouler, who carried out major alterations to improve its appeal to the visiting hunting fraternity. He installed a Mr Mason as the tenant.

In 1870 Alfred Dale was running the pub, originally shown as Burton End. He was listed as brewing in 1877, at what was now the Harborough Arms.

In 1884 Alfred John Dale, victualler, was advertising that it was *"replete with every convenience and comfort for hunting and commercial gentlemen and within 2 minutes walk of the station"*. Brewing probably ceased around this time, when a Mr Fuller became the tenant.

Now it is one of the few Bateman's pubs in the county.

Dixon, Thomas, *Rutland Arms, King Street.*

From 1835 to 1848 Thomas Draper was the victualler at the Rutland. By 1870 Thomas Dixon was at the pub, where he was shown as brewing in 1877. It was then run by his widow Mrs Ruth Dixon, shown as a victualler in 1884, but brewing would seem to have stopped.

In 1919 when included in the Adcock, Pacey Estate sale, the brewhouse was mentioned. It is now owned by the Pubmaster chain.

Green & Hacker, *Whissendine Brewery Company, Cheapside.*

In 1877, Adcock and Fast, of the Whissendine Brewery Company, were shown at Cheapside; however, this was only a depot. Although William Henry Green was shown as a large brewer and at the Midland Railway Stores, he had become the owner of the brewery at Whissendine which also supplied a shop at 3 Burton Street, near the station (see Whissendine entry).

From 1884 to 1892, they were listed as having offices at 30 Nottingham Street (F3361), with Henry Wall as the local agent. They had presumably bought the premises which had previously been used by the Tylers (see entry).

One local history book states that in the 1890s, a WA Heap brewed beer at King Street House, which he then retailed on Cheapside. However, this seems to have been at best what were termed botanical beers, or more likely mineral waters. In 1867, King Street House had been the home of Thomas Pickering Adcock.

Healey, Mrs Ann, *Crown, Burton End/Market Place.*

The Crown was for sale on 30th March 1813, with the owner being Mrs Healey. It was described as being newly built, with a brewhouse in the yard. However, the advertisement also suggested its possible conversion to a house. It was still in business in 1855, when kept by Robert Goodacre.

Knowles, George William, *The Wheatsheaf, 31 Thorpe End.*

In 1791 Thomas Warren was the victualler at the Wheatsheaf, but in 1813 J Sharman was advertising its planned closure to become an ironmongers.

However, a Wheatsheaf, shown as being on Sherrard Street, continued to trade, in 1835 being run by Henry Scorer. He was still at the pub in 1855, when he was also a corn merchant. At this time, the address was shown as Thorpe End.

The pub then seems to have been run by the Betts family, before passing to George Knowles. He was shown as brewing for 1884-88, although it may actually have been owned by HH Parry. On 15th April 1897, Knowles seems to have been involved in a transfer of ownership. Mention is made of George and Henry Langton, suggesting a connection with the Thorpe End Brewery.

However, on 6th April 1890, LB&M leased the pub for £130 pa from Mr Knowles, but in turn it was mortgaged to him. In June 1893, the landlord Thomas Walker was fined £1 for allowing customers to play dominoes for drink. The following year he was fined a further 10s for being *"helplessly drunk"* in charge of a cart.

Having given up possession on 6th April 1895, LB&M then came to a new arrangement on the 27th. This was to supply all ales and stouts in cask, except bitter, at 20% discount. The wording suggests that some brewing was still taking place. Mr Knowles paid off his mortgage in 1897.

Langton & Sons, *Thorpe End Brewery, Thorpe Road/Saxby Road.*

The George Adcock, mentioned above, may have gone into business on his own, but he seems to have died shortly afterwards, since in 1865 it was being run by his executors. However, in 1867 George Adcock was listed as a gentleman in Burton End, whilst Mrs Adcock was shown as a brewer in Sherrard Street.

In 1870 Adcock junior (Exec of):- mild, pale and strong ale and porter brewer. John Mowbray was the manager for the executors of the late George Adcock junior. In 1871, the Thorpe brewery was being run by JG Adcock.

The Thorpe End Brewery.

Photo: Author

The Thorpe End Brewery.

Photo: Author

J. S. LORD,
THORPE END BREWERY,
MELTON MOWBRAY.

PRICE LIST OF SEASON BREWED

MILD, STRONG, PALE ALE
AND NATIONAL STOUTS.

Brand on Casks.   s. d.
X........MILD ALE........1 0   Per Gal
XX.......DO.. DO........1 2   "
XXX......DO. DO.........1 4   "
XXXX..STRONG DO..........1 6   "
X.E.......DO. DO........1 8   "
P.A.....PALE DO.........1 4   "
I.P.A. INDIAN PALE ALE   2 0   "

The above Ales are supplied, in good condition, delivered free, in 6, 9, 18, 36, and 54 Gallon Casks.

NATIONAL STOUTS!

From the Melton Mowbray Times & Vale of Belvoir Gazette 1887.

The son George was shown as running the business in 1875, but this was probably a directory error, since in 1876 it was described as George junior (trustees) Thorpe Brewery and Sherrard Street. Similarly in 1877, the Thorpe End Brewery, was under the control of the trustees of Adcock junior, Sherrard Street, when George Henry Ellingworth was shown as the agent.

Around 1884, it was trading as Adcock, George junior & Company, Thorpe End Brewery and offices at 1 Nottingham Street. However, by 1887, John Shaw Lord was at the Thorpe End Brewery and Nottingham Street. He was advertising mild, strong and pale ale as well as national stouts. An indenture of 29th October then mentions both Lord and also George Langton. The following year the business was trading as Langton & Sons, brewery and maltings. However, one directory still listed JS Lord as brewer at the Thorpe End Brewery, as well as running the Eight Bells and the Half Moon, both of which were on Nottingham Street.

In 1890, Langton & Sons were shown at Thorpe End and 36 Nottingham Street, with their "Celebrated AK Ale". From 1892 to 1910, the central office was 36 Nottingham Street. In 1890, the Brewers' Journal reported that Harry Langton of the Thorpe End Brewery had "*invented an improved form of tap, in which a covering device in the form of a tongue extends to its aperture, opening and closing with the turning of the tap itself. The object of this simple contrivance is to prevent the accumulation of flies or other insects, dust, or mould in the aperture of the tap when turned off and not in use.*" (Brewers' Journal p111).

In 1891, they were negotiating with LB&M to supply the Princess Charlotte at Leicester with their beer, as long as they took 300 quarters of malt in return. The contract eventually was signed at 250 quarters, but apparently did not last for very long.

The background to the Langtons involvement in brewing seems to start in 1866 with Langton & Sons at the Union Brewery in Wandsworth, SW London. In 1876 this was trading as Joseph Langton & Sons. One of these sons may have been George Langton, since in 1878 one of George's sons, also called Joseph, was running the Dolphin Brewery at Cuckfield.

In 1894 George Langton was living in Dalby Road. Henry Langton, the brewery manager, was living at Claremont, also in Dalby Road. In 1896, George Langton retired from Messrs Langton & Sons and the partnership was dissolved. However, in 1900, it was still trading as Langton & Sons, still advertising their celebrated golden AK Ale, a light dinner ale, at one shilling per gallon. They were also bottling Bass, Guinness and Youngers.

On 3rd March 1901 the business was offered for sale at auction. However, interest must have been minimal, since it was for sale again on 23rd October 1906. It was also offered to Phipps of Northampton, where James Langton was a director. Presumably, this was another of George's sons and the same James Langton involved with various other breweries and a trustee of Blencowes of Brackley.

In 1906, the business was shown as being run by George and Harry Langton when they applied for a licence to sell wines and spirits from the brewery premises.

In 1910 Langton & Sons (F3360) was sold with 14 pubs - of which 13 have been identified. This was the same year that Joseph Langton sold the Cuckfield brewery. The tower brewery, with adjoining malthouse and kiln is still standing (SK758192).

Pollard, Walter, *Grapes, 10 Market Place.*

Although in 1919, this was an Adcock house, in 1922-5 Pollard was shown as the brewer of the beer retailed. It was known to the locals as the "*corner cupboard*" and was the tap for the Swan Inn. The site was said to have originally been a gin shop owned by a Mr Dixon.

In 1932 Arthur Ernest Arnesby was identified as the brewer and in 1936 Harry Hurst was still brewing at the pub. The pub is still trading.

Sturgess, John, *Malt Shovel, Sherrard Street.*

In 1855, John Sturgess was a maltster and pork pie manufacturer in Leicester Street. The Lord Warden at 32 Leicester Street, in 1870 was run by John Sturgess, who was also a wine and spirit merchant in Sherrard Street. In 1876, he was shown at the Malt Shovel in Sherrard Street and a maltster and wine and spirit merchant in Leicester Street. Then in 1877 a J Sturgess was listed as a brewer and maltster in Sherrard Street.

The Lord Warden was possibly the pub which All Saints Brewery were supplying in 1879 and which seems to have closed soon afterwards.

Taylor, William Charles, *Royal Oak, 5 Pall Mall.*

In 1891 William Taylor was only shown as a beer retailer, but the following year he was also listed as a brewer. This seems to have been at the Royal Oak, which was later demolished.

Turville, Thomas, *Jolly Butchers, King Street.*

The pub was built by a William Harrington, with Turville the brewer from 1877 to 1884. John Drury then took the Butchers, before it was run by Richard Freeman, and then Ada Freeman.

At the time of the Adcock Pacey sale in 1919, it seems to have been de-licensed, although the brewhouse was mentioned. The pub was next to the Generous Briton and the building was later Abbot's shop.

Turville, William, *Burton End.*

In 1884 William Turville was the brewer at the Queen's Head beerhouse, 27 Timber Hill, and then the victualler at the Red Lion, 38 Burton Street, both of which have been demolished. The Red Lion, which was de-licensed in 1928, had a malthouse standing next to it until the buildings came down in 1935.

Tyler, William, *29 Nottingham Street.*

In 1846, William Tyler was a maltster in Nottingham Street, then in 1855 William Tyler was shown as a coachmaker and maltster. The Tylers family home was at 30/31, where they operated as coachbuilders for nearly one hundred years.

In 1863 William was shown as brewing, and in 1870 was described as a coach builder, with horses and carriages for hire, brewer and maltster. However, in 1884, James Tyler was only a coach builder at No 29. The premises next door then seem to have become Green & Hacker's depot (see entry), and it seems that they had taken over the Tyler's brewing business.

Walker, Henry, *Noel's Arms, 31 Burton Street.*

From around 1835 to 1848 John Chambers was at the Noel's Arms, which is thought to date back to around 1800. It stands on the corner of Mill Street, at what was then shown as Burton End.

By 1870 Henry Walker was at the pub, where in 1877 he was listed as the brewer, although the pub seems to have been owned by Joseph Bailey and then Ernest Newton.

In 1884 Henry Charles Burrow was running the pub, but brewing seems to have ceased. It was in the Adcock Pacey estate when sold in 1919, and there is an indenture which suggests that, as early as 1860, they had an interest in it.

It was an Allied pub in the 1960s, but at some point it seems to have been owned by Ruddles, before being sold to Ind Coope in 1978. It featured in the 1979 Good Beer Guide, under the threat of demolition for road widening. However, it is still trading as an Ansell's pub.

Wilson, James, *Dog & Gun, 14 Pall Mall.*

In 1884 James Wilson was a coal dealer and running a beerhouse at No 11. In 1891, it was shown as No 9. Wilson was listed as the brewer for 1892-95. The pub was bought by Praeds of Wellingborough in 1897, but was in the 1909 compensation scheme. The owners received some £392 when it closed in 1914.

MOUNT SORREL

Bampton, George, *White Swan, North End.*

In 1835 Edward Hickling was running the White Swan, where in 1848 he was also in charge of the excise office. He is thought to have produced some of the earliest bottled beer in the county.

George Bampton was at the pub by 1855, when he was also a farmer. For the period 1892-1906, he was shown as a brewer and also as a rate collector. In 1922, it became an Everard's house, but was later demolished.

Leake Bros Ltd, *Castle Brewery, Green Corner, Main Street.*

Although there were no brewers listed in 1835 in the town, Joseph Priestley was shown as a maltster, whilst Elizabeth Priestley kept the Hammer & Pincer, which was still trading in the 1970s.

In 1870 Charles Francis Leake, established 1842, was listed as a wholesale and retail grocer and an agent for Burton ales. In 1884 he was still only a grocer. He died in 1892 and, on 27th September 1893, Leake Bros were trading as wine and spirit merchants. The following year, Leake Bros (Charles Rowley and William) were described as corn dealers, ale etc. agents. They were also agents for the Royal Insurance Company.

LEAKE BROS LTD
BREWERS — GROCERS — CASTLE BREWERY — WINE & SPIRIT MERCHANTS
MOUNTSORREL
NEAR LOUGHBOROUGH
Mineral Water Manufacturers and Corn Factors.
BRANCH:—GREEN CORNER, MOUNTSORREL.

The first mention of brewing seems to be in 1898, when Leake Bros were listed as brewers. In May 1899, Leake Bros Ltd was registered to acquire the business of Charles Rowley Leake and William Leake (F3420).

A 1900 advertisement shows the location as Green Corner, as well as brewers they were also mineral water manufacturers, corn factors and grocers. However, they would appear not to have owned any tied houses. Around the 1904, they were also running the Vine Wine Company at Wanlip Road, Syston. However, they were in voluntary liquidation on 18th July 1907.

In 1908 Ralph John Holland was at the Castle Brewery, but this was only with a wine and spirit business, despite an entry as a brewer in a directory for 1911. He was there until 3rd June 1914, when George Ward took over the licence, which lapsed completely the following year. The brewery, which was next to the mill, was demolished in 1959, for a boat yard.

Place, William.

In the 1826 poll book, Place was described as a brewer. His family were mainly farmers and wheelwrights and this seems to have been the only mention of brewing.

Simpson, Thomas, *Red Lion, Loughborough Road.*

In 1799, Simpson was moving from the Lion, which was described as having two good coppers, one of which was of 108 gallons, together with a 140 gallon mash tub. From 1835 to 1855, it was run by Joseph Antil. It was next to the bridge and was later closed.

NARBOROUGH **Bull, John,** *Red Lion.*

In 1799 Bull left the pub, which was owned by Nicholas Ward of Hinckley. The sale on 29th/30th April included the brewhouse, with a 60 gallon and an 18 gallon copper, an 8 strike mash tub and 10 casks of from 6 to 40 gallons. It was not listed in 1894.

NEWBOLD VERDON **Gilbert, Joseph.**

In 1846 Joseph was listed as a brewer and beerhouse keeper, but in 1848 was only a baker.

Raven, John.

In 1846 John Raven was a brewer and beerhouse keeper, but in 1848 was only a beer retailer.

OADBY **Clackett, Thomas.**

Listed as a brewer in 1835, but with no further details or entries.

Hurst, Isaac, *Black Dog, London Road.*

In 1800, the Black Dog and its brewhouse were for sale as a result of the death of the owner Mr Ludlam; however, the address was shown as Harborough Street. It was the oldest pub in the town, dating back to around 1753. It was rebuilt around 1783.

The Smalley family were brewing in the early part of the century and although it was bought in 1835 by William Watts of Leicester (see entry) brewing continued. In the 1840s and 1850s it was run by Peter Howard.

In 1870 Otto Juba was running the pub, but on the death of William Watts in 1875 he was given notice to quit. The pub, with stables and brewhouse was sold on 4th February 1875 to Mr Beales, the manager of the Leicester Racecourse Company. Isaac Hurst took over the pub and for the period 1877 to 1884 was brewing. He was shown as the victualler in 1888. However, in 1884 HP Curtis took over as the tenant.

In 1897, it was bought by the City Brewery of Lichfield; hence later passing into the hands of Wolverhampton & Dudley Breweries. Around 1930, J Stanhope at the pub was also an agent for Myatt's brewery at Wolverhampton and the pub on the corner of Albion Street and London Road is still trading as a Banks' house.

Ludlam, George, *New Inn, London Road.*

In 1848 George "Tibby" Ludlam, born 1817, was listed as a painter and by 1870 he was running the New Inn, which was built around 1864. For 1877-87 Ludlam was listed as the brewer until he left the pub in 1888. He was followed by Albert Durrad.

The pub was then bought by Thomas Fox (see entry), a beer wholesaler at the Fish & Quart in Leicester, who also owned the Travellers Rest. In 1899, it was bought at auction by Holes of Newark. As a result of their later take-over, it is now trading as a John Smith's pub.

Reay, Edward, *White Horse, 64 Leicester Road.*

The White Horse dated back to the mid 1700s and from 1765 to 1788 was run by the Ludlams. They were followed by John Spence, who was the victualler until around 1830. In 1835 John French was a farmer and running the pub, which was run by Mrs Lucy Ann French in 1855, until around 1859. The 1860s saw three victuallers succeed one another at the pub as follows:- Peter Waite, George Sturgess and William Derby.

James Batten had taken over by 1870, but by 1877 Edward Reay had taken the pub and was listed as the brewer. Thomas Walton was shown as the victualler in 1884, but there was no mention of brewing and that year it was bought by Langmore & Bankart. Hence, in 1901, it was an All Saints Brewery house, when they spent £590 on alterations. It was still trading in 1940, when it was valued at £10,000. It was demolished in 1973 and replaced by a new pub of the same name.

Ward, Jane, *Boot, New Street.*

This was a very short-lived affair. In 1838 it was run by Jane Ward and there was mention of a brewhouse at the rear, although this may have been primarily on a domestic scale. The pub was named after her husband's occupation as a shoe-maker. It had closed by 1859.

OAKHAM

Barnett, William, *White Lion, Melton Road.*

The White Lion dated back to at least 1791, when Thomas Banton was the landlord. In 1877, Barnett was listed as a brewer, when he was also shown as the victualler at the White Lion.

Bellares, William.

Listed as a brewer in 1791, but with no indication of his whereabouts. However, the Bellairs family of Norfolk seem to have had an interest in the Wharf/Castle Street maltings which had been owned by George Royce. In 1821, these had been supplying William Brown Edward, a brewer in Stamford, but had then been sold to John Pearson a local maltster and publican.

In 1868, the maltings, on what had become Burley Road, were to be demolished. Samuel Edward Mawby, described as a brewer's clerk seems to have been handling the paperwork involved with the property. However, he may have been employed at Langham, since the papers were held by the Wingfields, who were related to the Harrisons and Parrys involved with the brewery there.

Crowsons, *Patent Steam Brewery, Cross/New Street.*

The brewery was built in 1842, according to the datestone on the malting. It was described in 1846 as a recently started *"patent steam brewery with a new process"* (Union) started by James Crowson, a maltster as well as brewer. The business was trading as Crowson, John & Son, Patent Steam Brewery, Cross Street, and maltsters. Jas. Barrow Storey was described as the manager of the brewery.

John Crowson's home was shown as being in the Market Place, but the family is thought to originate from Lincolnshire. He ran the George Inn from 1828 to 1850, and was also shown as a maltster from 1842 to 1863. He was at the Crown 1855 to 1858. He was also a wine and spirit merchant from 1831, until he died on 9th November 1858, aged 64. He had two sons, William Cheltenham Crowson and John Crowson. The Crown on the High Street, dated back to at least 1760, when at that time it was run by William Gill.

In 1855 the location was shown as Cross Street and New Street, with Henry Workman as the managing brewer in New Street. William Thomas Bell, living in Church Street, was listed as a brewer in 1855 and seems to have replaced Mr Workman. In 1861, he was described as a professional brewer, aged 40, originally from Tonbridge in Kent.

In 1855 William Cheltenham Crowson was running the wine and spirit business at the Crown. Mrs Catherine Crowson was living in the High Street. John Crowson was a maltster in Cross Street.

A book on the town history (LIHS) records that the Patent Steam Brewery was advertised for sale in the Stamford Mercury in August 1856. The book states that it was bought by WR Morris of Luffenham, for £3,050. However, in 1862, the business was still listed as White, D & Crowson, J and John Crowson was still shown as a brewer and maltster at 121 New Street around this time.

Certainly, by 1866 the site had become owned by Morris Clarke & Company who moved their operations here from their Northgate brewery. It is possible that they continued to use both breweries until around 1870.

Grainstore, Davis' Brewing Company, *Grainstore Brewery, Station Approach.*

Set up in a derelict Victorian railway building, the Tap Room opened early in 1995, initially with a range of guest beers. Brewing started in November 1995 by Tony and Mike Davis. The former had some 30 years experience in brewing, including time at Charles Wells, before ending up as the Production Director and Head Brewer at Ruddles for 16 years. Tony's assistant brewer was Jamie Ramshaw.

The brewery has a 15 barrel plant, with a weekly capacity of 45 barrels. In addition to the Brewery Tap, they supply about 60 outlets within 40 miles of the brewery. The main beers are:-

Cooking Bitter	3.6%	Ten Fifty	5%
Triple B	4.2%		

A bottled beer - Best Man Bitter - has also been produced. The Triple B is also known as

157

**OAKHAM
(continued)**

Bunny Brown, after a previous manager of Morris' Rutland Brewery, who was so called because he would give a bun to any child who held his horse whilst he was visiting the brewery's estate.

The range also includes Tupping Ale 4.2%, brewed especially for the British Charolais Sheep Society.

Green, William Charles, *Cross Keys, 9 New Street.*

From 1900 to 1904 William Green was the brewer at the Cross Keys. Then in 1909, it was shown as being run by William Charles Green, with AC Green operating as a basket maker from the same address.

Although, Ruddles leased the pub in 1911, Albert Edward Butcher was identified as the brewer of the beer retailed in 1922-25. Thomas James King was the licensee from 1932 to 1949, and was still brewing in 1936. It was one of the last pubs in the area to brew, and there were some remains of the brewhouse at the rear (Peaty p165). It was described as a 300 years old Ruddles pub to be demolished for a road scheme in 1971. At the time it was run by the Pawletts, Ruddles oldest tenants. Mr Pawlett had married the niece of Tom King and had taken over the pub in 1949. It survived the road-building programme, but disappeared when the nearby Morris' brewery was demolished for that most valuable addition to any town, another supermarket.

Hanseatic Trading, *Manor House, Hambleton.*

Jim Pryor, with a brewing career which included, Bass, Bentleys, Fremlins, Courage and lastly Ruddles, became involved with setting up small breweries in Russia. This gave him the idea of reviving an historical product, stout which had been brewed for the Russian and Baltic trade. Perhaps the most famous example being Courage Imperial Russian Stout, brewed with a gravity of 10% to stand the journey.

In 1993, on retirement, he set up a small brew plant at his home in Oakham. Initially, he planned to export the beers and actually got as far as opening a shop in Volgograd. Difficulties with the Russian economy and growing interest in stouts and porters in the UK lead to him producing Black Russian a bottle-conditioned stout for Oddbins. However, his limited capacity meant that in 1996, production was transferred to McMullens in Hertford.

The beer used pale ale, brown, crystal and black malts with Fuggles and Goldings whole hops. It was 4.8% abv, with a strong bitterness of 35-40 units. It was stored in tanks for 2 to 3 weeks, then dry hopped before bottling. The secondary yeast in bottle would allow the beer to develop over 6 months. He was also producing a Bottle Conditioned Ale at 4.5% and Oddbins IPA 4.8%, all brewed by McMullens.

Morris Clarke & Company, *Northgate Street.*

In 1831, Clarke Morris, the son of John was in the census as a maltster and sometime after this the family became involved with brewing, trading as Morris & Co in 1840. In 1841, Edward Dumbleton, originally from Kent, was a brewer in Northgate Street, probably working for the Morris family. In 1846 John Morris was shown as a maltster in High St, one of five in the town. Dumbleton was then shown as a porter dealer in 1851, but still on behalf of the Morris'.

**OAKHAM
(continued)**

In 1855 Morris Clarke & Company were listed as brewing in Northgate Street. At the same time the Angel was kept by an R Clarke. That year, a John Rudkin Hall was shown as the brewer in Northgate Street, with his home in Northgate. His name suggests that his father may have married into the Rudkin family, maltsters in nearby Langham and who later provided the manager at Ruddles. Clarke's brother was called William Rudkin Morris, strengthening the probable family ties.

Clarke Morris had two sons:- William Clarke Morris and Charles Knoulton Morris. The name Knoulton came from Elizabeth Knoulton of Huntingdon who had married into the family. William Clark Morris was shown as a brewer in 1855, with his home in Jermyn Terrace. The directories show the business as Clarke Morris & Company brewers in Northgate, as well as Clarke Morris & William Rudkin Morris, who were also listed as coal and corn merchants. Clarke Morris died on 11th August 1857.

They then moved to Cross/New Street in 1866. William Clarke Morris was a farmer and grazier, living at Oakham Grange, Uppingham Road. In 1870, a Charles K Morris was shown as a maltster in Cross Street. William Cheetham Crowson remained as an ale and wine & spirit merchant at the Crown in the High Street. The 1871 census lists Robert Sharpe as a brewer in Cook's Yard, but there is no indication of whether he was employed by Morris.

In 1875 and 1876, Morris WC & CK were trading as the Rutland Brewery, New Street and also as coal, salt and seed merchants of Railway Yard. In White's 1877 directory, they were only shown as brewers in New Street.

In 1875, the Three Crowns and its brewery on Northgate Street was sold to Molesworth of Ketton for £580. However, the price suggests that this was a separate, much smaller, concern than that originally used by the Morris family.

The Brewers' Journal for 1883 p165 shows Custance & Furley at the Crown Hotel, operating as wine & spirit merchants partnership dissolved. Mr Custance had also bought the Red Lion in the High Street for £1,210 in 1880. Furleys seem to have continued to own several pubs, e.g. the Red Lion in 1913, for which they supplied the wine and spirits, but it is not clear from where they obtained their beer.

In 1891-5 WC & CK Morris were trading as the Rutland Brewery, New Street (F3758), with CK living in Catmos Street. Thomas Johnson was a brewery and coal agent in Cross Street, but there was no identification of a link with Morris.

In 1905 Morris' Rutland Brewery Company Ltd was registered, but around this time CK Morris seems to have died and on 23rd November the brewery was sold at auction. It was bought for £28,250 by Warwicks & Richardsons Ltd Newark. The property included a 10 quarter brewery and 12 quarter maltings, possibly operated by W Needham (also a miller at Thrussington). The sale also included the Rutland Arms beerhouse at the brewery, 18 freehold pubs and 3 annual tenancies.

The pubs were mainly in Rutland, but also included one at Horncastle, one at Car Colston and another at Hoveringham. The Oakham houses included:- Bell, Britannia, Roebuck, Royal Duke and the Railway. There was also an off-licence on the corner of Simper Street which had previously been the Rutland Arms. The house colour was a royal blue background with gold leaf block letters shaded brown and was still used into the 1950s.

Output is thought to have been around 2,000 barrels per year, with two brews a week of bitter and brown ale. Bottling of Guinness on a machine that could handle some six bottles at a time was the main bottling line! There were about 14 men employed at Oakham, with six horse drawn drays for local delivery.

Brewing ceased in 1907, but surprisingly the following year Morris' Rutland Brewery joined the Brewers' Society. This may be connected with the fact that, for licensing reasons, Warwicks continued to bottle Guinness under the "Harp" label by Morris. This was done in separate premises in Newark, until the business was liquidated in 1962.

The Oakham site was used as a depot until 1926, when it too closed. The buildings were then converted to a badminton club called the "Palace", later became a furniture store, and were demolished in November 1980 for yet another supermarket. The maltings in Cross Street are now a garage.

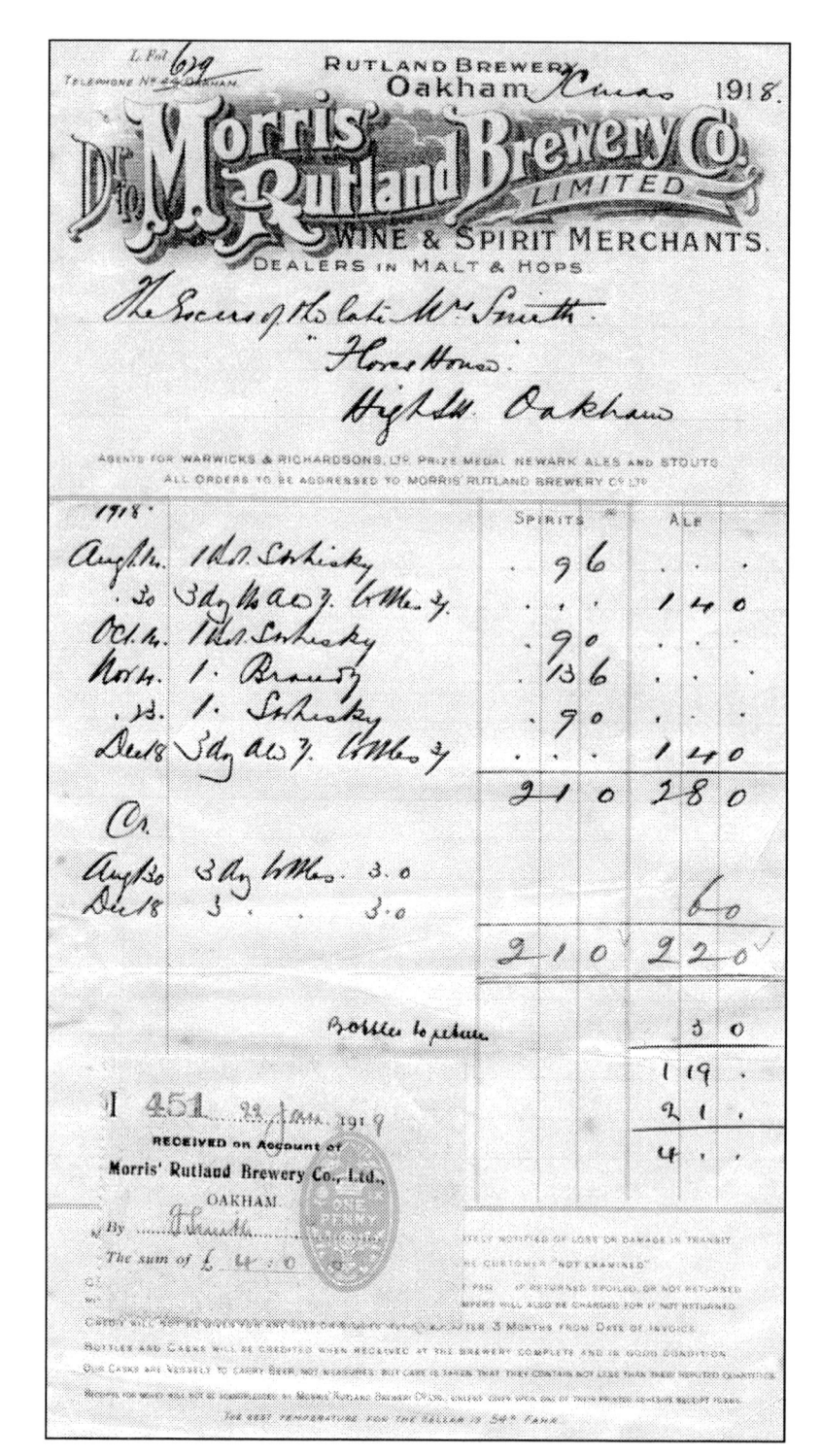

Invoice used in 1918.

From the Jack Feast collection

Oakham Brewery, *12-13 Midland Court, Station Approach.*

The Oakham Brewery, with a 10 barrel plant, was founded in October 1993 on a small industrial estate near the station. The founder was John Wood, formerly employed as a computer project manager.

In 1995 it was bought by Paul Hook, the owner of the converted barge Charter's Bar in Peterborough. John Bryan was employed as the brewer at Oakham, and the business expanded into the next door business unit. The addition of another fermenting vessel and 6 conditioning tanks, doubled the capacity to 30 barrels per week.

The beers were supplied to Charters and the Flower and Firkin pub in Peterborough, together with some 60+ free trade outlets in the East Midlands and East Anglia.

In 1998 the brewing plant was moved to a former unemployment office on Westgate in Peterborough. The new site was a US inspired brew-pub known as The Brewery Tap. With its 35 barrel plant, this is one of the largest brew-pubs in UK.

The Oakham Brewery.

Photo: Author

OLD DALBY

Belvoir Brewery, *Woodhill, Nottingham Lane.*

Colin Brown who had previous experience with Theakstons and Shipstones, started his own brewery on 6th June 1995 with a capacity of 25 barrels. His initial plan was to brew at Belvoir Castle, which once had its own brewery, hence the choice of name. The pronunciation gave rise to the use of "Beaver" for some of the beers.

The equipment largely came from the closed Shipstones in Nottingham, indeed the Star bitter and the mild are designed to replicate the bitter flavour of their old brews.

The brewer uses a full mash of the finest Maris Otter malt from one of the few remaining traditional floor maltings at Beeston in Nottinghamshire. For bitterness and aroma four varieties of Worcester whole hops are used and the brewery places emphasis on their use, including dry hopping of the casks.

Current output is around 30 barrels a week, supplying some 80 free trade outlets in the East Midlands. The regular beer range is:-

| Mild Ale | 3.4% | Star Bitter | 3.9% |
| Beaver Bitter | 4.3% | | |

There are also seasonal beers:-

| Whippling Golden Bitter | 3.6% | Old Dalby Ale | 5.1% |
| Peacock's Glory | 4.7% | | |

The latter obviously is named after the village, the Glory comes from the birds which roam the grounds of Belvoir Castle, whilst the Golden is named after "The Whippling" river which runs through the valley. The occasional/special brews have included:- High Flyer, Liquid Gold and Jolly Beaver. The range also includes Old Merry at 6%, based on an old recipe for a strong dark ale, which also incorporates *"some alternative ingredients"*!

In July 1998, they opened the Beaver Tap in Nottingham and also formed Beaver Inns to sell the beers. The brewery has recently been extended, with larger fermenters and the building of a bigger refrigerated storage space. The equipment for the latter coming from some of the recently closed regional breweries of Crown Buckley, Ruddles, Flowers, Bass Sheffield and Morrells.

**QUORN/
QUORNDON**

Earl, Mr, *White Horse.*

The White Horse dates back to around 1663, when it was run by William White. It was still owned by the White family in 1746, when reference was made to the home-brewed ale. In 1791, it went to John Gretton, who was a nephew of the Whites.

A Mr Earl placed the pub for sale on 6th November 1812, with brewery, and the following year it was run by John Bostock. It was then run by Thomas Hubbard from around 1846 to 1855 and brewing seems to have stopped around this time.

In 1896, it was one of the houses which HH Parry was looking to sell (see Harrison family entry). Then in 1910, CJ Needham sold it to CBB/Offilers. The pub is still trading as the "Old White Horse", an Everard's house, but at some point has been completely re-built.

Rumsby, James, *White Hart.*

In 1835 Ann Williams was at the White Hart. James Rumsby was shown as a maltster at the pub in 1870, which he had kept since at least 1846. He was listed as the brewer in 1877-87. In 1894 he was shown as a maltster and victualler, as well as a farmer. It was then run by Thomas Hubbard and brewing seems to have stopped around this time.

In 1910 it was owned by the All Saints Brewery and in 1940 was valued at £2,500. It is still trading as a free house.

RATBY

Aspell, George, *Plough.*

Listed in 1877 as the brewer and victualler at the pub.

REARSBY

Benskin, Edward, *Old House.*

A local history book suggests that around 1800, Thomas Dawson was a brewer/innkeeper in the village, whilst the Benskins were maltsters. In 1846, William Benskin was a maltster and miller in addition to running an un-named beerhouse. John Benskin was shown as running the King William IV. Around this time, Royle Woolerton was a stone mason in the village.

However, the Benskins involvement with brewing, then seems to be replaced by the Woolertons. In 1870, S Woolerton was listed as a grocer and the following year J Woolerton was shown as a brewer. In 1876 W Woolerton was the brewer, then the following year Spreckley Woolerton was a brewer, grocer and mason. He was shown as a large brewer and farmer in 1877, with Mrs Alice Benskin shown as a maltster.

In 1884 John Benskin was listed as a farmer and maltster and from 1891 Edward Benskin was shown as a brewer and maltster (F4235) to around 1921. The brewing took place in the outbuildings at the rear of the Old House.

Sarson, John.

In 1884 John Sarson was shown as a grazier, brewer and miller. It is not clear whether he was connected with the Leicester family, whose business was later bought by Everards. In August 1873 a John Sarson was the licensee of the Prince Leopold in Leicester.

ROTHLEY

Abbott, William, *Royal Oak, Village Green.*

In 1846 William Abbott was running a beerhouse and was also a brewer, but not in 1855 when Mrs Sarah Abbott was at the Royal Oak. It was then owned by Dawson Fowkes, until he died on 17th August 1868, leaving the property to his wife. John Boulton was at the pub from 1870 to 1884, but was supplied by the All Saints Brewery from at least 1882. It is now an Everard's house, but there would seem to be the remains of a brewhouse at the rear of the pub.

RYHALL
near Stamford

Crown Brewery, *Crown Street.*

In 1870, Thomas Mee, a tailor, lived at what was called the Crown Brewery, but neither he, nor the address, were listed five years later. The maltings on Essendine Hill were still used by Harts of Stamford in 1912, but in 1922 Malting House in the village was a private residence, whilst the Crown Inn was owned by Smiths of Oundle, as a result of their purchase of Bean and Molesworths of Ketton in 1900. The Crown had been valued at £400 in 1900, when it included a carpenter's shop and smithy, with the address shown as Crown Street. It was still trading in 1979.

In addition, Sismore and Gann operated as maltsters in 1846, whilst the Sismore family ran the Green Dragon. There are buildings at the rear of the pub, which could have been the old brewhouse and maltings.

The village is now included within Lincolnshire.

SALTBY

Harris, William, *Nag's Head, Main Street/ Stonesby Road.*

From around 1848 to 1855, Joseph Mount was running the pub, where in 1888, Robert

Ironmonger was also a shopkeeper. Then in 1895-96, William Harris was described as running the public house and also a shopkeeper. However, his invoices call this the "Saltby Brewery" suggesting that he was brewing for the pub and a small local trade. From 1898 the pub was run by William Henry Harris, until 1904 when Alfred Henry Skinner took over and brewing may have ceased.

The pub, with a next-door brick building which was possibly once the brewhouse, is still in business. Surprisingly, it still carries the external signs of a Ruddle's house.

SHEPSHED

Cotton, Mrs Mary, *Crown, Market Place.*

By 1870 Robert Cotton was at the Crown, where he was listed as a victualler in 1884. In 1892, Elizabeth Cotton was the brewer, followed by Mrs Mary Cotton as the brewer from 1895 to 1902. The pub is now an Everard's house which features in CAMRA's national guide.

Cotton, Thomas, *Sullington House, Sullington Road.*

In 1884 Thomas Cotton was shown as a farmer and victualler and then from 1892 to 1895 as a brewer. In 1898 Mrs Sarah Cotton was brewing at the pub, when a pint of the best bitter was said to cost a halfpenny. In 1906 it was bought by Marstons, but now trades as the Bull and Bush.

Gent, Thomas, *Kirk Hill.*

Brewing in 1892-95, Gent was initially a beer retailer. The location may possibly be the off-licence at 31 Kirk Hill Street, which was later bought by Offilers.

Start, Ann, *Bull's Head, Market Place.*

In 1809 on the death of Mrs Start, the pub with its capital brewing vessels, was for sale. For many years it was run by the Barretts, until 1855 when Joseph Dexter took over. However, there was no specific mention of brewing.

SILEBY

Barber, William, *Fountain Inn, Brook Street.*

From at least 1846 to 1855, Miss Ann Sarson was running the Fountain. In 1870 William Hand was at the pub. By 1884 William Barber was the victualler and from 1895 to 1923 he was shown as the brewer (F4628). Then in 1925 Horace Rowell was identified as the brewer of the beer retailed, but in 1932 there was no mention of brewing when the pub was being run by Florence G Rowell. The pub is still trading, with beers from Whitbread.

Hutchinson, James, *Black Swan.*

The pub, which was built some time after 1800, and its brewery, was for sale in May 1811. James Hutchinson was the landlord at the time.

Parkinson, Henry, *Plough, 10 High Street.*

The Plough dated back to at least 1802, when a Mr Barrodell was running the pub. Mrs Mary Wilkinson was the victualler in 1848.

By 1870 Edward Parkinson was a butcher and victualler at the Red Lion, whilst Harriet Parkinson was at the Plough, from at least 1855. From 1892 to 1921 Henry Parkinson (F4629) was brewing at the Plough, followed in 1922 by Charles Henry Parkinson.

In April 1923 it was bought for £4,600 by the All Saints Brewery, although two years later, Walter Croghan was still shown as the brewer of the beer retailed. The pub closed at some time after 1940 when valued at £2,500, and the building is now used for selling parts for motorbikes. However, the beam from which the sign once hung still protrudes from the frontage, albeit somewhat ravaged by the weather.

Parkinson, Mrs Eliza, *Red Lion, King Street.*

In 1884 Edward Parkinson was at the Red Lion and then from 1892 to 1895 Mrs Eliza Parkinson was listed as the brewer. In 1895 the Parkinsons were pork butchers and farmers and brewing seems to have stopped, although the family owned the pub until at least 1922. The pub was later closed and seems to have been demolished.

Prior, Alfred.

Listed by Friedrich for 1871, but with no other details.

Sharpe, William & Sons, *Steam Brewery, High Street.*

In 1808 a Mr Knight was at the Duke of York, followed in 1848, by Henry Smith a butcher. There was no mention of brewing at this time, but in 1812 a Mr Sharpe operated a malt office near to the North Gates, High Cross Street in Leicester and a Richard Sharpe junior was a maltster at Scalford in 1846.

In 1860 William Sharpe founded a brewery behind the pub. This was described as a four storey tower brewery with attic. In 1870, the business was trading as Sharpe & Sons, whilst William Sharpe was also shown as a brewer at the Duke of York.

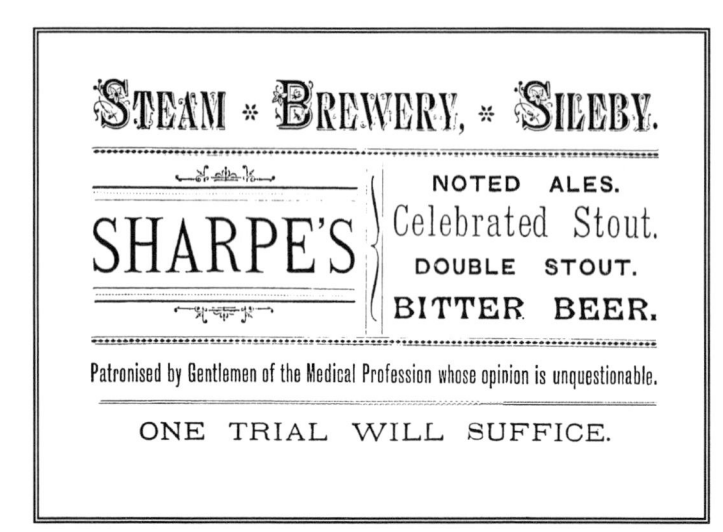

The business was run by his two sons William & Frederick, but their partnership seems to have been dissolved in 1876, although it was still listed as William Sharpe & Sons.

William Sharpe senior died on 9th September 1877; however, that year the business was still listed as William Sharpe & Sons at the Steam Brewery.

In 1881, Frederick Sharpe of the Sileby brewery was living at Syston, where John Sharpe was an ale merchant in the High Street. However, in 1884, Frederick was shown as living at Sileby House, Cossington Lane. William Henry Sharpe was shown as living at Hunting Box, Cossington End. Their stout was obviously popular in the area, since in 1883 they were supplying it to the All Saints Brewery in Leicester.

From a commercial directory dated 1889.

They were trading as W Sharpe and Sons around 1884-5 and in 1891 the business was trading as William Sharpe & Sons (F4630). Sharpe's stout was available at Thomas Fox's ale stores at Church Gate in Leicester. In 1893, they were involved with a court case concerning the responsibility for the payment of carriage on malt which was subsequently found to be of poor quality. The malt had been purchased at Leicester market and had become mixed with some of poor quality before being delivered to Sharpes (Brewers' Journal 1893 p107 Perkins vs Bell).

The remains of W Sharpe and Sons as they appear in the 1990s.

Photo: Author

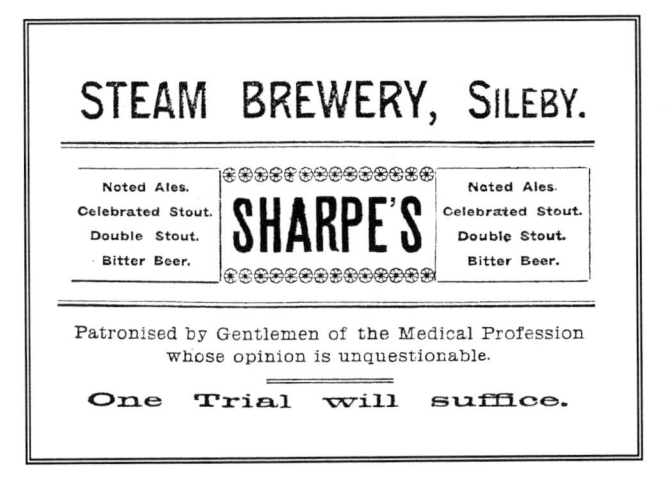

STEAM BREWERY, SILEBY.

Noted Ales. Celebrated Stout. Double Stout. Bitter Beer.

SHARPE'S

Noted Ales. Celebrated Stout. Double Stout. Bitter Beer.

Patronised by Gentlemen of the Medical Profession whose opinion is unquestionable.

One Trial will suffice.

From a commercial directory dated 18894.

In 1895, they were shown as brewers, maltsters and coal merchants. The estate rationalisation at LB&M saw the White Lion at Sileby transferred to Sharpes in exchange for them giving up the Earl Grey at Leicester, together with 2 cottages and the payment of some £500. However, the Cape of Good Hope seems to have gone from Sharpes to Strettons around 1902.

In 1905 the Head Brewer was Elijah Betts. He replaced a Mr Goss, who having fallen down the stairs and broken his leg, had died of pneumonia.

In 1912, William Sharpe & Sons, Steam Brewery, was registered as a Limited Company, but the following year was trading as Sharpes (late W Sharpe & Sons) Sileby Brewery Ltd. Their slogan was *"One trial will suffice"*.

Photo: Author

In September 1920, Sharpe's Sileby Brewery Ltd was bought by Strettons of Derby, with whom they already had strong trading links. As well as the brewery, and a malting in King Street, the sale included 15 licensed houses and 20 off-licensed. Oddly, the Duke of York was not included in the list of properties transferred, although it was one of their houses. The business was wound up in October 1921.

The brewery was thought to have closed in 1922, although it seems to be still listed in 1925. Strettons themselves were taken over by Allsopps who continued to use the maltings (SK602151) until the 1930s. After their sale by Allsopps, the maltings were operated by Plunketts until 1972. The buildings are almost completely intact at the rear of the Duke of York.

Sneesby, James Henry, *High Street.*

There is an entry for Sneesby brewing at an un-named pub in 1923 (F4631), but unfortunately no other details have been forthcoming.

SOMERBY

Parish Brewery, *The Old Brewery Inn, High Street.*

In 1846 the Three Crowns was kept by William Bull, brewer and maltster. However, in 1855 when kept by John Preston, there was no mention of brewing. It was owned by Brasenose College, until its sale in 1903. The pub was later owned by Ruddles in 1911, before becoming an Everard's house after the great 1978 sell-off. Full circle, it became the home for the Parish Brewery in 1990, when it moved from the Stag, Burrough (see entry).

In July 1990 brewing commenced at the new site, with a 20 barrel plant. Innovation in 1995 saw the production of Baz's Super Brew, a one-off 23% beer which was in the Guinness Book of Records as the strongest beer in the world. A slightly weaker bottled version is brewed by Bateman's for Jacktar Ltd, a London beer agency, which licences the name from Parish. Sadly that year saw the death of the brewer and business partner James Cantrell, aged only 42. The current range is as follows:-

Mild 3.5%	Wild John Bitter 4.7%
PSB 3.8%	Poacher's Ale 6%
Farm Gold 3.8%	Bonce Blower 11%
Somerby Premium 4%	

It supplies some twenty local free trade outlets as well as the Old Brewery Inn.

SOUTH LUFFENHAM

Fowler, Daniel & Son, *Boot and Shoe, The Street.*

Postcards of the village show the rear of the pub, with a signboard stating *"Genuine Home Brewed Ale"*, with Elizabeth Fowler as the licensee. This would seem to be where from 1876 to 1895, Daniel Fowler was listed as a baker, grocer and beer retailer. From 1876 to 1880 Donald Fowler was listed for the Boot & Shoe.

From 1895 they were trading as Daniel & Son and still retailing beer, but in 1904, the business was listed as the exors of the Fowlers and this seems to be the last entry for them. The pub, which has not been externally altered for over a century, is still trading in the village centre.

STATHERN

Brewsters Brewing Company Ltd, *Penn Lane.*

Brewster is the old English term for a female brewer. The brewery was started in January 1998, by Sara Barton who was trained at Herriot Watt, Edinburgh and then worked for Courage for 3 years. It uses a 5 barrel plant from the closed Wylye Valley Brewery in Wiltshire.

It is located on her father's farm, with a capacity of 10-15 barrels a week, with two fermenters and three conditioning tanks. The current production is about 5 barrels per week, with 100% natural ingredients including malt from the traditional floor maltings at Beeston. The current range, with descriptions from the brewster is as follows:-

- Marquis 3.8% session bitter light maltiness balanced by a dry hoppy finish.

- Bitter 4.28% premium pale ale well-balanced red ale with nutty malty character and an aromatic hop flavour from a mixture of Fuggles, Goldings and Northdown hops.

- Vale Pale Ale 4.5% premium pale ale brewed with amber malt.

- Golden Ale with a subtle biscuit malt flavour and citrus hop notes from the Northdown, Goldings and Cascade hops used.

- Monty's Mild 4% full bodied dark mild made with a blend of pale, chocolate and crystal malts as well as torrified wheat. Lightly hopped with Progress hops.

The latter was named after the brewery dog! There is also a range of seasonal brew such as Stocking 5%, the winter brew made from a mix of speciality barley malts and oat malt for extra body. They also produce Frau Brau a 5% cask-conditioned lager.

The village pubs the Plough and the Red Lion are worth trying for the beers. There is also an old maltings in the village at SK772308.

STONEY STANTON

Middleton, George, *Frank's Arms.*

In 1801 Thomas Allen was the victualler at the pub, which was for sale in the November as a result of his bankruptcy. This included the sale of his brewing vessels. This may be the same property which was described as *"a newly erected freehold pub and malting in the middle of the village, details available from Mrs Herrick"*.

In 1870 Sarah Ann Higgin was shown as a grocer and beer retailer, with Mrs Ann Lane running the un-named beerhouse in 1884. Then in 1892 George Middleton was shown as being at the Frank's Arms. In 1908 he was a beer and wine retailer and was also identified as a brewer. He continued to brew until 1920 (F4811). However, in 1922 he was listed only as a beer retailer. It is possible that this may have become the Francis Arms, Huncote Road.

STRETTON

Blake, Charles, *Ram Jam, Great North Road.*

The pub was originally called the Winchelsea Arms. Then at some period in the eighteenth century, Charles Blake returned from India with a recipe perhaps originally based on Rambooze - wine, ale, eggs, sugar - which perhaps gave the pub its new name.

In 1846 it was shown as Greetham, Rutland, kept by John Spring and then in 1855 by Mrs Sarah Spring.

SWANNINGTON

Hunt, Charles *Robin Hood Inn.*

Charles Hunt was a victualler and butcher at the Robin Hood from 1846. In 1870, Hunt was identified as a brewer at the pub. Mrs Sarah Lovett was the victualler in 1884, but with no mention of brewing. The rebuilt pub is still trading.

Williamson, Moses, *Bull's Head, 71 Main Street.*

In 1846-48 Moses was the brewer and victualler at the Bull's Head, but brewing was not mentioned in 1855 when it was kept by William King. Although no longer a pub, the building still stands as a private house.

SYSTON

Barker, Jack, *Bell Inn, 13 Melton Road.*

In 1848 George Brooks was the victualler at the Bell, followed by Henry Cooper around 1855. In 1870 Joseph North, was a surveyor and rate collector at the Blue Bell, shown as Leicester Road. From 1877 to 1884 North was shown as a brewer, he was still also a land surveyor and assistant overseer. In 1881 the location was shown as Melton Road.

From 1892 to 1925 John Wing was the brewer, but in the latter year John Barker was identified as the brewer of the beer retailed. On 21st May 1927, the licensee was a John Victor Barker, but this was probably the same person. From 9th August 1930 to 13th June 1932 Arthur Henry Mansfield was the brewer. JV Barker was again brewing to 9th December 1933, followed by George Albert Barker.

In 1942, JV's brother, Jack Barker, was still listed (F5003), but on 10th July of that year it was bought by Leicester Brewing & Malt, who installed Reginald North as their tenant. It closed on 1st January 1960.

Barradale, Perry William, *Syston Brewery, Queen Victoria, High Street.*

In 1884 William Charles Johnson was the victualler at the pub and identified as brewing in 1892. On 3rd June 1893, Barradale took the Queen Victoria in the High Street. The pub, together with the Malthouse on the Green, was owned by the Needham family, who were corn merchants. He was at the Queen Victoria pub until 4th June 1898, but at some point seems to have traded as the Syston Brewery, suggesting that he may have been operating on a wholesale basis (F4999). Certainly, in 1894 Johnson was again listed as running the pub and the Victoria seems to have been owned by HW Needham of LB&M around 1897.

In 1898, Arthur Alexander Butson was listed as living at the Brewery, Bath Street. However, he had previously been a hairdresser and this may simply have been the name of his house.

On 15th October 1899, Barradale moved to the Hope and Anchor on Wanlip Road. According to an article in the Leicester Mercury, based on a letter from his grandson, he employed a Billy Baum to help with the brewing. He was at the Anchor until 1st June 1901, when he moved to the Fox and Hounds, where he stayed until 1909, but there is no record of his brewing at the latter pub, which was supplied by All Saints Brewery in 1907.

In 1922 LB&M sold the Queen Victoria for £5,800 to Everards, who still own it, with what looks like the remains of the brewhouse at the rear. The Malthouse is still standing next to the Conservative club.

Booth, John Henry, *White Swan, Melton Road.*

In 1870 Samuel Bevan was a coal merchant and beer retailer on Lower Bridge Wharf, whilst the White Swan was shown as being on Leicester Road and run by George Randall from at least 1846.

Mrs Rachel Bevan was listed as brewing 1877-1895 and in 1881 JC Bevan was the victualler at the Bull's Head. In 1892 Samuel Bevan was listed as the brewer, but he may have died in 1891 and in 1894 Rachel Bevan was again shown as the victualler.

On 6th February 1897, Arthur Hyde took the licence and was listed as the brewer for the following year's directory. George Wallace Hitchcock was identified as the brewer in 1900 and was brewing until 1902.

For the period 1910-1920, John Henry Booth was listed as the brewer (F5001). However, in December 1897, the All Saints Brewery had bought the pub for £2,670 from Henry Booth. The purchase included the local fire station! It was not until 1916 that they sold the brewing plant from the White Swan, Syston, and the Coach & Horses, Kibworth, for £44. This suggests that they continued to brew until around 1915. In 1920 the pub was de-licensed for £1,248 compensation and sold in 1922.

Brown, Mrs Mary.

There is an entry in Friedrich for Mary Brown brewing in the period 1895-98. Unfortunately, other than involvement in the confectionery trade, no information regarding brewing has been discovered and it may be that this was at best a very small-scale off-sale trade.

Clark, Thomas, *Bull's Head, High Street.*

One of the earliest references to the pub was in 1799, when John Gray was running it. In 1808 it was run by a Mrs Wild and in 1848 by Mrs Elisabeth Potter.

By 1870 Thomas Clark was at the pub, where he was shown as brewing for the period 1877-87. In 1881 he was shown only as a victualler, but JC Bevan took over soon afterwards (see Booth entry). The victualler in 1887 was identified as Geary Willcocks but this was probably a mis-print, since in 1894 George Willcocks was listed. In 1919, it was a Sharpe's house at the time of the sale to Strettons.

Johnson, William Henry, *Green Brewery.*

In 1896 Walter Samuel Drinkwater was at this location, where two years later a Mr Bindley was a grocer and beer retailer. A Thomas Sikes actually founded the brewery, although he was only there for a short period of time from 1st June 1901 to 7th June 1902. He died, aged 87, in December 1909 in Nottingham. He was followed as the licensee by Mary Jane Abbott, but there was no record of her as a brewer.

In 1904, William Johnson was listed as a grocer and brewer, presumably the William Henry Johnson brewing 1906-10 and possibly related to the individual previously brewing at the Queen Victoria (see Barradale entry). Then in 1910 Henry Bindley was a grocer and beer retailer (F5000). In 1912-14 John Sidney Kemp was the grocer and licensee, but he was then followed by Ella Kemp, suggesting that he was on war service.

On 6th March 1920, Sidney Dixon McIver took over the licence and was listed as a brewer in the following year. He was also shown at Beaumanor Road, Leicester. However, on 2nd January 1923, Mrs Ada McIver sold the property for £1,500 to Henry Goodall. The documents mention the brewhouse in the converted cottages at the rear. Although brewing ceased, it continued to operate as an off-licence known as Goodall's Quality Stores until the 1960s. After a variety of uses, it is presently a fishing tackle shop, with the brewery building still at the rear.

From the Jack Feast collection

Leicester Brewery, *Unit 6, Half Croft, High Street.*

Tony Wheeler, aged 43 and a former wine merchant, and Clive Lawton aged 26, previously a brewer at Mansfield, founded the Leicester Brewery in May 1983 to brew keg beer for clubs. This was an investment of £125,000, which aimed to provide beer for clubs within an eight mile radius of the brewery. The aim was to produce 100 barrels per week at prices some 20% lower than the competition. This would result in a price of around 50p for the lager and 45p for the bitter.

They supplied their bright filtered beer to some 15 clubs and at their peak produced some 30 barrels per week. This consisted of two products:-

Old John Bitter	1035°
Sport Lager	1035°

However, competition was too intense and the business closed in 1985.

Riley, Ernest Ealing, *Dog & Gun, Chapel Street.*

In 1870 George Baker was a beer retailer, whilst Thomas Baker was a coal merchant, with various other side-lines. Then in 1883 Thomas Baker was the brewer at the beerhouse to 31st January 1903. He was followed as the brewer by his son Robert Carr Baker, who had been running the Gate Hangs Well.

Ernest Eliu Riley (F5002) was listed as brewing for the period of 1906-1930. In 1913 he was advertising his *"home brewed ales"*, but the following year Mrs Sarah Ann Riley was listed as the brewer, suggesting her husband may have been away on war service. From 1914 Ernest Ealing Riley, presumably their son, was actually the brewer until around 1930.

The Dog and Gun is still in business, with beers under the Ansells badge.

Webster, Thomas, *Fox & Hounds, High Street.*

The Fox dates back to at least 1846, when it was kept by Fras Knight. Jarvis Payne had taken over the pub by 1855. In 1870, it was run by Thomas Webster, described as a wine and spirits merchant, wholesale and retail ale and porter merchant and brewer. In 1884 Alfred Measures was the victualler, but with no indication of brewing.

By 1910, it was supplied by the All Saints Brewery, which carried out major alterations in 1925. In 1940 it was valued at £4,500 and is still in business with beers from Ansells.

THURMASTON

Bates Mr, *Plough.*

In 1804, Mr Bates was retiring from business and the pub, with brewhouse, was available to let from Edward Bishop. By 1846 it was run by Charles Winterton, whilst in 1855 Benjamin Garner was the victualler.

The brewing vessels at the "Old Plough" were for sale in 1864, as a result of Joseph Allen leaving the house.

Ballard, Edward, *Black Horse, Main Street.*

The Black Horse dated from around 1801 when kept by a Mr Smith. From 1835 to 1855, it was run by a William Smith.

In 1894, Thomas Wright was the victualler, then by 1904 Edward Ballard was identified as the brewer of the beer retailed. However, it had been owned by All Saints Brewery from 1902, when they seem to have paid Mr Ballard some £1,670 for the pub.

Nevertheless in 1922 Mrs Maria Mould was still starred in the directory as a brewer and similarly in 1925 Gordon Hartshorn was the brewer. Around the period 1932-36 George William Smith was listed as the brewer. The pub closed in 1938 and the de-licensed premises were sold.

Hurst, John Leonard Gilbert.

In 1923 Mr Hurst was brewing at an un-named beerhouse, but by 1925 he was only shown as a beer retailer.

Preston, Ralph, *Grocer's Arms.*

The Grocer's Arms beerhouse was run by Arthur Toon in 1884, although he was only described as a broker. By 1898 Mr Preston was running the pub and in 1913 was advertising his *"home brewed ales"*. The Grocers closed for compensation of £545 in 1917.

Smith, Richard, *Boat Inn.*

In 1837, Richard Smith was shown as the victualler at the pub, in connection with Samuel Daykin a maltster of Great Wigton. He seems to have inherited the property in 1835, from the will of John Smith, a victualler and coal merchant.

In 1857, the property seems to have been in the hands of Joseph Cooper Moore, presumably the same individual brewing in Cank Street in 1846. By 1869, John Goodman seems to have been the tenant at the inn.

THURMASTON (continued)

However, in 1875 it seems to have become owned by John Flude a victualler in Leicester (see entry). In 1883, John Flude was described as a coal merchant and the former inn was a private house, next to 3 cottages converted from the brewhouse and barn.

The last mention of the property was in 1911, when the land was purchased by the Peptine Maltine Ltd of Fairfax Street.

Smith, William, *Generous Briton.*

William Smith (see entry) was at the pub in 1884, when it may have still been brewing. In 1898 Alfred Wright was running the beerhouse, described as at the end of an alleyway. It was owned by NBC in 1922, and their papers for 1956 mention the brewhouse in the yard.

TWYFORD

The Featherstone brewery was originally located in the Saddle public house (see Enderby entry).

ULLESTHORPE

Proctor, Mr, *Red Lion.*

The Red Lion was for sale with brewing vessels in 1810. The following year it was again for sale because Mr Proctor was leaving the business. This may have been the end of the pub, as well as its brewhouse, since it does not feature in later directories.

UPPINGHAM

Askew, Joseph, *White Hart, High Street.*

Listed in 1855 as a brewer at the pub. In 1875, it was kept by Benjamin Freer, but there was no further mention of brewing. The pub later closed.

Compton, William, *Market Place/High Street.*

In 1855 W Compton was listed as a brewer, wine merchant and the agent for the County & Provident. In 1847, William Compton is thought to have bought what was later called "Drapers Bottling House", which stood at the rear of the Swan, from Leonard Bell. Although it is not clear whether this was used for beer or wine, it was used in connection with the Vaults in the Market Place.

By 1863 he was more clearly identified as William Compton, brewer in the High Street. However, in 1870 William was only a wine & spirit merchant in the Market Place and the High Street. This business traded until at least 1894. William died on 6th July 1896, when his home was Compton House, 68 High Street. The business at the Vaults seems to have been taken over by Robert Draper and then later by James Thorpe, and continued to operate as bottlers. The buildings are still standing.

"The Bottling House"

Photo: Author

Hart, William Garner, *Unicorn, 11 High Street East.*

The Unicorn dated from at least 1791. In 1857, when Hart bought the pub from Thomas Hickman, there was a brewhouse at the rear and which he seems to have continued to operate. In 1855, Thomas Hall had been shown as a maltster at the pub. In 1871, it was run by John Donaly, but there does not seem to be any mention of brewing. In 1914, it was taken by the Knight family, who continued to run it until it closed in 1974. The building was then used as a doctor's surgery. It is now a hairdressers, but the word "The Unicorn" are still clearly visible on the outside of the building.

Waggon & Horses, *Adderley Street/High Street East.*

The Waggon and Horses was not listed in 1870, which suggests that it may have changed name. Mrs Catherine Tomlinson was then running the beerhouse until 1902. NBC leased the pub in 1887 and bought it in April 1893. However, what would seem to be the old brewhouse is still standing at the rear.

WALCOTE

Red Lion.

In 1810, the Red Lion was for sale with brewhouse, details from Thomas Cooper a carpenter and joiner. In 1898 it was owned by the Lion Brewery of Northampton, but around 1929 it was sold. Having closed as a pub, which stood on the left as one entered the village from Lutterworth, it was later demolished.

WALTON

Buck, Thomas Palmer, *Windmill Brewery.*

In 1870, there was no mention of the pub, but by 1884 Thomas Palmer Buck was listed as the victualler. However, it seems to have been owned by LB&M, who apparently sold it in October 1895. It may have been one of the brew-pubs which were owned and supplied with malt by Needham and Crick. At this time LB&M were selling their country properties to concentrate their business on Leicester.

TP Buck's Original Brewery.

Photo: Author

In 1886 Buck was brewing at the pub as the Windmill Brewery. He continued until 1900, when he moved to Lutterworth (see entry). The pub was sold in the 1920s and was a Banks' pub when it closed in 1984. It is now a private house.

WALTHAM on the WOLDS

Lock, Mrs Sarah Ann, *Wheel, High Street.*

The Wheel dated back to at least 1846, when Henry Chester was the victualler. He was there until 1855. In 1894, William Hubbard was the victualler and also a farmer.

Mrs Lock was shown as the brewer of the beer retailed in 1904 and still running the pub in 1916. However, in 1909 compensation of £760 had been agreed and the pub later closed and there are no obvious signs of its location.

Rose, William Edwin, *Royal Horseshoes, Main Street.*

In 1846, John Hutchin was the victualler and was still there in 1855. Charles Rose was shown as a grazier and victualler in 1894. Then in 1904 Rose was identified as the brewer of the beer retailed, and seems to have remained there to around 1922. In 1925 John R Boyal was the brewer until 1936. The pub is still trading on the village cross-roads, with beer from John Smiths.

Welborn, Mrs Ann, *George & Dragon.*

The George was kept by Frances Musson in 1846. However, in 1855 it was owned and run by Thomas Welbourn and seems to have remained with the same family, although the spelling of their name seems to have changed over the years. In 1904 Mrs Ann Welborn was shown as the brewer.

In 1925 John Rudkin Morris was the brewer. The combination of names suggests that he may have had family links with Oakham (see Morris entry). However, brewing seems to have stopped by 1932.

WHISSENDINE

Green & Hacker, *Whissendine Brewery, The Nook.*

Although described as early nineteenth century, the first record of the brewery was in the 1870s, when it was trading as the Whissendine Brewery Company, selling *"Cottesmore Hunt Ales"*. It had been founded by a John Jones Fast, who was a builder here and at Melton Mowbray. By 1876 it was being run by Adcock and Fast, also at Cheapside and the Railway Stores, Melton Mowbray. The following year Thomas Pickard Adcock, brewer for the Whissendine Brewery Company, was also shown as a wine and spirit and porter merchant at King Street, Melton Mowbray. The manager at Whissendine was a Herbert Tompson.

The Whissendine Brewery of Green and Hacker

It seems to have been owned by William Henry Green in 1877. In 1880 it seems to have become Green and Hacker, and they were advertising their Cottesmore Hunt Ale, with stores at Nottingham Street. In 1881, whilst still trading as Green & Hacker, the partners at Melton were shown as Green and Johnson. Between 1884 and 1892, Green & Hacker's office was at 30 Nottingham Street (shown as F3361), with Henry Wall as the local agent.

From the Loughborough Almanac 1887.

GREEN & JOHNSON,
BREWERS,
WHISSENDINE BREWERY,

Beg to thank their customers for past favours, and respectfully solicit a continuance of the same.

Their fine Ales and Stout may be had at the following rates:—

	Per Gal.		Per Gal.
XXXX	2/-	X	1/-
XXX	1/6	XK BITTER ALE	1/6
XX	1/4	DOUBLE STOUT	1/4
AK	1/2		

Stores: Sparrow Hill, Loughborough. Agent: Mr. B. JOHNSON.

An 1890s advertisement.

The Cottesmore Hunt Ale.

GREEN & JOHNSON,

BREWERS, WHISSENDINE.

NOTED ALES AND STOUT.

Melton Mowbray Office, Nottingham Street.

The Whissendine Brewery of Green and Hacker

Then in 1891 it was trading as Green & Hacker, shown at Nottingham Street and the Railway Stores in Melton (F5564). There was also a shop and agency in Burton Street, Melton Mowbray. In July of that year, the properties were for sale and LB&M considered buying at the following prices:-

173

Railway Inn, Melton	£1,500
Bell, Asfordby	£800
Craven Arms, Leicester	£1,400
Rutland Arms, Leicester	£ 250 for 11 year lease

In February 1892, it was announced that the partnership had been dissolved. However, Green & Hacker were still shown as operating an off-licence at Burton Street, Melton. By 1893, the brewery had definitely closed (Goodwin 1993). The top was removed and the building converted to the Red House which is still standing (SK830142). However, although Green & Hacker was still listed as trading in 1895, this may simply be another example of directories being out-of-date.

WHITWICK

Grimley, Thomas Slater, *Grace Dieu Road.*

From 1877 to the 1880s, Thomas Slater Grimley was a cooper and beer seller at Wood Street, Ashby and William B Grimley was a cooper at Castle Donington or Ashby from 1875 to 1913.

However, for the period 1895 to 1902 he seems to have been operating from Whitwick, both as a cooper and briefly as a brewer.

Whitcraft, Mrs Hannah, *Three Crowns, Market Place.*

In 1800 the Three Crowns was for sale, the owner being the trustees/executors of John Jeffon deceased, the tenant William Whitcraft. In 1813 Mr Whitcroft (sic) was shown as running the pub. In 1848 Mrs Hannah Whitcraft then took the licence and was listed as the brewer in 1877.

In 1884 it was run by Edward Hood, who was also running the Forest Rock Hotel on Leicester Road, but there was no mention of brewing. The datestone over the entrance to the yard has the inscription 1881, suggesting that the pub was rebuilt around this time. It is still in business.

WIGSTON MAGNA

Chamberlin, William, *Travellers Rest, Bull's Head Street.*

In 1884 Chamberlin was running the beerhouse and listed as the brewer. He was brewing at the pub until around 1898, although he may have been there until 1900. The pub was closed for compensation of £1,200 in 1913 and was later demolished.

There was also a Travellers Rest shown under Oadby, which around 1884 was run by a Thomas Chamberlain. In 1894 it was an LB&M house, which was briefly owned by Thomas Fox (see entry) until it was bought by Marstons in 1901. It was later demolished for the building of the Oadby Owl.

Cleveland, Alfred, *Durham Ox, Long Street.*

The Ox was previously called the Woolsack and before that the Ram's Head. In 1846 it was kept by John Johnson and in 1870 by Isaac Hurst.

By 1875 Alfred Cleveland was at the pub and he was listed as the brewer in 1877. In 1881 Charles Collins was the victualler, but there was no indication of brewing. The Ox was compensated for £788 in 1926 and closed.

Forryan, John George, *King William IV, 7 Bell Street.*

From 1848 the pub was run by members of the Goodwin family until 1861. Then in 1870 Edward Murrell was the victualler.

The brewer for the period of 1877-84 was John Forryan, who was receiving wine & spirits from the All Saints Brewery. The Forryan's, a local family had a farm on the corner of Bell Street and Leicester Road.

In 1889 Isaac Hurst was running the pub, followed by Mrs Caroline Hurst. However, in 1899 the property was included in those owned by the trustees of the Midland Brewery, Loughborough, which suggests that it was a tied house and brewing had already stopped. The licence was transferred to the Nautical William on Aylestone Road. The de-licensed property was sold in 1957 to Kingsley Engines and the area is now covered by shops.

Hassall, William, *Bushloe End/Leicester Road.*

In 1848 Joseph Hassall was a maltster, then from 1876 to 1880 William was a brewer and beer retailer. White's 1877 directory lists William Hassall as a butcher, brewer and shopkeeper. In addition, around 1880-84 Joseph Hassall was a maltster and farmer in Bull's Head Street. In 1884, Henry & James Hassall were corn factors and merchants in Leicester Road.

Hurst, Mrs Mary, *Old Crown, Moat Street.*

In 1812 Mr Coltman was at the Old Crown, which in 1846 Charles Davenport was running and was described as 100 years old.

By 1855, John Hurst had taken the pub. In 1870 Mrs Mary Hurst was at the pub and shown as the brewer in 1877. From 1881 to 1884 it was owned by John Forryan and the Hurst family then seem to have moved to the King William, also owned by Forryan. In 1894 Albert Hill was the victualler, but there was no mention of brewing.

The pub was included in the Sharpes of Sileby estate in 1921 when Strettons bought the business (see entry). It is still trading as a free house.

Potter, Joseph, *Plough, Station Road.*

The Plough was kept by Elizabeth Burbridge in 1846, but by 1848 Joseph Potter was at the pub. He was shown as brewing from 1877 to 1891, when it passed to his widow Catherine and son, also called Joseph. The latter was the victualler in 1894.

In 1881, the address was shown as Bushloe End. The pub, which was rebuilt next to the framework knitting museum, is now a Marston's house.

Potter, Thomas Burbridge, *Bell, 64 Leicester Road.*

The Bell was described as newly built in 1801, when it was part of the sale of the property of the bankrupt Thomas Spencer, victualler and maltster. In addition to the Bell, the sale included the Black Horse, tenanted by William Vann and the Crown, tenanted by Lewis and Elizabeth Ruffell. The brewery vessels and casks were described as being in excellent condition and there was a malt office capable of 20 quarters per week.

However, these references seems actually to have been the Blue Bell in Bell Street, which was demolished in 1847. The licence was transferred to the new pub which was built in 1861, when the first landlord was a James Tabberer.

In 1870 the Bell in Leicester Road was run by William Cook. Thomas Potter took the pub around 1875 and was shown as the brewer in 1877. In 1881 he was still the victualler, but brewing may have ceased. By 1910 it was an All Saints Brewery house, which in 1940 was worth £4,000. It is still open as a Festival Ale House.

Vann, William, *Queen's Head, Bull's Head Street.*

In 1812 Thomas Gillam moved here from the Black Swan at Kilby Bridge, where he had previously been brewing (see entry). By 1848 William Vann was at the pub, where he was shown as the brewer in 1877. However, in 1859 Mary Ann Vann seems to have been running the pub.

In 1881, Mary was a widow of 70, living with her nephew William, who may therefore have been the brewer in the latter period. John Vann became the victualler in around 1884. By 1889 it was owned by Eady & Dulley; hence in 1929 it went to NBC and was still their property in 1956. It is still trading; however, it is has been very much rebuilt, although there remain some old buildings at the rear.

White, Benjamin, *Bull's Head, Bull's Head Street.*

The Bull dated back to 1617. In October 1811, the death of Samuel Freer led to the sale of his pub, the Bull's Head. The sale included a 20 and a 14 strike mash tub, 150 gallon copper and a smaller one, a 250 gallon vat and two excellent coolers. This suggests that his brewing was on a somewhat larger scale than many of the other pub breweries. The pub was taken by Thomas Gillam, previously brewing at the Black Swan, Kilby Bridge (see entry).

In 1848 Thomas Cooke was the victualler, whilst in 1870 Tony Evatt was both running the pub and a butcher. In 1877 Benjamin White was shown as the brewer at the pub where he was the victualler until around 1884, when he was 56. From 1891 to 1898 his wife Mrs Sarah White ran the pub and was listed as the brewer.

In August 1897, the Bull's Head was described as a fully licensed free public house. Together with two houses and workshops, it was sold on 29th September for £3,700 to NBC. In 1913 George Coleman was their tenant at the pub, which had presumably ceased brewing. Nevertheless, the NBC papers for 1956 stated that the brewhouse building was still intact, although the plant would have been long gone. The pub was demolished when Paddock Street was extended to Bull's Head Street.

WOODVILLE

Brunt, Bucknall & Company, *Hartshorne Brewery, High Street.*

In 1794 W Bucknall was a victualler in Leicester, but no definite links have been found, although in the 1830 poll book William Brunt was listed as a victualler at Hartshorne. The Hartshorne brewery was founded in 1832 and from 1846 to 1855, Brunt & Bucknall were listed as brewers in Woodville. Thomas Brunt was at the Nelson and also an earthenware manufacturer. A Thomas Brunt, a draper of Ashby, was also connected with property owned by Robert William Beard of the nearby Castle Gresley Brewery.

In addition in 1863, Samuel Bucknall was shown as a brewer and maltster at Broughton. In 1870, he was living at Small Thorne House.

The 1872 employment contract for Benjamin Staley the younger, of Swadlincote, lists the partners as Charles Brunt, Samuel Bucknall and Samuel Ratcliffe, brewers of Hartshorne in Derbyshire. However, Woodville itself was listed under Leicestershire at this time and the contract carries a Leicester seal. Staley's contract was for 4 years, starting at 16s per week rising to 18s. He would also receive a bonus of £5 at the end of the third year and £10 at the end of the fourth, However, he would have to pay £25 if he wished to leave their employ during the time of the contract. Clause 2 of his contract states that he *"will keep the secrets of the said partners"*, suggesting that he was employed in a reasonably technical capacity.

In 1876, the business was trading as Brunt, Bucknall, Ratcliffe & Betterton. The following year, both Samuel Bucknall and Henry Inman Betterton, living at Blackfordy, were identified as brewers at Woodville. The business was then trading as Brunt & Company, Hartshorne, operated by the partners Bucknall, Ratcliff & Betterton. It was shown as the Hartshorne Brewery, Woodville in 1887 (F859). One of the partners was Samuel Ratcliff the grandson of one of the founders of Bass Ratcliff & Gretton. He died on 28th June 1889, at Ashby-de-la-Zouch, leaving an estate of £47,628, including the brewery which was to be run by his sons Samuel and Charles Robert.

On 25 October 1890 Brunt Bucknall & Company was registered as a limited company with 49 freehold properties, 46 leasehold and 6 one yearly tenancies. It had capital of £60,000 in £10 shares, of which 5,000 were held by the vendors, together with a 5% debenture of £94,300. William Weare an ale and porter merchant in Leicester was advertising his stock of Brunt & Bucknall's celebrated Wooden Box Ales.

In 1894, Henry Inman Betterton, brewer, was still living at Blackfordby.

In March 1895, the Earl of Caernarvon, acting on behalf of his tenants, took Brunt Bucknall to court for polluting the Hartshorne brook with refuse and waste. The case also involved the other local brewery, Messrs Betteridge, but the case against them was dropped after an out-of-court agreement. The brook on the border of the county was described as foul and black, with a strong smell which was peculiar to breweries.

Brunt Bucknall & Co argued that they had historic rights, dating back to 1832, to use the water. Their case rested on the growth of housing in the vicinity and the effects of two slaughterhouses. The village was described as having some 73 houses and around 600 people. They admitted that the brewery had been extended by about a third in 1873 and that after a fire in 1875, the brewery had been rebuilt. The latter rebuild had been completed in 1877, including means for dealing with effluence, but had not increased capacity.

Henry H Betterton (another slight variation on names shown in the journals), the manager, who had been with the business since 1867, said that for the last 20 years annual output had been from 20,000 to 28,000 barrels. His evidence was supported by his son Arthur, who was also employed at the brewery and Charles George Markham, the Company

Secretary, since October 1873.

The arguments regarding previous usage by the brewery, their investment in new cleaning methods and the recent development in the village, won the case. The case may have been not unconnected with the extensive additional cellars, bottling department and stores for which Thomas Lowe and Sons builders of Burton had been given the contract in 1895. Unfortunately, on 11th December, Henry Inman Betterton, the Managing Director, died at his home in Woodville.

In June 1896, their annual worker's trip to Portsmouth involved some 300 people giving an indication of the size of the concern. The following year's trip was to Liverpool.

In 1896 they had offices and stores at Rutland Street, Leicester, run by Mr WE Chadwick, but by 1898 they also appear to have had premises in the High Street. In November 1896, they paid £3,000 to LB&M for the following properties:-

>Saracen's Head, Long Lawford   Woolpack, Union Street, Rugby on a long lease
>George, Kilby   Old Crown, Newbold

Around this time they also seem to have taken the Crown at Bulkington which was previously leased by LB&M. In 1899 they owned 81 licensed properties. S Ratcliff was Chairman, whilst SR Ratcliff was a director (this may be a mistake for CR). The Company Secretary GG Markham was also a director, together with HB Betterton and AH Betterton.

In 1900, the depot was shown at 1 Rutland Street, Leicester, whilst in 1904 WE Chadwick the district manager was shown at 7 Rutland Street, Midland Railway Stores and William Street. They were also expanding their Leicester estate, including the following:-

- Brickmakers, St George Street 1901
- Black Horse, Granby Street 1905
- Black Boy, 35 Albion Street 1912, leased

In 1913 they were still operating a depot at 61 Charles Street Leicester. However, in 1919 the brewery, and its 100+ pubs, was taken over by Salt & Company of nearby Burton on Trent. The deal was financed by mortgage debentures to be paid off from future profits. At the turn of the century, Salts themselves were financed by £170,000 share capital and a debenture mortgage of £600,000. In 1920, Brunt Bucknall bought the Jolly Sailor in Macclesfield.

The Brunt Bucknall & Company depot then moved to 7 Marlborough Street, Leicester, where Harry Knight was the district manager. They also operated from the LM&S stores in William Street. By 1922, they had moved the agency back to 61 Charles Street.

The Burton brewers generally were still in difficult financial times, partly related to the major purchases of tied houses at the end of the nineteenth century. The depression after the First World War added to the problems, and in 1927 Salts were themselves bought by Bass for £2½m and closed. The latter promptly sold the Woodville site for £5,000.

The brewery was opposite the Nelson, which is still trading as a Bass Pub. The brewery building was described in a local history book as being the most important building on the High Street. The brewery was closed soon after the take-over and many of the buildings demolished.

The bottling store was used from 1933 to 1972 by the Woodville Brotherhood Institute. It is still standing as Victoria House, 33 High Street, with "BB & Company 1896" high on the end wall. The offices were used as a coach depot for Viking Motors; hence the site is now called the Viking Estate. The off-licence recently closed, is now for sale.

The bar window at the Hare and Hounds in Ashby was etched with the brewery name until the mid 1970s.

Bucknall's bottling store.

Photo: Author

Thompson, William Thomas, *Wooden Box Brewery.*

Wooden Box was the name for the village until 1845, and Brunt Bucknall also used the term "Wooden-Box Ales" in their trade mark. In 1877 the village was still shown as Leicestershire.

In 1855 Joseph Thompson junior was a brewer at the Joiner's Arms, which he had run from at least 1849. His father was a manufacturer of earthenware. In 1876-77 Thompson Thomas & Thomas William were shown as running what had become the Wooden Box Brewery (F5779). TW Thompson then seems to have sold the business, since he went on to become the Head Brewer at the Derby Brewery Company for sixteen years. He died, aged 52 on 6 May 1908.

In 1870, T Betteridge was a beer retailer and butcher in Woodville and by 1881 the business had become T Betteridge & Sons, Wooden Box Brewery. In the period 1891 to 1898, the business was operated as T Betteridge & Sons. The court case mentioned above describes this as a smaller brewery than Brunt Bucknall. At this time, W Betteridge was also shown as an earthenware manufacturer in the town. On 31st December 1899, a CH Thorpe of Woodville was attending the Midland Counties Institute of Brewing Annual Dinner, but there was no indication of his role.

However, in April 1901, a Mr Thompson of the Wooden Box Brewery was writing to Offilers (see Cavendish Bridge entry), offering a beerhouse and two cottages at Coalville on 5% commission if a sale went through. Offilers declined, since they were *"not buying at present"*. In 1906 Thomas William Thompson was the last entry for the Wooden Box. A 1915 advertisement for the Shoulder of Mutton at Ashby Parve includes the availability of "Wooden Box Ales", but these could have been from Brunt Bucknall & Company.

Although there seem to be no signs of the brewery, the Joiner's Arms is still trading and on the opposite side of the High Street are the remains of a pottery kiln and small factory.

WORTHINGTON

Larrance, William, *Black Horse, Griffee Hill.*

In March 1806, Mr Larrance was leaving the business and selling the pub, together with a 50 gallon copper and 6 strike mash tub. This may be the pub which now trades as the Malt Shovel on the corner of the road to Griffydam.

WYMESWOLD

Barnes, Richard, *The Fox, Brook Street.*

Around 1835-55 William Wootton was the victualler at the Fox. Then by 1870, William Ford had taken over the licence.

In 1884-94, it was run by Mrs Elizabeth Hubbard (see entry) and in 1900-02 John Smith was identified as the brewer. Then in 1904, Richard Barnes was running the pub and shown as the brewer in 1906. However, the pub was closed for £486 compensation in 1907 and there are no signs of it nowadays.

Hubbard, John Henry, *Three Crowns, 28 Far Street.*

The Three Crowns dates back to at least 1810, when it was being run by a Mrs Fox. In 1835 Robert Curtis was the victualler, followed by Joseph Bampton.

By 1855 John Bakewell was at the pub, but in 1877 John Wootton Bakewell was shown as a brewer's agent. In 1894 it was run by Mrs John Mitchell.

The brewer for 1900 to 1914 was John Henry Hubbard (F5909) and in 1921 John Hubbard. Then around 1922-5 Robert Hames was the brewer, although he was still at the pub in 1932, there was no mention of brewing.

The pub is still trading and what looks like the remains of a brewhouse can be seen a the rear; although at some time the building has been converted to accommodation.

A

Abbey, John, 127
Abbott, Mary Jane, 168
Abbott, William, 162
Acresford Brewery, 5
Adcock & Fast, 151, 172
Adcock, George, 152
Adcock, George junior & Co, 153
Adcock, John, 29
Adcock, Pacey & Co, 149
Adcock, Thomas Pickard, 172
Adcock, Thomas Pickering, 149
Admiral Duncan, The, 120
Admiral Nelson, The, 67
Admiral Rodney, The
    Leicester, 94, 95, 118
Agar, Thomas, 28
Airman's Rest, The, 72
Albert Hotel, The, 62
Albert, The, 88
Albion Hotel, The, 142
Albion, The
    Leicester, 58, 105
    Loughborough, 131, 138
    Stamford, 55, 58
Aldwinckle, BW, 55
Aldwinckle, Mrs Louisa, 146
Ale Wagon, The, 92
Alford, John, 43
All Saints Brewery Co, 53, 123
Allcock, John, 29
Allen family, 116, 117
Allen, Edward Thomas, 127
Allen, George, 150
Allen, Joseph, 169
Allen, Thomas, 166
Allsop, James Samuel, 84
Anchor Brewery, 53
Anchor Inn, The, 31
Anchor, The
    Hathern, 23
    Thringstone, 16
Andrews, Arthur, 43
Andrews, Thomas, 43
Angel Hotel, The, 22
Angel Inn, The, 146, 147
Angel, The
    Ashby, 6
    Leicester, 93
    Loughborough, 128
    Oakham, 159
Anglo-Bavarian Brewery, 46
Angus, Mrs Mary, 150
Antelope, The, 77
Antil, Joseph, 155
Arguile, Richard, 4
Argyle, Frederick, 43
Arnesby, Arthur Ernest, 153
Artilleryman, The, 45
Ashby Woulds, The, 75
Askew, Joseph, 170
Aspell, George, 162
Atkin, Charles Thomas Pacey, 44
Atkins, Benjamin, 28
Atkins, Edward Skipwith, 44

Atkinson, George, 44
Atton, Celia, 11
Austin, Rowland, 44
Austin, William, 44
Axe & Square, The
    Countesthorpe, 57
    Leicester, 46
    Sanvey Gate, 94
Aylesbury Brewery Co, 58, 59, 74
Ayre, John, 27

B

Baggott, Mark, 27
Bagnall Brothers, 4
Bagnall, Thomas, 4
Bailey, Catherine, 147
Bailey, Mrs Mildred, 150
Baker, George, 169
Baker, Richard Westbrook, 36
Bakewell, John Wootton, 179
Ball, Henry, 12
Ballard, Edward, 169
Ballard, James, 44
Ballets, 150
Balloon, The, 75
Balmoral Hotel, The, 119
Bampton, George, 155
Bampton, Joseph, 179
Bandwagon, The, 75
Bankart, Samuel Nevins, 54
Bannister, Arthur, 142
Bannister's Brewery, 101
Bannister's Brewery, 142
Banton, Thomas, 157
Barber, Mrs E, 45
Barber, William, 163
Barfield, Lionel, 35
Barkby Arms, The
    Leicester, 44, 95, 127
Barker, Jack, 167
Barker, John, 167
Barker, William Robert, 121
Barker, William S, 23
Barley Mow, The, 141
Barley Sheaf, The
    Hinckley, 26
    Whetstone, 124
Barnes, Richard, 178
Barnett, William, 157
Barradale, Perry William, 167
Barratt, Joseph, 50
Barrett family, 163
Barrodell, Mr, 163
Barrow, Richard, 30
Barrow, William, 45
Barrs, William, 128
Barsby, Samuel, 45
Barton, Sara, 166
Barton, Sarah, 13
Bass, George, 24
Bateman, Hannah Jane, 45
Bateman, John, 45
Bates & Bishell, 52
Bates & Sons, 95
Bates family, 65
Bates, John, 6, 7, 65

Bates, Mr, 169
Bates, Son & Bishell, 98
Bates, William, 112
Bates, William & John, 97
Bath Hotel, The, 47
Batten, James, 156
Baum, John, 146
Baxter, John, 28
Bayley, Joseph, 148
Bayley, M, 147
Bean, W & Co, 31
Beard, Hill & Co Ltd, 45
Beardsmore, Arthur, 43
Beardsmore, John, 45
Beardsmore, William & Thomas, 24
Beaumanor Brewery, 87
Beaumont, William Humber, 45
Beaver Tap, The, 161
Bedford, George, 25
Beeby Brewery, 60
Beeby, Jos, 12
Beeby, Thomas, 46
Beeston Brewery Co, 51
Beeston Brewery Company, 46, 49
Bell & Crown, The, 12
Bell Inn, The
    Leicester Market Harborough, 147
    Syston, 167
Bell, The
    Asfordby, 174
    Oakham, 159
    Wigston Magna, 175
Bell, William Thomas, 157
Bellares, William, 157
Bellis, Thomas, 23
Bells of Burton Ltd, 45, 49
Belvoir Brewery, 161
Belvoir Castle, The
    Leicester, 77, 81
Belvoir Hunt Brewery, 127
Bennett, Miss Ann, 46
Benskin, Edward, 162
Berridge, William, 26
Berrington, William, 128
Berry, John Harley, 5
Berry, Thomas, 6
Betteridge, T & Sons, 178
Betterton, Henry H, 176
Betts family, 151
Bevan, JC, 168
Bevan, Samuel, 167
Bewicke Arms, The, 38
Bickley, John, 46
Biggs, Mrs, 46
Biggs, William, 47
Billington, Thomas, 9
Bindley & Co, 145, 150
Bindley, James, 113
Bingley, George, 10
Birchin, Robert, 96
Birchnall, Emma, 20
Birchnall, Robert, 1
Birchnell, Mrs William, 11
Birchnell, William, 11
Birkin family, 131
Birkin, Elijah, 128
Birkley, John, 46
Birkley, Robert, 53

Birmingham Breweries Ltd, 99
Birmingham Tavern, The, 94
Bishop Blaize, The, 140
Bishop, George, 10
Bishop, Mrs Louisa, 9
Bishop, Robert, 22
Bishop, The, 6
Bishops Blaize, The, 139
Bitter End, The, 129
Black Boy Inn, The, 131
Black Boy, The
   Leicester, 79, 177
Black Dog, The, 156
Black Horse, The
   Foxton, 21
   Frisby, 21
   Hinckley, 27
   Leicester, 78, 114, 119, 177
   London Road, 84
   Melton Mowbray, 23, 150
   Worthington, 178
Black Lion, The
   Belgrave, 9
   Illsley, 94
   Leicester, 93
   Loughborough, 88, 140
   Thurmaston, 44
Black Swan, The
   Kilby Bridge, 36, 175
   Sileby, 163
Blackamoor's Head, The, 138
Blackbird, The, 50
Blacksmiths, The, 131
Blake, Charles, 167
Blakeman, Thomas, 45
Blakesley, John, 26
Blakesley, W, 25
Bland, Elias, 22
Bland, John, 146
Bleasdale, Mrs Henrietta, 47
Blencowe Brewing Co, 6, 7
Blencowe, Peter, 7
Blencowe, William, 99
Blencowes of Brackley, 58, 59
Blood, Ann, 47
Bloor, Robert, 26
Blower, William, 46
Blue Bell Inn, The, 20
Blue Bell, The
   Hinckley, 26, 96
   Syston, 167
   Wigston Magna, 175
Blue Boar, The
   Hinckley, 25, 96
   Leicester, 84, 119
   Loughborough, 17
Blue Cow, The, 149
Blue Lion, The
   Leicester, 52, 95, 112
Blunt, William Henry, 144
Boat & Engine, The, 47
Boat Inn, The
   Loughborough, 129
   Thurmaston, 169
Boddington & Co, 67
Bolderson, J, 150
Bolton, Charles Edward, 35
Bonner, Mrs Louisa, 47
Bonner, Samuel, 10

Boot & Shoe, The, 166
Boot Inn, The, 26
Boot, The
   Hinckley, 27
   Oakham, 156
Boot, William Henry, 47
Booth, John Henry, 167
Bostock, J, 47
Bosworth, Thomas, 4
Bosworth, William, 146
Boultbee, Mr, 11
Boulton, John, 162
Bourne, Frederick Coutts, 34, 35
Bow Bridge, The, 80
Bower, The
   Leicester, 108
Bowker, James, 47
Bowl Turner's Arms, The, 114
Bowley, Oliver, 5
Bowling Green Inn, The, 5
Bowling Green, The
   Leicester, 84, 96, 112
Bowmar, Thomas, 4
Boyal, John R, 172
Boys & Styles, 36, 37, 51, 85
Brackley Brewery, 103
Braden, John Laws, 48
Bradgate Arms, The, 88
Bradgate Hotel, 2
Bradley, Thomas, 4, 6
Branson family, 87, 88
Branston, Sophia, 146
Branston, William, 147
Braunstone Gate Brewery, 81
Braunstone Hotel, The, 71
Bray, Richard, 48
Brewer's Arms, The
   Cropston, 20
   Leicester, 80
Brewery Tap, The, 160
Brewsters Brewing Company Ltd, 166
Bricklayer's Arms, The
   Leicester, 109
Bricklayers, The, 73
Brickmaker's Arms, The
   Leicester, 106
Brickmakers, The
   Leicester, 13, 177
Bridge Brewery, 67
Briggs, John George, 48
Briggs, William, 27
Brighton Arms, The
   Leicester, 65, 114
Brindsley, James, 113
Britannia Inn Brewery, 135
Britannia Inn, The
   Belgrave Gate, 57
   Loughborough, 135
Britannia, The
   Kegworth, 30
   Leicester, 54, 77
   Loughborough, 130, 135
   Oakham, 159
British Arms, The
   Leicester, 112, 119
British Charolais Sheep Society, 158
British Lion, The
   Leicester, 79, 96

British Waterways Yard, 20
Brookes, Jas, 11
Brooks, George, 167
Brooks, Thomas, 20
Brookside Inn, The, 6
Brotherhood, James, 48
Brotherton, John David, 128
Broughton & Broughton, 51
Broughton, Anne, 51
Brown, Charles, 48
Brown, George, 48
Brown, John, 49
Brown, John Stanyon, 49
Brown, Joseph, 121
Brown, Mrs Mary, 168
Brown, William, 49
Brunswick Brewery, 77, 85
Brunt, Bucknall & Co, 13, 176
Brunt, Bucknall, Ratcliffe & Betterton, 176
Buck, Thomas Palmer, 142, 171
Buck's Horn, The, 16, 17
Buckler, Eli, 25
Bucknall, W, 176
Buck's brewery, 145
Bull & Bush, The, 163
Bull Hotel, The, 74
Bull Inn, The, 11
Bull, John, 156
Bull, Thomas, 146, 147
Bull, William, 165
Bull's Head, The
   Ashby, 4
   Belgrave, 9
   Blaby, 10
   Broughton, 11
   Clipstone, 28
   Desford, 21
   Diseworth, 138
   Enderby, 21
   Hinckley, 24
   Kilby Bridge, 36
   Leicester, 47, 82
   Shepshed, 163
   Swannington, 167
   Syston, 168
   Wigston Magna, 175
Bumper, The, 61
Bunney, Mrs Elizabeth, 49
Burbridge, Elizabeth, 175
Burchnall, Mrs Ann, 11
Burchnall, Mrs Emma, 20
Burchnall, Samuel, 1
Burdett, James, 27
Burditt, John, 146
Burgess Inn, The, 43
Burgess, Daniel, 10
Burgess, Henry, 50
Burlington, The, 44
Burnhope, John, 50
Burroughs & Sturgess, 134, 135
Burrow, Henry Charles, 154
Burton Boat Co, 67
Burton Brewery Co, 54, 142
Burton, John Hunt, 50
Burton, Samuel, 128
Buswell, Frank, 145
Butcher, Albert Edward, 158
Butcher's Arms, The

Leicester, 94, 127
Butler, George, 50
Butt, Thomas, 50
Buttery, Ann, 44
Byard, John, 27

C

Caernarvon, Earl of, 176
Cafflin, Thomas, 63
Cambridge arms, The, 44
Canal Tavern, The, 88
Cannon Brewery, 58, 59
Cant, Joseph, 51, 52
Cantrell, Henry, 146
Cap & Stocking, The, 130
Cape of Good Hope, The
    Leicester, 126, 165
Cardington Brewery, 108
Carnall, John, 6
Carne Rasch, Frederick, 99
Carter & Bird, 131
Cartridge, William, 27
Carver & Bates, 98
Carver & Co, 97
Castle Brewery, 155
Castle Gresley Brewery, 176
Castle Tavern, The, 26
Cattell, Thomas, 114
Cattermole, Richard, 89
Cave, Jimmy, 145
Cave, William, 51
Cavendish Bridge Brewery, 13, 66
Caves Arms, The, 5
Challis, Charles, 116
Chamberlain, George, 51
Chamberlain, Thomas, 52
Chamberlin, William, 174
Chambers, John, 154
Champion Inn, The, 9
Chapman, George, 52
Charlesworth, William John, 6
Charnwood Brewery, 59
Chelsea Pensioners, The, 126
Cheney Arms, The, 37
Chequers, The, 57
Cherry Tree Inn, The, 119
Cherry Tree Steam Brewery, 141
Chester, Henry, 171
Chesterton, Thomas, 10
Childs, Alfred, 150
Childs, George, 144
Choice, John, 25
Church, Thomas, 144
City Brewery of Lichfield, 61
Clackett, Thomas, 156
Clark, Thomas, 168
Clarke, Job, 52
Clarke, John, 25
Clarke, Richard, 27
Clarke, Samuel, 52
Clarke, William, 13
Claypole, Diggle & Hardy, 130
Clayton, William George, 52
Cleaver, John, 136
Cleveland, Alfred, 174
Clewes, John, 52
Clifton, Charles, 53

Clock Warehouse, The, 88
Clowe's Arms, The, 82
Coach & Horses, The, 35
    Anstey, 4
    Kibworth, 57, 168
    Kibworth Beauchamp, 35
    Leicester, 48, 95, 115
    Lutterworth, 145
    Market Harborough, 146
    Markfield, 148
Coach Maker's Arms, The, 52
Cock & Co, 53
Cock & Langmore, 44, 53, 54
Cock & Moon, 54
Cock Inn, The, 143
Cock, The, 124
Coleman Brothers, 127
Coleman, Joseph Morris, 35
Coleman, Samuel, 60
Coleman, Thomas, 145
Collington, Thomas, 26
Collins, George, 60
Collins, John, 60
Collins, Richard, 60
Collis, George, 60
Collis, John, 61
Collis, John George, 48
Collison, Thomas, 61
Collison, Thomas Baxter, 61
Coltman, Edwin, 25
Coltman, The, 175
Coltman, William, 61
Compton, Mrs Saran Ellen, 61
Compton, William, 170
Concert Hall, The, 44
Cook & Stafford, 116
Cook, Thomas, 61
Cook, William, 128, 175
Cooke W & Co, 48
Cooke, Joseph, 9
Cooke, Thomas, 175
Cooke, William, 11
Cooper & Pettifor, 2
Cooper, Albert, 23
Cooper, George, 5, 24
Cooper, Henry, 129, 167
Cooper, Robert, 62
Cooper, Samuel, 129
Cooper, Thomas, 171
Cooper, William, 62, 129
Coronation Hotel, The, 115
Corrall, Mr, 10
Cort, Robert, 62
Cottage Inn, The, 44
Cotton, Jeremiah, 145
Cotton, Mrs Hannah, 150
Cotton, Mrs Mary, 163
Cotton, Mrs Sarah, 62
Cotton, Thomas, 163
Coulson, Mrs Susan, 62
Coulston, John, 150
County Arms, The
    Blaby, 71
    Leicester, 107, 108
Coup, William, 129
Coupland, William Frederick & Co, 1
Cow Pasture, The, 55
Cox, John Thomas, 62, 63

Cox, Thomas, 6, 63
Cox, William, 20
Cradock Arms, The, 71
Crain, John, 27
Crane, Thomas, 28
Craven Arms, The, 54, 174
Craythorn, Charles, 108
Craythorne, Edward Henry, 111
Crick, Throne, 99
Cricket Players, The, 85
Crofts, James, 27
Cross Keys, The
    Castle Donnington, 12
    Kegworth, 29, 30
    Kings Cliffe, 55
    Leicester, 113
    Loughborough, 141
    Oakham, 158
Cross, Charles, 63
Crow, John, 63
Crow, Samuel, 25
Crowhurst, Percy, 35
Crown & Anchor, The
    Hinckley, 27
    Leicester, 47, 48, 49, 60
Crown & Cushion, The
    Leicester, 50, 105
    Loughborough, 130
    Whitwick, 88
Crown & Dolphin, The
    Leicester, 69, 82, 83
Crown & Horse Shoe, The, 28
Crown & Thistle, The
    Leicester, 46, 64, 79, 108
Crown Brewery, 162
Crown Inn, The
    Burton Overy, 12
    Fleckney, 21
    Hinckley, 26
    Ryhall, 162
Crown, The
    Bulkington, 177
    Enderby, 46
    Hinckley, 26
    Kegworth, 29
    Kibworth Beauchamp, 35
    Leicester, 80
    Melton Mowbray, 151
    Oakham, 157, 159
    Shepshed, 163
    Wigston Magna, 175
Crowson, John & Son, 157
Crowson, William Cheetham, 159
Crowsons, 157
Crystal Palace, The, 125
Cufflin, Thomas, 63
Cumberland, James, 14
Cummings, George, 64
Curzon Arms, The, 85
Custance & Furley, 159

D

Dakin, Charles, 129
Dale, Alfred, 150
Dale, John, 43
Daniel Lambert, The, 126
Darby, William, 43

Dark Star Brewery, 7
Darman, William, 149
Davenport, Charles, 175
Davis' Brewing Co, 157
Davis, Tony & Mike, 157
Davy, WS, 23
Dawson, Thomas, 162
Daykin, Samuel, 169
Dayman, Edward, 64
De Montfort Hotel, The, 82
Deacon, Jonathan, 146
Deacon, Mrs Eliza, 64
Deacon, Thomas, 21
Dean, John R, 118
Denbigh Arms, The
   Lutterworth, 145
Denman, Thomas, 64
Derby Brewery Co, 178
Derbyshire, Frederick, 60
Devon Brewery, 23
Dew Drop, The, 30
Dewey, John, 23
Dewick, George, 64
Dexter, Edward, 64
Dexter, Joseph, 163
Dexter, William, 7, 20
Diamond Jubilee, The, 65
Dicks, Thomas, 65
Diggle, Samuel, 130
Dixie Arms, The, 85
Dixon, Thomas, 151
Dog & Gun, The
   Balby Gardens, 121
   Hinckley, 24, 27
   Loughborough, 132
   Melton Mowbray, 154
   Mount Sorrel, 30
   Syston, 169
Dog & Hedgehog, The, 85
Dog & Partridge, The, 99
Doleman, John, 1
Dolphin & Crown, The, 46
Dolphin Brewery, 23
Dolphin Brewery, Cuckfield, 153
Dolphin, The
   Leicester, 8, 85, 95
   Market Harborough, 146
Dormer, J, 20
Dover & Newsome, 58, 59
Dover Castle, The, 118
Dowell, Thomas, 26
Dracott, William, 65
Draper, Thomas, 151
Drinkwater, Walter Samuel, 168
Druid's Arms, The
   Loughborough, 129, 138
Drury, John, 154
Duddle, Thomas, 65
Duke of Bedford, The, 37
Duke of Cambridge, The, 114
Duke of Cumberland, The, 92
Duke of Devonshire, The
   Leicester, 61, 78
Duke of Northumberland, The
   Leicester, 51, 52, 79
Duke of Portland, The, 8
Duke of Rutland, The, 26
Duke of Wellington, The
   Leicester, 97

   Market Harborough, 147
Duke of York, The
   Leicester, 105
   Loughborough, 140
   Sileby, 164
Dulley, James, 148
Dulley's of Wellingborough., 52
Dumbleton, Edward, 158
Dun Cow, The, 21, 45
Durham Ox, The
   Leicester, 93
   South Luffenham, 32
   Wigston Magna, 174
Durham, L, 28

E

Eady, Joseph Chamberlain, 148
Eady, T, 150
Eagle Brewery, 34, 35, 97
Eagle, The, 132
Eames, R, 147
Earl Grey, The
   Leicester, 126
   Markfield, 58
Earl of Cardigan, The, 65
Earl of Lancaster, The, 119
Earl of Leicester, The
   Leicester, 51, 62
Earl of Stamford Arms, The, 62
Earl Stamford, The, 101
Earl, Mr, 161
Earp, Cornelius, 22
Earp, Henry, 112
East Falkland, 74
Easts of Milton Malsor, 22
Eaton, George Trussell, 13
Edgeley, Thomas, 65
Edwards, Mrs Susan, 65
Egerton Brewery, 149
Egglesfield, John, 22
Eight Bells, The, 153
Elephant & Castle, The, 65
Ellingworth, James Christopher, 12
Elliott Watney & Co, 53
Else & Froane, 123
Emerson, John, 10
Engine Inn, The, 95
Enson, John, 25
Erskine, The, 116
Evatt, Tony, 175
Everard & Co Ltd, 65
Everard, George, 65
Everard, Son & Welldon, 66
Everard, Thomas & William, 66
Everitt, Benjamin, 27
Evershed, Sydney, 5
Exeter Arms, The, 6, 7
Exeter Brewery, 15
Exeter's Arms, The, 55
Eyley, Benjamin, 50

F

Falcon Vaults, The, 54
Falcon, The
   Leicester, 53

   Long Whatton, 139
Fallen Knight, The, 6
Fardell, Matthew, 150
Farmer, John, 5
Farnell, Henry, 6
Farrers, Thomas, 130
Fast, John Jones, 172
Fatty Arbuckle, 89
Fayre & Firkin, The, 4
Featherstone Brewery, 21, 170
Fever, Mrs, 46
Field, William, 5
Findley, John, 77
Findley, Mr, 77
Fish & Quart, The
   Leicester, 62, 63, 156
Fisher, John Thomas, 130
Flag Tavern, The, 99
Flavell, John, 77
Flavell, Joseph Kilbourn, 77
Fletcher - see Flewitt, 78
Fletcher & Son, 13
Fletcher, James, 77
Fleur de Lys, The, 116
Flewitt, Charles, 105
Flewitt, John, 77
Flower & Firkin, The, 160
Flower, Charles, 78
Flude family, 125
Flude, John, 170
Flude, William, 78
Flying Horse, The, 30
Flying Scud, The, 57
Ford, William, 178
Fordham, Nora, 37
Forest Rock Hotel, The, 174
Forester's Arms, The
   Leicester, 45, 48, 75
   Loughborough, 139
Foresters, The, 52
Forrester & Son, 78
Forrester, William, 115
Forresters, The, 53
Forryan, John, 175
Forryan, John George, 174
Forsell, John Nicholls, 31
Forshaw's Quality Ale House, 137
Fortune of War, The
   Leicester, 63, 112
Fosberry, Mr, 12
Fosbery, Henry, 79
Foster, Charles, 79
Fountain Inn, The, 163
Fountain, The
   Leicester, 29, 90, 95
Fourpence & Firkin, The, 141
Fowler, Cornelius, 9
Fowler, Daniel & Son, 166
Fowler, Edward & Son, 130
Fowler, Richard, 9
Fox & Goose, The
   Great Glen, 22
Fox & Grapes, The, 63
Fox & Hounds, The
   Kibworth Beauchamp, 35
   Leicester, 45, 112
   Loughborough, 130
   Skiffington, 58
   Syston, 167, 169

Fox Hotel, The
  Leicester, 48
  Loughborough, 140
Fox Inn, The, 140
Fox, Charles Oliver, 79
Fox, Mrs, 179
Fox, Richard, 148
Fox, Samuel, 144
Fox, The
  Barrow, 124
  Lutterworth, 144
  Wymeswold, 178
Fox's ale stores, 164
Foxon, John, 97, 105
Foxon, Thomas, 64, 79
Foxon, Thomas Liggins, 113
Foxton family, 125
Francis Arms, The, 166
Frank's Arms, The, 166
Franks, Thomas, 35
Fraternity & Firkin, The, 141
Frearson, Samuel, 79
Freeman's Arms, The, 52
Freemason's Arms, The
  Leicester, 47, 78, 81
Freer, Samuel, 175
French, John, 156
Frith, Mrs, 28
Froane, Richard Pepper, 123
Full Moon, The
  Leicester, 95, 96, 108, 113
Fullback & Firkin, The, 141
Furmidge & Co, 22, 150
Furnival, George, 147
Fuzzock & Firkin, The, 141

G

Gadd, Septimus, 130
Gale, Jonathan, 130
Gamble & Gilbert, 79
Gamble, Henry, 79
Gamble, Wakelin, 21
Gardener's Arms, The, 65
Gardiner, John, 77
Garner, Benjamin, 169
Garner, Mrs Mary, 80
Garner, Thomas, 147
Gask, George, 80
Gask, George Samuel, 9
Gate, The, 146
Gates Hang Well, The, 169
Geary, Alfred, 1
Geary, William, 80
Gee, Charles, 80
Gee, William, 11
General Sir John Moore, The
  Sileby, 58
General Wolfe, The, 45
Generous Briton, The
  Leicester, 111
  Loughborough, 130
  Melton Mowbray, 150
  Thurmaston, 170
Gent, Thomas, 163
George & Dragon, The
  Leicester, 65, 86, 117
  Oldbury, 99

Waltham, 172
George & Talbot, The, 150
George Commercial Hotel, The, 49
George Hotel, The
  Hinckley, 27
  Leicester, 48
  Melton Mowbray, 150
George III, The
  Leicester, 47, 95
George Inn, The
  Hinckley, 27
  Oakham, 157
George IV, The
  Leicester, 113
  Loughborough, 140
George, The
  Ashby, 5
  Belton, 10
  Kilby, 177
  Stamford, 34
Gibbon, Richard, 80
Gibbs, Charles, 147
Gibson & Co, 53
Gilbert, Joseph, 156
Gilbert, William, 21
Giles, William, 130
Gill, William, 157
Gillam, Thomas, 36, 175
Gilling, Robert Charles, 80
Gladstone Vaults, The
  Leicester, 44, 122
Globe, The, 24
Glover, Henry, 81
Glover, Joseph, 22, 115
Golden Ball, The, 117
Golden Fleece, The
  Leicester, 88
  Loughborough, 131
  South Croxton, 37
Golden Lion, The, 46
Golden Lyon, The, 108
Golden Shield, The, 21
Goodacre, Robert, 151
Goodall's Quality Stores, 168
Goode, William, 26
Goodliffe, John William, 34
Goodman & Co, 81
Goodman, John, 169
Goodman, William, 81
Goodrich, Benjamin, 21
Goodrich, Henry, 81
Goodwin & Hobson, 53, 81
Goodwin, Cock & Co, 53, 54
Goodyer, Thomas, 81
Goulding & Son, 125
Grainstore Brewery, 157
Granby Inn, The, 150
Granger, William, 81
Grapes, The
  Market Harborough, 148
  Melton Mowbray, 153
Gray, John, 168
Greasley, Mr, 82
Greasley, William, 45
Great Central Hotel, The, 93
Great Central Railway, 67
Great Northern Hotel, The, 109
Greaves, John, 29
Green & Hacker, 151, 154, 172

Green & Johnson, 172
Green Brewery, 168
Green Dragon, The
  Leicester, 81
  Ryhall, 162
Green Man Inn, The, 82
Green Man, The
  Loughborough, 17, 129
Green, George, 26, 116
Green, Thomas, 82
Green, William Charles, 158
Green, William G, 127
Green, William Henry, 172
Greenwood, Edwin, 82
Gregory, William, 82
Grey Horse, The
  Loughborough, 129
Grey, Frederick, 130
Greyhound, The
  Hinckley, 25
  Leicester, 66
  Lutterworth, 145
Griffin, Edward, 82
Griffin, Edwin, 49
Griffin, The
  Leicester, 79
  Loughborough, 141
Grimes, James, 82
Grimley, Thomas Slater, 174
Grocer's Arms, The, 169
Grolsch Brewery Co, 41, 42
Grolsch Ruddles Brewing Co, 42
Groocock, Samuel, 83
Guildford, Henry, 48
Guildford, William, 22
Gurden, Cornelius, 83
Gutteridge, Henry, 83
Gutteridge, James, 17

H

Hack, Richard Thomas, 83
Haddon, Samuel, 83
Hagger, Thomas, 28
Half Moon, The
  Hinckley, 26
  Leicester, 58, 108
  Loughborough, 135
  Melton Mowbray, 150, 153
Halford, John, 4, 43
Halkin Holding, 90
Hall, John Rudkin, 159
Hall, Thomas, 147
Hall, William, 26, 27, 35
Hames, Robert, 179
Hammer & Pinchers, The, 155
Hampton Burrows, Charles, 113
Hampton, Claude, 82
Hand, William, 163
Handford, Mrs Catherine Kidney, 84
Hands to Pump, The, 99
Hannam family, 98
Hannam, Mary, 84
Hanseatic Trading, 158
Harborough Arms, The, 151
Harborough Hotel, The, 150
Harborough Lounge, The, 148
Hardy & Hanson, 17

Hare & Hounds, The
   Ansty, 1
   Ashby, 177
   Fulbeck, 11
   Leicester, 126
   Loughborough, 130
Harley, W&F, 132
Harleys, Messrs, 132
Harriman, John, 84
Harrington, William, 154
Harris, William, 162
Harrison, George, 36, 84
Harrold, William, 24
Hart, Redfern, 137
Hart, William Garner, 171
Hartridge, George, 30, 31
Hartshorne Brewery, 176
Harvey, Joseph, 131
Harvey, Thomas, 28
Hassall, William, 175
Hat & Beaver, The
   Atherstone, 144
   Leicester, 50
Hatter's Arms, The, 48
Haunch of Venison, The, 109
Hayler, Charles, 85
Headley, William Brookes, 20
Healey, Mrs Ann, 151
Healey, Thomas, 86
Heaton, William, 12
Heighton, Arthur, 61
Herbert, Thomas, 86
Heron, John, 144
Herrick, John, 36
Hicken, John, 26
Hickinbotham, Robert, 4
Hicklin, William, 86
Hickling, Edward, 155
Higgin, Sarah Ann, 166
High Cross Brewery Co, 83
Highcross Brewery, The, 83
Hill, J, 27
Hill, Thomas, 116, 147
Hill, Willoughby, 26
Hinckley Road Brewery, 48
Hipwell, William, 48
Hirons, John, 144
Hitchcock, George Wallace, 168
Hitchcock, Henry, 86
Hitchcock, Robert Wells, 86
Hoar, Barrie & Robert, 88
Hoball, 148
Hobgoblin Inns, 140
Hodgson, Howard, 89
Holland, Ralph John, 155
Holland, Thomas, 86
Holly Bush, The
   Hinckley, 25
   Leicester, 77
Hollywood Bowl, The, 111
Holman, John, 144
Holman, Richard, 89
Holman, Thomas, 150
Holmes, Herbert, 131
Holt, John, 86
Holt, John Alfred, 86, 87
Hood, Edward, 174
Hooke, Edward, 1
Hope & Anchor, The, 167

Hope Cottage Brewery, 87
Hopkins, George, 131
Horn of Plenty, The, 50
Horse & Groom, The
   Kegworth, 28, 30
   Rearsby, 58
Horse & Jockey, The, 114
Horse & Trumpet, The, 2
Horspool, George, 11
Hoskins & Oldfield, 11, 91
Hoskins Brewery plc, 88
Hoskins Wharf, The, 88
Hoskins, Tom, 87
Hotel Belgrave, The, 9
Hotel Inn, The, 92
Hotel Victory, The, 82
Hough, Joseph, 20
House Vaults, The, 56
Hubbard, John, 126
Hubbard, John Henry, 179
Hubbard, Richard, 150
Hubbard, Samuel, 92
Hubbard, Thomas, 48, 161, 162
Hubbard, WH & WS, 70
Hubbard, William, 171
Hubberthon, William Herrick, 36
Hudson, Henry, 147
Hughes, Henry, 92
Hughes, Mrs Elizabeth, 1
Hull & Everard, 65, 66
Hull, George, 24
Hull, James, 22
Hull, Thomas, 66, 116
Hunt, Charles, 167
Hunt, Samuel, 92
Huntsman, The, 120
Hurst family, 175
Hurst, Harry, 153
Hurst, Isaac, 156, 174
Hurst, John Leonard Gilbert, 169
Hurst, Mrs Mary, 175
Hutchin, John, 172
Hutchinson, James, 163
Hutt, Edmund, 92
Hyde, Arthur, 168

I

Illsley, Henry, 93, 126
Illston, John, 93
Ilsley, George, 6
Independent Family Brewers, 76
Ironmonger, Thomas, 26

J

Jackson, Sam, 6
James, Henry, 131
Jarvis Canning Co, 40
Jarvis, William, 147
John Barleycorn, The, 112
John O' Gaunt, The, 125
Johnes, Ebenezer, 46
Johnson family, 48
Johnson, Edward, 93
Johnson, James, 94
Johnson, John, 94, 174

Johnson, Thomas, 159
Johnson, William Charles, 167
Johnson, William Henry, 168
Joiner's Arms, The
   Leicester, 61
   Woodville, 178
Jolly Angler, The, 82
Jolly Anglers, The, 126
Jolly Butchers, The, 154
Jolly Potters, The, 12
Jolly Sailor, The, 99
Jolly Tar, The, 126
Jones, John Evans, 94
Jones, William, 22
Jordan, William, 35, 94
Juba, James, 94
Juba, Otto, 156

K

Keck's Arms, The
   Leicester, 79, 113
Kecks, 64
Kegworth Brewery Co, 29, 95
Kell, Walter, 95
Kellam, William, 95
Kelsey, William, 142
Kemp, George, 23
Kemp, John Sidney, 168
Ketton & King's Cliffe Brewery Co, 31, 34, 35
Ketton Brewery Company, 34
Ketton Steam Brewery, 34
Kidd & Hotblack,, 58, 59
Kilby, William, 95
Kimber, George, 45
King & Crown, The, 105
King George III, The
   Leicester, 47, 116
King Richard III, The, 97
King William IV, The
   Loughborough, 137
   Quorn, 139
   Rearsby, 162
   Wigston Magna, 174
King William, The, 146
   Wigston Magna, 175
King, Mrs Anne, 95
King, William, 167
King's Arms, The
   Nuneaton, 58
King's Head, The
   Leicester, 50
   Stamford, 55
Kinghurst, Samuel, 26
King's Head Inn, The
   Castle Donnington, 12
   Leicester, 86
King's Head, The
   Ashby, 4
   Hinckley, 26, 27
   Langham, 37
   Leicester, 48, 52, 64
   Loughborough, 130
   Lutterworth, 144
   Market Harborough, 148
   Melton Mowbray, 150
Kingston, Daniel, 95

Kingston, Mrs Ann, 95
Kington, William, 85
Kinnell & Hartley, 58, 59
Kirby, Thomas, 9
Kirchin, Robert, 96
Kirk & Soar, 108
Kirkstall Brewery, 15
Kisby, William, 96
Knapp, John, 96
Knight, Fras, 169
Knight, John, 125
Knight, Mr, 164
Knoulton, Elizabeth, 159
Knowles, Ann, 4
Knowles, George William, 151

L

Lamb, Henry, 131
Lamb, The
   Ashby, 5
   Market Harborough, 148
Lancaster Arms, The, 64
Lancastrian Castle, The
   Leicester, 64, 80
Lane & Robinson, 114
Lane, Mrs Ann, 166
Langham Brewery, 51, 85
Langmore & Bankart, 54, 123
Langmore, William, 105
Langton & Sons, 152, 153
Langton, George & Henry, 151
Lant, Thomas, 96
Lapworth, Henry, 96
Larrance, William, 178
Laughton, William Taylor, 116
Lavender, Egbert William, 145
Lawrence, Mrs Mary, 97
Lawton, Clive, 168
Leader, Thomas, 145
Leake Bros Ltd, 155
Leake Brothers, 97
Leake, John, 97
Leason, William, 145
Lee, George, 97
Leeds & District Clubs Brewery, 109
Lees, Henry, 12
Lees, John, 12
Leicester Banking Company, 54
Leicester Brewery, 70, 168
Leicester Brewing & Malting, 97
Leicester Gas Co, 47
Leicester Volunteer, The, 96
Lenton, Henry, 48
Lenton, Robert, 116
Letts, George, 105
Letts, Joseph, 147
Lewis, Samuel, 132
Lichfield Brewery Co, 59
Lichfield Tavern, The, 25
Light Hussars, The, 124
Limbert, Charles E, 129
Line, William, 145
Lion & Dolphin, The
   Leicester, 84, 107, 108
Lion & Lamb, The
   Billesdon, 10
   Leicester, 78, 125

Lion Brewery, Northampton, 171
Lippitt, HW, 70
Little Bowden Brewery, 147
Little Eaton Brewery Ltd, 16
Lock, Job, 25
Lock, Mrs Sarah Ann, 171
Lomath, John, 105
Long, John, 105
Lord Byron, The, 120
Lord Durham, The, 79
Lord Nelson, The, 14
Lord Raglan, The
   Leicester, 48, 115
Lord Rancliffe, The, 8, 60
Lord Warden, The, 154
Lord, James, 132
Lord, Mark, 105
Love, Samuel, 6
Lovett, Mrs Sarah, 167
Lowe, William, 105
Ludlam, George, 156
Ludlam, Mr, 156
Ludlams, The, 156
Lutterworth Brewery, 145

M

Ma Pardoes, 88
Magazine Inn, The
   Leicester, 48, 121
Malt Shovel, The
   Ashby, 6
   Barkby, 6
   Langham, 37
   Leicester, 49, 82
   Melton Mowbray, 154
   Worthington, 178
Malthouse on the Green, The, 167
Malthouse, The, 55
Maltster & Brewer Inn, The, 10
Maltster's Arms, The, 51
Man in Moon, The, 10
Manbres & Clarks, 54
Manchester Brewery Co, 78
Manning, Augusta, 33
Manor House, The, 12, 158
Mansfield Head Inn, The, 45
Mansfield Head, The, 112
Mansfield, Arthur Henry, 167
Mansfield, Mr, 21
Manship, Alfred, 44
Manton, John, 105
Markham, Betsy, 106
Markham, William, 106
Marlborough Head, The, 112
Marquis of Anglesey, The, 69
Marquis of Exeter, The, 55
Marquis of Granby, The
   Hinckley, 24, 26
   Leicester, 45, 121
   Loughborough, 128
Marquis of Hastings, The, 47
Marquis of Wellington, The, 47
Marshall Brothers, Huntingdon., 134
Marshall, Jos, 27
Marshall, Joseph, 25
Marston, Ann Maria, 48
Marston, Thompson & Evershed, 25

Mash Tub, The, 88
Mash, William, 145
Mason, James, 9, 26
Mason, Mark, 26
Mason, William, 21, 26, 150
Masons, 7
Masters & Allen, 116, 117
Masters, E & Co, 116
Matthews, Ann, 5
Matthews, Frederick, 106
Mawby, Ellen, 145
Mawby, William, 106
May, Thomas Henry, 82
McCann, William, 48
McIver, Sidney Dixon, 168
Measures, Mrs Margaret, 22
Measures, Richard, 22
Measures, William, 5
Mechanics Arms, The, 8
Melton Hotel, The, 2
Mermaid, The, 76
Merton College, Oxford,, 6
Middleton, George, 166
Midland Arms Hotel, The, 43
Midland Brewery Co Ltd, 8, 14, 106, 132, 174
Midland Hotel, The, 34
Midsummer Inns, 88
Milk Maid, The
   Leicester, 43, 106
Mill on the Soar, The, 75
Miller, Son & Watts, 107, 122
Miller, Thomas & Son, 107
Minton, James, 12
Mitchell, Henry, 107
Mitchell, John, 127
Mitchell, Mrs John, 179
Mitre & Keys, The
   Leicester, 52, 96
Moira Arms, The, 12
Molesworth & Bean, 33
Molesworth TC & Son, 31
Molesworth, Thomas Casswell, 31
Monk, Joseph, 21, 147
Monk, Richard, 49
Monk, Robert, 147
Moon family, 60
Moon, Cock & Co, 54
Moore, Joseph Cooper, 169
Moore, Maria, 50
Moore, Methuselah, 107
Moore, William, 26
Morley, Julia, 34, 35
Morris Clarke & Co, 157, 158
Morris, John Rudkin, 172
Morris, John W, 48
Morris' Rutland Brewery Co Ltd, 159
Moseby, William, 108, 113
Mosedale, Mr, 108
Mould, Mrs Maria, 169
Moulds, George, 145
Muddiman, James, 126
Muddiman, Mrs Elizabeth, 145
Munday, John, 37
Mundy Arms, The, 129
Munton, Thomas, 146, 147
Murrell, Edward, 174
Musson, Frances, 172

Mutton, George, 147
Myatt of Wolverhampton, 64, 78

N

Nag's Head, The
   Leicester, 63, 93, 123
Nag's Head, The
   Leicester, 46
   Saltby, 162
Naseby Hotel, The, 47
Nautical William, The, 174
Navigation Inn, The, 6
Navigation, The
   Ashby, 4, 30
   Barrow upon Soar, 138
Neal, Richard, 108
Neale, Charles, 145
Neath, Joseph, 36
Needham, 145
Needham & Crick, 37, 60, 85, 98, 171
Needham family, 167
Needham, J S & Co, 26
Needham, Matthew, 62, 63
Needham, Rowland & John, 28
Needham, William, 108
Nelson, The, 177
Netherton Ales, 88
Neville Arms, The, 57
New Crown, The, 12
New Inn, The
   Ashby, 6
   Belgrave, 9
   Castle Donnington, 12
   Cosby, 102
   Hinckley, 24, 25
   Kegworth, 31
   Leicester, 46, 109
   Loughborough, 131
   Oadby, 63, 156
New Jolly Angler, The, 8
New Jolly Anglers, The, 126
New Leicester Arms, The, 78
New Plough, The, 125
New Town Arms, The, 52
Newbatt, William, 20
Newton, Charles, 50, 109
Newton, John, 109
Nichols, Thomas, 109
Noel Arms, The, 149
Noel's Arms, The, 154
North Bridge Inn, The, 120
North Bridge Tavern, The
   Leicester, 91
North Leicester Brewery Co, 7
North, Herbert, 135
North, Isaiah, 136
Northampton Street Brewery, 84, 97
Northants & Leicestershire Clubs Co-op Bry Ltd, 109
Northwick Arms, The
   Ketton, 31, 34
Nottingham Brewery Co, 48, 78
Nunneley & Co, 54
Nunneley & Eady, 147
Nunneley, Joseph & Co, 148
Nutt family, 120, 145

Nuttall, Thomas, 7, 60, 85
Nuttall's Beeby Brewery, 85
Nuttall's brewery, 134
Nutting, Mrs Ann, 43

O

Oadby Owl, The, 174
Oakden, Edward, 23
Oakham Brewery, 160
Oakland, Emanuel, 111
Odd Fellows, The
   Leicester, 95
Oddfellow's Arms, The
   Leicester, 64
Oddfellows, The
   Kegworth, 30, 31
Oddfellows' Arms, The
   Ashby, 6
Offilers' Brewery Ltd, 13
O'Gaunt, John, 11
Old Axe & Square, The, 45
Old Black Horse, The
   Leicester, 80
Old Black Lion, The
   Leicester, 93, 116
Old Bowling Green, The, 96
Old Brewery, 1
Old Brewery Inn, The
   Somerby, 11, 165
Old Castle Inn, The
   Leicester, 118
   Loughborough, 129
Old Castle, The, 113
Old Cheese, The, 65
Old Crown, The, 21
   Newbold, 177
   Wigston Magna, 175
Old English Gent, The, 17
Old English Gentleman, The, 142
Old Flying Horse, The, 30
Old George, The, 4
Old Greyhound, The, 37
Old Horse Inn, The, 45
Old Horse, The, 66
Old King's Arms, The, 83
Old Mitre, The
   Leicester, 50, 109
Old Pack Horse, The, 128
Old Plough, The
   Birstall, 10
   Sutton Bonnington, 138
   Thurmaston, 169
Old Red Lion, The
   Earl Shilton, 21
   Huncote, 28
   Leicester, 61
Old Robin Hood, The, 83
Old Station, The, 99
Old Swan, The, 88
Old Talbot Inn, The, 131
Old Ten Bells, The
   Leicester, 49, 121
Old Three Cranes, The, 29
Old White Hart, The, 111
Old White Horse, The, 162
Olde Coach House, The, 90, 91
Oldershaw Brothers, 136

Oldershaw, Robert W, 136
Oldershaw, Thomas, 12
Olive Branch, The, 44
Olphin, Mrs Mary Parker, 111
Opera Hotel, The, 119
Oram, Thomas, 145
Orange Tree, The
   Leicester, 93
   Loughborough, 130
Orgill, John, 5
Original Brewery, 111
Orton, Arthur John, 26
Orton, Frederick John, 27
Orton, Samuel Thomas, 112
Orton, William, 27
Osborne, Robert, 29
Osborne, Thomas, 145
Oswin family, 43, 46, 126, 127
Oswin, Elizabeth, 146
Oswin, Harry, 6

P

Pacey, John, 12
Pacey, T, 112
Pack Horse, The
   Leicester, 97, 105
Pack, Thomas Small, 28
Paget, Thomas, 52, 112
Painter's Arms, The, 44
Palmer, William, 24
Papillon, Godfrey Keppel, 35
Parish Brewery, 11, 165
Parish, Barrie, 11, 21
Parkinson, Henry, 163
Parkinson, Mrs Eliza, 163
Parnham family, 43
Parry, Henry Harrison, 37
Patent Steam Brewery, 157
Paul, George, 112
Paxton, Charles, 6
Payne, Charles, 145
Payne, Jarvis, 169
Payne, Peter, 6
Payne, Thomas, 26
Peacey, John, 25
Peach, Henry, 107
Peacock, The
   Leicester, 50, 109
   Loughborough, 137
   Lutterworth, 144
Peat, John, 27
Pegg, John, 11
Pegg, Samuel, 112
Pelican, The
   Leicester, 49, 92
Penn, J & Co, 87
Penn, Jabez, 87
Penn, Thomas, 10
Peptine Maltine Ltd, 170
Perberdy, William, 112
Pettifor, Daniel, 2
Phantom & Firkin, The, 141
Phillips & Marriott of Coventry, 144
Phillips, St Martin's Brewery, 101
Phillips, Wallace, 120
Phipps of Northampton, 58, 59, 145
Physio & Firkin, The, 141

Pickering, William, 126
Pickwick, The, 93
Pied Bull, The
   Leicester, 53, 81
Pilgrim, Charles, 112, 118
Pincess Charlotte, The, 8
Pine Apple, The, 106
Pitfield Brewery, 7
Place, William, 155
Plant family, 47
Plant, William, 147
Plough Inn, The
   Hinckley, 24
   Loughborough, 140
Plough, The
   Ashby, 19
   Birstall, 10
   Hinckley, 24
   Ratby, 162
   Sileby, 58, 163
   Stathern, 166
   Thurmaston, 169
   Wigston Magna, 175
Plow & Crown, The, 125
Plowright, John Simkin, 22
Plumbers, The, 6
Pointsman, The, 78
Pollard, Walter, 153
Port Stanley, 74
Porter, Mr, 10
Porter's Lodge, The, 115
Potter, Elizabeth, 168
Potter, Joseph, 175
Potter, Thomas, 175
Potter, Thomas Burbridge, 175
Potter's Inn, The, 12
Pougher, Thomas, 113
Pountain, 14, 15, 17
Powdrell, William, 25
Powell, Mr, 9
Poyner, Charles, 21
Pratt, Knightley, 27
Pratt, William, 25
Preston, John, 165
Preston, Nathaniel, 113
Preston, Ralph, 169
Preston, Samuel, 113
Priest, William, 22
Priestley, Joseph, 155
Prince Albert, The, 62
Prince Blucher, The
   Leicester, 69, 119
Prince Leopold, The, 162
Prince of Wales, The
   Hinckley, 26, 27
   Leicester, 83, 106, 120
   Shepshed, 30
Prince Regent, The, 94
Princes Feathers, The, 24
Princess Charlotte, The, 153
Prior, Alfred, 137, 163
Proctor, Mr, 170
Pryor, Jim, 158
Pyed Bull, The, 53

Q

Queen Hotel, The, 82

Queen Victoria 1st, The, 61
Queen Victoria, The, 167
Queen, The, 116
Queen's Head, The
   Ashby, 6
   Barnwell, 57
   Hinckley, 24
   Leicester, 98, 119
   Loughborough, 135, 141
   Lutterworth, 145
   Melton Mowbray, 154
   Wigston Magna, 175
Queen's Head, The
   Markfield, 2

R

Railway Arms Inn, The, 36
Railway Hotel, The, 59
Railway Inn, The
   Ketton, 34
   Melton Mowbray, 174
Railway, The
   Oakham, 159
   South Luffenham, 32
Rainbow & Dove, The
   Leicester, 84, 88, 97
Ram Jam, The, 167
Ram, The
   Ibstock, 28
   Leicester, 118
   Loughborough, 127
   Lutterworth, 145
   Melton Mowbray, 150
Ram's Head, The, 174
Randall, George, 167
Raven, John, 156
Raven, Joseph, 120, 121
Rawdon Hotel, The, 12
Rawlings, Richard, 113
Ray's Arms, The, 88
Read, Alfred, 113
Reay, Edward, 156
Red Bull, The, 53
Red Cow, The
   Leicester, 71, 86
   Market Harborough, 147
Red Lion, The
   Desford, 57
   Gilmorton, 22
   Hinckley, 25, 96
   Huncote, 28
   Kibworth Beauchamp, 36
   Leicester, 62, 64, 80, 87, 106, 122
   Market Bosworth, 146
   Melton Mowbray, 154
   Mount Sorrel, 155
   Narborough, 156
   Oakham, 159
   Sileby, 163
   Stathern, 166
   Ullesthorpe, 170
   Walcote, 171
Redrup G & JA, 132
Redrup, George, 132, 133
Reynolds, John, 114
Richards, George, 114
Rifle Butt, The, 127

Rifle Butts, The, 60
Riley, Ernest Ealing, 169
Riseam, John, 137
Rising Sun, The, 97
Robert William Beard, 176
Roberts, John, 137
Robertson, Benjamin Charles, 126
Robey, Samuel, 137
Robin Hood Inn, The, 167
Robinson, Samuel, 26
Robinson, William, 114
Robinsons, 59
Robinsons of Burton, 50, 51
Rocket, The
   Leicester, 75, 97
Rodgers, Ann, 146
Rodwell, Austin, 21
Roe, Joseph, 6
Roe, Sir Thomas, 13
Roe, William, 145
Roebuck, The
   Leicester, 61
   Oakham, 159
Roper, Charles, 114
Roper, Samuel Henry, 93, 94
Rose & Crown, The
   Leicester, 66, 108
   Lutterworth, 144
   Market Harborough, 147
   Wymeswold, 30
Rose, William Edwin, 172
Ross, Joseph, 26
Rowbotham, William, 1
Rowell, Horace, 163
Royal Duke, The, 159
Royal George, The, 129
Royal Horseshoes, The, 172
Royal Hotel, The
   Broughton Astley, 22
   Long Eaton, 134
Royal Lancer, The, 95
Royal Oak, The
   Barkby, 6
   Barrowden, 45
   Bitteswell, 143
   Great Dalby, 22
   Great Glen, 22
   Leicester, 94, 119
   Melton Mowbray, 154
   Rothley, 162
Royal Standard, The, 79
Royal, The, 107
Ruddle & Co Ltd, 38
Ruddle, G & Company Ltd, 36
Ruddle, George, 37
Ruddles Brewery Ltd, 41
Ruddles, G, 87
Rudkin, George Henry, 26
Rudkin, Tom R, 36
Rudkin, William, 10
Ruffell, Lewis & Elizabeth, 175
Rumsby, James, 162
Rushby, George, 150
Russell Tavern, The, 82
Russells, of Gravesend, 15
Rutland Arms Hotel, 11
Rutland Arms, The
   Leicester, 113, 174
   Melton Mowbray, 151

Oakham, 159
Rutland Brewery, 31, 99, 159
Rutland Vintners, 75
Rylott, Arnold, 51
Rylott, J, 79

S

Saddle Inn, The, 21
Saddle, The, 170
Saffron Waldon Vineyard Co, 88
Sailor's Return, The
   Leicester, 81, 93
Salmon Inn, The, 64
Salt, William, 148
Saltby Brewery, 162, 163
Salutation, The, 134
Sanvey Gate Tavern, The
   Leicester, 63, 113
Saracen's Head, The
   Ashby, 5
   Leicester, 71
   Long Lawford, 177
   Loughborough, 128
Sarson, John, 162
Sarson, Miss Ann, 163
Sarson's Wine & Spirit, 69
Scanlon's Brewery, 7
Scorer, Henry, 151
Scott, John, 114
Scrimshaw, John, 144
Seale, Richard, 115
Sealy & Wilde, 34
Seven Stars, The, 99
Shakespeare Brewery, 36, 37, 51, 52
Shakespeare, The, 75
Shakespeare's Head, The, 51
Shamrock, The, 52
Shardlow Brewery Ltd, 20
Sharpe & Sons, 164
Sharpe, Mrs, 5
Sharpe, Robert, 159
Sharpe, Thomas S, 12
Sharpe, William & Sons, 164
Sharpes Sileby Brewery Ltd, 54, 165
Shaw, James, 20
Shaw, James & Thomas, 20
Shaws, 6
Shellard, Moses, 144
Shelton, William, 115
Shepherd, Elizabeth, 145
Sheppard, Thomas, 147
Sherriff, Bill, 47
Ship, The, 117
Shipstone Arms, The, 49
Shipstones, 114, 131
Shoulder of Mutton Hotel, The, 116
Shoulder of Mutton, The
   Anstey, 124
   Arnesby, 144
   Ashby, 4
   Lutterworth, 143
Siddons, John, 115
Sikes, Thomas, 168
Sikes, William, 6
Silver Street Brewery, 122
Simpson, Thomas, 155
Simpson, William, 6

Sir Robert Peel, The, 109
Sir Thomas White, The, 60
Sismore & Gann, 162
Six Packs, The, 147
Skandles, 93
Skerrit, Robert, 150
Smart, John, 115
Smeeton, William, 20
Smith family, 116
Smith, Charles, 115
Smith, George, 27, 137
Smith, Henry, 147
Smith, J & T, 29
Smith, James, 116
Smith, John, 147
Smith, John & Son, 137
Smith, John H, 11
Smith, Nicholas Loe, 23
Smith, Richard, 169
Smith, Samuel, 137
Smith, Stephen, 27
Smith, Thomas, 116, 148
Smith, William, 169, 170
Smith's Ketton Brewery, 34
Sneesby, James Henry, 165
Snow, John, 112
Southam & Allen, 116, 117
Southgate Brewery, 65, 66
Spade Tree, The, 30
Spence, Mrs Sarah, 9
Spence, Robert, 9
Spence, Thomas, 116
Spencer, Henry, 137
Spinney Hill, The, 30
Spinning Hill Tavern, The, 60
Spitalhouse Brewery, 126
Sportsman, The, 75
Spring, James, 116
Springthorpe, Thomas, 33
Springwell Mineral Water Works, 31
Springwell's Brewery Co Ltd, 30
Spriong, John, 167
St Leger, The, 85
St Martin's Brewery, 123
Stafford, George, 50, 116
Stag & Hounds, The, 11
Stag & Pheasant, The
   Leicester, 2
   Loughborough, 139
   Lutterworth, 144
Stag, The, 165
Stag's Head, The
   Leicester, 62
Staines, Albert, 117
Staines, John, 43
Stamford Arms, The, 1
Stanyon, Joseph, 117
Star Inn, The, 24
Star, The
   Leicester, 121
   Stockwell Head, 26
Start, Ann, 163
Staynes, Thomas, 117
Steam Brewery, 2, 30, 138, 142, 164
Steam Engine, The, 20
Stenson, Frederick Alan, 138
Stevens, Enoch, 117
Stevenson, Mrs Elizabeth, 118
Stirling Castle, The, 112

Stockdale Arms, The, 125
Stonehall, George Henry, 118
Street, Frederick, 139
Stretton, German, 139
Strettons Brewery, Derby, 59
Strugglers, The, 6
Sturgess, John, 154
Sturgess, Samuel, 21
Styles & Gill, 51
Sugden, Henry E, 24
Sullins, Peter & Co, 30
Summers, Samuel, 9
Sun Inn, The
   Leicester, 84
   Market Harborough, 147
Sun, The, 20, 120
Sutton Lodge Brewery, 11
Sutton, John, 27
Sutton, William, 5
Swan & Rushes, The, 46
Swan Inn, The, 153
Swan With Two Necks, The
   Leicester, 55, 96, 120, 122, 132
Swan, Isaac, 6
Swan, The, 155
Swan, William, 7
Swithland Leisure, 88
Sworder, John, 133
Sykes Brewery of Burton, 61
Sykes, Jas, 61
Sykes, Thomas, 68
Syston Brewery, 167

T

Tabberer, James, 175
Talbot, The
   Belgrave, 9
   Gilmorton, 22
   Leicester, 83, 115, 121
   Loughborough, 130
   Market Harborough, 148
Tallis, Charles, 116
Tansley, George, 139
Tansley, William, 140
Tap & Mallet, The, 137
Tarry, Adam, 119
Tarry, Isaac, 118
Taylor family, 119
Taylor, James, 28
Taylor, John Henry, 119
Taylor, Mrs Sarah, 119
Taylor, Thomas, 147
Taylor, William Charles, 154
Telegraph, The, 78
Ten Bells, The, 63
TH&M, 11
Thirlby, Thomas, 28
Thomas & Son, 107
Thomas, Mr, 21
Thompson, James, 119
Thompson, Thomas William, 178
Thompson, William, 34
Thompson, William Arthur, 127
Thompson, William Thomas, 178
Thorpe End Brewery, 151, 152
Thorpe, Joseph, 9
Three Bells, The, 147

Three Cannons, The, 47
Three Cranes, The
    Kegworth, 28
    Knighton, 36
    Leicester, 119
Three Crowns, The
    Ketton, 32
    Loughborough, 137
    Lye, 99
    Oakham, 159
    Somerby, 165
    Whitwick, 174
    Wymeswold, 179
Three Horse Shoes, The
    Loughborough, 137
    Melton Mowbray, 149
Three Nuns, The, 132
Three Tuns, The
    Barlestone, 57
    Bishops Castle, 88
    Hinckley, 27
    Kegworth, 29
    Loughborough, 132, 140
    Melton Mowbray, 134
Tidd, Charles, 49
Tiger Brewery, 73
Tiger, The, 112
Tilley, Alfred, 77
Tirrell, Joseph, 147
Tobago Lodge, The, 34
Tom Hoskins Brewery, 87
Tom Hoskins pub, 88
Tomlin, Mr, 10
Tomlin, William, 27
Tomlinson & Son, 72
Tomlinson, Mrs Catherine, 171
Tomlinson, William, 27
Tompkin, William H, 119
Toon, Arthur, 169
Toone family, 82
Toone, George, 126
Toone, William, 10
Topp, Mrs Mary, 27
Town Arms, The, 80
Town Seal, The, 46
Townsend, Fred, 120
Townsend, James, 120
Townsend, Thomas, 46
Travellers Rest, The
    Leicester, 156
    Oadby, 174
    Wigston Magna, 174
Travellers, The, 63
Trease, George, 133
Trent Brewery, 68
Trent Brewery Co, 68
Trent Navigation Co, 19
Trivett, Augustine J, 122
Trivett, William, 27
Trivett, William Henry, 146
Truman, Thomas, 140
Turk's Head, The
    Castle Donnington, 12, 136
    Leicester, 43, 60, 80
Turner, Edwin, 44
Turville, Thomas, 154
Turville, William, 154
Twell, William, 12
Tyler, Henry, 140

Tyler, William, 120, 154

U

Underwood, John, 28
Underwood, William, 140
Unicorn, The
    Loughborough, 130
    Lutterworth, 145
    Uppingham, 171
Union Brewery, Wandsworth, 153
Union Canal Co, 146, 147
Union Inn, The, 71, 146
Upper Brunswick Brewery, 77

V

Vale Brewery Co, 22, 23
Vale of Belvoir Hunt Brewery, 127
Vann, Mrs Elizabeth, 120
Vann, Richard, 83
Vann, William, 175
Varnham family, 43
Vauxhall Gardens, 47
Vears, William, 145
Veasey, Samuel, 121
Veres, George junior, 145
Vickers, Herbert, 44
Victoria Vinegar Brewery, 19
Victory, The, 69
Vine Tavern, The, 95
Vine Wine Co, 155
Vine, The, 78
Volunteer, The, 142
Voss, Edward, 144
Voss, Henry, 121

W

Waggon & Horses, The
    Ashby, 13
    Leicester, 92, 117
    Uppingham, 171
Wainwright, Thomas, 121
Wakeling, James, 121
Walker, Claud Wyborn Gordon, 35
Walker, Henry, 154
Walley, Leonard, 140
Walls, Richard, 140
Walton, Thomas, 156
Ward, Charles, 145
Ward, F, 35
Ward, Francis, 27
Ward, Frederick, 121
Ward, George, 155
Ward, James, 9
Ward, Jane, 156
Ward, Nicholas, 156
Ward, William, 36
Warden Arms, The
    Leicester, 60, 107
Warden, Thomas, 22
Wardwick Brewery, 134
Warren, Thomas, 151
Warwick Arms, The, 16, 17

Warwick Castle, The, 16, 17
Waterside Inn, The, 88
Watson, John, 150
Watts & Peach, 122
Watts & Son, 122
Watts & Sons, 54, 122, 123
Watts family, 120
Watts, Arthur William, 119
Watts, William, 132
Webb, Henry, 123
Webster, Thomas, 169
Webster, William, 10
Welborn, Mrs Ann, 172
Welch Brothers, 9, 43, 80, 123
Welcome Inn, The, 127
Wellington Brewery, 127, 136
Wellington Brewery, Gravesend, 35
Wellington Castle, The, 94
Wells of Bedford, 39
Wells, Frank, 125
Wells, John, 148
Wells, Sidney & Sons, 29, 95
Wells, William Henry, 125
Wesley, John, 43
West End Inn, The, 81
Westbrook, HB & AF, 122
Westcotes, The, 75
Western Hotel, The, 67
Weston, John, 36
Wheatley, Thomas, 25
Wheatley, William, 27
Wheatsheaf, The
    Crick, 58
    Leicester, 92
    Loughborough, 17, 130
    Melton Mowbray, 85, 151
    Thurcaston, 73
Wheel, The, 171
Wheeler, Tony, 168
Whincup & Son, 34
Whincup, Francis, 34
Whissendine Brewery Co, 100, 151, 172
Whitby, John, 140
Whitcraft, Mrs Hannah, 174
White Bear, The
    Hinckley, 24, 25
    Leicester, 60
White D & Crowson J, 157
White Hart, The
    Leicester, 86, 111
    Loughborough, 137
    Lutterworth, 145
    Quorn, 162
    Uppingham, 170
White Horse, The
    Hinckley, 25
    Leicester, 49, 119
    Loughborough, 140
    Oadby, 156
    Quorn, 161
White Lion, The
    Bilston, 99
    Leicester, 114
    Loughborough, 128
    Oakham, 157
    Sileby, 165
White Swan, The
    Leicester, 44, 64, 79, 95

Loughborough, 17, 127, 131
 Mount Sorrel, 155
 Syston, 57, 167, 168
White, Benjamin, 175
White, Jonathan, 126
White, Mr, 125
White, Simeon, 147
Whitehead, Henry Eggington, 67
Whiteman, Walter, 62
Whitwell, Henry, 126
Wicked Hathern Brewery, 24
Wicks, Arthur Hill, 15
Widdowson, H, 3
Wilcocks & Gadd, 130
Wilcocks, George, 135
Wild, Mrs, 168
Wildbore, William, 126
Wilde, Frederick & Henry, 34, 35
Wilford, Thomas, 35
Wilkinson, John, 49
Wilkinson, Mrs Mary, 163
Wilkinson, Samuel, 126
Wilkinson, William, 126
Willcocks, George, 141, 168
Willett, George, 135
Willett, Henry, 135
Willett, Jemima, 4
Willey, Joseph, 22
William Caxton, The, 75
Williams, Ann, 162
Williams, Jos, 144
Williams, Mrs Eliza, 28
Williams, Thomas, 141
Williamson, Moses, 167
Willis, Arthur Hill, 15
Willis, Goodwin & Co, 53

Willmot, Sir Henry, 13
Willow Tree, The, 113
Wilmot & Co, 66
Wilmot Arms, The, 16, 17
Wilmot, Philip Mann, 66
Wilson, Hugh, 30
Wilson, James, 154
Wilson, Thomas, 126
Wilton Street Brewery, 50, 116
Wiltshire Brewing Co, 88
Winchelsea Arms, The, 167
Windmill Brewery, 171
Windmill, The
 Gotham, 30
 King's Cliffe, 33
 Leicester, 28
 Loughborough, 136
 Market Harborough, 146
 Walton, 142, 143, 144
Windram, H, 126
Wing, John, 167
Wingfield family, 85
Winterton, Charles, 169
Withers, George, 141
Wood, William Liddard, 52
Woodboy, The, 64, 80
Wooden Box Brewery, 178
Woodford, Edward, 36
Woodford, Jonathan, 35
Woodman's Arms, The, 64, 121
Woodman's Stroke, The, 49, 82
Woodville Brotherhood Institute, 177
Woodward, Arthur, 25
Woodward, Mrs Emma, 141
Wool Comber's Arms, The, 62
 Leicester, 49

Wool Combers, The
 Leicester, 65, 106
Woolerton, Royle, 162
Woollereton, John, 93
Woolman, John, 127
Woolpack, The
 Hilmorton, 24
 Leicester, 112
 Rugby, 177
Woolsack, The, 174
Woolstapler's Arms, The, 84
Wootton, William, 178
Wootton, William Henry, 142
Wormleighton, William, 144
Wright, Alfred, 170
Wright, Charles, 127
Wright, Edmund, 20
Wright, George, 61
Wright, Mrs Ann, 142
Wright, Orson, 52
Wright, Thomas, 169
Wychwood Brewery, 140
Wylye Valley Brewery, 166
Wyvern Arms, The, 43

Y

Yeomans, Alfred H, 24
Yew Trees, The, 101, 102
York Castle, The
 Leicester, 43, 50, 62, 106, 114
York, Arthur, 127
York, John, 106

The Author

Mike Brown

After a career in the RAF, Mike now devotes most of his time to researching the brewing industry. His allegiance to Robbie's best bitter and the "County" might give some indication of his roots. His desire to complete a photographic record of brewing sites goes back to having walked past Charlie Creese's brewery to get to school every day. He only found out what the buildings had been after they had been demolished for yet another supermarket.

THE BREWERY HISTORY SOCIETY

The Brewery History Society was founded in April 1972 to bring together people with a common interest in the history of brewing, to stimulate research and to encourage the interchange of information. To this end members receive a quarterly Journal - Brewery History - which contains articles about brewers and breweries from as early a date as possible as well as more up-to-date news of mergers, take-overs and new small breweries. In addition, the Society publishes an informal newsletter through which members can exchange information and seek assistance in research puzzles.

Meetings are held in different parts of the country at which members can get together for a chat and a pint or two and occasional visits to breweries are arranged.

The Society has an Archivist whose responsibility it is to safeguard the books and research material acquired by the Society. He will endeavour to answer specific enquiries from both members and the general public, or will pass them on to the appropriate County Archivist. These are volunteers who take responsibility for correlating research within their own area whilst liaising with the Archivist. A Photographic Collection is maintained to which members are encouraged to donate copies of their own photographs. Copies of photographs in the collection may be purchased. The Society also maintains a Book Shop which holds a large stock of new and second-hand books on beer and brewing.

Upon joining, new members will receive a copy of the current Journal, a membership card, a list of fellow members and their interests, a copy of the Rules and Constitution and current Book Shop list.

Further details may be obtained from:-
THE MEMBERSHIP SECRETARY
Brewery History Society
Manor Side East
Mill Lane
Byfleet, West Byfleet
Surrey KT14 7RS

Also published by the Brewery History Society

A CENTURY OF BRITISH BREWERS 1890 to 1990
A directory listing, county by county, compiled by Norman Barber
ISBN 1-873966-04-0 - A4 Paperback

SOUTH YORKSHIRE STINGO
A DIRECTORY OF SOUTH YORKSHIRE BREWERS,
by David Lloyd Parry
ISBN 1-873966-05-9 - A4 Paperback

JUSTLY CELEBRATED ALES
A DIRECTORY OF NORFOLK BREWERS,
by Andrew P Davison
ISBN 1-873966-01-6 - A4 Paperback

WESTERHAM ALES
A BRIEF HISTORY OF THE BLACK EAGLE BREWERY, WESTERHAM,
by Peter Moynihan and K R Goodley
ISBN 1-873966-00-8 - A5 Paperback

BREWED IN NORTHANTS
A DIRECTORY OF NORTHAMPTONSHIRE BREWERY 1450 TO 1998,
by Mike Brown with Brian Willmott
ISBN 1-873966-06-7 - A4 Paperback

For more information on these and other brewing related publications please write to:

The Sales Manager
Brewery History Society,
Long High Top
Heptonstall
Hebden Bridge
West Yorkshire HX7 7PF